CHILDREN MATTER

CHILDREN MATTER

Celebrating Their Place
in the Church, Family, and Community

Scottie May
Beth Posterski
Catherine Stonehouse
&
Linda Cannell

William B. Eerdmans Publishing Company
Grand Rapids, Michigan / Cambridge, U.K.

Wm. B. Eerdmans Publishing Co.
2140 Oak Industrial Drive N.E., Grand Rapids, Michigan 49505 /
P.O. Box 163, Cambridge CB3 9PU U.K.

Printed in the United States of America

17 16 15 14 13 12 10 9 8 7 6 5 4

Library of Congress Cataloging-in-Publication Data

Children matter: celebrating their place in the church, family, and community /
Scottie May . . . [et al].
p. cm.
Includes bibliographical references and index.
ISBN 978-0-8028-2228-4 (pbk.: alk. paper)
1. Christian education of children. 2. Church work with children.
I. May, Scottie.

BV1471.3.C52 2005
259′.22 — dc22

2005050062

www.eerdmans.com

This book is dedicated to

Our Grandchildren

Shelby, Jeremy, and Sydney Vischer
Ian and Anna Bruns
Sophie, Lila, and Ava May Vischer

Kyra and Caleb Posterski
Rowan and Kieran Melles

Grand Nieces and Nephews

Erika and Drew Stonehouse
Catherine, Laura, and Graham Hutton
Caden Thoreson

And all the children whose faith has taught and blessed us

CONTENTS

PART III: HOW WE DO IT MATTERS

Introduction

THE STORY OF A BOOK

One summer afternoon a seminary professor began refining the syllabus for a course she would teach in the fall semester, "Ministry with Children in the Church." What book should she assign to help students grasp a broad view of the church's ministry with children? A look at the publication date for the text she had used in the past stimulated the exclamation, "I can't use a book that old to describe children's ministries today!" She had looked for a replacement before and nothing seemed to fill the bill, but she concluded another option must be found.[1] With that conclusion came an inspiration. In October, at a conference, she shared her idea with colleagues: "We could write that book together." And so, we slipped away from the conference for a few hours and Beth, Cathy, Linda, and Scottie sat around the table at a quaint ethnic restaurant in Toronto and began brainstorming what we thought needed to be included in what would become *Children Matter.*

What do we have to offer in such a book, we asked? We realized we had spent a lifetime doing children's ministry, as teenage and young adult volunteers, as professional Christian educators, curriculum developers, consultants, and as professors wrestling with the challenge of equipping students to "serve the present age"[2] of children. The privilege of doctoral study and research had been ours. God had given us the opportunity of

1. Judging from recent publications on children's ministries, others were sensing this same need a few years ago.

2. From Charles Wesley's hymn, "A Charge to Keep I Have."

travel, of observing and learning from children's ministries in large and small, rural and urban churches in many countries of the world. The churches we currently serve in as volunteers are in very different contexts, offering a variety of ministries. We represent different theological traditions, and yet we discovered a large plot of common ground in our theology of children's spirituality, faith, and formation. As we began working together we discovered in the team two prophet/teachers and two shepherd/teachers, who brought to light varied perspectives and ways to express the message we wished to communicate. We share a passion to see the amazing spiritual potential of children being nurtured in faith communities around the globe; to see those communities realize that they are not fully the church unless children are present.

As we began brainstorming what we thought needed to be included in this book, early in the conversation we agreed that it should provide both foundational understandings and practical insights on how to do ministry effectively with children. We also wanted to address the multicultural nature of the contexts in which the church finds itself in the twenty-first century and the importance of biblical content in the forming of faith for children and the adults who journey with them. The structure of *Children Matter* reflects these concerns.

Overview of the Book

Part I, "Foundations Matter," explores the foundations on which to build ministry. Chapter 1 launches this exploration by taking a look at common ministry metaphors. These metaphors picture perceptions and assumptions about children that — often subconsciously — influence the shape of what happens with them in the church. When we stop to take a fresh look at the foundations of our ministry, a good place to begin is with critical reflection on the metaphors — perceptions and assumptions — that presently guide our decisions and practices.

Chapters 2, 3, and 4 examine biblical, theological, and developmental foundations. From the study of Scripture in chapter 2, we gain a glimpse of God's heart for children and God's desires for children to be treasured, welcomed, instructed, and seen as models of faith in the home and the church. A review of various theological traditions and their understandings of children introduces readers to how church leaders across church history have interpreted and applied Scripture to ministry with children. Chapter 3 looks at how these theological perspectives can be lived out in ways that foster or hinder the spiritual responses and growth of children. Our beliefs about how children learn and develop in all areas of life are important aspects of our foundation for ministry. Chapter 4 presents insights from research in the human sciences that help us understand the Creator's design at work within children.

To wrap up Part I the reader reflects on the influence of both history and societies on how the church views children. Chapter 5 provides a brief overview of theological, philosophical, and social science perspectives across history, how they have shifted and impacted the church's care for children.

Part II, "Context and Content Matter," begins with a focus on how contexts impact the lives of children. Chapter 6 reminds us of the diversity of contexts in which churches are located and the diverse contextual realities that children in a given church may have experienced. To connect meaningfully with children we must be aware of and grow in understanding of the primary, secondary, and macrosocietal environments or contexts in which they live.

Contexts are formative. How welcome children feel and how fully they experience the church and family powerfully influence whether the context encourages or hinders their coming to Jesus. Chapter 7 identifies the faith community, the church, as a primary setting of faith formation for children and their families and examines the elements essential for that formation to occur. Chapter 8 looks at how the domestic church, the family, provides a nurturing environment for children and parents.

With chapter 9 the reader's attention shifts to the content important in the forming of a child's faith and the role of story in the child's grasp and processing of that content. Chapter 10 addresses curriculum — what it is, its role in making faith content accessible to children through their adult shepherds and teachers, and how to go about planning and evaluating the church's curriculum for children.

It is our hope that the reflection stimulated in examining the foundations of ministry and the insights gleaned regarding context and content will have practical value. However, Part III, "How We Do It Matters," specifically addresses practical suggestions for implementing the principles and perspectives gained in the preceding chapters. A chapter is dedicated to discussing a variety of models for doing ministry with children in worship (chapter 11), in teaching/learning settings (chapter 12), and in specialized ministries (chapter 13).

Too often, while trying to meet the demands of the children who are present in our churches, we fail to think of the children who are not there. Chapter 14 reminds us of God's concern for all children, those in the community whose parents do not bring them to church, children with special needs, and the children of the world. The importance of making the church a safe place for all children is also addressed.

Moving God's people into increasingly effective ministries with children calls for wise, Spirit-guided leadership. In chapter 15 the reader will observe a seasoned children's pastor leading a church into new understandings and practices that prepare the way for children to become and grow as followers of Jesus and experience the joy of serving God.

Acknowledgments

Early in our discussion of *Children Matter* we realized that we did not want this book to be a set of edited essays, as helpful as they might be. We wanted the richness of our backgrounds and personality differences to come together in conversation, to take us beyond our present understandings and enrich every chapter. Grants from the Wabash Center and the Louisville Institute, both funded by the Lilly Endowment, made this collaboration possible. We wish to thank the Lilly Endowment for contributing so significantly to this book.

We also want to recognize several persons who have helped with this project. Two students made time available to us in spite of their busy schedules. Laura Widstrom provided research assistance and initial writing for sections of chapter 5, and Alicia Satterly took on several tasks related to manuscript preparation. Ruth Goring did preliminary editing and provided us with significant insights and ideas for refinement at points.

Authors are blessed when their editors offer support and efficient, skillful assistance. Sam Eerdmans's interest in the idea of this book spurred us on in the writing task. Our first communication from Managing Editor Linda Bieze carried words of encouragement and the good news that *Children Matter* was on the fast track. With affirmation and efficiency Associate Managing Editor Jennifer Hoffman guided the manuscript through the production process. We say a heartfelt "Thank you" to the whole Eerdmans team with whom we have worked.

With gratitude we look back on the experience of bringing *Children Matter* into being. The hours spent together have wonderfully enriched us as we worked, discussed, and critiqued each other's perspectives in the process of refining each chapter. And God provided a treasured bonus — as is so often the case when we are doing God's work — the gift of growing friendship. It is our prayer that you, our readers, and your ministries will also be enriched through *Children Matter: Celebrating Their Place in the Church, Family, and Community.*

PART I

FOUNDATIONS MATTER

Chapter 1

METAPHORS SHAPE MINISTRY

Children matter! They matter to God. They matter to the church of Jesus Christ. They matter because of who they are: children are complete human beings made in the image of God. The church gathered is bereft without them. In fact, can the church be the church without children present? We have written this book because we love children, and we spend lots of time thinking about the kinds of experiences that churches create for them.

We wonder why ministry with children looks so different in various church traditions. We also wonder why children's ministry has changed so much since we were children. Do you think about these things too? Possibly the differences have to do with perception and assumptions — our perceptions of children and our assumptions about how they learn and how they relate to God. We don't usually use those terms; instead, we talk about such issues using word pictures or metaphors.

What's it like to teach "sponges"? How might it differ from teaching "pilgrims"? The children's ministry at our church seems like a "carnival." Shouldn't it be more like "school"? These words — *sponge, pilgrim, school, carnival* — are metaphors for situations in children's ministry and can help us begin to identify key differences among our perceptions and assumptions.

If the goal of children's ministry is to help children know God through Jesus Christ and to love, obey, and follow him all their lives, do our responses to the questions about metaphors make a difference? The answer is both yes and no. Yes, because the *way* we do ministry can affect children as much as *what* we teach them. Yet no, since God through the Holy Spirit can work in and through any circumstance.

To establish a shared understanding for our conversation throughout this book, this chapter examines common metaphors employed in speaking of ministry with children. But first, let's look more closely at the concept of metaphor.

A metaphor is simply a literary device using analogy or comparison that affects our perception of reality. Metaphors are powerful yet subtle. They shape what we do. Metaphoric platitudes such as "More is better," "We're number one," and "Knowledge is power" influence our thinking. George Lakoff and Mark Johnson in *Metaphors We Live By* identify a metaphor that affects how many live today: "Time is money."[1] This metaphor of time as a commodity has spawned numerous ways of speaking that we rarely question: "How do you spend your time?" "Quit wasting time." "You'll save time if you . . ." This economic metaphor affects our attitudes and behavior, even though each day has exactly the same amount of time. Time cannot be saved, wasted, or spent; time simply is.

The significance of metaphor is exemplified in Scripture. Through numerous word pictures, most of which are found in John's Gospel, we better understand the character of our Lord. He is the Good Shepherd, the Vine, Bread of Life, Living Water, the Door or Gate, the Lamb of God, the Alpha and Omega, the Way, Truth, and Life.[2] In reality Jesus is none of those things, yet metaphorically he is all of them.

Lakoff and Johnson recognize the role of metaphor when they state, "What we experience and what we do every day is very much a matter of metaphor. . . . We simply think and act more or less automatically along certain lines."[3] If their observation is accurate, not only do metaphors influence our understanding of Jesus but they also influence our ministries.

This chapter considers several aspects of metaphors regarding children's ministry:

1. George Lakoff and Mark Johnson, *Metaphors We Live By* (Chicago: University of Chicago Press, 1980).

2. See John 10:11, 14; 15:5; 6:35, 48; 4:10-11; 10:7; 1:29, 36; Revelation 1:8; 21:6; 22:13; John 14:6.

3. Lakoff and Johnson, *Metaphors*, p. 3.

- metaphors for teaching — some historical and some contemporary — which are "micrometaphors" because they refer to the relationship of an individual teacher with his or her group of children
- metaphors for the children's ministry itself, which are "macrometaphors" since they represent the entire ministry
- the causes and implications of those metaphors

No metaphor, micro or macro, perfectly represents a ministry setting or its people. Yet helpful insights result when the metaphors of a context are identified, because metaphors matter. They matter a lot.

An Exercise with Metaphors of Teaching

For several years Scottie traveled as an education consultant for churches. She conducted workshops and seminars to equip volunteers in educational ministries. Often she would include an exercise involving micrometaphors — metaphors for the teacher, the learner, and the curriculum or materials. A description of this exercise follows; you may want to try it with your church.

The Learner

Scottie asks volunteer Sunday school teachers to identify common metaphors for the learner or student. Nearly always, "sponge" is the first metaphor they identify. Following in quick succession are "blank slate,"[4] empty cup or vessel, clay, and even wet cement (from the title of a 1981 book, *Children Are Wet Cement*). From church to church, the responses have been amazingly consistent. She makes a list of these responses on the left side of a chalkboard.

Her next question is, "What do all these things have in common?" Someone says, "They can be shaped." Someone else may add, "They're incomplete," or "They need to be filled." Eventually someone says, "They are all passive objects."

4. In classical literature on education the Latin term for blank slate is *tabula rasa*, first used by John Locke in the seventeenth century to refer to learners or students.

Indeed they are. Not only that, they are inanimate objects. (It is true that at some point a natural sponge is alive, but not when we use it.) These metaphors for learners are common in the historical education literature, and there is a measure of truth in them. But a learner, regardless of age, is much more than a passive, inanimate object.

If Lakoff and Johnson are right about the power of metaphor, what might be the implications for the learning process if teachers in our churches view learners first of all as sponges? Implicit in this view is that learners sit and *soak up* what is being taught.

Scottie then asks the teachers whether these metaphors are biblical. Upon reflection, they realize that people are not usually imaged in these ways in Scripture.[5] (Admittedly clay is a metaphor from Scripture. But the context is different for this metaphor: *we* are clay, and *God* is the potter — Isaiah 64:8. That's very different from picturing a human teacher as a potter.) The Bible uses words such as *sheep, plants, seeds, pilgrims* — things that are alive, growing, and active. *Disciple* is not used in Scripture to refer directly to children, but it is implicit throughout the pages of both Testaments that God desires children to follow and obey him — to become disciples. Scripture frequently refers to learners of all ages as children — in other words, people. In the exercise, a list of metaphors such as these — sheep, seeds/plants, pilgrims, disciples, people[6] — goes on the right side of the board.

Then come some questions: Would I teach "pilgrims" the same way I would teach "sponges"? What difference does it make if I envision my learners as passive, inanimate sponges or as active, growing, relational, living beings? What are sponge-like activities? What are pilgrim activities? Does any of this matter?

If we think about what we're trying to do — to help children want to become followers of Jesus — we need to see them as pilgrims, different from sponges. Pilgrims are people on a journey that has a high purpose. Christians' purpose is to be lifelong followers of Jesus. If we view children as sponges, we expect them to sit still with their hands in their lap and their mouths shut while they "absorb" the Bible. If we view them as pilgrims, we

5. Note that Matthew 23:27 is an exception: Jesus calls the religious leaders whitewashed tombs.

6. Sheep (Isa. 53:6), seeds/plants (Mark 4:15-20; John 15:5), pilgrims (Ps. 84:7, 119:54), disciples (John 13:35).

will help the children enter into the story and interact with it in any number of ways. These differences matter because not only do we want children to love the Lord Jesus, we also want them to love his story — the Bible.

The Teacher

The same process happens with metaphors for the teacher. The left side of the chalkboard gets filled with words such as *expert, authority, boss, controller, evaluator,* and *funnel holder* (pouring lesson contents into the heads of learners). On the right side the words represent a different view of teacher: *shepherd, farmer* or *gardener, fellow pilgrim, guide, friend.*

In what ways is the role of teacher on the left side of the board viewed differently from the role implied on the right? What might be the difference in the relationships between the teacher and the learner in the two columns? What impact might that dynamic have on the learning that takes place?

Metaphors on the left side of the board indicate that the teacher controls or *acts on* the learner, whereas the metaphors on the right bespeak an interactive relationship that guides rather than controls the learning process. Some of the metaphors indicate a collegial relationship yet acknowledge that the teacher's life experience and maturity has him or her farther along on the journey. The metaphors on the right appear more in accord with biblical accounts of how the Lord Jesus related to his followers.

The Curriculum Resources

The last component of teaching considered in this exercise is the curriculum resources or material to be used.[7] When asked whether curriculum is more like a blueprint or like a roadmap, volunteers are sometimes evenly

7. Several years ago Scottie asked a group of Sunday school volunteers to identify a metaphor for the curriculum — the lesson plans. A man of about twenty-four blurted out, "A straitjacket!" He was teaching five-year-olds and felt confined and limited by what the lesson plans were asking him to do. This young volunteer felt that he had to follow the curriculum even though it didn't seem to be "working," because it was written by people "who know what they are doing" while he was "just" a construction worker.

divided. As they consider the difference between these two metaphors, it soon becomes apparent that *blueprint* goes in the left column, while *roadmap* goes in the right. Why is that? A blueprint must be followed precisely, or the finished product will not be what the architect intended. But lesson plans should be used more like a roadmap. A starting point is provided as well as the desired destination, but the teacher has options as to which route to take to reach the destination. The chosen route may be an exact, efficient expressway-like following of the lesson plan. Or it may include excursions along winding country lanes to see new sights — for example, adding creative experiences that may enhance the learners' knowledge and insight.[8] The two columns on the chalkboard end up looking something like figure 1.1 on page 9.

Learning can happen under either set of micrometaphors. No ministry is likely to adhere completely to the model suggested by either of these columns. Sometimes learning should look more like the left column, but most of the time it should look like the right. Ministries usually float somewhere in the middle. The leader of children's ministry must discern when learning experiences should be more passive and when active experiences are better.

Metaphors from Scripture tend to be active and intrinsically link learner and teacher: if learners are viewed as sheep, the teacher is a shepherd;[9] the seed or plant metaphor is linked to the gardener or farmer metaphor; pilgrim links with fellow pilgrim, disciple with guide. Exploring the seed/farmer metaphors yields further significant insights. If the farmer's goal is to produce a crop, what is the role of the farmer in the process? To prepare the soil, fertilize it, water the seeds and plants, and control weeds. Yet the farmer cannot cause the seed to grow. That growth comes from within the seed. The farmer can only prepare the environment in ways that will facilitate growth. This has meaningful parallels with the role of those who minister with children.

As volunteer teachers consider metaphors and their influence, they begin to see implications for their own teaching. Some learning activities — such as fill-in-the-blank workbooks, preformatted crafts, unscram-

8. There *is* a blueprint for children's ministry, but it is not the lesson materials. It is the Bible, the Word of God. The architect of this blueprint is God himself.

9. Interestingly, in recent years many churches have begun to call Sunday morning teachers "shepherds."

Figure 1.1. Metaphors and learning models

	Passive Metaphors	Active Metaphors
Learner	Sponge	Sheep
	Blank slate	Seed or plant
	Empty cup	Pilgrims
	Clay	Disciples
	Wet cement	Children/people
Teacher	Expert	Shepherd
	Authority	Farmer or gardener
	Boss	Fellow pilgrim
	Evaluator	Guide
	Funnel holder	Friend
Curriculum	Blueprint	Roadmap
Strengths	Familiar	Emphasis on process of growth
	Easy to assess	Supports learning by experience
	Seems more efficient	Encourages creativity
	Focus is on the content	Focuses on application
	Learning seems more objective	Seems more effective to some
		Seems to value learners more highly
Weaknesses	Tends toward rote learning	Less familiar
	Less opportunity for creativity	Harder to evaluate
	Less focus on the individual	Seems less efficient
	Less reflection happens	Initially a challenge to equip staff
	Expects conformity	Learning seems more subjective

bling memory verses, and Bible crossword puzzles — tend not to encourage children to wrestle with the meaning and application of biblical texts. Wise teachers use such activities sparingly.

When empowered by more active metaphors, teaching provides learners with continual interaction with the learning environment. It recognizes that children learn best through experiences they can make sense of and reflect on, and that they need to feel valued and accepted. We want children to realize that the Bible is a real book about God's involvement in the lives of real people whom he created and loved, who did real things at a real place at a certain time. These concepts are pilgrim-like. Learning in which teachers and learners are fellow pilgrims looks somewhat foreign, however, to most people involved in children's ministry. Chapter 12 further explores these types of learning experiences.

Metaphors and Children's Ministry Models

As we have seen, metaphors for teaching in children's ministry influence the relationship between the teacher, the learner, and the content that is God's Word. But there are also macrometaphors that influence the overall direction of a church's ministry with children. Although often more subtle or implicit, these metaphors tend to shape everything that is done, even without the awareness of the leadership staff. The dominant metaphor tends to become the ministry model.

The wide range of models for children's ministry could be represented by many metaphors. Some currently prominent metaphors or models will be discussed in this section: School, Gold Star/Win a Prize, Carnival, Pilgrims' Journey, and Dance with God. The last two metaphors may be unfamiliar in many churches, but they have qualities that make them worthy of careful consideration.

School Model

For more than two hundred years the most widely used metaphor for ministry with children has been school — hence *Sunday school.* The metaphor became so pervasive that "school" crossed over from being a metaphor to being the reality. The way the Bible is taught in countless churches is synonymous with schooling. The architecture, organization, and practices of many churches' programs are very school-like. This includes an emphasis on learning content — in this case, the Bible. It must be noted that many public schools today offer dynamic, effective teaching and learning for children. However, in churches in which the School metaphor is dominant, the teaching often focuses on learning content without a context.

The educational wing of churches sometimes reflects factory-like efficiency. The area may be divided into classrooms, usually carefully age-graded, with teachers and students sitting at tables. At the end of the school year, each grade moves to the next classroom and a new teacher. This process is reminiscent of a slow-moving assembly line as if children were on conveyor belts, to be made into "finished products" by eighth or ninth grade, when the "manufacturing" process is completed.

Carefully designed materials with unified themes and lesson plans were soon developed. They continue to be distributed widely, so that learners of the same age study the same lesson each week even if they live on opposite sides of the country. These materials, based on the Bible, are easy to follow so that even the novice teacher can feel successful. Questions are asked to ensure that "learning" is happening. Rewards often accompany correct answers. Weekly reviews and even quizzes attempt to motivate learning. The intent is to teach children the Bible so that they know it cognitively.

Many churches have no Sunday school during the summer; it is "vacation" time just as in regular school. In some churches Christian education ceases when a person "graduates" from Sunday school — when she or he has learned the Bible lessons in the curricular materials. The age of such termination varies from church to church. In some traditions it corresponds with confirmation.

None of this is wrong or bad, but the question must be asked: Is *schooling* the best way to accomplish the real purpose of most Sunday schools — to help children want to become followers of Jesus Christ? One of Sunday school's initial purposes was to teach children to read, a skill that involves decoding squiggles on a page. The purpose now, however, is mainly to introduce children to the Bible and Jesus Christ. Is this purpose really achieved through schooling methods? Could it be that the School model unintentionally treats the Bible like a textbook from which children extract information, just as they learn the names of rivers and oceans from a geography text?

Strengths

This model is very familiar. It is time tested, efficient, and easy to administrate. It focuses on *knowing* the content. The lesson plan is carefully prepared so the teacher knows what to expect. The use of objective learning makes assessment easier. If enough classrooms are available, large numbers of children may be accommodated. Some learners excel in this type of setting. Also, children may have opportunities for nurturing relationships with the teacher.

Weaknesses

Cognition is stressed, often with insufficient concern for the affective and character dimensions of the child.[10] Some children see little difference between Sunday school and regular school, so they respond to the content they learn in similar ways. Often there is little active or "authentic" learning.[11] The lesson aims often are not retained long term, though the Bible stories may be memorable. Recruitment is frequently challenging because volunteers do not feel qualified to be "teachers." This model tends not to acknowledge individual abilities or creativity, life circumstances or needs, nor the past and present work of the Holy Spirit within the child's life.

Gold Star/Win a Prize Model

Competition and rewards have become so prominent in American culture that we rarely question the effects they may have on learning and on children within the church. Based on the enthusiastic response evoked from children (and many adults), this model assumes that rewards are effective motivators for learning. Rewards have become commonplace because they appear to bring about the desired results.

10. "Education which is concerned only with intellectual development or in which the acquisition of information is a compulsive priority is less than Christian" (Ted Ward, "Metaphors of Spiritual Reality, Part 3," *Bibliotheca Sacra* 139, no. 556 [1982]: 291).

11. "Authentic learning" refers to learners' opportunities to engage in real tasks relevant to the content or in real-life activities that enhance application of the content to their own lives.

Rewards and competition are evident in many church activities for children: when Sunday school attendance is posted and rewarded with stickers; when "sword drills" and Bible quizzing are used regularly as games for learning the Bible; when we have contests to see who can bring the most visitors; when we give prizes for memorizing Bible verses. What often happens with this model is that the children of church leaders and good students are the winners, while fringe kids and those who struggle in school are overlooked or feel stupid or, worse yet, think that in God's eyes they don't measure up.

This model should raise concerns because of the seductive influence of rewards as well as the me-first attitudes aroused by competition, whether it is "me" as an individual or "me and my team." Leaders in children's ministry need to be aware of the implicit agenda that accompanies rewards and competition. When *extrinsic* motivation or rewards are introduced to promote learning, the quality of the learning as well as its value to the child can diminish.[12] When motivation is *intrinsic,* on the other hand, the child wants to learn because the content itself has significance and meaning. Leaders of children want the value of God's Word, not a token prize, to be preeminent. Extrinsic motivation tends to devalue the activity itself; the hidden message of a reward system is "I need to bribe you to get you to do this because you wouldn't want to do it on your own."[13]

The power of competition is evident when a contest promising a prize is introduced to a group of children. Often an intense desire to win, a measure of aggression, and sometimes even hostility emerge within the

12. Several years ago Scottie had a conversation with a youngster that she remembers vividly. The child, whom we'll call Emily, told Scottie that she had just learned a Bible verse. Emily recited it, and then Scottie asked her a couple of questions about the content of the verse. Emily answered them well. Next, Scottie asked her why it was an important verse to learn. Emily responded, "If I say two more, I get a T-shirt." The leaders of that ministry had missed a wonderful opportunity to explore with Emily what meaning this verse about the love of God might have for her. Instead they motivated her with a reward.

13. Alfie Kohn's *Punished by Rewards* (Boston: Houghton Mifflin, 1993) provides extensive research on the effects of extrinsic motivation. Furthermore, according to George R. Knight, "[I]f the aim of Christian education is the restoration of the image of God in fallen humanity, then the aim of Christian discipline — both in mind and conduct — is self-control rather than control by others" (*Philosophy and Education: An Introduction in Christian Perspective* [Berrien Springs, Mich.: Andrews University Press, 1988], p. 230).

group. Winning becomes all important, while qualities such as gentleness, kindness, and thinking first of others are disregarded. Inherent in competition is the attitude "For *me* to win, I have to beat *you*." This is contrary to the Christian character called for in the New Testament: "Do nothing from selfish ambition, . . . regard others as better than yourselves" (Phil. 2:3).

The Gold Star/Win a Prize model has reached such popularity in the United States that programs and materials are being exported to other countries. Unintentionally, competition is spreading to non-Western countries whose cultures value cooperation over competition and serving others more than winning or asserting oneself. Wise international leaders of ministry with children contextualize what they receive from the United States, adapting the materials so that they are compatible with the values of their own culture and, most of all, those of Scripture. The U.S. developers of these materials need to learn from other cultures what is valued in those contexts and how to modify their programs rather than assuming that American approaches are superior.

In ministry settings with street kids and children at risk, the Gold Star/Win a Prize model is often the method of choice. The children are encouraged to earn points in order to receive a Bible or other things to enrich their lives. This is unfortunate: at-risk kids, even more than others, need to experience gifts that they don't have to earn so that they can understand and receive God's grace, the no-strings-attached, grace-filled gift of the gospel.

Strengths

This model is very popular among competitive children. It usually produces excellent short-term results. Volunteers who enjoy competition eagerly serve in these ministries, easing recruitment issues. The model stimulates enthusiasm and may provide helpful motivation for some. Fast learners often excel in competitive learning activities.

Weaknesses

The Gold Star/Win a Prize model may be stressful for noncompetitive children. It is based on extrinsic rather than intrinsic motivation. It sometimes promotes "gorge and purge" learning and tends to devalue cooperative learning. Often the learning activities are strongly disliked by children who struggle in school. This model may overstimulate some children, encouraging an intense desire to win. Competition may create animosity between opposing teams. Individual competition and rewards may breed self-righteousness and attitudes of superiority in winners. Also, this approach may evoke a greater interest in the prize than in the content and its significance.

Carnival Model

To most North Americans the word *carnival* immediately conjures memories of fun, noise, rides, cotton candy, and lots of activity. Presently, one of the rapidly spreading metaphors or models in children's ministry in the United States could be called the Carnival model. Since the early 1990s there has been a growing belief among some groups that church should be the high point of the week for children. To many children's leaders, that means it must be fun. This view is more prevalent in large churches that have significant resources of people, space, and finances.

A visitor to one of these ministries may be struck at the outset by an atmosphere reminiscent of Chuck E. Cheese's, a restaurant chain that caters to children. Large, open spaces are full of games, activities, and crafts. Lots of color, energy, and happy noise fill the room. Children, lots of children, mill around engaged in their activities of choice. "Carnival" churches often have similar age-appropriate activities for preschoolers.

The fun opening time is followed by learning-oriented sessions divided by age levels. This may include large-group time, with a drama team and worship band that present the lesson through music and a skit. The final period is devoted to small groups, where learners receive more personal attention from an adult leader.

Another version of the Carnival model consists of an elaborately decorated large space where many children gather. The leaders want the children to have a fun, memorable time, but this variation begins with a production for the kids rather than games and activities. The large meeting area may feature a complex theme, painstakingly evoked on every surface of the room by skilled artists. Some sites feel like a 3-D cartoon setting because of their elaborate constructions with special visual and sound effects such as bells, whistles, mist, or moving props. One U.S. church has a real, full-sized fire truck in its elementary children's area. It's used as a play area, but the back of the fire truck is also where children are baptized.

Strengths

Teaching happens in the Carnival model, and that teaching is entertaining. A high value is placed on fun. Hundreds of children are drawn to these venues. Most children love coming to these events, and they often enthusiastically invite friends. The setting and skills of those who do presentations make the sessions highly engaging. The drama, music, and media creations are usually marked by excellence. This model enables object lessons and analogies to be used readily as teaching methods.

Weaknesses

There seems to be a disconnection between the environment and the purpose of the ministry. Much of what takes place closely resembles entertainment in the culture at large, which may make it difficult for children to experience awe and wonder before the majesty and holiness of God. Some children may feel overwhelmed or lost in such a setting if not assigned to a caring, attentive small group leader. It is costly to establish the environment. High commitment and skill are required from the presenters. Fun is good, but this model overemphasizes it.

Pilgrims' Journey Model

When Scottie's children were young, their home was on three acres of wooded hills. A favorite activity of the kids was to help their dad blaze trails through the woods — trails that became paths for all kinds of adventures. By watching and helping their father, they learned to clear underbrush, fell small trees, and remove stumps. They learned according to their age and ability; at first their tasks were simple, but in time they learned to do all the work themselves.

Recently Scottie's son Phillip took his children back to the family homestead in Michigan. There he showed them how to blaze trails in the "lost 20," a wilderness area of creeks, hills, and woods. It was the same place where his father learned to make trails from his father, who had learned from his father. Four generations have blazed trails there by now, "teacher" and "learners" working side by side.

People of different ages influence each other on journeys that last a lifetime. This kind of learning occurs in the Pilgrims' Journey model — learning that is experienced, not just talked about; learning that is part of life's journey. Learning always happens on this journey, whether it is intentional or not. The pilgrims — teacher and learners alike — are shaped or formed by the journey.

The Pilgrims' curriculum develops along the way, serving as a roadmap for the journey, with emphasis on the application of biblical truths to life. Examples of this learning journey can be found in Scripture: the Israelites' exodus from Egypt and subsequent wanderings in the wilderness; twelve men traveling with Jesus, learning to be his disciples; the apostle Paul's itinerant work in the company of associates. The Pilgrims' Journey model clearly takes up a biblical metaphor.

This journey is for the entire faith community, not only children, so that everyone in the community can come "to maturity, to the measure of the whole stature of Christ" (Eph. 4:13). The involvement of all ages is important because "children are educated in the faith most appropriately when they are relationally connected with adults in activities prized by those adults."[14]

The micrometaphors for the teacher in this model are guide and fellow pilgrim — someone who is familiar with the journey and walks alongside the learners. The ministry leaders are fellow pilgrims alongside the children but have more experience and knowledge of the journey. In the course of a lifetime many different people will fill this significant role, from parents and grandparents to pastors, youth workers, and neighbors.

The Journey is an educational model based on a curriculum of life and spiritual growth as set forth in Deuteronomy 6 and other passages, such as Philippians 1:6. This journey toward Christlikeness has intrinsic rewards — rewards of growth and learning — for both the learner and the teacher, though the journey affects each pilgrim differently. The teacher's goal is to help pilgrims learn in a life context. In the process everyone learns from each other.

From an educational perspective, Douglas Sloan's term "participatory

14. Barbara Kines Myers and William Myers, *Engaging in Transcendence: The Church's Ministry and Covenant with Young Children* (Cleveland: Pilgrim, 1992), p. 154.

knowing" helps explain the human process involved in this model.[15] This form of knowing can have long-term influence on the person as he or she matures. Sloan stresses that such deep knowing "comes through activity" — active encounters that continue to inform the learner over the course of life. These encounters are experiential, contextual, and "immersive," influencing the cognitive, interpretive, and faithing process of children and adults. Active encounters such as these look very different from what usually happens in other models. (See chapters 11 and 12 for ministry examples that demonstrate the Pilgrims' Journey and lead to "participatory knowing.")

Leaders who base their ministry model on this metaphor view children as individuals in unique places in their journey toward being lifelong followers of Jesus. This model acknowledges the process by which a child keeps "increasing in wisdom and stature" (Luke 2:52, NASB). Adherents of the Pilgrims' Journey model use passages such as this brief description of the childhood of Jesus to inform their purposes.

This model with its holistic educational foundation allows for a wide variety of learning experiences within the ministry. There may be times when leaders want to draw on other metaphors or models, such as the Carnival or School model, to accomplish specific purposes, while retaining the Pilgrims' Journey model as the overarching, driving metaphor.

Strengths

The Pilgrims' Journey model creates learning experiences that are part of life and that are formative for participants. This educational model is intentional about following principles of spiritual growth drawn from passages from both Testaments of the Bible. Teachers and learners are fellow pilgrims, with the teacher serving as guide and companion on the journey. The guides can be at ease in their roles because they know that they are not solely responsible for the success of the journey but build on others' contributions. This model enables persons of all ages to participate holistically. Experiences with God's story and the people of God are as significant as "knowing" the content. The model is flexible enough that other models may be used in appropriate situations.

15. Cited in Myers and Myers, *Engaging in Transcendence,* p. 4.

Weaknesses

Ministry leaders may have little experience with this model; it may also be challenging for volunteers. Learning may be hard to assess. The Pilgrims' Journey model is not as likely to attract masses of children as some other models do. Bible learning tends to be less "systematic" than it is in the School model.

Dance with God Model

This artistic, expressive model is a challenge to describe compared to the others. There is no vivid, easily recognizable context or experience that depicts this model. Whereas the Pilgrims' Journey is an educational model, the Dance with God metaphor represents a relational model — the relationship of the child "with the living God — enacted in this world."[16] The people in the child's life become agents for this relationship as the child grows in awareness of the presence of God. Like the Pilgrims' Journey, the Dance with God model includes the whole person, in his or her cognitive, affective, behavioral, and especially the spiritual dimensions.

The name and description of this metaphor comes from *The Orphean Passages* by Walter Wangerin.[17] He pictures a child's experience with God as a dance through stages of spiritual life, which he calls "faithing." Wangerin believes that from conception a person bears God's own image (the *imago Dei*), and thus the developing child has innate sensitivity to God. The dance begins soon after birth — "in the mists" — with the infant's earliest awareness of things. The rays of sunshine warming the bassinet. The feel and smell of the mother's body as she nurses the baby. A soft lullaby. The consistent, loving touch and sounds of the caregivers in the church nursery. Because of the grace of God, these kinds of things help begin the dance of the infant with the as-yet-unknown, unnamed presence and love of God.

> Who can say when, in a child, the dance with God begins? No one. Not even the child can later look back and remember the beginning of it, because it is as natural an experience (as early and as universally received)

16. Walter Wangerin, *The Orphean Passages* (Grand Rapids: Zondervan, 1986), p. 11.
17. Wangerin, *Orphean Passages*, pp. 20-53.

> as the child's relationship with the sun or with his bedroom. And the beginning, specifically, cannot be remembered because in the beginning there are no words for it. The language to name, contain, and to explain the experience comes afterward. The dance, then, the relationship with God, faithing, begins in a mist.[18]

After this initial stage comes the *naming* phase of the dance, in which names for God are introduced. Those caring for the little one at home and at church speak these names for God in prayer, song, and story but also through direct conversation with the child: "Pat-a-cake, pat-a-cake, God loves you"; "Jesus loves *you,* this I know"; "God gave you a wonderful smile." Very naturally, the child absorbs these names for God just as readily as Mama and Dada.

As the child grows into the preschool years, the dance continues with the *containing* phase — when the child begins to hear stories of God's character and actions that he or she begins to contain and retain. Home-based learning is reinforced by experiences at church.

The dance moves into the *explaining* phase as the child reaches school age. By now the child has been hearing and entering into God's story for a few years at home and church, enough so that he or she can retell and soon explain simple Bible stories to a friend or a younger sibling, sometimes play-acting Sunday school.

The final phase of the child's dance with God — *claiming* — comes in early adolescence, when the dance is claimed as his or her own. For Wangerin the child is saying, in essence, "I want this dance with God to continue the rest of my life." In some church traditions this stage equates with confirmation.

Wangerin goes on to explain that the music for the dance with God is controlled by the environment — the home and the church. And the music can die. When that happens, the dance stops. If the child never hears names for God, the music dies early in the child's life. If the child never hears stories of God, if the child never is able to retell those stories, or if he or she is not given opportunity to claim the story, the music dies.

This model reminds Scottie of a wonderful annual Lenten event in the congregation with which she worships: a Seder (Passover) celebration for all ages on Maundy Thursday. This meaningful observance uses the sto-

18. Wangerin, *Orphean Passages,* p. 20.

ries and symbolic foods that commemorate the exodus of the children of Israel from slavery in Egypt. It is a beautiful time of rehearsing the goodness of God among all ages and types of households of faith. At the conclusion of the Seder meal there is a time of traditional Jewish folk dancing — the "dance with God" represented for all to see. A nursing mother keeps time to the music as she pats her infant. A toddler is carried by her parent as they dance with others in the traditional circle. A preschooler half dances, half swings between his parents as his not-quite-coordinated legs try to keep up. A first-grader intently watches the feet of her mother and tries to mimic the movements. Older children move through the grapevine steps of the dance with ease and energy. Off to the side some young teens create their own circle, adding extra spins and gyrations. Congregants from eight decades of life dance together to music that celebrates God's deliverance of the children of Israel.

The child's dance with God begins "in the mists" and is sustained in community — the community of faith. In children's ministry, a congregation's choice of model influences the dance, and the ministry leaders are part of the orchestra that makes the music. But as in the Pilgrims' Journey model, no one, other than the Holy Spirit, is solely responsible for sustaining the dance for the child, for his or her "faithing" process. Many people through the years influence this dance, for the good and the not-so-good. Wangerin writes, "Faithing simply is not a series of propositions, or theses, conceptually joined together; it is a *progressive experience*."[19]

In the Dance with God ministry model, if for some children the music of the dance has stopped, learning experiences are provided to enable the music to resume. For other children, opportunities help sustain the music to aid the growth in faith. This means that ministries may not be tightly age-graded as in other models but more in line with stages of "faithing." Also, parents are encouraged to be actively involved at home and in ministries at church in order to help their children, whatever age they may be, grow in their relationship with God.

In ministry the Dance with God model often has a distinctive feel. The pace is slow. Voices are soft and gentle. Lighting may be subdued. Colors are soft. The space, full of materials for learning and worship, feels special. After an initial period of adjustment to this countercultural environment, children move about the space reflecting the attitudes and behaviors of

19. Wangerin, *Orphean Passages,* p. 13, emphasis added.

the leaders. Learning may look different in various contexts, but it always includes a Bible story, a response to the story, and opportunities to be with God.

Though this model may be somewhat difficult to conceptualize, it takes seriously the fact that children can have a relationship with God and that the faith community as well as the family has a vital role in sustaining that relationship.

Strengths

This model draws on the concept that a person grows in faith — that it's a process.[20] The Dance with God model has a high view of the child, acknowledging above all God's creation of and love for the child. Leaders assume that children are able to encounter God with a sense of awe and wonder, yet they acknowledge that children of similar ages will not be at the same place in their awareness of God. As in the Pilgrims' Journey model, learning experiences tend to be built around "authentic" tasks. Direct instruction in the traditional sense usually does not take place. Many people throughout the child's life help sustain the music for the dance.

Weaknesses

Unless leaders are intentional, this model may overlook the child's bent to sin and his or her need to acknowledge that sin. It also may fail to provide opportunities for the child who at an early age desires to make a commitment to follow Jesus. Because many contemporary North American parents feel ill-equipped to be involved in the spiritual nurture of their children, this model may not be as effective as it might if the parents and church could work together closely.

Roots and Implications of Metaphors

The way we minister with children is shaped by conscious and unconscious metaphors. These metaphors are formed by what we believe about

20. Here are a few Scripture references that support this model: 1 Corinthians 3:6-7; Ephesians 4:15; 1 Peter 2:2; 2 Peter 3:18.

children, about how they learn and experience God, and about what our ministry should be like. We need to be concerned about tendencies to look to popular culture for the metaphors and methods that shape the church experiences of children. Metaphors do not develop in a vacuum. They are influenced by historical traditions, economics, social structures, educational theory, and theology, in addition to other aspects of culture.

No metaphor is perfect, and all metaphors communicate values. But some word pictures are more compatible with biblical values and goals than others. As we analyze the metaphors identified in this chapter, the ideologies and assumptions that underlie them begin to emerge. These same metaphors support educational theories and somewhat predictable methodologies that influence the kind of learning experiences that will occur.

A church's micrometaphor for teaching should be harmonious with the macrometaphor for the ministry itself. These two categories of metaphors should also be compatible with the purpose statement of the ministry in order to assure that the intended learning and experiences will actually take place. But this is not always the case. Children's ministry leaders must analyze these issues. Leaders need to be aware that because metaphors and their accompanying methods have real power, they have the potential to inform, form, or deform learners.

Children's ministry becomes *informing* when the emphasis is placed on cognition, learning the content of the Bible, knowing the stories and facts of Scripture. The informing process has a place in all ministries, but it is inadequate if it is the primary focus of the ministry. The ministry is more *forming* when it seeks to involve the whole child, not just his or her intellect, in the journey until Christ is formed in him or her (Gal. 4:19). When forming metaphors drive the ministry, the teacher is a guide and fellow traveler. The role of guide is broader and more holistic than that of an expert in biblical content. A forming children's ministry is able to provide what is usually missing from an informing model.

A warning is in order at this point. Some metaphors for children's ministry may actually be *deforming*, particularly when they conflict with the purpose of the ministry. The ways this "deforming" happens are usually subtle. It happens when an essential aspect of ministry is either omitted or overshadowed by some facet of the metaphor, so that children get a distorted view of God and/or the Christian life.

Ultimately ministry is about *transforming* — the child's being transformed into the likeness of Jesus Christ. No model or ministry can do that. No person can do that. Transformation is the work of the Holy Spirit alone. All we can do is to help facilitate that process. Much of the time that means that we adults need to get out of the way so that the Spirit of God can do that work. Our responsibility is to create an environment in which the child can learn about and enter into God's story, respond to the Holy Spirit, and experience the presence and leading of God.

Summary

This chapter examines the influence metaphors may have in ministry with children. Micrometaphors represent the relationship between the teacher, the learners, and the materials in a small group or classroom setting. A macrometaphor is the primary or driving metaphor for the entire ministry. Though each of the metaphors may be used in appropriate ways within children's ministry, some macrometaphors are less effective than others. Even though many metaphors may be valid for ministry, it is essential that the accompanying methods or approaches be compatible with the goals and purposes of that particular setting.

The children's ministry leader has the challenging but important responsibility to ensure that there is harmony between the metaphor for the ministry, the educational approach and methodology, and the ultimate purpose of the ministry — that there is congruity between purpose and methods. Acknowledging that learning is one purpose of educational ministries, educational philosopher George Knight says that there are higher purposes that must be preeminent: "reconciling fallen individuals to God and one another and restoring the image of God in them. . . . Christian educators will use many, if not all, of the same methods as other teachers. They will, however, select and emphasize those methodologies that best aid them in helping their students to develop Christlike characters."[21]

Virtually all churches that regard themselves as truly Christian consider their children's ministry to be biblically based. Yet these churches provide widely differing experiences driven by contrasting metaphors and methodologies. Do these differences matter? Yes, for sure. But there are many, many factors that make it inappropriate to judge any ministry

21. Knight, *Philosophy and Education,* p. 229.

model as totally misguided. First and foremost is the fact that in spite of the inadequacy of our efforts, our sovereign, powerful God is able to bring reconciliation and redemption to any circumstance through the work of the Holy Spirit. Second, a caring adult's consistently representing the unconditional love of Jesus Christ to a child is a powerful force for helping that child know God. Such a loving relationship speaks more loudly to the child than any ministry metaphor.

No metaphor or model is necessarily wrong, but the ministry leader must be aware of the dominant metaphor and its inherent assumptions. This is hard to do. It's a challenge to be objective in identifying one's own metaphors, particularly if aspects of them may not enhance the spiritual growth of the child.[22]

Because the metaphors that underlie children's ministry matter, consider the following questions as you review this chapter and analyze your own ministry with children:

- Which metaphors best conform to God's redemptive story? (You may want to add additional metaphors to the brief list surveyed in this chapter.) In what ways, if any, do they transcend cultures, current educational theory, and fads?
- In what ways does each metaphor resonate with Scripture? Where is each inadequate?
- Within the macrometaphor for your ministry, what is the view of the learner? Is it a biblical view of children? What is the view and role of the teacher?
- In what ways does that metaphor shape how learning happens?
- What values are communicated through the metaphor? Do those values help the child toward Christlikeness?
- How is Scripture treated and presented to the learners?

22. Developing your own philosophy of ministry, though time consuming and requiring much thought, is a good way to identify significant factors that may enhance your ministry and help put your finger on methods that may impede the accomplishment of your goals. See chapter 13, "In Specialized Ministries," pp. 285-88, for help in developing your philosophy using a model developed by William Frankena.

Chapter 2

CHILDREN IN THE BIBLE

When Cathy talked with Michael on the phone, his little daughter — Cathy's great-niece and namesake — was only hours old. "She has already taught us so much about God," he exclaimed with wonder. "She hasn't done anything. She just lies there, and sometimes she fusses, but we love her so much."

Was this young father just carried away with the emotion of this wonderful moment, the birth of his first child, or was he in touch with God's plan for parents and children? What does God think about children and their place in the home and the faith community? To answer these questions, we need to explore what the Bible says about children. Where do they show up in the biblical narratives? How did the Jewish people of ancient times view children? What did Jesus have to say about them? What insights can we glean from the biblical text to guide our life and ministry with children? In this chapter we search for answers to these questions.

Children: A Blessing

God's first recorded words to Adam and Eve are a blessing, a blessing involving children. The biblical story begins with the account of God's creative acts. Describing God's work on the sixth day of creation, Genesis 1:26-28 tells us:

> Then God said, "Let us make humankind in our image, according to our likeness. . . ."
>
> So God created humankind in his image,
> in the image of God he created them;
> male and female he created them.
>
> God blessed them, and God said to them, "Be fruitful and multiply, and fill the earth and subdue it; and have dominion over the fish of the sea and over the birds of the air and over every living thing that moves upon the earth."[1]

God instructed the first humans to be fruitful, multiply, and fill the earth. The author of Genesis saw the God-given privilege of procreation as a blessing. From the beginning of the biblical record, then, children are considered a blessing.

Throughout the Old Testament we find positive views of children. Psalm 128:1-4 lays out the rewards that come to the person who serves God.

> Happy is everyone who fears the LORD,
> who walks in his ways. . . .
> Your wife will be like a fruitful vine
> within your house;
> your children will be like olive shoots
> around your table.
> Thus shall the man be blessed
> who fears the LORD.

According to the psalmist, children are an important part of the blessing given to those who follow God.

When Jacob and Esau meet after years of bitterness and separation, Esau asks, "Who are these with you?" Jacob responds, "The children whom God has graciously given your servant" (Gen. 3:5). When Joseph presents Manasseh and Ephraim to Jacob, he introduces them as "my sons, whom God has given me" (Gen. 48:9). Speaking through Joshua, God reminds the Israelites, "I gave [to Abraham] Isaac; and to Isaac I gave Jacob

1. All Scripture references are from the New Revised Standard Version, unless otherwise indicated.

and Esau" (Josh. 24:3-4). The Hebrew people saw their children as gifts from God, expressions of God's grace.

The psalms speak of children as a source of joy. In celebration of God, the psalmist says,

> He gives the barren woman a home,
> making her the joyous mother of children.
> Praise the LORD! (Ps. 113:9)

In Psalm 127 Solomon exclaims,

> Sons are indeed a heritage from the LORD,
> the fruit of the womb a reward.
> Like arrows in the hand of a warrior
> are the sons of one's youth.
> Happy is the man who has
> his quiver full of them. (Ps. 127:3-5)

Solomon believes that many sons bring happiness to a father's heart. He also notes that they are "from the LORD." Proverbs 17:6 declares, "Grandchildren are the crown of the aged."

Biblical authors consistently affirm that mothers, fathers, and grandparents find joy in children. God blesses us through children.

Children and the Covenant

God's story begins with the glory of creation and God's blessing on the first man and woman, a blessing that includes children. However, God's creatures quickly sin, disrupting their relationships with God and one another. Genesis 3–11 reveals the results of sin and God's activity in this sin-marred world.

A new chapter in God's story of redemption begins in Genesis 12: "Now the LORD said to Abram, 'Go from your country and your kindred and your father's house to the land that I will show you. I will make of you a great nation, and I will bless you, and make your name great, so that you will be a blessing. I will bless those who bless you, and the one who curses you I will curse; and in you all the families of the earth shall be blessed'"

(Gen. 12:1-3). God calls Abram into a covenant relationship, and Abram's part in the covenant is belief in God's promises and willingness to act on that faith. He acts in faith by following God, leaving the old life, and going to a new land and a new life that God will show him. When we look at God's part in the covenant, we discover that children are at the heart of God's promise. God promises to make a great nation of Abram, and through Abram and Abram's children God plans to bless "all the families of the earth."

As we follow Abraham's story (Gen. 12–22), we discover that the child Isaac is central to the covenant between God and Abraham. Without Isaac there would have been no covenant. God's design requires that the "great nation" come from a child whose life is a gift from God. His birth, to a ninety-year-old mother and a hundred-year-old father (Gen. 17:17), would be impossible apart from God's gracious intervention. In his relationship with Isaac, Abraham faces the challenge of living by faith in covenant with God. The long years of waiting for the fulfillment of God's promise to give him a son severely test Abraham's faith. He agonizes with God over the unfulfilled promise.

> After these things the word of the LORD came to Abram in a vision, "Do not be afraid, Abram, I am your shield; your reward shall be very great." But Abram said, "O Lord GOD, what will you give me, for I continue childless, and the heir of my house is Eliezer of Damascus?" And Abram said, "You have given me no offspring, and so a slave born in my house is to be my heir." But the word of the LORD came to him, "This man shall not be your heir; no one but your very own issue shall be your heir." He brought him outside and said, "Look toward heaven and count the stars, if you are able to count them." Then he said to him, "So shall your descendants be." And he believed the LORD; and the LORD reckoned it to him as righteousness. (Gen. 15:1-6)

Here we see the pain of a man who had no children to inherit his goods and carry on his line. At the beginning of this conversation, God's promise sounds hollow to Abram; his faith cannot see the possibility of God's fulfilling the promise. But when God reiterates the promise, Abram reaches out in faith again, and his belief is "reckoned as righteousness."

Even after this encounter with God, Abram's faith fails. Rather than waiting for God to act, Abram takes things into his own hands, trying to help God provide the needed son. But the birth of Ishmael, resulting from Abram and Sarai's plan, does not fulfill the covenant promise. Graciously, God does not abandon Ishmael or Abram because of Abram's failure to trust, nor does God hurry the plan. In faith Abram (whose name God changes to Abraham) waits another fifteen years for God to act.

Finally, Abraham and Sarah hold Isaac in their arms, the child who embodies God's covenant, God's powerful faithfulness. What joy!

The testing of Abraham's faith, however, is not completed. Some years later God comes to Abraham with a very difficult command: "Take your son, your only son Isaac, whom you love, and go to the land of Moriah, and offer him there as a burnt offering" (Gen. 22:2). Abraham obeys; he surrenders Isaac to God. He gives back the gift God has given, and God, who never planned to harm the boy, rescues him. In this full surrender of his child, Abraham proves his faith-filled commitment to God and God's covenant with him. God responds with a reaffirmation of the covenant. "I will indeed bless you, and I will make your offspring as numerous as the stars of heaven and as the sand that is on the seashore. And your offspring shall possess the gate of their enemies, and by your offspring shall all the nations of the earth gain blessing for themselves, because you have obeyed my voice" (Gen. 22:17-18).

God's ultimate blessing for Abraham is that through his children all the nations of the world will be blessed. He and his children have the great privilege of being partners with God in blessing the world. Through them the Messiah will come, bringing salvation for all.

In the biblical story we see parents and children together living the covenant. God continues to act in the world today, and as God's people, we also live out God's story. For us, as it was for Abraham, living in covenant relationship with God calls us to a life of faith and involves our children.[2] Concerns relating to our children test our faith, and we grow in

2. In drawing comparisons between Abraham and Isaac and Christian parents and their children, it is important to note some differences and similarities between God's covenant with Abraham and the new covenant of the New Testament. God's covenant with Abraham was with a particular family, whose bloodline as descendants of Abraham identified them as covenant people. Jews were born into this covenant, and male infants were marked with the sign of the covenant, circumcision. The new covenant is entered not by physical inheritance but by new birth through faith in Jesus Christ (John 3:16). Our faith, not our bloodline, marks us as God's covenant people. We have seen, however, that faith also characterized Abraham's covenant relationship

faith as we work with them and surrender them to God. We, and our children, can also be part of God's plan to bless the world, not by providing the lineage for Jesus, as Abraham and Isaac did, but in many other ways. We can know the fulfillment of being partners with God. And God's covenant is not just for adults. Children also participate in the covenant, sometimes by refining our obedience and faith, even before they have any understanding of covenant relationships.

As we follow God's people through the Old Testament, an erratic story unfolds. At times the people faithfully live according to God's laws, wanting to be covenant people. But they repeatedly turn from God to other gods, ignore God, and experience discipline intended to draw them back into relationship with God. Finally, God's rebellious people are carried into exile. Scattered amongst the people of other nations, many of them remember their covenant faith. They practice God's laws as best they can and in this way maintain their identity.

In the fifth century B.C., the exiles began to return to the land of Israel. Ezra and Nehemiah returned also, to lead in rebuilding the city of Jerusalem and in reforms that would renew the returned exiles as covenant-keeping people. The number of Israelites who had intermarried with non-Jews deeply distressed Ezra and Nehemiah. In their teaching they called the people to purity in their marriages, requiring that both partners be Jews.[3]

In *Children in the Early Church,* W. A. Strange explains this passion for marital purity begun in the time of Ezra and Nehemiah and continued into Jesus' time.

> The aim of this policy was to secure offspring who belong fully and without any ambiguity to the covenant people, a "holy race" as they are described in Ezra 9:2. In the Jewish culture of the first century, therefore, children had great importance in assuring the future of the community. Children conceived within purely Jewish marriages, and brought up strictly within the ancestral tradition, guaranteed a future for a community whose survival depended on loyalty to their covenant faith.[4]

---

with God. His faith-filled example therefore can speak powerfully to us as new covenant people desiring to live a life of faith and to nurture the faith of our children.

3. Ezra 9–10 gives a good picture of how intermarriage was viewed.

4. W. A. Strange, *Children in the Early Church* (Carlisle, Cumbria, U.K.: Paternoster, 1996), p. 11.

Sandra Richter also notes that through the exile the Jewish people had lost the national boundaries that had defined their identity. They therefore focused their concern on establishing social boundaries of a "holy race" and children formed by the tradition to maintain their covenant identity.[5]

Again we see children as central to the covenant. Their birth into a covenant family was important; furthermore, parents were responsible to be sure their children learned and experienced the ancestral traditions. The spiritual formation of children was crucial to the covenant people.

Children's Formation as Covenant People: A Nonformal Process

Concern for the spiritual formation of children appeared long before the return of the exiles to Jerusalem. As Moses prepared the Israelites to enter the Promised Land, teaching the faith to the next generation surfaced as a top priority. God charges Moses with the responsibility of teaching the commandments of God to the people. God's goal is that Moses teach the present generation in such a way that their children and their children's children will respect (fear) God and live out God's laws (Deut. 6:1-2). At the beginning of Deuteronomy 6, Moses places before the people the challenge of passing their faith, a lived faith, from generation to generation. As we look further in Deuteronomy, we discover how this can be done effectively.

In Deuteronomy 5 Moses reminds the people that God has made a covenant with them and given them commandments by which to live. Their part of the covenant is to keep the commandments, and God will keep the promises made to their ancestors and bless them. Moses begins his teaching in Deuteronomy 6 by calling all God's people to listen.

> Hear, O Israel: The LORD is our God, the LORD alone. You shall love the LORD your God with all your heart, and with all your soul, and with all your might. Keep these words that I am commanding you today in your heart. Recite them to your children and talk about them when you are at home and when you are away, when you lie down and when you rise.

5. Comments from Sandra Richter, assistant professor of Old Testament, Asbury Theological Seminary.

> Bind them as a sign on your hand, fix them as an emblem on your forehead, and write them on the doorposts of your house and on your gates. (6:4-9)

Before he addresses the teaching of children (vv. 7-9), Moses focuses each person's attention on his or her own relationship with God. In verses 4-6 Moses identifies three elements in a life of obedience to God that is fulfilling and winsome to others. First, the people need to know their God. Over time, they will not obey unless they accept and give allegiance to the one Lord, their God. Second, Moses lays before them the possibility of an obedience that flows from loving God completely, not a reluctant obedience but one motivated by love. Third, he challenges the people to internalize God's laws, to meditate on them and make them their own. Then God's commands will become an inner guiding force, not just external restrictions. When obedience flows from a transforming love relationship with God, others sense that love and are drawn to it. Such a relationship prepares a person for teaching the next generation.

Notice that Moses commands the people to teach God's commandments to their children in the flow of life (6:7). Reciting the commandments and talking about them with the children is to take place at home, when the family travels, at bedtime, and first thing in the morning. In other words, conversation about God and God's laws should not be confined to a formal teaching setting. It should flow freely, spontaneously, at any time and in any place. In this way God becomes an integral part of the family's life.

Symbols are also used to teach children (6:8-9). When Jewish fathers prayed, they strapped key verses from the Law to their left hand and forehead. Over time Jewish families established the tradition of placing selected verses in little boxes, mezuzahs, by the door of their house. Each time they passed through, the Jews touched the mezuzah, and thus they were reminded many times a day of God's Law.[6]

Reciting the commandments to children and surrounding them with concrete symbols introduces them to God's laws, but that is just the beginning of the teaching. To understand God's ways, children need to see the commandments lived out. Again and again Moses reminds the Israelites that they are to observe, do, and keep God's decrees (Deut. 6:1, 2, 3, 17, 18).

6. *The Wesley Bible* (Nashville: Thomas Nelson, 1990), p. 263n.

Obedience will result in a lifestyle different from that of the non-Jewish people around them. Children will notice the difference and want to know, "What do these rituals and actions mean?" Notice, Moses does not say "*if* your children ask" but "*when* your children ask" (Deut. 6:20). A God-honoring life of integrity causes children to ask about that life, and when they ask, they are ready to listen and learn.

Look at the answer Moses instructs the people to give: "When your children ask you in time to come, 'What is the meaning of the decrees and the statutes and the ordinances that the LORD our God has commanded you?' then you shall say to your children, 'We were Pharaoh's slaves in Egypt, but the LORD brought us out of Egypt with a mighty hand'" (Deut. 6:20-21). Children best comprehend truth when it comes to them packaged in story. What the children need to hear, in answer to their questions, is the story of what God has done in the lives of the Jewish people, how they were slaves but God had delivered them. In the story the children can discover their powerful, faithful God. The story gives meaning to their religious observance, and it gives the children their identity as people with whom God has made covenant.

Whose lives should the children observe? Is it just the parents whom the children should hear telling the stories of God? Deuteronomy 6 is addressed to Israel (vv. 3-4). Although verses 7-9 appear to describe family activities, most of the chapter calls for a response from the whole faith community. Parents do have a significant role to play in the spiritual formation of their children. But God does not intend for one man and one woman to carry the full responsibility for their children's spiritual formation. God's plan, seen in Deuteronomy 6, is that the faith community support the family and together they nurture the children. Children will see many adults living in loving obedience to God. They can ask questions of people they admire and hear many stories of God at work. In such a vital community, parents will be strengthened and grow in their commitment to God.

Before we leave Deuteronomy 6, look at verses 10-12.

> When the LORD your God has brought you into the land that he swore to your ancestors, to Abraham, to Isaac, and to Jacob, to give you — a land with fine, large cities that you did not build, houses filled with all sorts of goods that you did not fill, hewn cisterns that you did not hew, vineyards and olive groves that you did not plant — and when you have

> eaten your fill, take heed that you do not forget the LORD, who brought you out of the land of Egypt, out of the house of slavery.

Several times in Deuteronomy, Moses expresses this fear. On three occasions he challenges the people not to forget God, and within a few verses of the warning he commands them to teach their children (Deut. 4:9-10; 6:7, 12; 11:16, 19). The juxtaposition of these verses is significant. When we recite God's commandments to our children and talk with them about God in the flow of everyday life; when we remember the importance of the life our children see us live; when we tell our children the story of God at work throughout history and in our lives, it is hard to forget God. Teaching the faith to children strengthens the faith of adults.

Did you notice that Moses fears for the people in *good* times? He knows that when they are enjoying the good gifts God has given them, it will be easy to take God for granted, to forget their need for God. When we feel self-sufficient, we often let God drift to the periphery of life; we continue to give God an hour or two on Sunday mornings, but the rest of our lives have little in them to stimulate the faith questions of our children. Keeping our focus on God, enjoying and serving God with our children takes intentional diligence, especially in times of success and ease. The needed diligence may be fueled by a commitment to pass on the faith to our children.

Children's Formation through Ritual, Experience, and Questions

God called the people of Israel to a way of life, not just to the observance of a few religious rituals. This way of life flowed from a heart of love for God and others. As a part of that way of life, however, God did prescribe religious rituals. These rituals were also means of teaching children and keeping the memory of God's mighty acts alive for all the people.

Each year the Israelites celebrated three major feasts: Passover, Feast of Weeks, and Feast of Tabernacles.[7] The whole family and their servants celebrated these feasts together as intergenerational events. The Feast of

7. Descriptions of the feasts are found in Exodus 12, Leviticus 23, and Deuteronomy 16.

Weeks was a time of thanksgiving, an opportunity to praise God for providing the harvest. Even in this time of joy, the ritual reminded the people of their days as slaves and of God's ongoing faithful provision for them.

Through the Passover and the Feast of Tabernacles, the Israelites reenacted their history. They ate the symbolic Passover meal together, the children asked questions, and the adults retold the story of God's delivering them from slavery in Egypt.

The Feast of Tabernacles began with everyone waving branches and praising God together. The families built shelters of branches and lived in them for seven days. How children loved this celebration. The fun events, however, had the purpose of ensuring that each generation of Israelites knew that their ancestors had wandered in the wilderness but God had faithfully led them into the Promised Land.

During Bible times these feasts were national celebrations. Everyone who was able gathered in Jerusalem for the feast. Excitement ran high. As they worshiped their God and remembered God's mighty acts for them, the people of God were bonded together. As a result, in those gatherings children developed a deep sense of identity.

Jewish children knew their history, as they experienced it in the feasts year after year. Through these repeated rituals, they grasped what they were ready to learn as they grew and developed.

The feasts gave adults opportunities to tell the story of God's acts when the children's minds were curious. God commanded Joshua to create another stimulus for telling the story. When the Israelites crossed the Jordon into the Promised Land, a man from every tribe carried a large stone from the riverbed where the priests' feet had stood. They erected this pile of stones as a sign that would prompt children to ask, "What do those stones mean?" Joshua instructed the people, "Then you shall tell them that the waters of the Jordan were cut off before the ark of the covenant of the LORD. When it passed over the Jordan, the waters of the Jordan were cut off. So these stones shall be to the Israelites a memorial forever" (Josh. 4:7).

Are you seeing a theme? The lifestyle of God's people, the feasts, and certain visual markers in the land all caused children to ask questions. In these teachable moments, adults told the story of their powerlessness and God's deliverance, faithfulness, and plan for the covenant people.

In our homes and faith communities, what leads children to ask questions about God, the Christian life, and faith? How might we plan to re-enact the stories of God from the Bible, history, and our own lives so that our children know and identify with these stories?

Covenant People Being Formed Together

As noted, the feasts were intergenerational events. Throughout the Old Testament we find children present with their parents in times of solemn national commitment and crisis as well as in times of high worship and celebration.

Shortly after they entered the land of Canaan, Joshua summoned the people to Mount Ebal (Josh. 8:30-35). He built an altar, offered a sacrifice to God, and then, with the people watching, wrote words of the Law on stones. Next, he led the people in reaffirming their covenant with God and read to them the words of the Law. The children were present, included in the gathering of the covenant people. The action, concrete symbols, and participation in the covenant affirmation held great potential to engage the mind and heart of a child.

During King Jehoshaphat's reign, a great enemy army moved toward Jerusalem (2 Chron. 20:1-28). The king called the people to fast, gather in Jerusalem, and seek God's help. Children came with their parents. They heard the king pray. In his prayer he praised God's greatness, told the story of God's past deliverance, and then, realizing that he was powerless against the enemy, confessed, "We do not know what to do, but our eyes are on you." The children experienced that atmosphere charged with fear and hope. Then they heard Jahaziel prophesy, "Thus says the LORD to you: 'Do not fear or be dismayed at this great multitude; for the battle is not yours but God's'" (2 Chron. 20:15).

God did give the victory, and the next day everyone returned to the temple praising God. What a wonderful way for children to learn about their powerful God. They were present to sense the human hopelessness and the need for God, to hear God's promise, and to experience the joy and celebration of the promise fulfilled.

When the walls of Jerusalem were rebuilt after the exile, Nehemiah led the people in a great celebration (Neh. 12:27-43). Two choirs marched on top of the walls, singing. Harps played and cymbals crashed. The choirs met at the temple, where the people rejoiced and the priests offered sacrifices. The children also rejoiced. One can picture boys and girls running along the wall, keeping up with the choir and orchestra, mixing joyfully with the crowd at the temple. Yes, the children were there, surrounded by praise to God and probably joining in the worship.

In the New Testament, children come to see and hear Jesus and receive a lunch of bread and fish when Jesus feeds the five thousand (Matt. 14:15-21; John 6:8-11). According to Matthew's account, on Palm Sunday children followed Jesus into the temple, shouting, "Hosanna to the son of David" (Matt. 21:15). It would seem they had joined in with the triumphal procession as Jesus entered Jerusalem. In the temple they carried on the praise they learned from the adults along the road. And Jesus affirmed their praise as God-ordained (Matt. 21:16).

From these Old and New Testament examples we see that children participated with adults in the spiritual life of the faith community. Through their participation they were being formed as covenant people.

A New Covenant

As our survey of children in the Bible leads into the New Testament, we enter a new chapter in God's story. The covenant related to the law and given through Moses was an important part of God's plan. However, God's promise to Abraham, and through Abraham to the whole world, could not be fulfilled through a covenant of law. A new covenant was needed. Jeremiah prophesied, "The days are surely coming, says the LORD, when I will make a new covenant with the house of Israel and the house of Judah" (Jer. 31:31).

The unfolding of the new covenant began with the birth of a baby, Jesus. The angels announced the good news to the shepherds: "To you is born this day in the city of David a Savior, who is the Messiah, the Lord. This will be a sign for you: you will find a child wrapped in bands of cloth and lying in a manger" (Luke 2:11-12). The new covenant required that God come and live among us to show us grace and truth (John 1:14). And God did not walk onto the human stage as an adult; Jesus came as a baby and lived out a complete childhood. He experienced helplessness, loving care, obedience to parents, and the process of growing in divine and human favor (Luke 2:52). The incarnation powerfully affirms the significance of childhood.

Jesus and Children

In the Gospels we do not find a large number of verses relating to children. However, given the cultural setting of the New Testament, where children were seldom noted, they are surprisingly present in the life and ministry of Jesus.[8] Although scholars of Jesus' day considered it a waste to spend time with children outside of teaching sessions, Jesus seemed to enjoy being with children.[9] On one occasion Jesus used an illustration from the dramatic play of children (Luke 7:31-35). He apparently took time to notice children and to watch their activities. He healed children (Luke 8:54-55), took them in his arms and blessed them (Mark 10:16), and included children in his teaching. What Jesus had to say about children, as we will see, was central to his teaching.

Matthew, Mark, Luke, and John, as they wrote their Gospels, faced the challenge of selection. Of all the things that Jesus said and did, what was most important for their readers to know? The writers of the Synoptic Gospels all chose Jesus' teachings regarding children as essential:

- Jesus sets a child in the midst of the disciples as the symbol of humility and greatness. (Matt. 18:1-5; Mark 9:33-37; Luke 9:46-48)
- Jesus warns those who would cause a child to stumble. (Matt. 18:6-16; Mark 9:42-48; Luke 17:1-2)
- Jesus blesses the children. (Matt. 19:13-15; Mark 10:13-16; Luke 18:15-17)

John does not include these events in his account of the good news. However, John highlights children as metaphors to help his readers understand entering into relationship with God (John 1:12; 3:3-6).

Not only is the presence of Jesus' teaching on children in the Gospels significant, but the emphasis in those teachings heightens their importance. A major focus in Mark's Gospel is discipleship. Mark 8:27–10:45 addresses what it means to be a follower or disciple of Jesus. At the center of this major block of teaching on discipleship, Mark places Jesus' teaching on children.[10] Understanding what Jesus says about children is at the heart of being a true disciple of Jesus.

8. Strange, *Children in the Early Church,* p. 38.
9. Hans-Ruedi Weber, *Jesus and the Children* (Loveland, Ohio: Treehaus, 1994), p. 19.
10. Strange, *Children in the Early Church,* p. 49.

After being tempted, Jesus left the wilderness and began his ministry, "proclaiming the good news of God, and saying, 'The time is fulfilled, and the kingdom of God has come near; repent, and believe in the good news'" (Mark 1:14-15). Jesus' teaching and preaching focused on the kingdom of God, and he turned to children to help him explain the new ways of God's kingdom. Jesus held up children as models who show how to enter the kingdom and who make clear the values of the kingdom.[11]

The disciples were obsessed with greatness. Jesus repeatedly found them discussing who would be the greatest in the new kingdom they expected him to establish. How could Jesus help their culture-blinded eyes see the reversed values of God's kingdom? "Jesus, aware of their inner thoughts, took a little child and put it by his side, and said to them, 'Whoever welcomes this child in my name welcomes me, and whoever welcomes me welcomes the one who sent me; for the least among all of you is the greatest'" (Luke 9:47-48).

Jesus shocked the disciples by setting a mere child in the place of honor, beside him. Children in the world of Jesus had no status; they were the weakest and most vulnerable in society. Yet Jesus placed a child in the place that should have been reserved for a prominent and favored person. Joel Green states, "Jesus thus turns the social pyramid upside down, undermining the very conventions that led the disciples to deliberate over relative greatness within the company of disciples and, indeed, that had led the disciples away from any proper understanding of Jesus' status."[12] After setting the child by his side, Jesus called the disciples to welcome the little one. Welcoming usually meant giving hospitality, serving and honoring a guest.

Luke 9:48 gives a glimpse of Jesus' heart for children. Jesus and God the Father identify with children. To welcome and serve a child is to welcome and serve Jesus and the One who sent him. We also see that Jesus set a high standard for welcoming children. His followers are to welcome children in Jesus' name, with a commitment to the child and in a way that is consistent with the heart of Jesus.[13]

At the end of verse 48, Jesus summarizes the reverse values of the kingdom: "The least among all of you is the greatest." He spoke these

11. Strange, *Children in the Early Church,* p. 48.

12. Joel B. Green, *The Gospel of Luke,* New International Commentary on the New Testament (Grand Rapids: Eerdmans, 1997), pp. 391-92.

13. Green, *Gospel of Luke,* p. 392.

words with a child standing by him representing the least, who are to be considered great and receive honor and service in the kingdom.

In Matthew 19:13, Mark 10:13, and Luke 18:15, we see the disciples' struggle to grasp and live the new kingdom values Jesus taught. When people brought their children to Jesus for his blessing, the disciples responded out of their cultural values. Jesus was busy with the important folk — adults, scribes, Pharisees, and maybe some Romans. He had no time for insignificant children, they assumed. However, to their great surprise Jesus became indignant with them, not with those trying to trouble him with the children.[14] Jesus wanted his disciples to see with new eyes and not be looking out for the concerns of the great ones — those who would be inconvenienced if Jesus took time to bless children. He wanted them to have eyes that see the little ones, their example, desires, and needs.[15]

Jesus wanted children to be able to come freely to him, and he commanded the disciples not to stop them. "Let the little children come to me, and do not stop them; for it is to such as these that the kingdom of God belongs" (Luke 18:16). The kingdom of God belongs to them; they have every right to come to the King.

Jesus added, "Truly I tell you, whoever does not receive the kingdom of God as a little child will never enter it" (Luke 18:17; Mark 10:15). Children, Jesus implied, show us how to enter the kingdom. A child has no way of earning entrance to the kingdom. In Luke's Gospel the story of Jesus blessing the children follows the parable of the Pharisee and the tax collector praying in the temple (Luke 18:9-14). Like the tax collector, children do not come to God with a list of good works intended to prove they are worthy of salvation.[16] They come empty-handed.

Luke 18:16 brings to mind Jesus' statement in Matthew 5:3, "Blessed are the poor in spirit, for theirs is the kingdom of heaven." Children are the poor to whom the kingdom belongs as a grace gift from their loving God.[17] How then must we enter the kingdom? We are to come like a child, with empty hands and no merit of our own, trusting the God of grace.

In the story of Jesus blessing the children, we see one more feature of Jesus' ministry: he takes the children up in his arms, lays his hands on

14. Weber, *Jesus and the Children,* p. 25.
15. Weber, *Jesus and the Children,* pp. 37-38.
16. Strange, *Children in the Early Church,* p. 52.
17. Weber, *Jesus and the Children,* p. 29.

them, and blesses them (Mark 10:16). Touch was a part of Jesus' blessing of the children, communicating his acceptance and love.

Jesus took children and their faith quite seriously. Matthew 18:6-7 makes this very clear: "If any of you put a stumbling block before one of these little ones who believe in me, it would be better for you if a great millstone were fastened around your neck and you were drowned in the depth of the sea. Woe to the world because of stumbling blocks! Occasions for stumbling are bound to come, but woe to the one by whom the stumbling block comes!" Who are "these little ones who believe in me"? As we have seen, Jesus used children as a symbol of all the vulnerable, powerless persons of low status who are important in the kingdom of God. "Little ones" therefore can include adults. However, as Jesus spoke these words a child stood beside him. The actual child was also the focus of Jesus' words, one of the little ones who believe. In this statement Jesus validates the faith of children: they can truly believe in him.

Commenting on Jesus' teaching on causing little ones to stumble, Strange states, "What happens to a child, and to a child's faith is a matter of great consequence to those who are in the kingdom of God. The truth about children is . . . in God's sight their worth cannot be exaggerated."[18]

In these passages about children, Jesus repeatedly holds up the child as an example of kingdom values and responses. By doing so, Jesus reveals the great difference between the kingdoms of the world and the kingdom of God. The Greeks and Romans viewed children as raw material to be formed, or uninformed beings to be educated. Jews believed children needed teaching and discipline so that they would learn to live like their ancestors and the adults in the faith community.[19] However, Jesus holds up children as teachers for adults. Within the kingdom of God, adults are challenged to be open to learn from children and others who are the least.

Were children needed as models for only the first followers of Jesus? Weber says, "Jesus' attitude toward children (and Jesus' teaching through children) was so new and astonishing that his disciples could not grasp it. One even wonders whether the Christian Church since then has fully understood these amazing actions and sayings."[20] Grasping and living the reverse values of the kingdom still challenge followers of Jesus in the

18. Strange, *Children in the Early Church,* pp. 57-58.
19. Strange, *Children in the Early Church,* p. 49.
20. Weber, *Jesus and the Children,* pp. 20-21.

twenty-first century. Like Jesus' first disciples, we need children in our midst, showing us how to trust our gracious God and encouraging us to live kingdom values by welcoming, respecting, and serving the least among us, who are greatest in the eyes of God.

Loving Care of Children

Certainly there's no question about it: children were valued in the Jewish community. However, it is possible to value children for what they offer and not value each child in the present. Some women looked to their children for their own validation. As Leah names her sons, we see her hope that the children she bears will win Jacob's love. "Leah conceived and bore a son, and she named him Reuben; for she said, 'Because the LORD has looked on my affliction; surely now my husband will love me.' She conceived again and bore a son, and said, 'Because the LORD has heard that I am hated, he has given me this son also'; and she named him Simeon" (Gen. 29:32-33). Fathers desired children to ensure the continuance of the family line, and the faith community invested in children to ensure the continuance of the covenant people.

Such utilitarian valuing of children sometimes did exist in ancient Israel, but the Bible also gives us pictures of children who were dearly loved. Abraham loved his son Ishmael and longed for God to bless him. In Genesis 17:15-16, God promises that Sarah will give birth to the son through whom the covenant will be fulfilled. Abraham responds, "O that Ishmael might live in your sight!" (Gen. 17:18). When Abraham had to send Ishmael away, his distress was great for the son he loved (Gen. 21:11). Abraham's misguided action, trying to help God fulfill the covenant promise, had consequences. One of the most painful results was having a son, Ishmael, whom he could not love and nurture into adulthood.

Isaac and Rebekah loved their children. Isaac loved Esau, and Rebekah loved Jacob (Gen. 25:28). Jacob, we are told, loved Joseph — more than any of his other children (Gen. 37:3). The Bible presents an open, honest account of the strengths and weaknesses of God's people. In this family we see love but also the results of unwise love that is focused on one child more than another. Human love is never perfect.

The most beautiful biblical pictures of loving care for children appear in the parent-child metaphors and similes used to give glimpses of God.

For a metaphor to have meaning, it must recall a reality known to the hearers. The use of these metaphors therefore implies that many Jewish parents did love their children tenderly and attentively.

In Psalm 103 David uses the father metaphor to picture God:

> As a father has compassion for his children,
> so the LORD has compassion for those who fear him. (v. 13)

In Psalm 131 David turns to a mother-child image:

> But I have calmed and quieted my soul,
> like a weaned child with its mother;
> my soul is like the weaned child that is with me. (Ps. 131:2)

Remembering the tenderness and love he has seen between a mother and her baby, David pictures himself as a weaned child calmly resting in God's arms.

Hosea paints a beautiful picture of God as parent.

> When Israel was a child, I loved him,
> and out of Egypt I called my son.
> The more I called them,
> the more they went from me;
> they kept sacrificing to the Baals,
> and offering incense to idols.
>
> Yet it was I who taught Ephraim to walk,
> I took them up in my arms;
> but they did not know that I healed them.
> I led them with cords of human kindness,
> with bands of love.
> I was to them like those
> who lift infants to their cheeks.
> I bent down to them and fed them. (11:1-4)

Here we have God modeling how children should be loved. Love includes instruction, tender touch, healing, kindness, meeting needs, and continuing love in the face of rebellion or rejection.

Jesus also turned the attention of his hearers to an example of good fathering: "If you then, who are evil, know how to give good gifts to your children, how much more will the heavenly Father give the Holy Spirit to those who ask him!" (Luke 11:13). Jesus assumed that the fathers in the audience gave good gifts to their children, or at least knew of fathers who did. However, Jesus wanted his hearers to realize that God's love and giving goes far beyond that of the best father.

In these word pictures of God as the perfect parent, we see the kind of love our children need from us. But there is more. As Cathy's nephew Michael discovered in the first hours of his baby's life, children and our relationship with them lead us into wonderful new discoveries about God and our relationship with God.

Implications for the Twenty-first Century

We come away from the study of Scripture amazed by God's great valuing of children and the breadth of insights the Bible offers to guide our ministry with children in the twenty-first century.[21] What will we do with these insights from the Old Testament and the teachings of Jesus? Let us look at our ministries with children through the lens of Scripture. How well is God's vision for the nurture of children being lived out in our homes and congregations?

The biblical material explored in this chapter raises the following questions.

- Are our approaches to the nurture of children in harmony with Scripture?
- What place do we give to children in our faith community?

21. As we have seen, much of the more specific biblical guidance for teaching the faith to children comes from the Old Testament. Some may ask, is it appropriate to apply those guidelines to teaching the Christian faith? The covenant of the New Testament is not totally disconnected from the old covenant. Paul identifies Abraham as the father of the bloodline and the faith-line covenant peoples (Rom. 4:11-12). Abraham's righteousness came through faith, and God desired that Abraham's descendants be people of faith. God's promise that through Abraham's descendants all nations would be blessed was fulfilled in Jesus. We become people of the new covenant only through faith in Jesus. Old Testament insights, however, help us see how to set the stage for our children to come to faith.

- How open are we as adults to learn from children?
- How well do we use the spiritual formation methods seen in the Old Testament?
- How well prepared are young parents to nurture their children?
- How well prepared are our congregations to welcome and nurture children?
- What can be done to equip parents and congregations to provide settings in which God's children, young and old together, are formed as faithful people of God?

In sections 2 and 3 we will explore a wide range of ways to implement biblical patterns in our homes and in churches of different sizes and settings. Our intent is not to tell you how to do children's ministry in your church but to give you options and resources to discover what is best for the children in your congregation.

Often those who minister with children feel like second-class citizens in the church. Accurately or inaccurately, we have assumed that others don't place much importance on what we do. Is that how God sees it? Our study of Scripture reveals that those called to minister with children are entrusted with some of the most important work in God's kingdom. So thank God for your honored vocation, and humbly seek to better understand how to serve God's precious little ones.

Chapter 3

THEOLOGY AND CHILDREN

Pastor Henderson dipped her fingers in the baptismal font, placed her hand on little Matthew's head and declared, "Matthew Aaron Jones, I baptize you in the name of the Father, the Son, and the Holy Spirit. Amen."

Pastor Mills held Sarah Beth in his arms and announced, "Sarah Beth Schmidt, we dedicate you in the name of the Father and the Son and the Holy Spirit. Amen."

Both Matthew's parents and Sarah Beth's are committed Christians, offering their children to God and committing themselves to raise their children to know, love, and serve God. Why was one baby baptized, the other dedicated?

Infant baptism and dedication are not the only issues that raise questions among parents and children's ministry leaders. When should my child be given the elements in the Lord's Supper? What happens to young children who die before asking Jesus to become their Savior? Will they go to hell? When can a child be saved? Can young children really experience God? Who is responsible for the spiritual nurture of children?

Faithful Christians hold a wide range of beliefs about children and their faith, about sin and grace, and they would give differing answers to these questions. In this chapter you will not find guaranteed right answers to these questions; however, we trust that as you read you will uncover insights to guide you in evaluating your theological understandings of children and their relationship with God. The chapter examines three theological traditions, their perspectives on children, and how those perspectives influence the spiritual care of children. We will also look briefly at children's experiences of God and the gospel record of how the first followers of Jesus became Christian; the chapter will end with a discussion of God's part and our part in the spiritual formation of children.

Can Children Really Experience God?

Do children really experience God? Can they have a genuine relationship with God? Here are the responses of two eight-year-olds to the question "Have you ever felt God close to you?"

> "Yah. Um, it sounds pretty silly, but when I'm lying in bed, my covers are his arms and my pillow was his chest. I feel like he's around me."[1]
>
> "It feels like someone's just sitting by you. And it's nice to know that it's Jesus, or God."[2]

Those who work with children are often moved by such beautiful expressions of a child's joy or peace in God's presence. Scripture too tells of young children who experience God. Samuel, after he was weaned, was given to the Lord to serve at the tabernacle and grew up in God's presence (1 Sam. 1–3). In a time when the Lord spoke only rarely to the people of Israel (1 Sam. 3:1), God chose to speak to the child Samuel; he was the one who could hear God's message for the people. An angel told Zechariah that John the Baptist would be filled with the Holy Spirit from birth — from within his mother's womb (Luke 1:15). As David, Jeremiah, and Paul looked back over their lives, they saw God at work from before they were born. Acknowledging that God had kept him safe from birth, David declared that God had been his God since infancy (Ps. 22:9-10; 71:6).[3] The prophet Jeremiah was known by God and consecrated to him before Jeremiah was born (Jer. 1:4-10). Even the apostle Paul realized that in spite of

1. Stated by a child aged eight years eight months, from unpublished research by Catherine Stonehouse.

2. Stated by a child aged eight years eleven months, from unpublished research by Stonehouse.

3. These two passages from the psalms are especially fascinating. Psalm 51:5 is a key verse for arguing for "original sin." Psalm 22 is a psalm of David, as is Psalm 51. He acknowledges both the depth of his sinfulness and his awareness of and trust in God from birth.

his early persecution of Jesus' followers, he had been set apart from birth and called by God's grace (Gal. 1:11-17).

Both in Scripture and today, then, we see that children can experience God. But does such experience make a child Christian? How do any of us become Christian? What answers do we find to these questions in the Gospels?

How Does a Child Become Christian?

The Gospels recount stories of those who first knew Jesus. How did their relationship with Jesus and commitment to him develop? One thing we do *not* see is a uniform pattern for becoming a follower of Jesus. Although the first disciples shared some similar experiences, each person's relationship with Jesus developed through a unique set of encounters, experiences, and responses.

For many, a relationship with Jesus began with an invitation. "Follow me" was the invitation Jesus most often gave. He addressed it to Philip (John 1:43), Peter, James, and John (Mark 1:17; 2:14), as well as to others as he taught.

Some of the first disciples heard the invitation, "Come and see." Andrew and a companion, probably John, were disciples of John the Baptist who one day heard him announce, "Look, there is the Lamb of God." Andrew and his friend began following Jesus and asked where he was staying; Jesus replied, "Come and see." They went and spent time with Jesus. Andrew was so impressed with what he saw that he hurried off to tell Peter. "We have found the Messiah." After being called to follow Jesus, Philip told his good friend Nathanael about him. "Can anything good come out of Nazareth?" Nathanael asked. Philip replied, "Come and see" (John 1:35-46).

As the disciples came to Jesus and followed him, they had opportunity to see how Jesus lived and what he could do. Seeing Jesus' power caused the disciples to ask, "Who is this man?" They learned from Jesus and got to know him, and over time they came to believe in Jesus as the Messiah. Their early belief was challenged, however, and many stopped following Jesus. But the Twelve, and several women, chose to continue to follow (Luke 8:1-3; John 6:66-69). In the crisis of Jesus' arrest, trial, and crucifixion, some of the disciples failed, losing their hope that Jesus was God's promised Redeemer. They did not fully understand who Jesus was and why he had come until after the resurrection. As the disciples followed Jesus, then, over time they came to believe more and more fully.

John's Gospel focuses on belief as the crucial element in one's relationship with God: "To all who received him, who believed in his name, he gave power to become children of God" (John 1:12). In John 20:31 we discover the book was written so that its readers might come to believe that Jesus is the Messiah, the Son of God, and that through believing they would have life in his name. Through belief in Jesus his followers entered into a special relationship with God and received new life.

For the first followers of Jesus, coming to faith, or belief, was a process. At various points each person made responses to Jesus. Early or later in their relationship they declared their faith in him. Their early expressions of faith were real, and Jesus affirmed them (Matt. 16:16-17; John 11:27). However, as they walked with Jesus and experienced the unfolding of God's plan, they realized how much more there was to understand and even discovered points at which their beliefs needed to change.

When did these first followers become Christians — Christ's ones? When did they receive new life from God? It seems they entered on a journey of becoming, a process of experience and learning that led to crucial choices and responses, which in turn opened them to new learning and growth. Perhaps some, if not all, of the disciples could identify a point when they truly believed and made a critical commitment to be a follower of Jesus. As we look at the accounts of their lives, we cannot know when that critical response was made. We can, however, see the importance of all their experiences and responses in building their relationship with Jesus and making them Christian.

The drama of John 21:15-19 gives us an important glimpse into what Jesus values in his followers. After the resurrection we find Jesus talking with Peter on a beach. Three times he asks, "Do you love me?" Each time Peter affirms his love, Jesus responds, "Feed my sheep," or "Feed my lambs." Peter is the disciple who denied Jesus. Yet it seems Jesus is more concerned about Peter's continuing love, translated into action, than about how perfectly he "kept the faith" or how he began his relationship with Jesus. Because of his love for Jesus, Peter did repent of his sin with bitter tears, and that was important. But in this scene of reconciliation Jesus focuses on the importance of Peter's continuing love and calls him to live out his faith in service to others.

Jesus' comments about children relate in interesting ways to the stories of the first adult disciples. Jesus commanded the disciples, "Let the children come to me, and do not stop them" (Matt. 19:14; Mark 10:14; Luke 18:16). Children were invited to "come and see," to experience Jesus. As they spent time with him, they got to know and love Jesus.

We noted that as the disciples followed Jesus they came to believe in him, and their belief brought them into a special relationship with God and the experience of new life. The Gospels do not give us stories of children in the process of coming to faith, but as noted in chapter 2, Jesus referred to children as "little ones who believe in me" (Matt. 18:6; Mark 9:42). Most young children believe easily and love sweetly. These are gifts Jesus accepts as precious and real. As was true for the adult disciples, the child's belief and love need nurture, development, and the maturing that takes place as one follows Jesus. We might think of the child's belief and love for Jesus as the embryo of faith, a most crucial reality, a beginning but real relationship with God.

But, you may wonder, what about sin? How does sin affect a child's relationship with Jesus? It cannot be denied that children sin (Gen. 8:21); that is evident empirically as well as theologically! However, neither the narratives of the Bible nor the teachings of Jesus make reference to a particular child's sin. Jesus never directly speaks of a child's sin, nor does he imply that a child does *not* sin. Does Jesus not care about sin? John the Baptist refers to Jesus as "the Lamb of God who takes away the sin of the world" (John 1:29). Jesus *is* concerned about sin, but that is not where he begins in establishing a relationship. Jesus does not focus his attention on the sins of children; he simply opens his arms to them and blesses them.

How do children become Christian? The Bible does not tell us how children actually come to faith. The Gospels do not give us a specific set of steps or pattern for a child's response to God. Instead Jesus challenges us, along with the disciples, not to hinder or stop children in coming to him. The invitation "Come and see, come and experience my blessing," is extended to children. As children meet Jesus in the stillness of their bedroom, or in the sense of someone "sitting by you and knowing it's Jesus," and in the stories of Scripture, they can come to know and love him. The early belief of the young child can be nurtured and grow into the maturing faith of a faithful disciple of Jesus. At what point along that journey is the child Christian? Can we know, or do we need to? Jesus' message seems to focus not on those questions but on the need to encourage the child's coming to him, to be careful not to hinder that coming, and to celebrate the child's love for him.

All Christians want to pass on the faith to the next generation, but views on how to do that differ widely. In the next section we will look at some Christian traditions and their understandings of how that is done.

Theological Traditions

The understandings of children and their faith have a long history in many Christian traditions and denominations, sometimes dating back centuries. The church's theology influences its practices. Therefore it is helpful to consider the role a particular theology plays in the life of a local church.

Fully exploring the complexities of theological traditions, however, is beyond the scope of this chapter. We will look at only three traditions and only a slice of the perspectives within each of them. Few of us will find ourselves precisely described in any of these three accounts, but hopefully what follows can help us think theologically about children.

In *He Shines in All That's Fair: Culture and Common Grace,* Richard Mouw posits that every theology has a corresponding sociology. "We can fully understand the claims of a theological perspective only if we attempt to see what it would look like if those claims were fleshed out in the life of a community."[4] In other words, the church's view of God and his people affects the way its members relate to and interact with each other as well as the ministry practices they develop. If Mouw's position is correct, then the church's theology regarding children matters a great deal, because it shapes the practices that help form our children.

Here are some crucial theological questions for children's ministry leaders: How does your church's tradition view children? Is the child a sinner under God's judgment until reconciled through salvation? Or is the child "safe" because of Christ's redemptive work on the cross? The Bible says that the children of believing parents are holy (1 Cor. 7:14); nowhere does it teach damnation of the very young. Just how, then, is the church to view children?

The theological issue of *original sin*[5] and the faith community's beliefs

4. Richard Mouw, *He Shines in All That's Fair: Culture and Common Grace* (Grand Rapids: Eerdmans, 2001), p. 74.

5. Although the term *original sin* is not found in Scripture, "one cannot miss the idea of inherited sinfulness in the Old Testament" (Henri Blocher, *Original Sin: Illuminating the Riddle* [Grand Rapids: Eerdmans, 1997], p. 31).

about *grace* are at the heart of our theology of children. These two theological issues significantly influence beliefs about children in regard to baptism, confirmation, the Lord's Supper, being part of the faith community or being separate from it. Differing views on these matters lead to contrasting sociologies or ways of ministering and relating to children. The differences among theologies and practices range widely.

Over the centuries, theological writings on original sin, grace, and baptism have been extensive, divergent, and potentially confusing.[6] In spite of these complexities, there is wide consensus on two doctrines: all people sin, and God is the source of all grace.

Original sin infects all human beings because of the sin of Adam and Eve. Some churches believe that the effects of original sin are addressed through infant baptism. Other churches hold that original sin separates the child from God, and they desire to bring the child to God at as young an age as possible through prayers of confession and repentance of sin. Many holding this view believe children are not culpable until they reach the "age of accountability."[7] Still other churches see Christ's redeeming work on the cross as sufficient for supplying grace, often referred to as prevenient grace, which keeps young children safe from the damnation of original sin, should they die before they claim faith in Christ as their own.

The concept of the grace of God also has somewhat complex facets. Views of grace become especially significant in church practices and theologies regarding children. Theologians define grace as an undeserved blessing bestowed by God, God's activity that flows from his nature. For those of the Reformed tradition, grace encompasses two categories: *common grace* and *special grace*. Common grace is the favor God shows toward all humans; it is common to all, evident in sunshine, rain, and crops for food. Special grace "is the grace by which God redeems, sanctifies, and glorifies." Im-

6. See the excellent work *The Child in Christian Thought* (Grand Rapids: Eerdmans, 2001), edited by Marcia Bunge, for a survey of the complexities of theological positions regarding children since the time of the ancient Hebrews.

7. Age of accountability is an extrabiblical concept based on Romans 14:12, which states that every person will be accountable or responsible to God. For some, this verse implies that there is a chronological period in which a person is not yet accountable for his or her actions, although the age of the transition from innocence to culpability is not identifiable as a fixed point. Some use verses such as Deuteronomy 1:39 and Isaiah 7:16 as support for a time of innocence before the age of accountability.

parted only to the elect or the redeemed, it is God's initiative; it starts with God. It is prevenient, efficacious, irresistible, and sufficient.[8] Christ reconciles us to himself through this special grace.

Those who follow the theology of John Wesley, that is, those in Methodist and Wesleyan denominations, nuance four experiences of grace somewhat differently: prevenient, justifying, sanctifying, and glorifying grace.[9] Prevenient grace (also called preventing grace by Wesley) is God's uncalled-for, seeking, wooing love. It is offered to all and makes possible our response to God, but can be resisted or ignored. Justifying grace happens when, in repentance, we experience forgiveness of our sins in response to God's graciously drawing us to himself. Sanctifying grace occurs as the Holy Spirit begins transforming us into Christlikeness. Finally, at death we experience glorifying grace as the effects of sin and the fallenness of our humanity are healed.

Out of our views on sin and grace come beliefs about baptism. According to Gregory Boyd and Paul Eddy, the various positions on Christian baptism demonstrate the breadth and complexity of the issues involved.[10] Historically, infants have been baptized by sprinkling or pouring water on them. In Catholic theology and also traditional Lutheran churches, this is to eradicate original sin. For the Eastern Orthodox it is to enjoin the one baptized to the church. Presbyterian churches view it differently, believing that baptism is similar to circumcision in the Old Testament, a means by which children are included in the covenant God has made with his people.

> Other forms of Protestantism believe baptism is reserved for people who have made a personal decision to believe in and follow Jesus. . . . Here, too, there is a variety of understandings. A few groups who practice adult baptism believe that baptism is God's means of remitting sin in a believer's life. Others hold to a more Presbyterian view, seeing it as the rite that publicly initiates a person into God's covenant. The most

8. P. E. Hughes, "Grace," in *Evangelical Dictionary of Theology*, ed. Walter Elwell (Grand Rapids: Baker, 1984), pp. 479-81.

9. Catherine Stonehouse, "Children in Wesleyan Thought," in *Children's Spirituality: Christian Perspectives, Research, and Applications*, ed. Donald Ratcliff (Eugene, Ore.: Cascade, 2004).

10. Gregory Boyd and Paul Eddy, *Across the Spectrum: Understanding Issues in Evangelical Theology* (Grand Rapids: Baker, 2002), p. 202.

> prevalent understanding among those who practice adult baptism, however, is that it is an outward public testimony of God's inward work. This is the most common view among Baptists.[11]

In Boyd and Eddy's survey of baptismal practices we find three major perspectives on baptism. In this chapter the theologies behind these perspectives will be referred to as *sacramental, covenantal,* and *conversional.*[12]

Sacramental traditions include Episcopal, Anglican, Methodist,[13] Lutheran, and Roman Catholic churches. Among them a sacrament is often described as an outward, visible sign of an inward, spiritual grace. The sacraments themselves, baptism and the Lord's Supper (the Eucharist) in particular, are seen as means of conveying grace to the recipients. The role of the priest or pastor as an agent of grace is more significant for Catholics than for Protestants in this tradition.[14] Many practices of this tradition have their origins in the early centuries of Christianity.

The covenantal tradition began shortly after the Protestant Reformation. Presbyterians, Christian Reformed, and Reformed congregations represent this tradition, regarding themselves as people of the covenant. Their views on the sacraments, especially baptism, focus on covenant. A covenant in this context "denotes a gracious undertaking entered into by God for the benefit and blessings of [human beings], and specifically of those [persons] who by faith receive the promises and commit themselves to the obligations" involved.[15]

According to theologian Dennis Okholm, God has had but one covenant with his people — *a covenant of grace,* first implied in Genesis 3:15 and extending until today. Circumcision was the sign of the covenant in Old Testament times for incorporating male children. Baptism is the corre-

11. Boyd and Eddy, *Across the Spectrum,* p. 202.

12. The term *evangelical* is not being used as a category, because Christians who identify themselves as evangelical can be found in each of these categories.

13. Methodists, those from the Wesleyan tradition, in unique ways may combine the three traditions. They may hold to a sacramental view of infant baptism, recognize that children enter into the covenant of faith, and see the need for a child's conversion if the baptismal grace is lost.

14. Timothy Phillips and Dennis Okholm, *A Family of Faith: An Introduction to Evangelical Christianity* (Grand Rapids: Baker, 2001), pp. 173-80.

15. Gleason Archer, Jr., "Covenant," in *Evangelical Dictionary of Theology,* ed. Walter Elwell (Grand Rapids: Baker, 1984), p. 276.

sponding sign for both genders in the New Testament (see 1 Cor. 12:13; Gal. 3:27-28). Okholm explains,

> In baptism a covenant is established between God, the child, and the church (along with the parents). The promise of the gospel is announced to the child (who does not comprehend it at this point) with the intention that the child will "complete" his/her baptism in future faith and repentance (marked by a public declaration of his/her acceptance of the church's faith at the end of the confirmation process). The congregation and the parents promise to raise the child in the nurture and admonition of the Lord so that the child will always know Jesus Christ as Lord and Savior and will grow in the knowledge. Thus, there is less emphasis on a "moment" of conversion and more emphasis on the child's growth in knowledge and commitment to Jesus Christ. In fact, we do not "make" Jesus Lord and Savior as if by some democratic vote; he *is* both, whether we acknowledge it or not. . . . In the covenant view, then, the entire congregation acts as the "godparents," nurturing the child in all areas of the life of the church.[16]

Conversional groups include Baptists, many Pentecostals, Bible churches, and other conservative or fundamentalist denominations. Many conversional denominations contain subgroups that have come into being since 1850. This tradition does not acknowledge sacraments but administers *ordinances* of believer's baptism and the Lord's Supper or Communion. These ordinances are symbols for the participants rather than means of receiving grace. A person enters into a relationship with Jesus Christ through individual repentance of sin and then acceptance of Jesus Christ as personal Savior.

To understand better the differences between these major positions and their implications for ministry practices, we will consider some stories of children from these traditions.[17] Each tradition is represented by

16. Dennis Okholm, personal communication, April 12, 2003.

17. Though the names and specifics of these stories are fictitious, they are based on interviews Scottie did for her doctoral work and subsequent research. Therefore the patterns, implications, and outcomes of the stories are actual. See Scottie May, "Reflections on Childhood Religious Experiences: Patterns of Similarity and Variability in Perceptions of Adults from Three Evangelical Churches," unpublished document (Ann Arbor: University Microfilms International, 1993), no. 9334539.

two stories — one positive and one less so. The stories also demonstrate the significant interdependence of life in the faith community and life within the home. This interdependence creates the sociology or way of spiritual life for children.

The Sacramental Tradition

The sociology of the theology that shapes this tradition views the sacraments as key markers in a child's life to be celebrated by the congregation, but especially by the family. These events are often commemorated annually.

Amanda's Story

Amanda is born into a devout, third-generation Episcopal family. At two months of age, she is baptized at her church to remove the effect of original sin. This sacrament begins the process of salvation that Amanda must later confirm and own for herself. Amanda's parents select godparents — her aunt and uncle — who present her for baptism and then vow to model for Amanda the Christian life, to pray for her, and to help her develop Christian character. This event is cause for significant celebration for Amanda's family as they welcome her into the Christian fold: she is now free from the curse of innate or original sin because of the special grace imparted to her through the sacrament of baptism. Every year Amanda's parents and godparents acknowledge the anniversary of her baptism.

In Amanda's toddler years, her parents carry her in their arms each time they go forward to receive the elements of the Eucharist. Every Sunday she receives a blessing from the one who distributes the elements. As Amanda grows, she looks forward to this moment of special touch and blessing to which she has become accustomed.

Education in the Christian faith begins at church when Amanda is almost school age. But all along she has been part of the congregation that gathers to worship on Sundays. Her parents model their faith before her every day at home. She learns to pray almost at the same time as she learns to talk. Her parents read Bible stories to her, sing simple songs of Jesus with her, and celebrate the Christian holidays, taking care to explain their meaning as she asks questions.

Amanda receives special instruction to prepare her for receiving the elements of the Eucharist for the first time. By now she is eight years old. This First Communion is a strong memory for Amanda. It is a marker that says to her that she has begun to receive God's dynamic grace in deeper ways. Later, in early adolescence, she begins another series of special lessons preparing her for confirmation — the time when she proclaims her faith in Jesus Christ as her Savior. This sacrament allows her all the privileges and responsibilities of a full participant in her local congregation. Amanda's family and godparents celebrate her First Communion and confirmation by presenting her with mementos.

By eagerly welcoming Amanda in the worship service, her congregation gives her opportunity to see God's people meeting together; she experiences the mystery, awe, and wonder inherent in the worship symbols and the liturgy. Amanda's parents wisely talk with her often about the message or homily preached on Sunday morning. Amanda also gets to "eavesdrop" as her parents discuss the message, asking each other clarifying questions. The education leaders of the church take great care that all along the way Amanda enjoys attractive, engaging learning experiences that help her "enter into" the Scriptures age-appropriately, so that she loves and understands them.

Not surprisingly, as a young adult Amanda has a strong, committed faith in Jesus Christ that she desires to live out through his power, though in her later teen years she struggles for a time with questions and doubts about her faith. The structures of the sacramental tradition and the faith of those closest to her provide the means for her becoming a devoted follower of Jesus. From her earliest memories she knew of the Lord Jesus' love for her. She had faith in him, trusted him, and loved him in return.

Sebastian's Story

In a different town, Sebastian attends a church of the same tradition as Amanda's, but his experience is not much like hers. His family is also third-generation Episcopal, but for them that means that church is a place they *go* from time to time rather than something they *are* — part of the people of God.

Baptized as an infant, Sebastian has godparents and a celebration just as Amanda does, but the similarities stop there. Sebastian's parents do not live their faith at home. They say that it's private, not to be talked about. So

Sebastian does not hear names for God or stories of God's character and actions. The family "says grace" at special mealtimes such as during the holidays. The major Christian holidays are about the only times they attend worship services. Nearly a thousand people are members of Sebastian's church, but fewer than two hundred attend on most Sundays. Sebastian and his family know hardly anyone in the church.

Unfortunately, Sebastian's church does little to challenge his family to think more about their faith. Often the sermons focus on current social issues and how thoughtful people should respond. Scripture is not regularly the focus, nor is the need to live holy lives. Classes prepare Sebastian for First Communion and for confirmation, but the volunteer teachers are ill equipped for the task. The primary mode of instruction consists of filling out workbooks and reciting memorized answers to questions about doctrine.

Not surprisingly, as a teenager, Sebastian sees his religion as irrelevant, so he stops going to church altogether. Even though the structures of his church were the same as those of Amanda's, the way the life of faith was lived out at home and church made all the difference. No one at home or church helped Sebastian see the relevance and significance of being Christian. He has been unable to experience mystery, awe, and wonder, or the presence of God as a living Person who desires a relationship with him. He is unaware of God's grace, except for common grace in its broadest sense.

The Covenantal Tradition

The commitment and influence of the church form the sociology of this tradition. The strength of covenant theology is evident in the eager welcoming of the child into the "church family." The emphasis is placed on how the communal life of the congregation affects the choices of the individual.[18]

Kobi's Story

Kobi's family is relatively new to the Christian faith. His grandparents were not followers of Jesus, but his parents became Christian during their college years. Because a relationship with Jesus Christ made such a differ-

18. Michael Horton, "Reformation Piety," *Modern Reformation* 1, no. 4 (2002).

ence in their lives, being part of a church is very significant for Kobi's parents. As newlyweds, they chose a church from the covenantal tradition because they wanted their nuclear family to be an intentional part of the larger family of God.

When he is eight weeks old, Kobi is baptized, just like Amanda and Sebastian. But for those in the covenantal tradition, this rite means something different. This tradition regards original sin, which is innate within Kobi, as already covered by the prevenient grace of God.[19] His baptism is a sign of God's covenant or promise that Kobi is part of the family of God to be cared for, taught, and nurtured, primarily by his parents but also by all the members of the congregation. Such covenantal baptism is a sign similar to that of circumcision, given by God to the ancient Hebrews (see Gen. 17:9-14).

Kobi also has godparents who take part in his baptism. His parents choose their close friends to have this special supportive role in Kobi's life. But the whole family of God at Kobi's church bears special responsibility — covenantal responsibility — for his spiritual growth. It is covenantal because during his baptism they all promise before God that they will help in Kobi's formation to be a follower of Jesus.

After his baptism, a reception is held in the church hall for the family. Scores of congregants join in welcoming Kobi to the "family." There are other evidences of the closeness of this faith community. When the family of God worships together, Kobi is always welcomed in the service by the pastor and the people, as are all the children of the church. As Kobi grows, he is regularly part of congregational gatherings: potlucks and dinners, weddings, birthday celebrations, and even funerals. He is encouraged to participate in the full life of the church. Everyone in the congregation has a vested interest in him. The people regard him as their child; he comes to regard them as his church family in every sense of the word. He loves being at church because he feels so valued and loved. His covenantal baptism truly made him a member of the family.

As it is for Amanda, education is part of Kobi's life in the church. For him it begins earlier. His classes teach him who God is and what he has done. Kobi has special instruction in order to participate in the Lord's

19. Because of the presence of prevenient grace, churches within this tradition may also regard this form of infant baptism as a sacrament. Still other covenantal churches "dedicate" their infants to God without the rite of baptism.

Supper, but the observance does not have quite the same significance as it does in the sacramental tradition. When he reaches early adolescence, he participates in confirmation. He claims his faith in Jesus Christ as his own, acknowledging God's special and dynamic grace at work in his life. Because he has been surrounded by godly, faithful people who pray for him, encourage him, guide him, and correct him, his identity has been and is being formed in the likeness of Christ.

As a teen, Kobi reflects back on his childhood church and says that it is just as much home to him as his own house. Accompanying this view of his church is the security of knowing how loved he is by God. Kobi says that this makes it easy to love God in return. Because he has experienced the wonder of unconditional love from his parents and the church family, even when he disappoints God by sinning, Kobi knows that nothing he does can separate him from God's love.

Lucy's Story

Unfortunately Lucy's faith experience is not much different from Sebastian's. Lucy's parents are not very serious about their faith. Her father grew up in a conversional tradition, while her mom was sacramental. After they married they did not attend church until Lucy was born. When it comes time for Lucy to be baptized as her mother is accustomed to, they pick a "neutral" church down the street — one that is different for both of them. Because her mom grew up in a sacramental tradition, she assumes that baptism means the same thing in their new church as it does in her childhood tradition. She is not curious enough to ask if being "covenantal" indicates that the meaning of the rites might be different.

At Lucy's baptism there are no godparents, because "it's not that big a deal." Mom breathes a sigh of relief: Lucy is Christian and "safe" from eternal damnation. Sadly, this covenantal church has little involvement in the family's life. It has departed from its tradition, with faithless results for Lucy.

The Conversional Tradition

Markers for the sociology of the conversional tradition hinge on the belief that it is through confession of sin, repentance, and faith in Jesus that one is converted and becomes a Christian, a follower of Jesus Christ. This may be referred to as a salvation experience, or accepting Jesus as your personal Savior, or asking Jesus into your heart. This tradition tends to emphasize the actions of the individual and how they then may be able to influence the faith community and the world.[20]

Maria's Story

For twenty-five years Maria's extended family has attended an independent conversional church. Her mother was saved as a young child, her father at the age of ten. Maria's parents both have a deep, passionate love for Jesus Christ. Their faith is very important to them, and they are active in their church, attending regularly. Before they had children, they prayed daily that their children would be saved while they were young and want to serve God their whole lives. Their daily prayers have supported Maria all her life.

When she is a few months old, Maria's parents dedicate her to God in front of the congregation. The pastor challenges them to live godly lives before her, teaching her and leading her to saving faith in Jesus.

Maria's parents lovingly and faithfully nurture Maria, just as Amanda's do. One day when she is four years old, Maria tells her mother she has a yucky feeling because she took a piece of candy when her mother had told her not to. Maria's mother explains that this feeling happens when we sin. It is God's way of letting us know we need to make things right with him. Maria asks Jesus to forgive her for taking the candy. Then, guided by her mother, she asks Jesus to come and live in her heart and help her want to do the right thing. Her mother then tells Maria that she is now a Christian and will go to heaven when she dies. She suggests that Maria tell her father as well as her Sunday school teacher what she has done. Her parents and teacher express their joy in the fact that now Maria is saved.

Maria regularly attends Sunday school, where she learns about the Bible and memorizes Bible verses. The importance of being saved is emphasized in the classes, as is the urgency of telling others about their need to accept Jesus as personal Savior. Maria takes her faith seriously and tells many of her school friends about Jesus.

20. Horton, "Reformation Piety."

Maria also attends children's church, while adults attend their worship service. Most major church events include a separate program for children, designed to accommodate short attention spans. Maria begins attending the adult service when she is about twelve. Her parents now allow her to partake in the monthly celebration of the Lord's Supper.

When Maria is fourteen, she asks her parents if she can be baptized. They encourage her to do so, but first she must meet with the pastor to explain how she knows that she is a Christian. Her account of her faith qualifies her for believer's baptism. At her baptism, she gives her testimony before the congregation — how she accepted Jesus as her Savior when she was four years old. She relates how much better she felt after confessing her sin and how confession still helps her whenever she sins.

Maria's older sister has no memory of ever accepting Jesus as her Savior. She says that because of their parents' teaching and example and the importance of their church in their lives, she cannot think of a time when she did not believe in and love Jesus. Her faith is just as strong as Maria's.

Children in Maria's church do not become members until they are adults. So Maria waits until she is twenty. But because she spends a great deal of time at church, she feels completely at home there. After officially joining the church, she is able to vote on issues of church business, teach Sunday school, and hold offices. Maria's love for and commitment to Jesus Christ is great. In response to an urging she has had since she was six, she is preparing to go to a needy country as a missionary to tell others about Jesus, something her parents and her church fully support.

Jake's Story

When Jake is three years old, his parents have a dramatic conversion experience at a revival service. Prior to this, his parents had no interest in God. The preaching convicts them that they are heading to hell — a destiny without God. Their salvation experience changes the way they live, think, and relate to people, especially each other. They had been living what they describe as sinful, hedonistic lives. Jake's parents begin to attend the church where the revival was held. On their very first Sunday in attendance, they are baptized to confirm the decision they made. They are enthused about their new freedom in Christ and eagerly begin to study the Bible.

Not long thereafter Jake's parents realize that Jake has not been saved.

The thought of their young son going to hell when he dies is dreadful. At home they begin to point out to him that his disobedience is sin and that God is unhappy when we sin. They ask prayer from the pastor and Jake's Sunday school teacher for his salvation.

Jake hears many lessons about his sin problem and what that means. When he is five, his Sunday school teacher asks him if he has asked Jesus into his heart. He shakes his head no. She helps him pray the sinner's prayer, having him repeat the words after her. The prayer goes something like this: "Dear Jesus, thank you for dying on the cross for me. Please forgive me for my sins. I am sorry for them, and with your help, I will change and not do them again. I accept you as my Lord and Savior. Please come into my heart. Thank you for saving me. Amen." The teacher encourages him to tell his parents what he has just done. With tears of joy, Jake's parents hug him and give praise to God for his salvation.

His parents frequently remind him that when he does wrong things he must confess them right away so that his heart will be clean again. Jake does this eagerly, because he doesn't want to be punished for unconfessed sins. Lessons at church often stress the need to be saved, in case a regular attender has not yet made that decision or a visitor is unsaved. Personal salvation is the only part of the biblical story that Jake remembers hearing.

As Jake gets older, his parents remind him regularly of the day he was saved. They want him to remember that day because their own conversion is so memorable to them. But Jake frequently forgets to be good, so over and over he confesses his sins and asks Jesus into his heart — just to be sure he's saved. Jake begins attending the worship service with his parents. After the sermon there is always an altar call when people who want to be saved go forward. Jake is concerned that since he prayed to receive Jesus in Sunday school with his teacher, maybe he didn't do it "right." So from time to time he goes forward — just to be sure. Occasionally the church shows films about Jesus' return, when those who aren't saved are unable to be with him in heaven. Jake doesn't want to be left behind, so he prays to accept Jesus again — just to be sure.

In young adulthood his faith is very important to him, but he is fearful that he is not measuring up to God's expectations. He feels guilty that he doesn't pray enough, read his Bible enough, tell others about Jesus enough. Jake isn't baptized until he is twenty-four, because he has felt that he is not a good enough Christian to witness publicly to being a follower of Jesus. He goes to church, but he is not always comfortable there. He is sure he does not measure up to the members; they are much better Christians than he is.

Interestingly, Jake's cousin has no memory of getting saved, even though she grew up in the same church as Jake. She always has loved and believed in the Lord Jesus as her Savior. But her youth pastor insists that she needs to know when and where she became a Christian. He tells her to pick a date and a place and write them in her Bible, so she will know for sure that she is saved. This still seems odd to her.

The "Unclear" Tradition

With the proliferation of fast-growing independent churches in recent years, there is an accompanying uncertainty about what tradition, if any, should be followed with children. This rise in new churches is often driven by a desire to reach unchurched people with the gospel — the emphasis usually being on reaching adults. In these settings, separate spaces and experiences for children are common.

Some church leaders believe that tradition, liturgy, and sacraments confuse unchurched people rather than attracting them. Therefore many of these churches seem to be tradition and liturgy free. This nontradition policy influences children's ministry. Without the guidance of historical tradition, but given that Christian parents want their children to follow in the faith, each church must determine how a child comes to faith based on its own understanding of Scripture.

Scriptures Supporting the Various Traditions

While, as stated earlier, there is no passage that explains specifically how a child comes to faith in Jesus Christ, a helpful text is the apostle Paul's description of the way training and Scripture formed Timothy: "But as for you, continue in what you have learned and firmly believed, knowing from whom you learned it, and how from childhood you have known the sacred writings that are able to instruct you for salvation through faith in Christ Jesus" (2 Tim. 3:14-15). Timothy learned the Scriptures, those contained in the present-day Old Testament, from his mother and grandmother (see 2 Tim. 1:5), no doubt even before his more formal synagogue schooling began about age five.

Each of the three traditions we are considering is able to support its views based on certain texts, though these passages do not directly speak of children. In some cases the same verses are used by different traditions to support differing positions.[21] Scholars in each tradition have developed careful arguments and scriptural explications. Here are a few from each tradition that are relatively easily understood by nontheologians.

Sacramental Tradition

Besides many centuries of church tradition, several biblical passages uphold the sacramental position on baptism, though none refers directly to children. Speaking to Paul, a brand-new follower of Jesus, a disciple named Ananias says to him, "Get up, be baptized, and have your sins washed away, calling on his name" (Acts 22:16). In an early sermon in Acts, Peter says, "Repent, and be baptized every one of you in the name of Jesus Christ so that your sins may be forgiven; and you will receive the gift of the Holy Spirit" (Acts 2:38). Following a reference to Noah and the flood, Peter says in his first epistle, "This water symbolizes baptism that now saves you also — not the removal of dirt from the body but the pledge of a good conscience toward God. It saves you by the resurrection of Jesus Christ" (1 Pet. 3:21, NIV). These texts appear to say that baptism brings salvation by removing sin.

Covenantal Tradition

Foundational for covenantal theology is the first chapter of Ephesians, in which Paul acknowledges God's predestination and adoption of his children. Because we cannot readily identify those God has adopted (see Matt. 22:14), churches holding this position welcome children into the safety of the faith community for their nurture. The view of grace as held by the covenantal position regards God as the initiator in salvation. God's grace

21. One such passage is Ephesians 2:8-9, which is used in the covenantal tradition to demonstrate God's grace in salvation, while the conversional tradition emphasizes that "works" such as baptism and other sacraments do not contribute to one's salvation.

seeks out the elect, because he does not want anyone to perish (2 Pet. 3:9). "We love because he first loved us" (1 John 4:19). Paul says that everyone is in need of God's salvation: "The righteousness of God [comes] through faith in Jesus Christ for all who believe. For there is no distinction, since all have sinned and fall short of the glory of God; they are now justified by his grace as a gift, through the redemption that is in Christ Jesus" (Rom. 3:22-24). Peter states that it is through the grace of our Lord Jesus that we are saved (Acts 15:11). Later, Acts 18 notes that it is by grace that people believe. Twice in Ephesians 2, Paul writes that it is by grace that we are saved. "For the grace of God has appeared, bringing salvation to all" (Titus 2:11).

As noted earlier, in the covenantal tradition one manifestation of God's special grace is prevenient, going before any human action. A significant reference to prevenient grace occurs in the Old Testament. The prophet Hosea describes God's initiating work toward his children, the Israelites, in the form of an allegory (Hos. 11). In spite of the Israelites' straying from God, he helps them learn to walk, holds them in his arms, heals and feeds them. Note too that prevenient grace is a crucial element in the Wesleyan theology of childhood. Wesleyans, who own elements from all three traditions discussed here, see evidence of God's initiating grace in passages such as Hosea 11, John 1:9 ("the true light, which enlightens everyone"), and 1 John 4:9-10, 19, where John speaks of God's love coming before our love responses. As God's light and love shines in each heart, prevenient grace draws the child toward God.

Conversional Tradition

In the familiar passages on which this tradition focuses, the power to become a child of God comes from believing on his name, resulting in eternal life (John 1:12; 3:16). This salvation comes only through the name of God's Son, Jesus Christ (Acts 4:12). Confession of sin brings God's forgiveness and cleansing (1 John 1:9). Verses from the epistle to the Romans, sometimes referred to as the "Romans road to salvation," support the conversional view. These state that no one is righteous; everyone sins (3:10, 23). Though the penalty for sin is death (6:23), God loves us and died for us (5:8), so in Christ we are not condemned for our sin (8:1). If we confess, believe, and call on his name, we will be saved (10:9-10, 13). The first thirteen verses of Romans 5 bear a similar message. While Paul and Silas are imprisoned in Philippi, the jailer asks, "Sirs, what must I do to be saved?" The men reply, "Believe on the Lord Jesus, and you will be saved" (Acts 16:30-31).

What Does All This Mean?

Theological traditions vary, and we focus on different Bible passages to support our beliefs. What can we learn from one another? It is very helpful to look at our own theology and the practices that flow from it through the lenses of the other traditions. In our ministries with children, what important elements are weak or missing? In the accounts of Amanda and Sebastian, Kobi and Lucy, Maria and Jake, what do we discover about the ways children come to faith in Jesus Christ and what is important for their ongoing life of faith?

These contrasting stories illustrate a crucial fact: for a tradition to benefit children, it must be *lived out* in loving commitment. It is not enough for the congregation to post a statement of beliefs or to stand during an infant baptism or dedication and promise to nurture the child in the faith. Those beliefs and that formal pledge must be lived out week after week, across the years, in the halls, sanctuary, and classrooms of the church, in the home, and wherever the adults and children of the church interact in the community.

In three of the stories *devout Christian parents,* committed to their children and their spiritual well-being, play an important role in their children's lives. They realize that they are part of the church, the body of Christ, and they involve them in the Christian community; they also build into family life an enjoyment of Bible stories, prayer, and music focusing on Jesus' love. Most important, devout parents such as these live their faith before their children, letting them see what it means to be Christian, even how Christians deal with failures and disappointments.

The *congregations* that nurture the faith of children actively support them and their parents. That support takes different forms. Worshiping communities invest time in *celebrating faith markers* such as baptism or dedication. Parents and a Sunday school teacher receive with joy the news of a child's conversion. In some traditions parents are encouraged to select godparents for their children, and some parents find support in a Sunday school class or small group. Amanda's and Kobi's congregations *welcome children in the worship service;* children come to the Lord's Table to receive the elements or a blessing and gain a deep sense of belonging to the people of God.

Several of the children in our stories receive *early education in the faith,* both at home and at church. Here it is crucial that children meet a loving God in the stories of Scripture and through loving relationships with God's people. In chapters 7-12 of this book we will examine in some depth the kinds of relationships, worship, and learning that help children develop a strong, healthy, growing faith. For children who are baptized, their education *prepares* them *to affirm and claim their faith as their own.* Baptism begins a process of coming to faith, a process of learning, spiritual growth, and transformation that we trust will continue for a lifetime.

We have been looking at the stories of children growing up in Christian communities and homes. But what about children who do not have parents and congregations that can provide them with the gifts we have listed? The following is one person's story rather than a composite.

Janna's parents were good people who believed in God and attended church each Sunday as their service to God. While they were in the worship service, Janna attended Sunday school, and then the family went home. Devotional practices and conversations about God, however, were not part of family life. From an early age Janna was hungry for spiritual things. Whatever the Sunday school or confirmation class teacher suggested, she did, and as a sixth-grader she began staying by herself for the second worship service following Sunday school. Her church seemed to pay little attention to children and their needs until they became older teens. Her child's heart hungered for more than what she found at her church.

Several of Janna's school friends attended a church that offered special activities for children, and she loved to go along when they invited her. Their church's pastor focused significant attention on children and youth and really cared about them. Along with the fun and special relationships, that church seemed to offer more to satisfy her spiritual longings. During her middle school years Janna regularly attended Sunday evening youth activities with her friends, and her growing desire to follow Jesus led to her baptism in the new church. Unfortunately, however, none of the adults around her considered the importance of helping her talk with her parents about her desire for baptism. When the parents learned what she had done, they were hurt and could not celebrate with her. The trauma of the events surrounding her baptism ended Janna's involvement with the new church, but not her walk with Jesus. Years later Cathy met her in a seminary class as she responded to God's call in her life.

Neither church in Janna's story equipped or supported her parents for their role in her spiritual life. Although both churches assisted her with some parts of her spiritual journey, they also failed her. But God was at work planting spiritual hunger, and she sought to know more about God. The Holy Spirit led her and she followed. She went to seminary with a passion to prepare for ministry with children who have no one to care for their souls, children outside the faith community.

Upon Janna's graduation from seminary, God did not release her to serve in a middle-class white church. God took her back to the poorest elementary and middle schools in her city, to live among racially diverse children and be the presence of Jesus there. Recently God led Janna and her husband to a new church that was established to provide relevant ministry in its community of lower-income and new immigrant families. As a volunteer, Janna provides leadership for the planning of ministry with the children, using insights not just from her seminary training but from her own years of working with and caring for children the world considers to be the least.

The story of Janna shows us that the grace and power of God is not limited only to circumstances that are ideal — situations in which the home and the community of faith are working in harmony. There are countless stories that tell of God's intervention to help a child encounter God with awe and wonder in spite of human obstacles or apparent spiritual neglect.

From the experiences of children in the three theological traditions examined in this chapter, we see the important roles played by faith communities and families in the spiritual formation of children. Still, in devout Christian families and healthy Christian congregations, some children come to faith, but others do not. Then there are children like Janna, who seek and find God in spite of limited support. How do we understand these dynamics? What is God's part, and what is our part?

Our Part and God's Part

God grants us the privilege of partnering with the Holy Spirit in helping children "come and see" Jesus. We can point children to Jesus by helping them enter the stories of Scripture and follow Jesus there, getting to know him, love, and believe in him. Through the stories of Scripture we can tell the wonderful news of our loving forgiving God, so that when children become aware of their sin, they know where to go for forgiveness.

At some point each person must acknowledge his or her own sinfulness, personally recognize his or her need for a Savior, and claim Jesus Christ as that Savior. We do well to allow the Holy Spirit to do the work of the Spirit — forming, convicting, and transforming. In order for children to respond to the Holy Spirit, we need to create space for silence and help them become comfortable with it. We can help them practice listening prayer and model it ourselves. And we have the privilege of providing opportunities for children to come face to face with the living God — in other words, to *experience* God, not simply learn *about* God. Without pressuring or prescribing how a child should come to faith, we can invite children to respond in love to Jesus.

Providing ministry settings in which we "let the children come" to Jesus, meet and respond to God, may require a different approach to children's ministry. We will need to encourage adults to *be with* children, to journey with them as Christ is being formed in all of us. Likely there will be a challenging learning curve to figure out what this means within a given church's tradition. But the resulting "sociology" may encourage more lifelong, committed followers of Jesus — an outcome that could include the Sebastians, Lucys, and Jakes in our churches.

Jesus commanded his disciples to welcome children. We too are called to welcome children into a faith community where God's presence is real, where children can experience that presence and the love of God through God's people. That welcome must be extended to children in our church families and also to children from families who do not attend church. Jesus' final words to his disciples, the Great Commission, challenge us to care about the children in our Jerusalem, Judea — our church and neighborhood — and around the world. We are called to help them all become followers of Jesus.

God gives us significant roles to play in the lives of children, but it is God who meets the child, becoming real to him or her. God desires a relationship with each child more strongly than we desire it for him or her and is reaching out to all children. From the beginning of life, with grace God draws the child toward Jesus. In the stories of Scripture, the events of life, and the community of faith, Jesus graciously meets children personally.

The Holy Spirit helps children get to know Jesus and to grow in their beliefs, guides them to comprehend what they are ready for, and calls them to new commitments.

Without the support of caring adults and a vital faith community, most children lose the memory of God's early approaches to them or never come to understand what God was trying to say. The noise and sufferings of life can drown out the music of the dance with God. Children may be hindered from coming to God; Jesus made that very clear (Matt. 18:7). But whenever a child has a relationship with Jesus, it is because God has initiated that relationship.

As was true for the first disciples, the growing child's relationship with Jesus must be dynamic and changing, continually in process. As children grow and develop, they become interested in new aspects of their faith; they may discover misunderstandings and struggle with new questions. Children who respond to God's love are beginning the journey of a deepening relationship and a growing understanding — the process of becoming more and more like Jesus. Parents and caring adults in the faith community have the privilege of joining children on that journey, sometimes showing the way, often learning from them. And on this journey with children, God's Holy Spirit always walks with us as the real guide and teacher.

Chapter 4

THE CHILD'S DEVELOPMENT

The pastor startled us into attention when he started his sermon with "All God's children got rhythm. That's the way God made us." Life reflects that rhythm. Sleeping and waking. Work and rest. Going to school and earning a living. Gathering as a community to worship God, being nurtured in faith and going out to serve others.

The rhythm in God's design is seen through the trajectory of growth from infancy to early childhood, from middle childhood to youth and on to adulthood. As we minister to children we must respect and adjust to the rhythm of the child's development. The intention of this chapter is to address current understandings of child development — especially concepts that have special relevance for our church communities.

Developmental psychologists have studied children in a quest to understand the path they follow in moving through childhood. Since every child is immensely complex and each one an individual, explaining childhood with one grand theory is not possible. However, scholars can open our eyes to new understandings of how children think and feel and act, especially, as Barbara Kines Myers says, if we use their work as "lenses and not blinders."[1] To give context to some of the developmental concepts we will address, consider the following scenario.

During a family meal at Christmastime, grandparents and parents lis-

1. Barbara Kines Myers, *Young Children and Spirituality* (New York: Routledge, 1997), p. 2.

tened in on a conversation between four-year-old James and seven-year-old Hannah.

James: Jesus and God are the same, you know.
Hannah: No, James. God made the world, not Jesus.
James: No, Hannah. Jesus made some things.

What does careful listening to this conversation tell us about these two children? What might have prompted James's initial comment?

Around the room were signs of the Christmas season. Candles cast a soft glow. The tree sparkled with angels, lights, and decorations made and collected over the years.

James studied the nativity scene on the table. Perhaps it was the baby Jesus in Mary's arms that started his thinking. Or maybe it was his seasonal immersion in Christmas pageants, carols, and stories at school, church, and home. Maybe he had caught a comment in church about the Trinity.

Why might the seven-year-old sister contradict her younger brother? Older sisters do that! But there is more to her definitive statement "God made the world, not Jesus" than simply correcting her brother. She was in the midst of celebrating the birth of Jesus, and she knew that the world had been created before that event. Her recently acquired cognitive ability to put events in order may have led her to reason that God and Jesus are not the same.

James, not ready to concede his point, responded, "Jesus made some things." It appears that he does not reason in the same way as his older sister. Both of the children are attempting to understand the nature of God. Clearly their theological views are not fully formed. They are children who think like children. They don't question that God is real, but they are struggling to understand the mystery of God.

While developmental theorists cannot tell us everything about how children experience the presence of the Lord or how children are captured by the message of God's love and mercy or how they are animated to care for others, they do widen our perspective. Jean Piaget's precise study of cognitive development led him to a theoretical framework for understanding how children think. Several of the experiments he designed continue to be used by contemporary researchers. As a psychoanalyst, Erik Erikson concentrated his studies on psychosocial development across a lifetime. He identified conflicts and crises that are experienced at various stages of development, reminding us that normal development does not proceed smoothly or painlessly. Lev Vygotsky highlighted the connection between social/cultural interaction and cognitive development. Lawrence Kohlberg's identification of levels of moral reasoning, James Fowler's stages in faith development, and David Hay and Rebecca Nye's exploration of childhood spirituality all add to our store of knowledge. These scholars and others give us insight into the interchange between James and Hannah. They help us comprehend the nature of children and respond in appropriate and meaningful ways.

We will look first at key developmental observations in infancy and toddlerhood, early and middle childhood, and then at perspectives on the spiritual development of children.

Infants and Toddlers

The newborn infant enters the world remarkably equipped to form relationships. Baby and mother quickly make eye contact. As mother or father hold the baby in their arms, the infant is at just the right distance to focus on the parent's eyes — between seven and ten inches.[2] Parents snuggle the newborn and make welcoming and soothing sounds. The baby's reflex is to turn toward the touch of mother's breast and begin to suck.

The love relationship or attachment between mother and child, as well as father and other close caregivers, begins at birth but is strongly evident by about seven or eight months, when the baby begins to demonstrate separation and stranger anxiety. Although the baby's distress may feel like rejection to people who are just trying to be friendly, developmentalists consider the seemingly magnetic pull toward mother and father to be a good sign. The strong attachment response means that the baby has learned to distinguish the special people in his or her life from people the baby does not know.

One of the places where an infant may be left with an unknown person is in the church nursery. In some churches, nursery workers change

2. Grace Craig et al., *Children Today,* Canadian ed. (Scarborough, Ont.: Prentice Hall/Allyn and Bacon Canada, 1998), p. 142.

from week to week. For their comfort and confidence, babies and their parents should be able to count on at least some of the nursery caregivers being the same caring and responsive people every week.

A baby's temperament and experience with people other than immediate family influence the intensity of the stranger-anxiety response. In North America, children are considered to be the primary responsibility of their own parents, and in some families a baby's experience with people outside the family is limited. In other societies, the whole community plays a more prominent role in raising children. Brenda is a Canadian living and working in Uganda. Her experience of having a child in Africa speaks to the way children are cared for by many people in the community. Perhaps her son will not be as distressed as many North American children as he moves through the attachment phases.

> Five months ago I had a baby. In Africa.
>
> The delivery was no different than any in Canada with one exception. There was a live and loud turkey outside the window of the birthing room.
>
> Gobble gobble gobble, our son Rowan was born.
>
> Ugandans congratulated me by saying "Thank you. You've done good work." Rowan's welcome-to-the-world gifts included a rooster (twice over) and a papaya.
>
> After two months of maternity leave, I returned to work. I am breastfeeding, so Rowan comes with me wherever I go, including on village visits. This is a culture where children are always welcome and where their squeaks and squawks during a meeting barely raise an eyebrow.
>
> Rowan is an object of fascination in the village — a live "case study" for those who have never seen a white baby before. My mothering is also on show. One older woman remarked with wonder, "they suckle just like our babies." It's a universal design.
>
> Despite the commonness of parents and children the world over, having a child in Uganda is different than in suburban Canada. The moment Rowan greeted life in Africa, he became part of a community — parented in some way by all.
>
> I heard a baby crying in the village last week and stood up to see who it was. My Ugandan colleague said, "It's not your child. But it is your child. Because every child is your child." That's why when people

> say goodbye to me, they say "take care of our baby." It's also why Rowan gets passed from hand to hand, and everyone welcomes the chance to play a part in his nurture.[3]

Research on attachment theory by John Bowlby, Mary Ainsworth, and others concludes that following the time of separation and stranger anxiety, children settle into a reciprocal relationship with their family, confident in the consistency of their parents' care.[4] Their anxiety in new situations and around new people lessens. In fact, toddlers who are securely attached to their parents are able to confidently move out to explore their world and make friends with other children and adults. They keep connected with their family by an invisible bond. It's as if they know where they belong, where home is, and this frees them to get on with other tasks of learning and life.

Around the first birthday, children take their first steps and utter their first recognizable words. From this time on there is an explosion of exploration and expression of language. At first a child's speech is understood only by those in the family, and it takes a child several years to master the grammar, pronunciation, and everyday use of language.

One of James's first recognizable words was "ba." Depending on the context and inflection, "ba" could mean "Where's the golf ball?" or "Roblyn" (his dog) or something else in his immediate environment. His family had the task of figuring out what he was really trying to say and responding to his intention rather than the precision of his vocabulary. Participating in what seems to be a miracle as a child learns to communicate in spoken language is a great privilege for adults. Gordon Wells likens the language interaction between parents and their children to playing ball.

> What the adult has to do for this game to be successful is, first, to ensure that the child is ready, with arms cupped, to catch the ball. Then the ball must be thrown gently and accurately so that it lands squarely in the child's arms. When it is the child's turn to throw, the adult must be prepared to run wherever it goes and bring it back to where the child really intended it to go. Such is the collaboration required in conversation

3. Brenda Melles, "An African Son," *Newsletter from Arua, Uganda,* May 2002.
4. Craig et al., *Children Today,* p. 199.

> with the adult doing a great deal of supportive work to enable the ball to be kept in play.[5]

How the adults in the toddler's life, including those in the church community, speak to him helps to shape the child's burgeoning language. If children hear cursing, they learn to curse. If they hear thankfulness, they learn to be thankful. As young children interact with older children and adults, they learn how to ask questions and carry on conversations. Through story, conversation, and prayer, their vocabulary begins to incorporate words and concepts that are important in their family and church.

Infancy is a critical time of beginnings: beginning to form relationships, especially with immediate family, beginning to walk and step away from adults to explore home and beyond, beginning to learn to speak the language of the family. According to Erikson, the strong relationship between infants and parents and other caregivers forms the base for all future relationships.[6] A healthy relationship between child and parent is grounded in trust and love. In the loving family, infants catch the first reflection of God's love for them. The fortunate child grows up in the family and faith community surrounded by grace.

Preschoolers

Three-, four-, and five-year-old children are on the move. They are looking for answers to their questions. They are learning to play and they are playing to learn.

Through play, children experiment with clay and water and building blocks and thus learn about the properties of materials around them. Through play, children learn about cooperation and the early demands of friendship. As they become more skilled, they engage in "pretend" play, sometimes developing quite elaborate dramas — most reflecting their own experience at home and in the community. Through play, children learn how to get along, how to share scarce resources, and how to deal

5. Gordon Wells, *The Meaning Makers: Children Learning Language and Using Language to Learn* (Portsmouth, N.H.: Heinemann, 1986), p. 50.

6. See chapter 3 in Catherine Stonehouse, *Joining Children on the Spiritual Journey* (Grand Rapids: Baker Books, 1998).

with the anguish of hurts, both emotional and physical. They need continuing direction and support in their attempts at playing together.

As preschoolers become more adept in verbal communication, we are able to hear some of their thinking processes. Discovering how children think is a challenge for scholars. Most have concluded that young children process information differently from older children and adults: they try to understand how things work but not by using adult logic.

Young children's language learning progresses at a rapid pace. But they are still mastering the definitions of words, and they tend to interpret words literally. Think of a child who has come back from a fishing trip where fish were lured onto a hook and pulled out of the water into the boat to die; imagine her mental images when she later sings the song, "I Will Make You Fishers of Men." The three- or four-year-old child does not grasp the meaning behind the "fishers of men" metaphor that Jesus gave to his adult disciples.

Piaget's groundbreaking work on cognitive development continues to provide a base for understanding how young children process information.[7] He determined that human beings are born with the tendency and ability to explore and make sense of the world. As they expand their experience and discover new ideas, they build increasingly complex structures of meaning. Based on his controlled experiments and careful observations of children, Piaget concluded that infants, preschoolers, school-age children, and adolescents think in qualitatively different ways. In particular, he found that between five and seven years there is a marked shift in how children think. This change is demonstrated by an experiment he designed; it can be readily duplicated.

> The materials needed are: a pitcher of juice, two measuring cups of equal size, and two different shaped clear glasses one of which is tall and slender and the other short and broad. Invite the child to pour the same amount of juice into each of the measuring cups. Be sure that the child agrees that the amounts are the same. Then instruct the child to pour the juice from the one measuring cup into the short and the other into the tall glass. Ask the child whether the two glasses now have the same amount of juice or if one has more. A four-year-old will almost al-

7. See chapter 4 in Stonehouse, *Joining Children,* for further discussion of Piaget's concepts of cognitive development.

ways say that the tall glass has more because the juice comes up higher. A seven- or eight-year-old will likely say that they have the same amount of juice because nothing has been added or taken away.

Piaget called the ability to transfer information about amounts from one situation to another and back again *conservation*. Before children have mastered this cognitive skill, they draw intuitive conclusions based on what they see at the moment rather than by looking back over the process. Once children have moved into the next stage of thinking — the *concrete operational* stage, in Piaget's terminology — they are able to reason backward and forward and are not bound by present appearance.

James and Hannah in the story at the beginning of this chapter are in different cognitive stages, according to Piaget. Hannah is moving into logical sequential reasoning, which she applies to her understanding of God. James is free to wonder about Jesus as Creator without the restriction of consistency in the sequence of creation and Jesus' birth.

Because preschool children are limited in their capacity to make logical connections between different situations, metaphors are often inexplicable to them. For example, "The Bible is a flashlight; it shows us the way to walk" is not understandable for a four-year-old.

Young children are learning about morality as they learn about other realities. Kohlberg's research into moral development concluded that children think about moral decisions differently from adults.[8] Young children tend to choose actions to avoid punishment or limit physical damage. Surprisingly, they believe that the greater amount of physical damage, the greater the wrong. In other words, the intent of the person is not as important for judging moral action as the results of the action. For example, when presented with a story about two children, one who broke a dozen cups by accident and another who broke one cup in anger, young children will say the first child was the "baddest."

It is only as children move into middle childhood, that they begin to factor in whether or not a bad deed was done "on purpose" or "by accident" as they make their moral judgments. Since children at that stage are especially concerned about fairness, the wise teacher is scrupulous about being seen to be fair with every child in the class.

8. See Stonehouse, *Joining Children*, chapter 5, for further discussion of Kohlberg's work.

Moral development includes more than how we think about right and wrong. It is about moral action and forming a reliable and sensitive conscience. Young children are starting to understand about right and wrong, but they are also exploring ways to consider the needs of others in their play and life interactions. They are forming a guiding conscience that will be sensitive to shame and guilt when they do wrong. Wise adults will be careful not to impose guilt or shame on young children for actions that are part of normal growth. For example, a child may be upset and disruptive because he is hungry. Mom or Dad may be busy with trying to finish a task but the child is hungry and thirsty and wants attention now. Or a child may drop and break a treasured item because his or her small muscles are still being developed.

Much of the developmental research related to young children has focused on how children think. Clearly children process information differently from adults. But when it comes to feelings, children are more like adults than we sometimes recognize. They experience stress, fear, delight, compassion, wonder, and are often more open about their feelings than are adults. Although they may not be able to fully grasp a theological idea, they can freely enjoy and participate in the worshiping community.

School-Age Children

As children move into their formal schooling years, their relationships and exposure to ideas and skills broadens. Erikson calls the middle childhood years (from six to eleven) the age of "industry versus inferiority." Children on a healthy developmental trajectory learn hundreds of skills such as reading and writing, riding a bicycle or inline skates, playing a musical instrument or organized sports. Wherever children live in the world, at this age they are acquiring knowledge and skills that are important in their society.

The dark side of this stage of life, from Erikson's perspective, is that children are especially vulnerable to losing self-confidence. Instead of developing a sense of competence and certainty in their abilities, they may begin to feel inferior. The teacher, parent, or children's ministry leader has a vital responsibility to protect the children in their care and not to diminish their confidence.

Vygotsky, a Russian psychologist, was especially interested in how children become *enculturated.* That is, how do children learn the values, language, and stories of their community? He recognized that children are not cooked up in batches like cookies; rather each child, even in the same family, brings distinctive abilities and experiences into the learning kitchen. Children are remarkably capable of learning without direct instruction. Toddlers will try and try again until they make a puzzle piece fit. But if an adult or older sibling suggests turning the piece in a certain way to make it fit, the child masters the problem more readily. Vygotsky calls the differential between what children can do on their own and what they can accomplish with the support of a more experienced child or adult the *zone of proximal development* (ZPD). "Vygotsky used the analogy of fruit and blossoms. The level the child can reach in independent work is like the fruit — it is already developed. The level the child can reach with guidance is like the blossom. The teacher can help the child turn the blossom into a fruit. 'What a child can do with assistance today, she will be able to do herself tomorrow.'"[9]

Gifted teachers are always aware of what the child knows and can do on his own and are creative in challenging the child to move to the next level of knowing and doing. Vygotsky gives us a structure for valuing both the ability of the learner and the significant contribution the teacher can bring to the process of learning.

Beyond the influence of individual teachers and families, Vygotsky's work also accounts for the significant role that cultures and the broader society play in how the child comes to understand the world. Diverse societies value different skills and often have quite distinct approaches for helping children realize important values and proficiencies.

Vygotsky's writing challenges us to tune in to what children have discovered on their own and to provide a bridge for their further learning. Even more important, he reminds us of how influential the social, physical, and spiritual environment is to a child's healthy development.

There is an enormous change between children entering middle childhood at around six years of age and moving into puberty at about eleven or twelve. During these years, they develop stronger communication and relational skills. Their knowledge of the world and understanding of moral

9. Craig et al., *Children Today,* p. 44; quoting Lev Vygotsky, *Mind in Society: The Development of Higher Psychological Processes,* ed. M. Cole et al. (Cambridge, Mass.: Harvard University Press).

and spiritual concerns expands. Their physical abilities strengthen, as well as the depth of their understanding of others.

Current research is nuancing our understanding of developmental theory. Without losing awareness that children at different ages think and act differently, the emphasis has shifted to understanding development as a continuous process. For example, Robbie Case has been called a neo-Piagetian. His research has led to the conclusion that cognitive development is much more fluid than initially thought and that children can in some measure be taught skills beyond what would be expected for their age.

Another movement in research is a swing away from an emphasis on nurture to focus on the place that genetics play in a child's development. Our understanding of child development keeps growing as research adds new pieces to the puzzle.

Recent work in neurobiology looks at a vital additional component in the learning process: emotions. Although all parts of the brain function interdependently, the limbic system (including the amygdala, hippocampus, and hypothalamus) is particularly relevant in governing emotions. For some time we have been familiar with the hemispheric functions of the neocortex. Overly simplified in lay terms, the "left brain" is the speech and analytic center, while the "right brain" is the creative and relational center. Based on groundwork laid by many other researchers, Daniel Goleman's significant work in *emotional intelligence* explores the role of emotions in the development and learning of a person as well as the significance of the limbic system in that process.[10] Emotions and feelings originate primarily in the limbic system, as do some aspects of personal identity and memory function, all of which relate to what an individual learns and how the person feels about that learning.[11]

Spiritual Development Research

Serious investigation of spiritual development in recent years has recovered a neglected area of research. Rightfully this work recognizes that the

10. Daniel Goleman, *Emotional Intelligence* (New York: Bantam, 1995).

11. See discussion of the work of Antonio Damasio in chapter 11 of this book, "In Worship," pp. 224, 226.

spiritual nature of a person is at least as important as the physical, cognitive, emotional, and social dimensions.

However, researching children's spiritual development is a little like trying to capture the wind in a box. As the Scriptures say, "The wind blows where it chooses, and you hear the sound of it, but you do not know where it comes from or where it goes. So it is with everyone who is born of the Spirit" (John 3:8).

Not surprisingly, developing a plausible methodology for studying the deep well of spiritual life is immensely difficult, especially when we are trying to understand *children's* spiritual experience. Spirituality is multi-textured. It influences how we think, what we value, how we act, and especially where we place our trust.

One difficulty in studying spirituality is that it is often based on what respondents remember and how they interpret their experience. All experiences are not remembered in the same way. Memory depends, for example, on the intensity of the experience and its later value for the person. The way people recall an experience is colored by their religious instruction in a particular tradition, their earlier experiences, their religious beliefs, and the current importance of that experience to them, as well as where, and to whom, they talk about it.

A further complication in this study is that children, especially young children, have limited language for expressing their spiritual experiences. Children who are raised in secular contexts may not have *any* vocabulary to talk about their spiritual awareness.

Although researching and writing about children's spiritual development is tough, a number of scholars have undertaken significant studies. We will look at only a sampling of the research here.[12]

James Fowler is an American scholar who is largely responsible for opening the door to serious investigation of faith development as a critical piece of human development.[13] He begins with the conviction that faith, defined as "a dynamic pattern of trust in and loyalty to a center of value, to an image of power, to a shared master story," is a basic human quality that

12. See David Hay, Rebecca Nye, and Roger Murphy, "Thinking About Childhood Spirituality: Review of Research and Current Directions," in *Research in Religious Education,* ed. Leslie J. Francis, William K. Kay, and William S. Campbell (Macon, Ga.: Smyth and Helwys, 1996), pp. 47-70, for a comprehensive review of childhood spirituality research up to the date of publication.

13. Stonehouse, *Joining Children,* chapter 7, discusses Fowler's work.

may be expressed through different religious forms. Fowler's faith development framework seeks explanations for how children and young people construct their religious knowledge. He has examined the faith processes of people in different religions — Christianity, Judaism, Islam, and others — and looked for common and identifiable stages that persons follow in their faith journey. The faith stages pertaining to children that Fowler identified are *primal faith, intuitive-projective faith, mythic-literal faith,* and *synthetic-conventional faith.*

Fowler calls the primal faith of very young children a prestage for faith development. He contends that a basic disposition to trust in the very young child is foundational, we might say, the "embryo of faith." Around the age of two, children move into intuitive-projective faith. During this period, faith is experienced intuitively rather than with formal logic. The first conscious images of God form at this time.

Around six or seven, children begin to develop a mythic-literal faith. They build a repertoire of story, ritual, values, and expectations for moral behavior from their faith community. Between the ages of eleven and fifteen, there is a transition to a new faith stage that Fowler calls synthetic-conventional faith. At this point, young people's ability to use abstract thought deepens their capacity to consider social, global, and theological issues. At the same time, interpersonal relationships are increasingly important. Teens become acutely aware of what friends, parents, teachers, youth leaders, and others expect of them. Many young people yearn to find a deeper relationship with God.

Fowler's stages of faith seem to reflect the spiritual path of many children raised in Western Christian families. But when Beth has invited college and seminary students to compare their personal faith journeys with Fowler's theoretical framework, those who grew up in a culture where another world faith and ideology predominate often say that this model does not adequately represent their experience. They tend not to resonate at all with the stages of faith that Fowler identifies. This serves as a reminder to be careful about expecting children everywhere to fit into our developmental theories.

Perhaps the reason for the disconnect between theory and life among these students is that faith is so closely aligned with religious beliefs. Separating the two may be purely an academic exercise. Sofia Cavalletti, an esteemed Italian Hebrew scholar, has spent a lifetime studying the spiritual life of children. Her position is that spirituality and religiousness are so closely bound together that it is not valid to consider one without the other. "To want to stay on a level of religiousness deprived of content would be tantamount . . . to wanting to speak a language without using a spoken tongue. If we intend to talk about God we must use a language, and the language with which we speak of God takes the name of an actual religion."[14]

Kalevi Tamminen, a Finnish researcher, conducted a major longitudinal study of the religiousness of children and adolescents.[15] He interviewed about three thousand Finnish children over a six-year period beginning in 1974. As much as possible, the same children were interviewed again in 1976 and 1980. Since 95 percent of people in Finland identify themselves as Lutheran, the vast majority of the children and teens in the study had some Christian church and education experience. Tamminen affirmed that most children and adolescents identified personal religious experiences defined as "an experience to which a sense of dependency on or a link with God/the divine and the transcendent is connected." However, he found that as they moved into adolescence, they became less certain of their beliefs and began to be more critical in their religious assessments.

In Great Britain, David Hay and Rebecca Nye contend that many contemporary children have lost the necessary vocabulary to speak about spiritual experience.[16] Hay and Nye have developed a qualitative research approach that analyzes children's conversations both verbally and symbolically. The researchers are looking beyond the words the children use and are paying special attention to the dimensions of awareness, mystery, value sensing, and meaning making. They have found in many cases that overtly religious language is absent but there is a clear presence of "spiritually significant experiences" in their transcripts. They demonstrate that recognizing children's spiritual awareness requires a well-tuned ear and heart.

The challenge of understanding God's design for healthy children continues. The study of the spiritual lives of children is unfinished.

Developmental research and theory help us to understand that chil-

14. Sofia Cavalletti, *The Religious Potential of the Child* (Chicago: Catechesis of the Good Shepherd Publications, 1992), p. 27.

15. Kalevi Tamminen, "Religious Experiences in Childhood and Adolescence: A Viewpoint of Religious Development between the Ages of 7 and 20," *International Journal for the Psychology of Religion* 4, no. 2 (1994): 64-83.

16. Hay, Nye, and Murphy, "Thinking About Childhood Spirituality," p. 67.

dren think like children, not like adults, and to marvel at the way children learn the language of their family and community — the language in which they can hear the stories of the Scriptures and express with growing confidence what they understand. It reminds us of the importance of loving care in the life of children; this sets the tone for experiencing the grace of God. It helps us to recognize how children are thinking about morality and how their conscience is being grounded.

Nourishing the growth of children in all aspects of their lives requires an understanding of human development. However, we can never know everything about the wonder of God's greatest creation, the child. As Myers marvels, "Just when I think I understand young children, I meet a little person whose actions prompt a sense of wonder, puzzlement or perplexity in me about what might be going on in this unique mind."[17]

17. Myers, *Young Children and Spirituality*, p. 2.

Chapter 5

HISTORICAL ROOTS OF MINISTRY WITH CHILDREN

What happens when the human race loses the ability to have children is the focus of P. D. James's chilling novel *The Children of Men.* Conflicts and intrigue develop around gaining possession and control of the last child to be born. The novel highlights the reality that the existence of any community is dependent on each new generation of children.

So it is for the church. Children are essential to the life of the church — yesterday, today, and tomorrow. Throughout the Scriptures we see again and again that the survival of the faith community is dependent on each new generation of children. And it becomes the responsibility of family and community to pass on to their children the story of God's creating, redeeming, and sustaining grace and power (Deut. 4:9; 6:4-9; 11:19; Prov. 22:6; Eph. 6:4).

The mandate to make God known to our children and our children's children extends to us today. But the way this scriptural directive is carried out looks quite different in the contemporary church than in the early days of the Christian church. The challenge of this chapter is to explore some of what has happened in the intervening millennia to bring us to our current children's ministry practices.

Life in the twenty-first century is not the same as life in the first century. In each generation God's people have sought to effectively carry out their responsibility of passing the truth about God on to their children. In different times and different places, particular people have been empowered by the Spirit of God to be leaders in thinking and action in this enterprise. Each successive era has had significant Christian leaders who have contributed to the church's understanding of who children are and what it means to teach them about living as followers of Jesus. The influence of these theologians and church leaders has sometimes shaped the way the whole society has responded to children. At other times, the Christian education of children in the church has been reformed in response to the predominant philosophical and educational theories of the period. The challenge is to be discerning about what is right and good and true and not be blown about by the "wisdom" of the day.[1] Followers of Jesus consistently return to the Scriptures to realign their efforts with the call to serve children in the name of Jesus.

The pages that follow offer a panorama of the history of the church and children. We will catch glimpses of how shifts in theological, philosophical, and social science perspectives have been reflected in how children are treated in the Christian community. Consideration of the impact of changing educational practice and socioeconomic-cultural realities will help us to understand the roots of present ministry practices with children.

The Early Church (A.D. 1–500/600)

What we know about children in the early church comes largely from incidents scattered throughout the Gospels and epistles and augmented by what we read about the times in other documents. We have glimpses of the childhood of Jesus and of John the Baptist. There are references to children being in the crowds who came to listen to Jesus teach (John 6:9; Matthew 14:21). Of particular interest are the stories about Jesus welcoming children and his teaching about children being models in the kingdom of God. Some of Jesus' healing miracles involved children. The raising from the dead of Jairus's daughter (Mark 5:21-24, 35-43; Matt. 9:18, 23-26; Luke 8:40-42, 49-56) and the healing of the royal official's son (John 4:46-51) are two such incidents.

As the early followers of Jesus established their identity as Christians, they regularly met together. At first there were no separate church build-

1. "Do not be conformed to this world, but be transformed by the renewing of your mind, so that you may discern what is the will of God — what is good and acceptable and perfect" (Rom. 12:2).

ings, so they gathered in homes or out of doors. Prisca and Aquila, for example, hosted a group of believers in their home (Rom. 16:5). After Paul and his companions arrived in Philippi, on the Sabbath they "went outside the gate by the river, where [they] supposed there was a place of prayer" (Acts 16:13). They found a group of women gathered for prayer and sat down to speak to them. It is likely that children were present at all these meetings.

In the early church, children formed part of the households who came to trust in Jesus. It seems that in at least some congregations, children were not merely passive spectators on the edge of what was going on but were taught and encouraged alongside the adults during the course of the church's meeting for worship.[2] We know this because the letters to the Ephesians and the Colossians specifically address children about their responsibility to their parents (Eph. 6:1-4; Col. 3:20). The same letters speak about the expectation of the early church that parents — especially fathers — will take the leadership in bringing children up "in the discipline and instruction of the Lord" (Eph. 6:4).

As W. A. Strange reminds us, the "New Testament spans a wide variety of places and culture and so we should perhaps speak of the worlds rather than the world of the New Testament."[3] The early Christians lived in a variety of places around the Mediterranean. There were wealthy and poor families, children who lived in cosmopolitan cities like Rome and children who lived in the country. They spoke different languages and had different cultural traditions. The first Christians were predominantly Jewish, but the church soon included an increasing number of Gentiles.[4] An anonymous writer of the late second century expressed eloquently how Christians were in the world but not of it:

> For Christians are not distinguished from the rest of mankind by country, or by speech, or by dress. For they do not dwell in cities of their own, or use a different language, or practice a peculiar life. . . . But while they dwell in Greek or barbarian cities according as each man's lot has been cast, and follow the customs of the land in clothing and food, and

2. W. A. Strange, *Children in the Early Church* (Carlisle, Cumbria, U.K.: Paternoster, 1996), p. 74.

3. Strange, *Children in the Early Church,* p. 2.

4. James E. Reed and Ronnie Prevost, *A History of Christian Education* (Nashville: Broadman and Holman, 1993), p. 4.

> other matters of daily life, yet the condition of citizenship which they exhibit is wonderful, and admittedly strange. . . . Every foreign land is to them a fatherland, and every fatherland a foreign land. (*Epistle to Diognetus* 6.1-5)[5]

There does, however, seem to be some continuity of experience from which to draw conclusions about what a child's life might have been like in the time of the early church. As it is for children everywhere, childhood was a time to prepare for adult responsibilities. "Girls had to learn to manage the household. Boys had to learn the work of their fathers, whether in the fields or in a trade."[6] In the Jewish community, not only did boys learn about trade and commerce, but they also received instruction in the Hebrew Scriptures. They were expected to memorize large portions of the Law and to understand the text as explained by their teachers. Girls, on the other hand, were not permitted to learn to read or write or to study the Law.

What was different about being raised in a Christian home rather than a pagan home? For one, the Christian child, like Jewish children, would be protected from infanticide, which was common in the ancient world, especially for newborn girls and children with disabilities. It is significant that in A.D. 374 the Christian Roman emperors Valentinian, Valens, and Gratian made infanticide a crime punishable by death. One aim of the consolidation of Christianity in the Roman Empire was to extend the protection of the law over the lives of young children.[7] Christians had inherited from Judaism a positive attitude toward their children. Jesus' interest in children and concern for them could never be totally overlooked by his followers.

We have very little detailed information about how the early church set about the task of nurturing children in the faith. But we do know that "the church grew by evangelism as well as by biological growth, as successive generations accepted the faith of Christ. Justin Martyr, writing a defense of Christianity around 155 a.d., could point to 'many men and women of sixty and seventy years of age, who became disciples of Christ from their childhood' (*I Apology* 1.15)."[8] By the middle of the second century there were many men and women who had been brought up in the church.

5. Quoted in Strange, *Children in the Early Church*, p. 81.
6. Strange, *Children in the Early Church*, p. 12.
7. Strange, *Children in the Early Church*, p. 112.
8. Strange, *Children in the Early Church*, p. 83.

As the church grew, it became evident that new believers needed a greater measure of instruction about the Christian faith. Gentile believers, especially, would have had little background in the story of creation, covenant, sin, and redemption found in the Scriptures. So a formal process of preparation for initiation into full membership in the church was needed to bring consistency of doctrinal understanding and integrity of Christian practice. In addition, early believers often faced severe persecution, and solid biblical knowledge would help them stand their ground. These factors led to the establishment of catechumenal schools. Over a two- or three-year period, candidates for baptism moved through three stages of preparation. First they were *hearers* who listened to the reading of Scripture and to sermons. Then they became *kneelers,* because they remained for corporate prayer after the hearers were dismissed from class. Finally they joined the *chosen* people, who received intensive training in doctrines and church liturgy and were prepared to receive baptism.[9] It is assumed that older children were included as students alongside the adults. Candidates who successfully passed their examination were welcomed, baptized, and allowed to break bread with the congregation.

The catechumenal form of Christian education "reached its peak of popularity around A.D. 325-450. It declined in effectiveness once it became expected of children to be baptized and when pagans, lacking genuine motivation for joining the faith, were commanded by law to attend church."[10]

Christian boys in the first centuries attended secular schools.[11] But by the end of the second century, many Christians became concerned about their sons' exposure to heretical philosophies of Greek and Roman origin while at the same time recognizing the value of education. In response, they established catechetical schools, a context for learning that integrated religious values, philosophy, and high moral standards. The catechetical schools were associated with local church congregations but welcomed both Christians and non-Christians into the community of

9. Michael Anthony and Warren Benson, *Exploring the History and Philosophy of Christian Education* (Grand Rapids: Kregel, 2003), p. 108, referring to Charles B. Eavey, *History of Christian Education* (Chicago: Moody, 1964), p. 84.

10. Anthony and Benson, *Exploring the History and Philosophy,* p. 109.

11. Cynthia K. Dixon, "Who Nurtured the Child?" paper presented at the First International Conference on Children's Spirituality, University College, Chichester, Australia, July 2000, p. 6.

study. The curriculum included Bible, theology, literature, philosophy, history, science, and critical thinking and rhetorical debating skills. The most prominent catechetical school was in Alexandria, Egypt, but later others were established in Jerusalem, Antioch, Edessa, Nisibis, and Constantinople.[12]

By the end of the fourth century, the theological question of whether infants who died without being baptized were condemned was causing intense controversy in the church. This issue was highlighted when the spiritual status of infant martyrs was considered. Augustine (354-430), the influential bishop of Hippo in North Africa, wrestled with this question, studying the Scriptures and considering his responsibilities to the children under his pastoral care. He wrote about the question of the innocence or innate depravity of infants and children in his *Confessions.* His articulation of the doctrine of "original sin" — based on such biblical texts as Psalm 51:5, "Indeed, I was born guilty, a sinner when my mother conceived me," and Romans 5:12, "Sin came into the world through one man, and death came through sin, and so death spread to all because all have sinned" — was critical to his resolution of the issue. He reconciled his belief that everyone is "born in sin" with the abhorrent idea that God would consign a baby to hell by posing the idea of the non-innocence of babies. Although infants possess no personal sin, he said, they are infected by the original sin of Adam. As children mature, they become more and more accountable for their sins. But still, when pressed about the tragic fate of unbaptized infants, he sadly consigned them to eternal punishment. His position was that infants should be baptized, because "it would be cruel to exclude infants from baptism; they too needed access to baptism for the forgiveness of sin."[13] Augustine's writing about the status of childhood (non-innocent), the nature of the human (created in the image of God but corrupted by Adam's sin), and the ritual of baptism (important for infants especially if their life was in danger) "formed and transformed Christian attitudes toward children" for centuries.[14]

12. Anthony and Benson, *Exploring the History and Philosophy,* p. 111.

13. Martha Ellen Stortz, "'Where or When Was Your Servant Innocent?': Augustine on Childhood," in *The Child in Christian Thought,* ed. Marcia J. Bunge (Grand Rapids: Eerdmans, 2001), p. 91.

14. Stortz, "Where or When," p. 79.

The Medieval Church (500-1500)

By the fifth century, infant baptism was well established in the church. As a support to parents, godparents were named who would share in the responsibility for teaching the faith. Parents and godparents were admonished from the pulpit to carry out the instruction of their children in the home.

Since few Christians could read, oral traditions were crucial for teaching and learning. "Formal teaching centered on the Apostles' Creed, the Lord's Prayer, and the Commandments along with some moral instruction."[15] Although oral instruction was a primary means by which children learned, they also were educated through popular practices of piety such as holy days, processions, wayside shrines, pilgrimages, and adoration of saints. Processions and passion plays, along with other forms of religious drama, enriched their understanding of the Christian life. In northern Europe, Romanesque and Gothic churches were built with stained-glass windows, carving, and statues illustrating biblical scenes. Worship in a visually rich Christian environment was part of the faith formation of children at this time.[16]

During the Middle Ages, monasteries emerged in both the Eastern and Western church. These schools of asceticism (self-denial and even self-punishment) and Christian life served to preserve and develop instruction in the Christian faith. Children of the nobility and sometimes of the poor studied along with monks and clerics. Monastic instruction was guided by moral and religious purposes and included reading, writing, arithmetic, singing, and the elements of Christian doctrine.[17]

In the early years of the ninth century, formal education outside of monasteries was minimal. Charlemagne (742?-814), who was crowned emperor of the Holy Roman Empire on Christmas Day in 800, sparked a major educational revival when he insisted that every cathedral and monastery establish a school. In addition, he decreed that priests must use the vernacular, making prayer and Scripture accessible to the ordinary person. When Charlemagne chose Alcuin of York to lead the palace school, he se-

15. Beverly Johnson-Miller, "Medieval Education," in *Dictionary of Christian Education*, ed. Michael Anthony (Grand Rapids: Baker, 2001), p. 454.

16. Johnson-Miller, "Medieval Education."

17. Johnson-Miller, "Medieval Education," p. 455.

lected an innovative educator. Alcuin introduced new teaching methods that included positive motivation, simplification of complex concepts, valuing individual gifts, and conversation. Since Charlemagne himself was one of his students, Alcuin's influence was extensive.[18]

Concern for the eternal safety of young children continued in the medieval era. The times were dangerous for children, with many dying in infancy. Christian parents feared — and their fears were nurtured by the church — that if their infant died without being baptized, the child would be eternally condemned. Since clergy were not always present when a baby was deathly ill, laypeople were given instruction so that in an emergency they could perform a baptism.[19]

By the tenth and eleventh centuries, local parishes were abundant, and it was now reasonable to expect that a family have access to clergy within a short time after the birth of a child. The church then clarified baptismal procedures. The expectation was that infants be baptized within the first seven days following their birth. If the child should happen to die unbaptized during that first week, the parents were simply required to do penance. If the child died unbaptized after the initial grace period, the consequences increased: penance was accompanied by a monetary fine.[20]

During this time, the role of godparents began to take on more significance. It was thought that the responsibility of raising a child ought to extend beyond the immediate family. Godparents were a required component of a baptism, although the requirements to serve in this position were far from rigid. Siblings, servants, and even unofficiating clergy were eligible to serve in this capacity. One particular responsibility of the godparents was to make certain that the parents of the child were living godly lives. Essentially, they took on a role of lifelong accountability for both the parent and the child.[21]

Infant baptism was well accepted, but there was disagreement during this era as to whether it was appropriate to offer the elements of the Eucharist to a child.

18. Johnson-Miller, "Medieval Education."

19. Nicholas Orme, *Medieval Children* (London: Yale University Press, 2001), p. 24.

20. Orme, *Medieval Children,* pp. 23-24.

21. Orme, *Medieval Children,* p. 202.

> Eleventh- and twelfth-century liturgical texts provide for bishops or priests to administer it to newly baptized infants. By the end of the twelfth century, this practice was dying out. There was now a belief in the Real Presence: the view that consecrated bread and wine were not merely memorials or symbols of Jesus but changed their nature to become his body and blood. This dictated greater reverence. One had to guard against the elements being spit or regurgitated, and a conviction grew among Church leaders that you needed to believe in the Presence to receive communion rightly. Children came to seem to be too young to understand what they were getting.[22]

Behavioral expectations for children continued to be quite rigid during the medieval era. Submission was expected. It was customary for children to remove their caps and bow toward their parents. In response, parents would have the opportunity to bless their children, similar to what one would experience in church.[23] Social problems of the era were blamed on parents who had not properly raised their children to respect God and his laws.

The Renaissance and Reformation (1500-1700)

The impact of the invention of the printing press with movable type by Johann Gutenberg (c. 1400-1468) cannot be overstated. Ten Bibles could now be printed as cheaply as one could be copied by hand. This invention became a historical turning point that changed society and eventually changed the direction of Christian education. It opened the door to the increased availability and affordability of books, the expansion of libraries, and increasing literacy, and it sparked the translation of the Scriptures into vernacular languages. Indeed the printing press set the stage for the Protestant Reformation.

In 1517, the Protestant Reformation was set in motion by the nailing of Martin Luther's ninety-five theses to the church door in Wittenberg. The radical changes that came about in the church through the influence of Luther (1483-1546) and other Reformers of the time are well known, but

22. Orme, *Medieval Children,* p. 214.
23. Orme, *Medieval Children,* p. 84.

many of us are less aware of the emphasis Luther placed on children in his preaching and writing.

Luther believed that Scripture fully supported the practice of infant baptism:

> For Luther, salvation occurs when baptism is received, as long as one recognizes that what makes it saving is the ongoing reorientation of human life that it effects. Luther's emphasis on the daily return to baptism shows that the claim "I am baptized" does not so much identify a specific event in time as describe a lifelong condition. The two most defining relationships in a baptized person's life are with the God of the gospel and with the church. To use baptism aright is to immerse oneself in the various means of grace — worship, prayer, proclamation, sacraments — so that one is constantly exposed to the working of the Spirit. Apart from the church, this is impossible.[24]

From infancy until the age of understanding, at seven, Luther placed the responsibility for nurturing a child's faith on both parents and the community as a whole.[25] He noted that the elasticity of the child and preadolescent functions as ideal soil in which to plant important ideas of faith. Unlike any other time in life, these formative years are critical in establishing the foundation for a faithful adulthood.[26]

Among Luther's many contributions to the church are his large and small catechisms. The large catechism was intended for pastors and adult leaders.[27] "His *Introduction* and *Shorter Catechism,* known as the 'Jewel of the Reformation,' were written to provide Christian parents with guidelines and a basic curriculum for teaching their children in the home."[28] Luther placed a high value on continual study of and reflection on the catechism texts:

24. Jan Strohl, "The Child in Luther's Theology," in *The Child in Christian Thought,* ed. Marcia Bunge, p. 143.

25. Strohl, "Child in Luther's Theology," p. 134.

26. Steven Ozment, *When Fathers Ruled: Family Life in Reformation Europe* (Cambridge, Mass.: Harvard University Press, 1983), p. 147.

27. Harold W. Burgess, *Models of Religious Education* (Nappanee, Ind.: Evangel, 2001), p. 52.

28. Robert F. Lay, *Foundational Documents for Christian Teachers and Ministers* (Upland, Ind.: Robert Lay and Taylor University, 2004), p. 173.

> I, too, am a doctor and preacher, as learned and experienced as all those may be who have such presumption and security; yet I do as a child who is being taught the Catechism, and every morning and whenever I have time, I read and say, word for word, the Ten Commandments, the Creed, the Lord's Prayer, the Psalms, etc. And I must still read and study daily, and yet I cannot master it as I wish, but must remain a child and pupil of the Catechism, and glad so to remain.[29]

Not only did the Protestant Reformation revolutionize the church, but its influence spilled over into the broader society. Through the leadership of the Reformers, the whole educational system across Europe would change. Prior to this time, schools had been under the strict control of the Roman church leaders. From Luther and other Reformers' perspective, these schools were largely failures. Luther placed a high value on education and believed that all children, rich and poor, boys and girls, should attend school. There they would study the Scriptures, the classical languages, and Hebrew as well as German, history, poetry, singing, instrumental music, and mathematics. He believed that only if children were educated could they give their full service to God and the community.[30] Luther preached sermons and wrote scathing letters to civic leaders pushing for funding and the establishment of schools throughout Germany. In 1524 he wrote to the leaders of cities in Germany, urging them to establish and maintain schools in order that the Roman Church not maintain the power it had traditionally held over education. His argument went like this: "If it is necessary, dear sirs, to expend annually such great sums for firearms, for roads, bridges, dams, and countless similar things, in order that a city may enjoy temporal peace and prosperity, why should not at least some money be devoted to the poor needy youth?"[31]

This period was especially rich in Christian thinkers, theologians, educators, preachers, and writers. The Moravian bishop John Amos Comenius (1592-1670), for example, was an influential Christian leader and educational theorist who paved the way for new ways of thinking about children, their development, and their education.[32] Comenius believed in

29. Quoted in Lay, *Foundational Documents,* p. 174.
30. John Elias, *A History of Christian Education* (Malabar, Fla.: Krieger, 2002), p. 87.
31. Quoted in Elias, *History of Christian Education,* p. 87.
32. Anthony and Benson, *Exploring the History and Philosophy,* p. 216.

a holistic education that would begin in infancy and continue through life. He introduced new systematic and sequential ways of approaching curriculum design, advocating the organization of curricular material in a progressive flow from easy to most difficult.

Comenius was appalled by the common teaching method of forcing children to memorize and recite material of which they had little understanding. He contended that children would learn more effectively if education were conducted in a gentler manner. Comenius is well remembered for producing what we know as the first picture book for children: *Orbis Sensualium Pictus,* published in 1638.

> Noting the contrasting ages at which beasts of burden and persons mature, Comenius deduced that God must have given the years of youth to humans for the purpose of education. Thus Comenius encouraged the establishment of common schools. Although he acknowledged the importance of the home in a child's education, he argued that most parents had neither the leisure nor the ability to teach their children properly in the strictest sense. Children of both sexes should be given a universal education that would include the arts and sciences as well as languages, morals, and theology.[33]

Some have said that Reformation Europe was the context in which parental authority and the art of parenting were most highly respected. It is true that there were expectations of responsibility of both the mother and the father in the rearing of a child. While the child was young, the mother-child bond remained primary. However, when the child reached the age of six or seven and was capable of responding to regular discipline, the father stepped in to fulfill the primary role of disciplinarian.[34] As in previous eras, overindulgence was believed to spoil children and lead them to a life of crime and laziness. The remedy was understood to be a stern upbringing, without coddling, allowing the challenges of life to nurture character.[35]

During the Enlightenment period — the time between 1648 and 1789 — Western culture underwent a transition from respect for religion to skepticism. Enlightenment thinkers preferred the world of facts to reli-

33. Reed and Prevost, *History of Christian Education,* p. 232.
34. Ozment, *When Fathers Ruled,* p. 132.
35. Ozment, *When Fathers Ruled,* p. 133.

gious enthusiasm. There was an emphasis on reason, science, scientific inquiry, progress, and a new openness to free thinking.[36]

Various philosophers offered serious challenges to the theologians and Christian educators of the day. One of these was John Locke (1632-1704), an English philosopher who rejected the theological idea of the innate depravity or innate goodness of the person. He proposed that a child is born as a *tabula rasa* or blank slate on which the experiences of life, school, home, church, community, and nature will write the life story. Locke considered that thought comes from reflecting on the sensations arising from interaction with the world.[37]

The Early Modern Period (1700-1900)

During the two centuries called "early modern," there were further shifts in thinking about the education of children. Jean-Jacques Rousseau (1712-1778) was especially influential in reshaping views of the nature of childhood. His writing on the innate goodness of children was in stark contrast to both the theological concept that children are "born in sin" and the "blank slate" perspective of John Locke. Rousseau proposed that human beings are not born in a state of depravity but are contaminated as a result of living in a morally corrupt society. His compelling 1762 novel *Émile* captured the attention of philosophers and educators. The story chronicles the life of a boy who grows up in a natural environment, free from the damaging influences of society. The book presents an elevated view of children and suggests a way of parenting and educating that moves away from stern discipline to leaving children free to learn what matters when they are ready. The book begins with a statement that succinctly states Rousseau's view of the child: "Everything is good as it leave the hands of the Author of Things; everything degenerates in the hands of man."[38]

Rousseau's ideas fed into a society open to a Romantic view of children and the family. An abundance of writings on childcare, medicine, and morals, which upheld Rousseau's view of children, followed.[39] His

36. Anthony and Benson, *Exploring the History and Philosophy,* p. 231.
37. Anthony and Benson, *Exploring the History and Philosophy,* p. 238.
38. Quoted in Anthony and Benson, *Exploring the History and Philosophy,* p. 242.
39. Dixon, "Who Nurtured the Child?" p. 9.

ideas sparked a radical reordering of educational practice. Several educational experiments flowed from the influence of Rousseau's writing, including schools founded by Johann Heinrich Pestalozzi and by Friedrich Froebel, who is known as the father of the kindergarten.

Also during this period, Christian leaders began to pay new attention to the plight of disadvantaged children — the poor, the illiterate, the orphan. The Industrial Revolution moved many families from small communities to crowded cities. Parents were now working away from home, and many children were also in the workforce. As a result, new problems related to the needs of children emerged. No longer was the extended family or village there to respond to the orphaned or sick child or the family in crisis. During the mid-1800s, it was estimated that in London alone there were thirty thousand children who lacked a proper home and adequate care.[40] Schools were not generally provided for these children, partly for economic reasons and partly because the upper class feared that educating the poor might encourage them to step out as entrepreneurs or scholars and thus disrupt the hierarchy of the social class system.

However, schools for street children, called Ragged Schools, now began to turn up in major cities around Europe. These schools generally depended on the support of kindly philanthropists.

The Sunday school too arose in response to the plight of working poor children. Robert Raikes, a newspaper publisher from Gloucester, England, is known as the father of the Sunday school. Raikes had spent the better part of his early adulthood working with adult prisoners and street people. Frustrated at their lack of progress toward a better life, Raikes determined to shift his focus.

In England at the close of the eighteenth century, poor children were expected to spend six days a week working in factories. On Sundays, when they were free from their responsibilities of work, lower-class children tended to roam the streets, causing trouble and disturbing local businesses. Raikes, a member of the Church of England, saw the situation as an opportunity. He focused blame for the behavior of the children on the ignorance of society towards their needs. "He began with the idea that vice is preventable."[41] Determined to take proactive measures, Raikes hired his

40. G. F. A. Best, *Shaftesbury* (New York: ARCO Publishing, 1959), p. 112.

41. Henry J. Harris, *Robert Raikes: The Man Who Founded Sunday School* (London: National Sunday School Union, 1959), p. 60.

first Sunday school teacher in 1780 or 1781. His intent was to train the factory children to read the Scriptures and, in doing so, to impress upon them values of morality and good behavior.

Initially there were difficulties, particularly as the boys who had been chosen were extremely unruly. It was said that some arrived with logs of wood or weights tied to their legs to prevent them from running away. Another story is told of a boy who sneaked a badger into class and set it loose at the appropriate moment to startle the teacher.[42] Nevertheless, it soon became apparent that the Sunday school experiment was a success. Being a newspaper man, Raikes had a natural venue for diffusing information; however, he was also a patient man, and he waited three full years before beginning to communicate the Sunday school concept and the results. "He was not a man in a hurry, and he was so astonished at the results that, it seems, he could hardly believe they were real."[43] Once the information had become public, Raikes received a steady stream of inquiries about his approach to Sunday school. Since it was costly to print the full Bible as his curriculum, Raikes printed a book, *Sunday School Scholar's Companion,* which included simple Bible lessons.[44]

Poor children in many English cities had the same struggles as those in Gloucester, and so Raikes's Sunday school idea spread quickly. A Baptist draper, William Fox, was particularly dismayed by the reality that there were so many children in England who were not learning to read. He saw in the Sunday school a way to further his dream that all poor "Englishmen" would be taught to read.[45] In 1785, along with several other influential men, Fox began what would popularly be called the Sunday School Society to promote the spread of Sunday schools. Its motto was "To prevent vice, to encourage industry, to diffuse the light of knowledge, to bring men cheerfully to submit to their stations."[46] (The class bias and condescension underlying this motto was consistent with the times.) The society instituted by Fox raised funds to pay the salaries of Sunday school teachers and to purchase supplies for the classes.

42. Harris, *Robert Raikes,* p. 71.

43. Harris, *Robert Raikes,* p. 75.

44. Illadel Sherwood, *200 Years of Sunday School in America* (Nashville: Dynamic Manuscripts, n.d.), p. 49.

45. Harold W. Burgess, *The Role of Teaching in Sustaining the Church* (Anderson, Ind.: Bristol House, 2004), p. 64.

46. Sherwood, *200 Years of Sunday School in America,* p. 26.

After a time the funds raised by Fox were depleted, however, and the society was quietly dissolved.[47] In its place, the London Sunday-School Union began. The aim of the union was "to promote the opening of new schools, and to furnish literature suited for Sunday-schools at a cheap rate."[48] In 1841 it began publishing a series of Sunday school lessons that were broadly used. By 1880, one hundred years after the first Sunday school began, the number of Sunday scholars in Great Britain was reported as 6,060,667.[49]

The support of John Wesley and the Methodist movement helped to give impetus to the establishment of the Sunday school. Wesley exhorted preachers to spend time with children and directed them to formalize a group if at least ten children were in regular attendance. It did not matter to Wesley whether a particular preacher had gifts and abilities suited to working with children. What mattered more was willingness to fulfill what he believed was a responsibility of ordained ministry.[50] Wesley was convinced that many children experienced genuine faith during their formative years.[51] This belief fueled his investment in the spiritual instruction and nurture of children. Ministry to children was an essential part of being a Methodist preacher.[52]

Wesley encouraged parents, both fathers and mothers, to take seriously the religious instruction of children. Wesley's mother, Susannah, had been a significant influence in the lives of her children. She placed a high value on the systematic teaching of her sons and daughters, spending personal time with each one every week. Susannah Wesley had organized classes in her home for her children and servants, and other members of the community were welcomed to these "kitchen meetings." John Wesley valued his mother's methods and sought her wisdom as he guided the education of children in the Methodist movement.[53]

47. Burgess, *The Role of Teaching,* p. 65.

48. Burgess, *The Role of Teaching,* p. 65.

49. Burgess, *The Role of Teaching,* p. 66.

50. Richard Heitzenrater, "John Wesley and Children," in *The Child in Christian Thought,* ed. Marcia Bunge, p. 298.

51. Susan Etheridge Willhauck, "John Wesley's View of Children: Foundations for Contemporary Christian Education," Ph.D. diss., Catholic University of America, 1992, p. 231.

52. John Wesley, *The Works of John Wesley: Complete and Unabridged,* 3rd ed., vol. 8 (Peabody, Mass.: Hendrickson, 1984), p. 316.

53. Catherine Stonehouse, "Children in Wesleyan Thought," in *Children's Spiritual-*

By 1790, Sunday schools had begun to take firm root in America. As in England, the Sunday schools were initially not controlled by any religious affiliation. However, the Sunday schools in America quickly grew and became recognized by the churches as a primary tool for the instruction of children.

At first, Sunday schools in America followed the English pattern of charity for the poor; they were established to serve children and adults, including African Americans, who were denied education elsewhere. Scripture continued to be the central text, and memorization was emphasized.[54] However, largely due to the influence of Presbyterian minister Lyman Beecher, who encouraged the rich to send their children to Sunday school, the Sunday school began to be seen no longer as a charity but for everyone.

In many communities as America expanded westward, the Sunday school was the "first organized expression of the church."[55] Many of them became incorporated into the local churches that followed.

By the 1830s, enrollment in public schools had grown to the point that Sunday schools no longer held primary responsibility for the education of children. Thus the Sunday schools now refocused on evangelical training and functioned as the religious complement to the public schools.[56]

Differences in doctrinal emphases regarding children coming to faith had been present since Reformation days. But the polarization of the conversion/nurture issue surfaced with a vengeance during the mid-nineteenth century's Second Great Awakening. Powerful preachers such as Charles G. Finney (1792-1875) conducted revivals and camp meetings across America, calling for repentance and encouraging a public declaration of faith.[57] The expectation of a radical conversion was often accompanied by "hellfire" appeals. The evangelists' zealous attitude and commitment to personal repentance and assurance of acceptance by God through Christ left a lasting mark on the evangelical church's ministry to children.

The revivalists rejected infant baptism as a way for children to come to

---

ity: Christian Perspectives, Research, and Applications, ed. Donald Ratcliff (Eugene, Ore.: Cascade Books, 2004), p. 134.

54. Maris A. Vinovskis, "Schooling and Poor Children in 19th-Century America," *American Behavioral Scientist* 35, no. 3 (1992): 313-31.

55. Burgess, *The Role of Teaching,* p. 8.

56. Vinovskis, "Schooling and Poor Children," p. 320.

57. Reed and Prevost, *History of Christian Education,* p. 304.

faith. Spiritually, children were considered to be no different from adults. To many conversionists, the conversion and subsequent nurture of children were more important than the conversion of adults. Conversionists viewed the child as having a whole life ahead to work for God, so a child who was converted would likely be less entrapped by sinful habits and would have more potential for godly flexibility.[58] Thus children were urged, just as adults were, to undergo an emotional repentance and a conversion experience.

Horace Bushnell (1802-1876), an American clergyman, reacted against revivalistic techniques for bringing children into a relationship with God.[59] His text *Christian Nurture,* published in 1847, challenged the notion that children exist outside of God's grace until their spiritual capacity has reached maturity. Bushnell suggested that a child could be raised in such a way as to "grow up a Christian, and never know himself as being otherwise."[60] His writing prompted consideration of new ways of thinking that would deeply affect the way adults went about instructing children in the faith.[61] Bushnell's ideas also served to challenge the commonly held notion that the church has the primary responsibility for teaching children of the faith. Bushnell said the family is the critical component in faith education and encouraged parents to take seriously this responsibility.[62]

Bushnell's position on passing faith to the next generation created considerable reaction. It was strongly opposed by the theologically conservative revivalists but was embraced by more liberal sectors of the church. In spite of conservative opposition, his views on the importance of nurture became foundational for much of modern Christian education.

Sunday school curriculum continued to be a concern of religious educators. By the middle of the nineteenth century, many denominational Sunday school unions and publishing houses were producing materials. In 1872 a committee was organized with the goal of establishing a curriculum

58. E. P. Hammond, *Early conversion: Showing how children and young people can be led to Jesus and prepared for church membership — with many practical illustrations and stories which others can use, with the help of God's Spirit, in securing these blessed results* (London: Passmore and Alabaster, 1900).

59. Burgess, *Models of Religious Education,* p. 82.

60. Horace Bushnell, *Christian Nurture* (reprint; New Haven, Conn.: Yale University Press, 1967), p. 4.

61. Dixon, "Who Nurtured the Child?" p. 17.

62. Marcia Bunge, ed., *The Child in Christian Thought,* p. 22.

plan that would bring some continuity to biblical study and would be accepted by many denominations, unions, and local Sunday schools. In January 1873 the first series of "Uniform Lessons" was inaugurated. The curriculum ran on a seven-year cycle, rotating through important scriptural texts. Methodists, Baptists, Presbyterians, and other Christians in the English-speaking world would read and study the same lesson on a given Sunday. Although adults studied the uniform lessons, the lessons were especially important for children. Independent publishers were not supportive of this perceived monopoly, but many church leaders decided that a uniform curriculum was the most promising curriculum-organizing structure.[63]

The Modern Period (1900-Present)

Maria Montessori (1870-1952) was an Italian physician and a devout Catholic whose life and work bridged the nineteenth and twentieth centuries. While working with mentally challenged children in Rome, she developed a distinctive educational approach that placed the child at the center. "Montessori believed that children had a natural inclination toward learning because of their inquisitive nature and creative spirit."[64] Out of this belief, she sought ways to create a learning environment where children could explore and learn under the guidance of teachers who would facilitate the child's self-discovery. The environment was to be carefully prepared with specially designed learning materials accessible to the children. Child-size furnishings and thoughtfully arranged learning centers would help children learn within a "climate of social interaction with others."[65] Montessori's work is directly reflected in some contemporary Christian education approaches such as Catechesis of the Good Shepherd, developed by Sofia Cavaletti, and Young Children and Worship (1989) by Sonja Stewart and Jerome Berryman. In addition, Montessori's emphasis on the prepared environment and her appeal for teachers to be attentive to children's readiness to learn has had a broad influence in Christian education.

63. Robert W. Lynn and Elliott Wright, *The Big Little School* (Nashville: Religious Education, 1980), pp. 100-103.

64. Anthony and Benson, *Exploring the History and Philosophy,* p. 351.

65. Anthony and Benson, *Exploring the History and Philosophy,* p. 351.

Some have called the twentieth century the century of the child. During this time, there developed a new recognition that childhood (and adolescence) is a special time of life that should be valued for its own sake and not just as a preparation for adulthood. Especially in the Western world, there was an explosion of toys, games, clothes, books, programs, sports, and media produced especially for children. Church and parachurch groups instituted a number of club programs for children: Girl Guides, Boy Scouts, Child Evangelism Fellowship, Awana, and Pioneer Girls (which became Pioneer Clubs), to name a few. Vacation Bible schools, summer day camps, programs for children in crisis, after-school programs, and many more responses to the needs of children were established. Many schools with a clear Christian focus were started to serve families from both Protestant and Catholic traditions.

The twentieth century was also marked by the influence of the physical and social sciences in all fields of study. For the first time, psychological analyses were done on a large scale, examining countless variables of human existence and making claims of authority based on scientific evidence. In the early part of the century, childrearing manuals emphasized control and routine. Infants' and children's feeding and bowel schedules were to be managed. This mode of thinking was strongly supported by behavioral psychologist John Watson (1878-1958). Watson was convinced that the infant and child were malleable, and with proper control and direction, the child's nature could be re-formed. His famous quotation gives the flavor of his position on the nature/nurture debate.

> Give me a dozen healthy infants, well-formed, and my own specified world to bring them up and I'll guarantee to take any one at random and train him to become any type of specialist I might select — doctor, lawyer, merchant-chief, and yes, even beggarman and thief, regardless of his talents, penchants, tendencies, abilities, vocations, and race of his ancestors. (1930)

In his 1928 text on infant and child care, he explained that the ideal child is one who is trained to be totally compliant. Watson went so far as to suggest that there might be better and more scientific means of raising children than by keeping them at home with their parents. Watson suggested treating children as if they were small adults, giving firm and objective directions. Children ought not be hugged or kissed, and they ought not be held on one's lap. Parents may shake hands with their children each day, and when they have done something quite admirable, parents might additionally pat their child on the head. Watson condemned the sentimentality with which many parents approached childrearing and suggested that those who utilized his methods, even for a short time, would be exceedingly pleased with the results.[66]

Then Dr. Benjamin Spock's *The Common Sense Book of Baby and Child Care,* published in 1946, turned the prevailing wisdom of parenting upside down.

> In post-war America, parents were in awe of doctors and other childcare professionals: Spock assured them that parents were the true experts on their own children. They had been told that picking up infants when they cried would only spoil them; Spock countered that cuddling babies and bestowing affection on children would only make them happier and more secure. Instead of adhering to strict, one-size-fits-all dictates on everything from discipline to toilet training, Spock urged parents to be flexible and see their children as individuals.[67]

Spock's book was translated into thirty-nine languages and was the standard parenting manual for decades. Although books on parenting are not directed toward programs that minister to children, parenting expectations in the society at large spilled over into the way Christian education was conducted.

Another development in the modern era was the establishment of publishing companies whose sole focus was responding to the need for quality Christian education materials. A number of companies began to produce materials that were marketed across denominational lines.

Each company had its own story. David C. Cook, for example, was a Chicago businessman who reached out to those in need after the Great Chicago Fire in 1871. After establishing a number of mission projects, he realized that there was a need for Christian education materials. So he began printing "Our Sunday School Quarterly," which included Bible lessons and hymns. From this beginning, the David C. Cook Publishing Com-

66. Dixon, "Who Nurtured the Child?" pp. 17-18.

67. "Dr. Benjamin Spock, 1903-1998," accessed December 2004 at http://www.drspock.com/about/drbenjaminspock/0,1781,00.html.

pany was formed. In 1933, Mr. and Mrs. Victor Cory worked together with Clarence Benson of Moody Bible Institute and his Christian education class to begin printing a series called the All-Bible Graded Sunday School Lessons. "All-Bible" was in response to the concern that science was replacing the Bible as central to Christian education. The goal of the Corys' material was to apply biblical truths to the daily lives of children and adults, under the motto "The Whole Word for the Whole Life." Thus Scripture Press Publications was born.

Meanwhile, across the country at First Presbyterian Church of Hollywood, California, Henrietta Mears was newly appointed as director of Christian education. Because she was unable to find suitable Sunday school materials that were biblically based, age appropriate, and attractive, she and her associates began to write and mimeograph their own curriculum materials. Other churches heard about what she was doing. By August of 1933, the demand was so great that the decision was made to reproduce the curriculum materials using a printing press. Thus Gospel Light Publications was formed under the motto "Planned, Christ-centered, and graded to meet the needs of each age."[68] Other curriculum publishers have followed these pioneers, so that now the choice of curriculum materials is extensive.

Today it is estimated that at least 32 million Americans regularly participate in a Sunday school program. One would be hard pressed to find a church that does not offer some kind of Sunday school program, although the curriculum and space and time organization may look quite different from place to place. Marlene Lefever, curriculum specialist, contends that the Sunday school is the largest volunteer organization in the world, with untold numbers of adults teaching children Sunday after Sunday, year after year.[69]

Conclusion

How we teach children about the things of God is bound up with how we understand education in general. Education is dramatically different today from the way it was in the first century. One critical difference is that

68. Sherwood, *200 Years of Sunday School in America*, pp. 51-67.

69. Marlene LeFever, address at the National Sunday School Convention, Dallas, Tex., May 2002.

we have moved from education for the privileged in society to education for all children. Christian leaders have been influential in this movement toward universal education. There are now opportunities for both boys and girls, rich and poor, to participate in studying the Scriptures. One implication of universal education is that we expect all children to be able to read and write by about eight years of age. In contrast to the recitation and oral approach to learning of earlier centuries, children's ministry is now visual and print oriented.

Over the centuries, philosophical views of learning and parenting have ranged from the assumption that children are blank slates needing to be taught to be productive members of society to the idea that children have the seeds of greatness and should be nurtured without any imposition of adult expectations. Particular cultures and periods have sometimes emphasized strict, harsh, punitive approaches to teaching children, while at other times and in other places the approach has been gentler — more creative and understanding. The balance between the role of the church and the family in the Christian teaching and nurture of children has been understood in various ways as well.

In earlier eras, children were often viewed as miniature but immature adults. In contrast, in the modern period, social science and educational research concluded that childhood was a distinctive period and that developmental concerns influenced all aspects of children's lives, including their faith formation. The methods employed in Christian education have almost always reflected the communication approaches and technology of the day.

The church today continues to be concerned about the next generation of followers of Jesus. Reflecting on how Christians across the centuries have carried out the task of passing the gospel from generation to generation is instructive to us. We see that the approaches have changed but the intention that children be carriers of the faith has not. We see that the church has found distinctive ways to respond to the concerns of its time. At many points in history, new perspectives on educational theory and practice began with Christian educators and then influenced the wider society. Christian leaders in society and the church have led the way in responding to the physical and social and spiritual needs of children — not always perfectly or with completely pure motives, but nonetheless they have made a difference in the lives of many children.

Children's ministry is solidly grounded in our theological understanding of the gospel of Christ and the place of children in the community of faith. The challenge is to keep central our commitment to the God of the Scriptures while connecting to the real lives of children in ways that are meaningful for them — to determine what God expects of us in and for our time.

PART II

CONTEXT AND CONTENT MATTER

Chapter 6

CHILDREN IN CONTEXT

A mission church in Sri Lanka has been formed with a number of new Christian families, most of whom have come out of the Sinhalese Buddhist religious tradition. This beautiful country surrounded by the sea has been wracked by civil war for more than a decade. (At the time of this writing, a peace agreement has been reached between the warring groups.) The minister's wife is especially concerned about nurturing the faith of the twenty-five or so children in the church.

A large church in New York City has a long-established ministry. Some families in the church lost someone dear to them in the World Trade Center disaster of September 11, 2001. Some of the parents were involved in the rescue operations. The children's pastor must find a way to nourish the faith of the children amid their sorrow and fear for the future.

A church in a town in Ontario, Canada, is shocked to learn that one of its leaders is being accused of negligence in his responsibilities as director of the town's water filtration system. Thousands have become ill with the *E. coli* virus, and seven people have died. Schools and community programs are closed for the rest of the school term as the town grapples with the water crisis. The church's children are confused to learn that a prominent member of their church community is facing court action.

Every church has its story. A story happens at a particular time and place and with a distinct cast of characters. Just as each person is unique, each church and community is distinct. How is ministry to children affected by their context? How do the circumstances surrounding children in their families, their church, their community, and their country influence the way we carry out ministry? This chapter offers ways to help us better understand the context where God has called us to minister.

Theologian Millard Erickson reminds us that the differences found among church communities are not just a phenomenon of the twenty-first century; the early church was also highly diverse: "We sometimes forget that the biblical period did not consist of a uniform set of situations. The temporal, geographical, linguistic, and cultural settings found within the canonical Scriptures vary widely."[1] Yet the gospel of Christ is for all time and for all people. The Christian communion includes people of every socioeconomic status, culture, nationality, ability, gender, and age.

Our task is to translate and demonstrate messages of faith to children for their particular time and place. The tension is to respect the truth and timelessness of the scriptural message while at the same time being sensitive to the diversity of children's circumstances.

A Model of Contextual Sensitivity

How then do we come to understand a child's context and then consider this reality in our ministry decisions? As Uri Bronfenbrenner notes, there are different layers of contextual influence.[2] Like a set of Russian nesting dolls or layers of an onion, various environmental systems enfold us. To understand their impact, we must expose each one.

Family provides a child's immediate environment. The child's family may consist of mother and father, several or no siblings, cousins, aunts and uncles, grandparents. Stepparents and half-sisters and -brothers may be grafted into the family. Or the child may live alone with his or her mother. Resources may be plentiful or meager. Faith may have a pivotal place in the life of the family — or not. Many parents are separated from their children for long hours or even days because of the demands of their work. On the other hand, some parents work from home. Families develop their own ways of celebrating important occasions. The family shapes children's lives, but each child also helps to shape the family. When a new baby comes into a family, it is never the same again.

1. Millard J. Erickson, *Christian Theology* (Grand Rapids: Baker, 1985), p. 121.

2. Uri Bronfenbrenner, *The Ecology of Human Development* (Cambridge, Mass.: Harvard University Press, 1979).

The cultural heritage of the family is passed on to children. Sometimes this includes a home language different from the majority language. Values of the cultural heritage shape the ethics and values of the family. Sometimes a family is isolated in an unfamiliar cultural landscape. Other times families from a particular heritage congregate in communities and churches.

Besides the family, other highly influential *primary environments* for a child may be the school, the church, and the daycare center. With few exceptions, every child in North America attends school, yet the forms of the schools vary. Some children are in public school, others attend private school, others are home-schooled. School is the social space that brings together the greatest numbers of people engaged in a similar purpose — at least minimally — to learn to read, write, and understand mathematics.

An important social context for many children is the church their family attends. Churches also come in many varieties. Besides having distinctive theological perspectives, they may be urban or rural, large or small, denominational or independent, new or old. Services may be in English or Estonian or Mandarin or Urdu or German or Spanish or Swahili or another language. The congregation may enfold children into the whole life of the church or provide separate programs for children or aim to do both.

Not only do the family, the church, the school, and other primary environments influence the child, but the relationships between them matter. For example, a family's commitment to church determines whether or not the child will go to church. Being part of a church sometimes poses economic challenges. For instance, children from a family with limited income may feel that they don't fit at a more affluent church because of their clothes or their family circumstances. Other children's teasing too often reinforces their feeling of not belonging. Parents may be pressured to come up with fees for special programs or particular kinds of clothes for church activities. Church programs for children also make demands on a family's schedule. Further, parents who are significantly involved in church activities may be in meetings several evenings each week and therefore unavailable to read bedtime stories, pray with their children, and tuck them into bed.

If a family is enthusiastic about its church involvement, its children are more likely to enjoy being part of the church. Also, churches that recognize the challenges of parenting and provide support for parents will be inviting places for families. Parents often choose a church with their children in mind. They look for a congregation where children are ministered to effectively and where their children will find a place to belong.

Beyond a child's primary environments and the interplay between them, there is another layer of context. This *secondary level* of environment includes settings and organizations that lie beyond the child's immediate experience yet still make a difference in the child's life. For example, the child may never visit a parent's workplace, but the hours the parent works and the time it takes to get to work affect the time the family has together. The children may never meet relatives who live far away, but the parents' experiences growing up with these people influence how they parent their own children. If the parents have good childhood memories of church, they are likely to want their children to be part of a church community.

In our culture, the media have a powerful influence on the life of the child. Even though some parents are diligent in controlling the on/off button of the television, exposure to television is almost universal in Western societies. Research by G. A. Comstock has found that the average American schoolchild watches twenty-eight hours of television per week.[3] Increasingly the computer, serving as teacher, entertainer, communication vehicle, and information source, is shaping children's view of the world. Besides cyberspace, children continue to expand their knowledge and understanding through books, music, and videos. Children coming to church bring with them a plethora of impressions and information from the media. Some of it is wholesome and beautiful and true. Some is not.

We tend to be very aware of the impact of family and the media on our children. What we don't notice so often is how the *macrosocietal system* also affects a child. For example, we recognize the disruptive power of family divorce for children — not only in their own family but also in their friends' families — but may not be aware of the paralyzing fear that trickles down to a child when the larger society is preparing for or engaged in war. We are horrified by parents who neglect their children but not so concerned when government policies require families in developing

3. G. A. Comstock. "The Medium and Society: The Role of Television in American Life," in *Children and Television*, ed. G. L. Berry and J. K. Asamen (Newbury Park, Calif.: Sage, 1993), pp. 117-31.

countries to pay school fees and buy books and uniforms for their children. In this case, families with meager resources face the dilemma of deciding which of their children will go to school. The result is that masses of bright children from very poor families are not being given even a primary education. Government actions may appear to be adult affairs, but their impact on children can be powerful.

The influence of the larger society's laws, values, history, and economic circumstances and policies cannot be understated. Children might seem to be sheltered by their family from the impact of the macrosystem. And in some ways they may be — at least for a while. But the macrosystem reaches into every person's life, even into the experience of faith. Clearly, the place of faith within a society, along with the presence or absence of freedom of worship, has a powerful impact on children's religious experience.

From the Ministry Leaders' Perspective

To be effective as children's ministry leaders, we must pay attention to children's primary, secondary, and macrosocietal environments. If we listen to people in the church and the broader community and learn to value the traditions that are markers of our unique place, we will be in a position to build on what God has done there. But if we bound ahead with little knowledge and respect for what has gone before, disruption and confusion may limit meaningful ministry.

A place to start in understanding our context is to get to know *who is here*. Who are the children and families? Who are the leaders? Whom has God brought to this church community? Paying attention to the particular needs, experiences, and gifts of the people who are here gives perspective to our decisions about how we minister.

- Leaders of a Korean Canadian church realized that many new immigrants were moving into the church's neighborhood. It happened that the pastor of children's and youth ministry was a qualified teacher of English as a second language. He began a Saturday English conversation class that attracted many adult learners. At the same time, he organized a tutoring program in which church young people worked one-on-one with children of the ESL students on their schoolwork.

As a result, friendships formed between the children and their tutors, families became comfortable in the church building, and some began attending worship services.[4]

- A large church with 750 children in Sunday school identified about twenty children who had special needs that made it difficult for them to participate fully in the regular programs. These children were disrupting the learning of other children. The Sunday school leaders decided to find an adult partner for each of the children with special needs. The partners would welcome the children and participate with them in all parts of the program. With this system, the children were comfortably integrated during the singing and worship times, but when the teaching and learning times began they became restless and disruptive. Too often the partners had to take them out into the hallway and wait there for the Sunday school time to be over. Although parents wanted their children to be fully integrated in the program, the leaders decided to organize a separate learning time for these children filled with music and drama.
- In a church in an affluent area, the children were pressured by school expectations and extracurricular activities. Parents were very busy in their demanding workplaces. Families enjoyed being together at church because during the rest of the week they were separated so much. However, the church's structure required families to part: the children would go to Sunday school and the adults to the worship service. At the end of the service they would meet to go home again. It seemed that the church was dividing the family rather than bringing it together. The answer for this church was to begin an intergenerational worship service once a month. Further, the children's ministry director began to seek occasions to create celebrations for children and adults together.

Besides asking who is here, we might ask who is *not* here.

- Towering over a lively suburban church was a large public housing complex. Hundreds of children called these apartments home, but not more than one or two attended the church a few steps away. A

4. Personal conversation with Peter Kim, January 2003, about Toronto Korean Somang (Hope) Presbyterian Church.

> new pastor for ministry with children and youth inspired young adults in the congregation to develop a program for children, Kids Company. One night a week, children from the community and some church children met to play games in the gym, work on a musical play, learn Bible stories, eat, and have fun. Gradually a number of the neighborhood children were drawn into the life of the church.

Another question to ask is, What is the story of the ministry to children in this place? Who knows it? Who carries the memory of the community in their mind and heart? What do the children say about what they appreciate in the church and what they hope for in ministry?

Of course, each person has his or her own chapter to recount. Engaging a broad cross-section of a congregation in telling stories can help us learn the complete story of the church and its children. The point is to discover what the community believes about children's ministry and how that has been expressed over the years.

As we come to understand a particular place of ministry, it is helpful to know how the church is positioned in the community at large. The way the apostle Paul spent his initial time in Athens as recorded in Acts 17 is instructive. He models the value of getting to know the broader community as a precursor to context-sensitive ministry.

> Those who conducted Paul brought him as far as Athens; and after receiving instructions to have Silas and Timothy join him as soon as possible, they left him.
>
> While Paul was waiting for them in Athens, he was deeply distressed to see that the city was full of idols. So he argued in the synagogue with the Jews and the devout persons, and also in the marketplace every day with those who happened to be there. . . . So they took him and brought him to the Areopagus and asked him, "May we know what this new teaching is that you are presenting?" . . .
>
> Then Paul stood in front of the Areopagus and said, "Athenians, I see how extremely religious you are in every way. For as I went through the city and looked carefully at the objects of your worship, I found among them an altar with the inscription, 'To an unknown god.' What therefore you worship as unknown, this I proclaim to you. . . . For 'In him we live and move and have our being'; as even some of your own poets have said." (Acts 17:15-28)

As Paul waited for his partners in ministry, he walked around Athens, talked to people, engaged in discussion. He intrigued people enough to be invited to speak to a leading group of thinkers and debaters. When he spoke he was able to refer to what he had seen (an altar to an unknown god) and what he had read ("as even some of your own poets have said"). He began with what they knew of God and then went on to speak about what they did not yet know. He respected their experience and understanding as he spoke further about God, the Creator and Redeemer of the world.

What can we learn from this about getting to know a new community? The temptation is to become so engrossed in running programs that we don't pay attention to the broader context. Following Paul's example, we might go to the local library, the mayor's office, the nearest coffee shop, the dry cleaner's, the bank, the daycare, and the school. We might attend Little League games and check newspapers and flyers to find out what community programs are offered for children, especially during a holiday break. We might ask a resident to accompany us on a walk through the neighborhood. As we come to know our community better, we will discover distinct opportunities and challenges that give us an enlarged vision of ministry.

A further way to tune in to the children's world is to explore their media experience. One children's pastor rather sheepishly confessed that she watches kids' TV shows.

> Not necessarily with any great purpose of applying it to children's ministry. I just enjoy them. They somehow make me catch the children's culture. I watch them like the kids do — boys and girls. And I watch programs that are about school, like *Arthur.* This is something that I really find helps me to understand children's experience in school. The shows highlight the pressures that children have around school and friendship and family and increase my awareness and sensitivity to children.[5]

To refresh yourself on children's culture, watch children's TV programs for fun and to discover what connects with children. When watching pro-

5. Shirley Yung of Scarborough, Ontario, Chinese Baptist Church, personal conversation, April 2, 2002.

grams with children, notice what captures their attention and what does not. Note the kinds of programs that appeal to children of a particular age. Are there differences between boys and girls? What is being communicated, and how is it being communicated? Attend to subtle negative messages such as the use of violent means to solve problems or villains represented as handicapped persons or foreigners.

Beyond media messages, what is happening in the society at large also affects children. As one example, we will consider here the effects of pluralism — people of different cultures living in close proximity.

Increasingly the United States and Canada are nations where people from many cultural heritages live and work and worship together. Worshiping together might at least be expected among Christians who take seriously Jesus' prayer for unity in the church (John 17:20-23). However, in many cases followers of Jesus form churches that are monocultural, where people who are not of that culture do not feel welcome. On the other hand, some churches have been intentional about bringing together people from different backgrounds to form an inclusive faith community.

Churches that to the outsider seem monocultural are sometimes a complex collection of cultures. For example, a church in Toronto includes Chinese from Hong Kong who value traditional Chinese culture mixed with some British influence; Chinese from Taiwan who keep more or less to Chinese traditions; Chinese from mainland China who have been influenced by Marxism, Taoism, and other religions and have had little exposure to Christianity; and others who have lived in Canada all their lives. Services are held in Mandarin, Cantonese, and English. Programs for children are usually in English, with translation given for children who do not yet understand English. Children's ministry leaders must be able to communicate with parents who speak either Cantonese or Mandarin.[6]

Children who attend churches like this one are often caught between two cultures. Sometimes the values of one culture complement the values of another, but sometimes they conflict. The expectations of the children's parents may differ from what they encounter at school or in the church from North American–trained teachers and ministry leaders. These children often face a crisis of identity. Parents may be confused by the ideas and behaviors that their children encounter in the society. The

6. Irene Cheung, "Church with Three Languages," paper for Children's Ministry course, Tyndale University College and Seminary, Toronto, March 2003.

church should seek to be a safe place for parents and children to discuss their concerns.

Although it is not easy to sort out who we are and where we belong when we have one foot in one culture and one in another, knowing more than one language and understanding more than one culture is a great gift. Moses was a bicultural child whose language and cultural experiences were profoundly helpful to him as an adult. Without his childhood training in the Egyptian court along with his mother's Hebrew instruction, he would have been less prepared to follow God's call to lead the children of Israel out of slavery (see especially chapters 2–13 of Exodus).

The church can play an important part as a place of welcome and a place to belong for multicultural children. In the church we find our primary identity as followers of Jesus, whatever our language or culture. From that common place, we can learn from each other what it means to live a life of faith in circumstances that are different from our own. Many of us would do well to follow the lead of the children's pastor of a Chinese church in Toronto. To expand her understanding of cultures different from her own, she has intentionally built a friendship with a person from a very different cultural background. Her life has been enriched and her eyes opened as they listen to each other's perspectives on life and faith.

Whatever the community we serve, we should pay close attention to the visual symbols that are used in curriculum and in the church building, to see how well they represent the whole Christian family. In particular, is the diversity of the people we intend to serve represented and honored in the stories we tell and the pictures we show? The visual images we use may have quite a different effect from what was intended.

After viewing a film about the life of Jesus, an African Canadian young person said, "There wasn't even a black dog in the film!" Every actor was white, sending him the message that there is no place for a person like him in the family of God. Rather than being drawn to follow Jesus, he felt excluded. Giving children and adults from a range of cultural backgrounds a voice in decision-making will help to keep us from making such ineffectual presentations of the gospel.

Children's lives are embedded in primary, secondary, and macrosocietal environments. The more in tune we are with the world around us, the more able we will be to minister meaningfully to children and their families. Of course, cultures and communities are not static. Neighborhoods change over time. Staying relevant requires vigilance. But effective children's ministry requires cultural literacy. Even in places where there are few other cultures represented, children benefit from learning about children who live in different circumstances from their own. The more we understand and appreciate the people and place where God has placed us, the more able we will be to carry out God's call to minister to the children of that place.

Chapter 7

CHILDREN IN THE FAITH COMMUNITY

Once upon a time there was a small, struggling southern California church without a pastor. In an attempt to revive the church, the elders called a new leader who had been in youth ministry for over twenty years. Upon arriving, Pastor Josh began doing ministry the way he had always done it, developing a relationship with every person in the congregation, and encouraging every generation to relate to each other on many levels. Because of the atmosphere created by the new leader, the church became increasingly diverse, generationally, ethnically, and economically.

Scottie's daughter and her family began attending this church shortly after Pastor Josh arrived there. During occasional visits, Scottie was able to experience the unique way that he served the church. One Sunday morning she saw Pastor Josh, in crisp khakis and starched white casual shirt, "shooting hoops" with some school-aged boys. Having taken care not to work up a sweat, he then took a few minutes to quiet himself before starting the worship service. Pastor Josh knew the names of the boys with whom he was playing. Because of this relationship, he was able to nurture them in significant ways as he led worship and delivered his sermon. Scottie's grandchildren looked forward to being at church, even simply accompanying their parents to a committee meeting. Their names were known and they were nurtured by the members of the congregation.

A fifty-something man in the congregation had a passion for gardening. He proposed that the church create a garden on its property. The idea caught on, and the people — families, singles, and older folk — began gathering on Saturdays to clear and till the land. The next Palm Sunday, the entire congregation processed from the sanctuary to the back garden, singing and carrying banners specially created for the celebration. The whole church family enjoyed a picnic dinner spread around the edges of the garden. Then came the planting time.

Everyone participated in planting their favorite vegetables, berry plants, and border flowers in the freshly tilled straight rows. During the long growing season, people of all ages came in the evenings and on Saturdays to hoe and weed the garden. When harvest time came, every household shared in the bounty, and the congregation gave the surplus to the homeless and others in the community.

One Christmas Eve, Grandpa Henry sat in a rocking chair on the sanctuary stage, reading a Christmas story to the many children surrounding him. It was hard to tell what was the greater attraction: the story or Grandpa Henry. After the service, Scottie's daughter told her his story. He had been part of the church for a long time. Because he loved children, he always kept a supply of wrapped candy in his pockets and generously gave it to all comers. But Grandpa Henry had a malignant brain tumor. As his medical bills escalated, the family came close to losing everything. The people of the church came together and decided to cover the family's mortgage for as long as necessary so they would not lose their home. This is just one of many ways the church family had rallied around Henry.

Eventually Grandpa Henry succumbed to his disease. The people of the congregation, under the leadership of Pastor Josh, turned Henry's memorial service into a celebration. The whole church was present, including the children who had sat around his rocker to listen to the Christmas story. Balloons instead of flowers surrounded the casket.

During the funeral, Pastor Josh prepared the congregation for an "open microphone" time. People of all ages lined up to tell what Grandpa Henry had meant to them. Children eagerly told stories and expressed gratitude to God for him. Some of them, including Scottie's granddaughter, were so young that they had to be lifted by a parent in order to be seen from the pews. The children got to take the balloons home to remember Grandpa Henry.

This church was a vital community nurturing the faith of children, teens, and adults. What made it so effective? Several factors seem to have been operative:

- All people were welcome and shown respect.
- The pastor loved and cared for the people, and they knew it; in turn, they loved and cared for each other.
- Church life was thought of and treated as family life.
- The emphasis was on people and their relationships with God and each other rather than on programs.
- The pastor empowered the people to create and own ways of relating to each other.
- Because children were present in every part of church life, they were formed by the faith of the members of the congregation.

Is your church like this one, or are you thinking, *Oh, if only I could find a church like that?* Few of us would not long for such a vital faith community in which to grow spiritually and serve Christ, in which to raise our children. Unfortunately, in our individualistic, age-segregated, busy society, where churches are sometimes run as large corporations, many of us have given up the vision of whole faith communities welcoming and nurturing the spiritual life of children. But participation in a vital faith community is essential to the Christian formation of the young. We must rekindle the vision and discover ways of bringing it to reality in our churches, whatever their size.

After a brief review of God's design for community, seen in Scripture, we will examine the characteristics of communities that nurture children and adults to become all God desires them to be. The chapter will also explore how to build and sustain communities that fully embrace children, celebrating the gifts they bring to and express through the faith community.

Created for Community

As we read Scripture, we do not search long before finding clues pointing to the importance of community. If we have eyes to see it, the evidence shows up in the creation story.

"Then God said, 'Let us make humankind in our image, according to our likeness'" (Gen. 1:26). Here we discover that God is an "us," a relational Being, in community. As we read on through the Scripture we come to know the triune God, Father, Son, and Holy Spirit, three in one, loving and working in perfect harmony for the redemption of all creation and the restoration of the kingdom of God. The Gospels reveal the beautiful relationship that exists between Jesus and his Father and God's plan for the Holy Spirit to continue the work of Jesus on earth.

Genesis 1:26 also tells us we are created in the image of God. To be in the image of God is to be created for community, with potential to be in relationship with God and with others. We need community for our wholeness, to become all we are created to be.

In the act of creation God established human community. The expanded creation story of Genesis 2 tells us that God said, "It is not good that the man should be alone; I will make him a helper as his partner" (2:18).[1] In Eve, God gave Adam one like himself, "bone of my bone and flesh of my flesh" (Gen. 2:23), to be in union with him, to be a strength and support to him, as he would be for her. God blessed this first couple and gave them the command to be fruitful and multiply (Gen. 1:28), to bring children into this community of man and woman.

God provided the community of family for the nurture of children, and God's intention is for that community to be stable and intimate. A man is to leave his father and mother and cling to his wife (Gen. 2:24). Here is long-term commitment to a relationship in which two become one, providing a unified, harmonious community for the nurture of their children. A community that is stable and loving, and supports its members across the years: this is God's creation design.

The Faith Community in the Old and New Testaments

As we move on through Scripture, however, we find that the nurturing community of the nuclear family is not sufficient in itself. We see God calling the people of Israel into relationship with Yahweh and working to form them as God's people. As the Israelites prepared to enter the Promised Land and become a nation of God's chosen people, Moses challenged them to live in obedience to God's laws for their good and for the sake of

1. It is important to realize that the word translated "helper" in Genesis 2:18 does not mean "subordinate assistant." The word used here is most frequently used in the Old Testament to refer to God as helper. In other uses it refers to a stronger army on which Israel calls for help.

their children (Deut. 6:1-25). God intended that the life of a God-honoring community and nation would nurture the faith of children.

God also instructed Moses and other leaders to gather the people regularly for learning and worship. They came together to hear the commandments of God for the first time (Exod. 34:32), and every year thereafter the people gathered in the place of worship for festivals to remember God's deliverance from slavery, to give thanks for God's bountiful goodness (Deut. 16:1-17), and to seek atonement for sins (Num. 29:7-11). Whole families participated in these gatherings. As we saw in chapter 2, Jewish children had the great privilege of learning the stories of God's goodness as they worshiped with the whole faith community. They knew who they were in that community through its stories and the reenactment of them. Throughout the Old Testament we see the crucial influence of the faith community in the spiritual nurture of children (for example, Josh. 8:30-35; 2 Chron. 20; Neh. 12:27-43).

As we move on into the New Testament, we discover that the gathered faith community was important to Jesus. In our only glimpse of Jesus' boyhood, he is in Jerusalem with family and friends for the feast of the Passover. He is there because faithfully every year Mary and Joseph took their family on the journey from Nazareth to Jerusalem to celebrate this feast with the whole community (Luke 2:41). But by the time he was twelve, for Jesus this trip to Jerusalem was much more than a family ritual. He identifies the temple as "my Father's house," and we see him, on his own initiative, turning to the religious leaders to test his developing understanding of God. He listens, he asks questions, and he amazes the leaders with his insights (Luke 2:46-49).

Mary and Joseph saw to it that Jesus was nurtured in and by the faith community, and we see him as an adult attending the synagogue and returning to Jerusalem every year for the feast of the Passover. As a child Jesus experienced the faith community, and as an adult he modeled participation in it.

After Pentecost the faith community took a new form for the people of God. Although believers in Jerusalem continued going to the temple and spent much time together there, they also met in homes for fellowship and prayer. They sold their possessions and shared with those in need (Acts 2:42-47). As Christians spread out from Jerusalem, they met regularly in homes. Whole households, including children, gathered as the church to learn, worship, and enjoy one another.

By God's design we are created for community, to learn and grow together. Nurture begins in the intimate community of the family, yet God does not intend for the family to nurture the faith of parents and children on its own. God draws us into a faith community where parents and children will be nurtured, instructed, and supported, a community that works together in service to God and the world God loves.

Faith-Nurturing Communities

Every community influences its children, for good or for ill. What elements come together to create a community that nurtures a vital, healthy, growing faith in children and adults? Both the character of the people who gather and the activities the group chooses determine whether or not it becomes a health-giving community.

The Character of the Community

At the heart of a healthy congregation lies love for God, and from that love flows obedience to God's commands, genuine worship, and love for one another. There is integrity between worship and life, words and deeds. Children who observe and are embraced in the love of such integrity discover what it truly means to be Christian. They see the meaning of the words they hear in church lived out before them through the week. They learn that love for and obedience to God touch every part of life, and they come to know a God who is present and active in all the challenges, joys, and sorrows they face.

Are churches today demonstrating this integrity of worship and life, word, and deed? After studying the North American church over more than two decades, George Barna expresses deep concern for the typical church.

> The stumbling block for the Church is not its theology but its failure to apply what it believes in compelling ways. The downfall of the Church has not been the content of its message but its failure to practice those truths. Christians have been their own worst enemies when it comes to showing the world what authentic, biblical Christianity looks like. . . .

> Those who have turned to Christianity seeking truth and meaning have left empty-handed, confused by the apparent inability of Christians themselves to implement the principles they profess.[2]

Not only seekers but also children need to see the principles of the Christian faith lived out. God desires to gather a diverse, multigenerational people who demonstrate the character God expects, a community of people who live in ways that accomplish God's purposes in the world. Such communities can nurture genuine faith.

Healthy congregations will have a clear sense of their identity as children of God, disciples and friends of Jesus, chosen to participate in God's work in the world. They will be loving communities, expressing love to children and adults in the church, to neighbors in the surrounding community, and to the world.[3]

As did the church described at the beginning of this chapter, nurturing congregations will experience disappointment, pain, and suffering. But together, by God's grace, they will find a way through. To provide our children, and ourselves, with a faith-giving community, we do not have to be perfect, to have arrived. God simply calls us to faithfully follow Jesus, growing as disciples. Wherever we are on the journey, God has a place of service for us.

The character, integrity, and spiritual vitality of the faith community will affect children profoundly. Those who care about the spiritual growth of children will care about the spiritual vitality of the whole congregation.

What Builds and Sustains Community

Persons created in the image of God long for genuine community, yet many in our individualistic, mobile society have never found it. People drift from group to group, church to church, because they quickly discover that simply putting people together in a room does not make them a community. Even fun activities shared in a group often leave us aware of our unmet hunger for community.

2. George Barna, *The Second Coming of the Church* (Nashville: Word, 1998), p. 5.

3. In Deuteronomy 6:5 and John 15:5, 8, 14, 16-17, notice that God's people, Jesus' disciples, are to have a sense of identity as God's children and friends of Jesus.

What kinds of groups bring about true community? What can our congregations do to build community for our children? What will real faith communities be like? Christian ethicist Christine Pohl has identified four elements she believes are essential for building and sustaining community: hospitality, gratitude, truth telling, and promise keeping.[4] Let's look at how each of these elements could affect children and set the stage for them to meet and know God in the faith community.

The word *hospitality* may bring to mind a delicious meal served on fine china; however, this is not how Christians across the centuries have understood hospitality. The Christian tradition of hospitality is the practice of welcoming strangers, particularly the vulnerable, the poor, and the needy, into a safe place as guests being served by welcoming hosts.

In *Making Room: Recovering Hospitality as a Christian Tradition,* Pohl defines "strangers" as "those who are disconnected from basic relationships that give persons a secure place in the world."[5] Although most children in our churches are not strangers who lack a "secure place in the world," within many churches children are invisible and not considered except in programs designated for them, and they may be disconnected from all but their peers and a few adults who work with them. In chapter 2 we noted that Jesus chose a child to represent the least, the most vulnerable and invisible, in society (Luke 9:46-48). And when Jesus speaks about children it is in terms of welcome: "Let the little children come to me. . . . Whoever welcomes this child in my name welcomes me" (Luke 18:16; 9:48). This is the language of hospitality. Children need welcome to grow in faith. Much that has been learned about welcoming strangers — the poor, the needy, the displaced — can help us see how to offer children hospitality in the congregation, how to make them truly welcome.

Hospitality is offered when we welcome another into a place that is important to us, a place that feels safe and comfortable and where the person experiences acceptance, friendship, and respect. To express welcome and respect we must notice others, giving them our full attention and being willing to listen to them. Hospitality requires time for sharing

4. Christine Pohl, faculty member at Asbury Theological Seminary, has been studying these elements — how they are lived out or violated in the faith community and the implications of those actions. Her insights will be published in an upcoming book to be released by Eerdmans.

5. Christine Pohl, *Making Room: Recovering Hospitality as a Christian Tradition* (Grand Rapids: Eerdmans, 1999), p. 13.

our lives and our stories, time for our lives to be visible to those being welcomed.[6] True respect is based on belief in the equal value and dignity of all persons. It recognizes that each person in a relationship has gifts to offer and that each needs the gifts of the other.[7] Across the centuries, hospitality has been a sacred practice among Christians. They look for Jesus in those they welcome, expecting God to teach and bless them through their guests.[8]

How would our churches change if the whole congregation, not just the children's Sunday school teachers, took seriously Jesus' admonition to welcome children — if as a congregation we truly offered hospitality to children? What places and activities of importance to adults need to be opened to children? Other than in children's programs, how often do we turn our full attention to children? Who listens to them? Where are friendships built between children and adults? As a congregation, do we really see children as persons of value and dignity equal to teenagers and adults? Do we expect to receive gifts from them in the family of God, to see Jesus in them and hear his voice through them? The church will be a nurturing community for children when they experience it as a place of gracious hospitality.

How do we become a community of generous hospitality? It does not happen instantaneously but develops through small acts of welcome and respect, practiced faithfully over time. Giving attention to learning hospitality through these faithful practices with our children will equip us to broaden our hospitality to others. And as our children live within an environment of hospitality, they will become persons committed to making others welcome.[9]

I noted earlier that most children in our churches are not "strangers" in the full sense of the word. However, in the towns and cities around our churches there are many children who truly are strangers in need of our welcome. God calls us to extend hospitality to these children, and in doing so we will provide children of church families with opportunities to learn the ways of God's kingdom.

Health-giving hospitality grows out of *gratitude* for the loving wel-

6. Pohl, *Making Room*, p. 13.
7. Pohl, *Making Room*, pp. 6, 72.
8. Pohl, *Making Room*, p. 68.
9. Pohl, *Making Room*, pp. 175-76.

come we receive from God. When out of gratitude for God's love we love others, they are able to see God in us. What a marvelous gift we are privileged to offer! However, if gratitude is missing and we serve grudgingly, we will be exhausted and will often hurt those we try to serve.[10]

A grateful spirit focuses on gifts received from God and from others and keeps us aware of our own neediness. This awareness protects us from thinking more highly of ourselves than we ought and helps us remember the value and dignity of others (Rom. 12:3-5). Biblical writers refer to adults as "children" of God.[11] We have much to gain by seeing ourselves as standing with our children as grateful recipients of God's grace and care. The psalmist David celebrates the God who like a Father has compassion for "those who fear him," a God who understands the limitations and potential of his child (Ps. 103:13-14). True gratitude for God's patient understanding of us inspires and energizes us to express patient understanding to the children in our midst, giving them a comfortable place in the community.

Gratitude creates an atmosphere of joy and peace. Shared gratitude bonds us together in a joy-filled community.

The practice of *truth telling* also builds community. A real community does not have to keep secrets. We can tell others who we are and what is going on in our lives because the welcome of those around us will hold us safely. In Sunday school one morning, during a time of reflection on the "dark places of danger" in the Good Shepherd story, a little girl blurted out, "We're getting a divorce."[12] She could speak the painful truth and be enfolded in the teacher's love as well as in the love of the Good Shepherd.

Truth telling means we do not try to hide from children the hard stuff of life or the difficult mysteries of God. Wendy faced surgery for the removal of a brain tumor. The children's director at her church, wanting the children involved in expressions of concern and prayer, invited Wendy to come and talk with them. She readily agreed. Two children dragged a rocking chair into the center of the room for Wendy, and they all sat around her on the floor. She told them what was about to happen and

10. Pohl, *Making Room,* p. 172.

11. The term is used by Jesus (Matt. 5:9) and often by the apostle John (John 1:12; 11:52; 1 John 3:1, 10; 5:2) and the apostle Paul (Rom. 8:14, 16, 19, 21; 9:8).

12. "Celebrate Sunday School, 4 Million Teachers Strong" (Elgin Ill.: David C. Cook, 1988), Video.

why. Then she asked if they had any questions. The predictable question "Are you afraid?" was answered seriously and honestly.

A less predictable question from a nine-year-old boy: "Are you angry?" It caused Wendy to pause and think. "Yes," she said finally. "Sometimes I am angry that I have this terrible thing in my head that could take me away from my family and all that I love. I get angry when I ask God to take it away and nothing happens." As she talked about her fears, the children ministered to her through their concern and honest questions.

After Wendy returned to the worship service, the children got busy making encouragement cards for her. Many volunteered that they would pray for her.

Wendy had her surgery. The children's director had known from the first that if Wendy died, her death would have to be talked through with the children. But she lived, and after some months she came back to the children's area. She sat on the same rocking chair while the children gathered around her, eager to hear what had happened. Wendy explained what she could of the experience and praised God for his gracious kindness to her and her family. She told the children that whenever hospital staff or visitors asked who had made the cards taped all over the walls in her room, she always said, "The children at my church made them. They are praying for me." She thanked them for their ministry to her.

Wendy experienced grace as the children of her church were given opportunity to minister. Processing fear, anger, suffering, and sorrow in community builds bonds among children and adults and matures the faith of all.

In the church we are committed to telling the truth about God. We tell our children the story of God at work in creation, bringing redemption throughout history, and still at work in our times and lives. It is important that we tell the Story truthfully and appropriately. Children and adults can enter the stories of Scripture together to meet God in them and hear what God has to say to each one.

As children hear and comprehend more and more of the biblical story, they will have questions. In a truth-telling community the imperfections of biblical characters and the mystery of God's ways will not be denied. Adults will help children process their questions with respect and honesty and will celebrate new insights.

As we enter the stories of God together, experience God, share our discoveries, and honestly process our questions, a deep sense of community is built. We can tell the truth about our journey with God, celebrating what we know and acknowledging that we all still have much to learn.

Promise keeping is also essential for community. Nothing destroys community faster than betrayal, or an unwillingness to commit ourselves to one another in the first place. Yet many children live in a world of broken promises. Who will promise to be there for them? Will the church give the gift of promise keeping to provide a nurturing community for children? Before promises can be kept, they must be made. What promises do children need from the church, and in what forms do we make those promises?

Children need promises of hospitality. We keep these promises as children are made welcome in places that are important to adults and when adult friends, teachers, shepherds, or small group leaders invest in relationships with children, giving the gift of presence on a regular basis over time. Children also need our commitment to truth telling.

We make promises in rituals of infant baptism or dedication. In one baptismal ritual the pastor addresses the congregation, expecting its response.

> Do you, as Christ's body, the Church, reaffirm both your rejection of sin and your commitment to Christ?
>
> *We do.*
>
> Will you nurture one another in Christian faith and life and include [this family] now before you in your care?
>
> *With God's help we will proclaim the good news and live according to the example of Christ.*
>
> *We will surround [this family] with a community of love and forgiveness, that they may grow in their service to others.*
>
> *We will pray for them, that they may be true disciples who walk in the way that leads to life.*[13]

This ritual leads the congregation to make significant promises to the child and the parents. In other rituals the congregation is asked to stand, signifying a commitment to support the family and provide spiritual nurture for the child just dedicated to God.

Do we take these promises seriously? As leaders in the church, do we

13. *The United Methodist Book of Worship* (Nashville: United Methodist Publishing House, 1992), p. 96.

do anything to help the congregation think about the promises being made and guide them in keeping them? If the teenagers in our congregation were to read the ritual used in their baptism or dedication, would they say, "Yes! My church kept those promises," or would they feel betrayed?

A congregation's promises to children are also reflected in policies and ministry plans. We promise to provide children with a safe environment, to protect them against abuse. Staffing policies for children's ministries can be designed to provide adequate personnel for relationship building. Job descriptions and covenants for children's ministry volunteers can articulate the commitments that will produce a faith-nurturing community. How many job descriptions for pastors contain promises related to the spiritual nurture of children? Once we articulate our promises in our policies, we must keep them.

Mission statements and slogans that a church publishes are promises being made to the whole congregation, including the children. Such statements elicit a negative response in those who do not find that the promises are being kept for them. As persons concerned about children, we need to take stock regularly. Are we delivering on our vision and mission statements when it comes to children?

One of the challenges we face is the hesitancy of many adults to make commitments. How often do we hear, "You can put me down as a substitute, but I can't promise to be there every week"? We encounter many people who enjoy attending church but resist becoming a member, making a commitment. Yet true community calls for commitment, promises made to one another and kept. As leaders we face the task of guiding contemporary adults into an understanding of community, its importance, and the value of their commitment to the lives of children.

Children in the Faith Community

Wednesday evenings the adults of Cathy's congregation meet in a prayer service or seminar, the teens gather in youth group, and the children in Christian Life Club. But on Wednesday, September 12, 2001, no one went to age-level activities.[14] Children, teenagers, and adults all gathered in the

14. This was the day following the terrorist attacks on the World Trade Center in New York City and on the Pentagon in Washington, D.C.

sanctuary to hear God's words of comfort, to pray, and to be together in God's presence. We all knew we needed one another.

In times of crisis we become acutely aware of our need for community. But when life is relatively calm, we may be happy in our age- and interest-segmented groups, forgetting the importance of community. God designed the faith community to be a means of grace. The processes through which faith and a life of faith are nurtured and grow require a community in which they can be seen, practiced, and understood.[15] Children are nurtured most effectively in communities where they feel a sense of belonging, where they are able to participate in its life and ministry, and where adult members model a vital faith.[16] In this section we will examine the gifts children receive in community and the gifts they offer.

True Belonging

We noted earlier that the twelve-year-old Jesus identified the temple as his "Father's house" (Luke 2:49). He had a deep sense of belonging to God and felt at home in God's house with God's people. All children need that sense of belonging to God's people in the community of faith.

A sense of belonging grows as children build relationships with adults and other children in the church, as they receive love and in turn love others. As children are welcomed into and participate in various facets of the congregation's life, their sense of belonging grows. Children who know they belong observe the lives of adults they are coming to know and admire and want to be like them. As new families come to the church, then, they should be welcomed wherever they enter, then caringly guided toward full involvement.

If children belong only to a Sunday school class or a midweek club, the church's formative influence in that child's life is limited. Unfortunately, in many churches today almost all activities for children and teenagers are with their peers and the few adults who lead the programs. The young belong only to their peer group, and when they graduate from

15. Craig Dykstra, *Growing in the Faith: Education and the Christian Practices* (Louisville: Geneva, 1999), pp. 40-41.

16. See Lawrence O. Richards, *Children's Ministry: Nurturing Faith within the Family of God* (Grand Rapids: Zondervan, 1983), pp. 74-78.

youth group, they graduate from the church. With their peers they go off to find a spirituality that suits them, leaving behind the congregation to which they never belonged.

The church will be a positive influence in the development of its children to the degree that they are seen *as part of* the church, not just attached to it through programs, no matter how well conceived or entertaining these programs are.[17] Children need churches committed to the nurture of the whole child for the whole of childhood.

Meaningful Participation

One of the basic premises of Craig Dykstra's *Growing in the Faith* is that children — and persons of all ages — "come to faith and grow in faith and in the life of faith by participating in the practices of the Christian community."[18] Children need to participate in the worship, learning, and works of service and outreach of the congregation. They benefit from involvement in the Christian disciplines of prayer and spending time with God. Growth is healthiest when children participate in these meaningful activities along with persons who have developed understanding and skill in the practices and are able to guide and teach the children.[19] The rituals of a church — worship, the sacraments, times together as the family of God, and special traditions at various time in the year — should capture the essence of the community's faith. If that faith is to be embraced by the next generation, children must be "included as participants in all the community rituals."[20]

The child's participation needs to go beyond simple presence and observation, important as those are. Children grow spiritually and in their sense of belonging and identity with the faith community as they contribute. Older children can read the Scripture lesson in Sunday wor-

17. We are not advocating that programs be abandoned. Nearly everything we do in ministry is in relation to some program structure. However, programs become unproductive when they become the end and not the means, or, as Don Posterski has often said, when programs rather than people become the channels for ministry.

18. Dykstra, *Growing in the Faith,* p. 44.

19. Dykstra, *Growing in the Faith,* pp. 44-45.

20. John H. Westerhoff III, *Will Our Children Have Faith?* rev. ed. (Toronto: Morehouse, 2000), p. 55.

ship, the children's choir can lead the congregation in praise to God, and in some traditions children serve as acolytes, preparing the congregation for worship.

Probably more children than we realize are ready to take responsible roles in the faith community. When eight-year-old Billy heard a call for new ushers, he responded. The head usher took time to train him, impressing on him that often the first contact people have with a church is with an usher.

Soon Billy's mother called the children's minister and asked what had happened to make such a difference in her son. "Billy made us take him shopping to buy him a suit!" she said. "He has never worn anything but a T-shirt, jeans, and running shoes." Billy knew he had an important responsibility, and he wanted to look like and be like Mr. Brown, the head usher.

Often we view children's participation as a learning experience for them. It is that but also much more. Children should be involved in the work of the church because they have gifts to offer: the joy their presence brings as they visit an elderly shut-in, their energy and faithfulness as they pick up papers and straighten songbooks each Sunday after worship, the musical ability of the gifted fifth-grader who accompanies the children's choir. Along with adults, children grow spiritually through expressing their faith and love for God in service, when as members of the church — not just *future* members — they do the work of the people of God.[21]

Being Formed through Experience and Education

John Westerhoff believes that faith cannot be taught; it can only be inspired. Such inspiration comes as "faith is expressed, transformed, and made meaningful by persons sharing their faith in a . . . community of faith."[22] Pastors and church leaders have often thought that children must understand the concepts of the faith before they can experience it. However, children learn first and most profoundly through experience. They also learn through imaging, through hearing stories and using their imag-

21. Gretchen Wolff Pritchard, *Offering the Gospel to Children* (Cambridge, Mass.: Cowley, 1992), pp. 141, 143.

22. Westerhoff, *Will Our Children Have Faith?* p. 19.

ination to process those stories and their experiences. Finally, children learn using "signs," conceptual language.[23]

When children are present, experiencing life in the faith community, they sense the joy, wonder, and awe of those around them as they worship together. They sense God's presence, even if they cannot name it. And they watch and imitate the adults and teenagers they see worshiping, relating to others in the community, and serving.[24] Experiencing the faith community is crucial to the faith formation of children.

To understand that experience and give it meaning, however, children need education. The faith community has the privilege of leading children into the stories of Scripture, where they meet God and begin to discover God's character and God's ways. In those stories they also hear God's call to live a life of love, purity, and obedience to God, a life that makes a difference in the world. Children grasp the meaning of stories and their experiences first intuitively and affectively. As they develop, they organize their knowing into concepts and begin to understand theological words as they integrate what adults teach and say with what they have known through experience and story. Marva Dawn claims that the "Scriptures cannot be known unless there is a genuine Christian community in which to study, memorize, and obey them."[25] Education and experience in the community of faith must go hand in hand.

One Sunday morning the children's minister asked four-year-old Kim what she had learned in Sunday school. The story had been about David and Saul and the effects of Saul's hostility toward David. Kim thought for a moment, then responded, "To stop a fight, somebody has to stop first, even if the other person did the wrong thing." Kim was not simply parroting adult words. She had somehow grasped, from the story and her interactions with the adults around her, an important aspect of character.

Through their experiences with the people of God, children will learn what it means to be Christian and how to make a difference in the world. This raises serious questions for those leading the church's ministry with children. What are children in our congregation observing, experiencing,

23. Westerhoff, *Will Our Children Have Faith?* p. 61.

24. Pritchard, *Offering the Gospel,* p. 143.

25. Marva Dawn, *Is It a Lost Cause? Having the Heart of God for the Church's Children* (Grand Rapids: Eerdmans, 1997), p. 32.

and learning? Are they seeing Christian character, the life God desires for Christians to live?

Children, Essential to the Community

Not only do children need the community of faith, the community needs children. When Moses summoned all the Israelites to renew their covenant with God before they crossed over into the Promised Land, the children were in that great gathering of covenant people (Deut. 29:2, 10-11). Today the church, the Christian covenant community, is the fundamental expression of the people of God. And the church is fully the church — the people of God — only when children are present. God's people learn the meaning of responsibility and selfless care as they minister to children. We see faith in fresh ways when we invite children to process their experiences with us, and we experience grace as God ministers to us through them.

The essence of a community lies in the life and faithfulness of its people. Without children, life and faithfulness have no meaning beyond one generation. As Neil Postman put it, "Children are the living messages we send to a time we will not see."[26] Without the need to prepare that living message, to model and explain the faith to children, adult faith is impoverished.

Christ is made known to the world through the worship, discipleship, service, learning, and witness of the people of God. When asked who is greatest in the kingdom of God, Jesus drew a child into the group of gathered disciples to teach them the ways of the kingdom. And Jesus promised to be with his people in some mysterious way when they welcome children (Matt. 18:3-5). Children *must* be involved authentically in the activities of the people of God and helped to become responsible participants in the life of the church, or the church will fail to incarnate Christ and to see truly the kingdom of God.

The Mystery of Formation in the Community

How does God meet children in the faith community? The way God meets with human beings will ever remain a mystery. God meets children in the

26. Neil Postman, *The Disappearance of Childhood* (New York: Vintage, 1994), p. xi.

same way God meets adults — through the mystery of the Holy Spirit's work, through relationships among the people of God, through the revelation of God's will and purpose in Christ and the Scriptures.

Three-year-old Stephen said to his mother one day, "Mommy, I can believe in God because I don't understand him." While we, like Stephen, accept the mystery of God's relationships with people, certain activities can serve as vehicles for our growth and understanding. Adults who desire to pass on the faith to the next generation will accept the mystery and develop authentic practices for faith communities.

Relationships in Community

On Brandon's first Sunday at Cathy's church, he spent the worship hour with other three-year-olds and two adult worship leaders. When his parents came for him, an adult brought him to the door and, with a warm smile, said to him, "I'm so glad you came this morning. Come again, darling."

Brandon's face broke into a big smile; he looked up at his mother and exclaimed, "She called me darling!"

In a little more than an hour the worship leader had begun to build a warm relationship with a three-year-old who realized that he was special to her.

Personal, meaningful relationships are crucial for nurture in the faith community. We might think of relationships as the nerves that carry messages of love, understanding, insight, and pleasure from person to person in the body of Christ. Without relationships, few messages reach their intended receiver. Thomas Groome challenges religious educators to view their students not as objects to be shaped but as persons for relationship.[27]

The Gift of Relationships

The Christian formation of children is fostered through a variety of relationships. Children need to know and be known by adults who care about

27. Thomas H. Groome, *Christian Religious Education: Sharing Our Story and Vision* (San Francisco: Harper and Row, 1980), p. 263.

them, invest in them, and give them opportunities to see adults living as Christians. Healthy, warm relationships with both men and women contribute profoundly to children. Given the many single-parent families in our milieu, the church can give children the gift of meaningful relationships with adults who in a small way fill the void left by the mother or father who is absent from their home.

Based on a legitimate concern for protecting children from sexual abuse, some churches do not allow men to work with young children. But children need the experience of learning with and from men, worshiping with them and knowing that they love Jesus. Especially little boys need to know that real men love and serve God. They need to see and experience the nurturing warmth of men who model what it is to be a Christlike man. Our policies must protect children from abuse while releasing both men and women to love, teach, and nurture children.

Building relationships with other children in the faith community enhances a child's sense of belonging and joy in being at church. Children who are rejected by their peers or who simply do not build friendships among church peers usually drop out as soon as they have that choice. As you work with children, be alert to those who are outsiders, those who do not know how to relate constructively with their peers. Rejection causes great pain, which over time can swell into anger and explode in violence. But if relational struggles are noted early and adults provide the support and guidance needed to develop positive relational skills, these children can be drawn in and nurtured by the community.

A healthy peer group, developed in the church during childhood, can support preadolescents as they move into middle school and face intensifying pressures from a non-Christian society. As children move toward adolescence, knowing, trusting, and being accepted by their peers becomes essential for them to talk freely and honestly in the church group about their faith and life. Times for children to have fun together and become friends are not just an enticement to get them to church. Such activities can build supportive relationships that will enhance their Christian formation and life.

Children are also blessed through relationships with persons in a wide age range, from teenagers to senior citizens. Cathy saw that beautiful mix of ages one morning during Vacation Bible School week. Teenagers and college-age youth stood on the church lawn, ready to engage with the children in an outdoor game. A woman in her sixties and a man in his thirties were set to help the children build birdhouses, while teenagers and middle-aged and older adults prepared snacks in the kitchen. The extended family had gathered to serve the children, enjoy time together, and build relationships as the children learned more about Jesus.

Although children profit greatly from participation in worship and other congregational events, relationships grow over time in smaller face-to-face groups. The relationships built in small group settings enhance experiences of being together as the larger faith community. In the gathered congregation children see faces they know, people who love them and greet them by name, and they know that they belong. They are bonded to the congregation through the relationships developed as they participate in the life of the faith community in a variety of settings.

Yet children and adults can be together in a room and not develop significant relationships. How do we get to know one another, become important to each other? Relationships build through small acts of attentiveness and interest, something as simple as an adult's looking deep into a child's eyes and saying, "I'm so glad you're here." In the press of doing ministry we can too easily overlook such small acts of personal care.

Formative relationships are built as adults take an interest in the lives of children and what is important to them, as we listen to their joys and their disappointments. This kind of sharing can take place as children arrive for an activity, if adults are prepared in advance and free to just visit with the children. Opportunity for sharing between children and adults needs to be built into our ministries. Time for conversation is a wise investment. Significant relationships usually take time to develop. Adults who commit themselves to minister with children once a week for a year or more give them a gift of faithful friendship.

But, you may be asking, how do we get enough adults involved with children to build these important bonds? Here are just a few suggestions. Draw together a team of persons to work with children, allowing individuals to take ministry roles that fit their gifts and available time. Anthony never saw himself as a teacher, but for several years he served as "the grandpa" with the two- and three-year-olds each Sunday morning. Enlisting department grandparents, aunts, uncles, or shepherds — roles many people accept more readily than the role of teacher — can enrich the lives of children and adults. When first- through sixth-graders meet together each Sunday, children have contact with some members of the ministry team over a period of several years (chapter 12 discusses this approach). This provides opportunity for significant relationships to build. Also, give persons opportunity for short-term service with children. Often that limited experience begins their journey toward a more extensive ministry commitment.

The blessings of relationships between children and adults go both ways. Scottie tells of one eight-year-old boy who blesses her every Sunday. "He stands beside me and looks at me until I notice him. Then, with an ear-to-ear smile, he says, 'Hello, Mrs. May,' and gives me a hug." She feels blessed.

How do we build nurturing relationships with children? Through intentional acts of attentive caring over time and by trusting God's Spirit to work in those relationships, bonding us together.

Relational Bridges

The transition from elementary school to middle school, from children's ministry to middle-school youth ministry, can be difficult for preadolescents. Too many children do not make that transition in the church and simply drop out, wandering away to face adolescence without the support of a faith community. Youth and children's ministry leaders need to plan together for this transition.

During the latter part of fifth grade, children need to begin getting acquainted with the youth team. Invite persons who work with middle-school youth to participate in a few events where they can get to know the fifth-graders. Some churches have fifth-graders and adults who know them join in some summer activities with sixth-, seventh-, and eighth-graders. Such a plan can also give the middle-school youth opportunities to practice hospitality. Relationships built with workers and older children before moving into middle school can greatly enhance the newcomers' comfort and the likelihood that they will become participating members, blessed by the youth ministry of the congregation.

A Story about Community

Too often our view of the church gets in the way of building community and meaningful relationships. We get so busy running the "corporation" and managing programs that children, relationships, and community get lost.

For several years Linda worked with congregations and theological schools in Canada. After one particularly difficult board meeting, she wrote "If Churches Were Parks."

> If we tore down our church buildings and replaced them with parks, would the buildings be missed? If churches were parks, there would be trees and grass and places for pleasant walks, neighborhood families enjoying the changing seasons, and our "old ones" sitting on benches telling children stories of their lives and faith.
>
> In the fall, as the leaves changed from green to yellow, orange and red, we could invite our friends and neighbors to corn roasts and BBQs; invite them to laugh with us, talk with us, and enjoy the beauty of God's creation — in the park. We could leave the children something wonderful in a world gone mad.
>
> In the winter we could roll in the snow with the neighborhood children, throw snowballs, create snow sculptures, and get to know each other again as we walked under trees heavy with hoar frost. At Christmas we could string colored lights, decorate a Christmas tree, savor the story of the nativity, and sing carols under quiet stars.
>
> If churches were parks, we would have to forsake our games of power and our dreams of empire for pleasant walks, snow forts, corn roasts, Christmas trees, carol sings, Easter pageants, and heart-to-heart talks with those who need to know why we still believe in God. If our churches were parks, all people could gather there; they could come whenever they wished, for there would be no locked doors or security windows on our parks — no stained-glass windows to hide behind. Members of the church eating lunch in the park could strike up a conversation with a business person, university student, or shopper resting before heading home, or admire the multicolors of a group of teenagers and ask them if they are afraid of the world we have created for them, or angry because of the future we may have taken away from them.
>
> Of course we would find pain in our parks: lonely people, unhappy children, sullen youth. We might confront those trying to buy drugs in our parks. We might fear those who would hurt us and steal from us. If our churches were parks, we would have to confront the world outside our buildings. We would have to be those who make peace and speak of

> redemption and hope rather than those who hide behind fortress walls and wish the world away.
>
> When God started the world, He put his man and woman in a park. He chose to walk and talk with his creation in a park. When we were cast out of the park, we began to build towers, empires, cities, and temples. We had to acquire and possess — not only the present but the past and the future. We found ways to control our world and other persons. It's hard to do this in a park.

Obviously the "park" image cannot be pressed too far, but it does suggest that there are certain qualities that should be nurtured in congregations — especially when children are present. How much of the park do children find in our churches?

Conclusions

Children's ministry is enjoying heights of interest not experienced since the early twentieth century, but what will children find in our ministries? Will they be brought into programs focused on keeping them happy and entertained, or will the ministry leaders wrestle with vital questions about how the church can best serve children? Will the leaders be concerned about the church's attitude toward children? Will the congregation see children not just as the church of tomorrow but as *part of* the church of today? Will the congregation find ways to engage children in significant learning, authentic worship, and responsible service in and through the church's community? Will they realize that children are learning from the way the church lives out its faith? Will church leaders set aside the model of church as an efficiently run, fast-growing corporation? In the power of God's Spirit, will they seek to lead the people gathered by God in their faith community to embody and practice together the identity and character God expects?

When the church answers yes to these questions, through their experiences with the people of God children will learn what it means to be Christian and how to make a difference in the world.

Chapter 8

CHILDREN IN THE FAMILY

"Cathy, this is Silvia," announced the voice from the answering machine. "Could you give me a call? Kurt and I would like to talk with you about what more we can do to disciple Noel." Silvia was not a Sunday school teacher asking for help with a challenging eight-year-old. Noel was Silvia's daughter.

During the bedtime ritual one evening, Noel had said, "Mommy, I miss being with God." She reminisced about children's worship in her old church, where she had had time and quiet to be with God. Her mother listened to her and began to seek ways to provide her with such treasured times with God.

Cathy suggested that Silvia set aside a special place at home where Noel could go just to be with God. A few months later Cathy visited their new home and was given the grand tour. The first stop? Noel's bedroom, where she showed Cathy her special place to be with God. Earlier in an interview, Noel had talked about how her daddy read to her from the Bible at bedtime. As he read she would ask questions, and they took time to discuss the answers.

Here was a young couple that cared deeply about the discipling, or faith formation, of their children. They did not depend on the church to ensure that their daughters became Christians, although the family did attend church together. These young parents took seriously their privilege and responsibility of discipling their children. They gave their girls a gift of immeasurable value.

Kurt and Silvia are in touch with God's plan for the faith formation of children. In Deuteronomy 6 we saw that God intends the home to be the primary context for teaching children the ways of God. "Recite [God's words] to your children and talk about them when you are at home and when you are away, when you lie down and when you rise. Bind them as a sign on your hand, fix them as an emblem on your forehead, and write them on the doorposts of your house and on your gates" (vv. 7-9). The home is the most natural setting in which these activities can take place, a home where parents love the Lord their God with all their heart, soul, and might (Deut. 6:5). But the home is to be supported and nurtured in a vital faith community. This chapter explores the home-church partnership for spiritual formation, its power, and how it can work today.

Family: The Primary Context for Faith Formation

When we listen to children like Noel, we discover that they seem to naturally and easily believe in God. They want to know about God and enjoy God's presence. In her excellent book *Family: The Forming Center,* Marjorie Thompson refers to this as a "mysterious . . . seemingly innate, untaught knowledge of God."[1] What provides children with this early knowing? Writing in the 1700s, John Wesley spoke of "what is vulgarly called natural conscience. But," he claimed, "this is not natural: It is more properly termed preventing [prevenient] grace."[2] Wesley believed that God extends grace before a person calls for God's help and that this grace is at work in the heart of every person.[3] From the beginning of life God's grace is active; the dance with God begins, and spiritual formation is under way.

But does spiritual formation simply unfold in response to grace, or are other factors at work? Robert Mulholland claims that "every action taken, every response made, every dynamic of relationship, every thought held, every emotion allowed: these are the minuscule arenas where, bit by bit . . . we are shaped into some kind of being. . . . [L]ife is by its very nature, spiri-

1. Marjorie J. Thompson, *Family: The Forming Center* (Nashville: Upper Room, 1996), p. 15.

2. John Wesley, *The Works of John Wesley: Complete and Unabridged,* 3rd ed., vol. 6 (Peabody, Mass.: Hendrickson, 1984), p. 512.

3. John 1:9 is one verse that supports Wesley's view on prevenient grace. He saw the "light that enlightens everyone" as evidence of God's grace reaching out to every human being.

tual formation."[4] God's grace in our lives makes spiritual formation and growth possible, but children and adults are formed in the minuscule events of daily life, and those who have the most intimate relationships with children will influence their formation most profoundly, for good or ill. The home, then, is at the heart of spiritual formation for children and for their parents, and that formation takes place in the flow of everyday life.

Formative Relationships

If asked, "How do you nurture the faith of your children?" many parents might answer, "We pray at meals and at bedtime, read the Bible together, and go to church." Although these are significant experiences for children, *relationships* with parents and other significant adults provide the most formative influences for children.

Thompson pictures the spiritual life as "not one slice in a large loaf of reality but leaven for the whole loaf."[5] This image helps us see that we cannot separate out the spiritual and somehow nurture it apart from the rest of life. How children are developing physically, mentally, emotionally, and in their sense of self affects their spiritual development. The ways family members relate to one another day in and day out are profoundly formative. How does this work?

Human beings see themselves in the mirror of others' responses to them. As the nursing baby looks into the mother's eyes, what does he or she see? Do the eyes reflect love and joy? If so, the baby sees himself or herself as a loved and lovable person. When parents or caregivers respond to toddlers with wise boundaries and with love, mercy, and grace, the children feel noticed, valued, and secure. They also discover that others have expectations for them. When we listen to children and take time to play with them or read to them, they realize they are important to us. If we are present when they need us and meet their needs, children can release their fears and rest in our trustworthiness.

Most children seem to assume that God is like their parents and other significant adults. Boys and girls whose parents and families have given

4. M. Robert Mulholland, *Shaped by the Word,* rev. ed. (Nashville: Upper Room, 2000), pp. 25-26.

5. Thompson, *Family: The Forming Center,* p. 13.

them good gifts see God as one who also gives such gifts. Unfortunately, any inability of parents to give healthy love may also color the child's picture of God.

Children begin to form their image of God at an early age. Between eighteen months and age three, children are curious about their world, full of questions regarding how it works. Seeing the world through the eyes of their experience, they assume someone makes things happen. Children seem to have a sense that there is a "Great Other" behind the wonderful world in which they live.[6] In their families, from friends, or at church they hear the name of God, connect that name with the One they are aware of, and continue constructing their understanding or image of God. This is not a conscious act, but naturally children build their image of God drawing from their experiences. And since young children have an active imagination they have no trouble believing in unseen beings, including God.

Through our relationships with very young children we participate in their spiritual formation. God desires that in the arms of their parents children first experience unconditional love and grace. Such parental grace, limited as it is, prepares the child to hunger for and receive God's grace.[7] Parents have the awesome privilege of being "God's love with skin on" for their children. The way parents love and relate to their children, day in and day out, in good times and bad, is the most powerful influence on their formation.

The family is the spiritual formation crucible not only for children but for parents as well; spiritual formation is not a one-way street. When we are tired and impatient with our children, yet they love us anyway, we see God's grace. Our children also show us our need for continued transformation.

One morning in the break between Sunday school and the worship service, a young pastor came down hard on his two-year-old son for something the child had done. As the worship service began, the congregation sang the first hymn and God spoke to the pastor. "You treated your little son unjustly; he was just being a two-year-old, you know. The problem wasn't with him, it was with your pride. You were embarrassed over

6. For more on the child's beginning awareness of God, consult Ana-Maria Rizzuto, *The Birth of the Living God: A Psychoanalytic Study* (Chicago: University of Chicago Press, 1979), pp. 7, 44-45, 178.

7. David Seamands, *Healing Grace: Let God Free You from the Performance Trap* (Wheaton, Ill.: Victor, 1988), p. 46.

what people would think." As the congregation continued singing, the pastor walked down to the pew where his little son stood and asked for and received forgiveness.

If we let God convict and forgive us at the points where we fail in our parenting, and if we open our eyes to see God in our children, parents and children together will be formed in the image of Christ. Thompson says the way we relate to one another is the most important spiritual discipline in the life of a family.[8] Healthy, health-giving relationships reflect God's love through seemingly simple but demanding practices. Thompson discusses six crucial practices: presence, acceptance, affirmation, accountability, forgiveness, and hospitality.[9]

By *presence* Thompson means more than physical presence. She calls us to intentionally focus on the other person through true listening, learning from the other, and caring about the other's joys and needs. Presence requires us to tune out distractions and be willing to set aside our agenda for the good of the other.

"Presence" brings to mind a picture of Jesus turning from the adults who clamored for his attention to welcome the children, take them in his arms, and bless them (Mark 10:13-16). Jesus did his work as teacher, preacher, and healer, but he also took time to be present to children. And our children can experience the presence of Jesus when we turn our attention to them and bless them with our time and our touch.

We give children a glimpse of God's heart for them when our *acceptance* of them is unconditional. Children need to know that they are loved and treasured no matter what they do. This does not mean that we approve of all their actions. A child's behavior is often inappropriate or destructive and needs to be named as unacceptable, but this can and must be done while respecting the child as a person of worth. Because we love our children, we cannot allow them to do things that would be destructive to themselves and those around them. Wise discipline is an expression of the child's worth and our acceptance of him or her. In the frustrating moments of parenting it is often difficult to see more than a negative behavior, to express acceptance for the child while putting a stop to the behavior. Unconditional acceptance calls for developing appropriate response skills and also the love and patience God can give us as we seek strength and grace.

8. Thompson, *Family: The Forming Center,* p. 59.
9. Thompson, *Family: The Forming Center,* pp. 59-67.

In addition to acceptance, children need *affirmation*. Healthy families discover and celebrate the uniqueness of each member, their gifts of personality, interests, and skills. Parents don't expect all their children to be the same; they find ways for each one to develop his or her own gifts and interests. They carefully avoid comparing children or using the strengths of one to point out the weaknesses of another. Children learn to notice and appreciate the special gifts of others as they live with affirming adults.

It is not enough to affirm children in general terms; they need guidance to discover their special gifts. A group of middle-school girls reported, "Our parents tell us we can become anything we want to be. But nobody helps us know what we would be good at or what we would enjoy doing."[10] Watch for a child's natural aptitudes, talk together about them, and give the child opportunities to develop in areas of strength. Often persons become aware of their gifts through service. When families engage in serving, they may discover gifts God has given them to be used for the sake of others.

Accountability is caring enough about people to confront them when their attitudes and conduct have been destructive. Permissive parents often intend to act in love, but failing to honestly name a destructive behavior and hold children accountable for it is not love. On the other hand, attacking children and berating them for what they have done inflicts deep wounds. Children need parents who speak the truth from a heart of love (Eph. 4:15), who will hold them accountable for their actions while lovingly standing by them.

Jesus taught his disciples to pray, "Forgive us our debts, as we also have forgiven our debtors" (Matt. 6:12). *Forgiveness* is at the heart of our relationship with God and relationships in the family. In the closeness of family life we often hurt one another. Tired, busy parents, distracted by their own agendas and seeing situations through adult eyes, can cause their children pain. Children can also wound their parents and siblings. Some families face major betrayal and abuse that need the healing of forgiveness.

Forgiveness is not forgetting a wrong done or saying, "Oh, it really doesn't matter." Forgiving is a process that begins with acknowledging the reality of the pain and injustice inflicted on us. The journey then leads us to the place of choosing to release our need to judge the other, our resent-

10. From a conversation with Marcia Bunge, 2002.

ment, and our desire to make the other person pay. Released from these burdens, we intentionally begin to rebuild the love essential to the relationship.

True forgiveness is not easy and cannot be forced. It takes time, even for the small hurts of family life, and for deep wounds a wise and caring guide is usually needed. When it comes to the difficult process of forgiving, God does not leave us to our own resources but offers the strength we need. Children often model for adults the beauty of forgiving. Forgiveness and reconciliation are signs of God's presence in a home.

It is important to note that in the case of abuse, we do not want to unwittingly make children feel that they must forgive the abuser and not do anything about their situation. Children must be protected. By law persons working with children are required to report abuse or suspected abuse. Children must know that forgiveness does not call for one to keep secrets or stay in a hurtful relationship. Churches are often prone to trust the remorse expressed by those caught in the sexual abuse of children and too easily offer forgiveness too soon.[11] Our teaching on forgiveness must be wise and include advocacy for children.

The final practice mentioned by Thompson is *hospitality,* welcoming into our homes friends and persons beyond the circle of those close to us. As Jesus wrapped up his teaching to the crowds shortly before his arrest, he described the final judgment.

> Then the king will say to those at his right hand, "Come, you that are blessed by my Father, inherit the kingdom prepared for you from the foundation of the world; for I was hungry and you gave me food, I was thirsty and you gave me something to drink, I was a stranger and you welcomed me." . . . Then the righteous will answer him, "Lord, when was it that we saw you hungry and gave you food, or thirsty and gave you something to drink? And when was it that we saw you a stranger and welcomed you . . . ?" And the king will answer them, "Truly I tell you, just as you did it to one of the least of these who are members of my family, you did it to me." (Matt. 25:34-40)

11. From a comment by Rev. Marie M. Fortune in the video "Hear Their Cries: Religious Responses to Child Abuse," produced by Center for the Prevention of Sexual and Domestic Violence, Seattle, 1992.

Jesus invites into his kingdom those who give food and water to the needy and welcome strangers into their homes. For the righteous in this parable, hospitality had become a way of life. They did not even realize that their care for "the least" was care for Jesus.

Mulholland defines spiritual formation as "a process of being conformed to the image of Christ for the sake of others."[12] Hospitality is practiced "for the sake of others" and is an important, though often overlooked, aspect of spiritual formation. How does self-giving hospitality become a way of life? An excellent starting point is in the home, where children and parents together experience the joys and challenges of welcoming others, enjoying them, loving them, and meeting their needs.

Unfortunately many parents, focusing on their own desires and what they think is best for their children, ignore the needs of others and become self-centered. But focusing only on the needs and desires of our own family is not actually in the best interest of our children. When planning holiday celebrations, do we think of including persons who have no family with whom to celebrate? When deciding on schooling for our children, do we consider the contributions our family, both children and parents, could make to the public school? If we have a good income, are we sensitive to the children who will be left out if church events cost too much? As a family, do we share our time and resources with others?

One day as Jesus taught, someone announced, "Your mother and your brothers are standing outside, wanting to see you." Jesus surprised the crowd with his response: "My mother and my brothers are those who hear the word of God and do it" (Luke 8:20-21). For Jesus, family is larger than parents and siblings. As followers of Jesus we are called to care about God's larger family, including other people's children as well as our own. As we live out Christian hospitality, the Holy Spirit conforms us all in the likeness of Christ.

Good Enough Parenting

Talk of parents and their roles in the spiritual formation of children can be overwhelming. Busy young parents may find it hard to imagine adding

12. M. Robert Mulholland, *Invitation to a Journey: A Road Map for Spiritual Formation* (Downers Grove, Ill.: InterVarsity Press, 1993), p. 15.

more to what they already do for their children. "And how perfect do I have to be?" they may ask. The practices discussed above may seem possible only for the very wise and perfect.

However, children do not need perfect parents, simply good enough parents.[13] To support our children in their spiritual formation, we simply need to be on the journey with them, learning and growing, willing to say "I'm sorry" and to seek God's transforming grace, love, and strength. There is room for parents to grow and learn new skills. Actually ongoing growth is essential, since children and their needs change as they grow and pass through various life phases.

We noted earlier that spirituality is the leaven in the loaf of life, not a separate slice of it. One significant way children are formed is by the way they are parented. Basic parenting forms the spirit of the child. When parents lovingly care for their baby, faithfully responding to the infant's cries for help, and when they keep promises, their children learn to trust, and that ability to trust provides the foundation for faith in God.

Behavioral boundaries designed to give children appropriate freedom while protecting them and creating a pleasant, respectful atmosphere in the home significantly influence them. As they live by the rules of the home, children experience the value of laws and respect for others. When they break the rules, they discover that actions have consequences, and wise discipline allows them to experience those consequences. For example, if Jane uses her crayons to color on the wall rather than on the paper provided, Mommy lays out her options: she may color on the paper, but the crayons will be put away if she colors on other things. Through discipline children can also experience the mercy of the second chance even as they learn about consequences. And every time children bear the consequences of their actions, we should then enfold them in loving arms and assure them, "I love you very much, even when I cannot let you do naughty things." This is grace.

Wise, loving, consistent discipline lays the foundation for children to understand God's laws, judgment, mercy, and grace. Such discipline helps children become persons who respect others, take responsibility for their

13. The term "good enough parents" is inspired by Donald W. Winnicott's use of the term "good enough mother" in his *The Maturational Processes and the Facilitating Environment: Studies in the Theory of Emotional Development* (London: Hogarth/Institute for Psychoanalysis, 1965).

actions, and avoid destructive behavior. Spiritual formation is taking place through the give-and-take of life in the family with good enough parents.

Although wise, loving Christian parents are a wonderful blessing to a child, children from very difficult home situations can also have a beautiful understanding of God. Some children who live with constant fighting and turmoil in their family "hang on to God and learn to trust him" once they come to know Jesus. They express confidence in God's love and know God is there for them in times of need.[14] When children are given time to process Bible stories in settings such as children's worship and are free to respond as they choose, profound and meaningful artwork and application of biblical truth may be done by children wrestling with difficult things such as the death of a sibling or the separation and divorce of their parents.[15]

When parents are unable to give children what they need, young ones can still find comfort and nurture in God's presence. Some children, though not all, experience God as the loving parent they do not have. Robert Coles, after thousands of hours of conversation with children, marvels at how some children develop amazing strength of character and values in situations that totally destroy other children.[16] Coles also notes that faith and the teaching of their church sustain children and give them strength.[17]

When parents are unable to give what a child needs, don't assume that God is not there. Look for evidence of God's presence in the child's life, and find ways for the family of God to surround the child with love and support.

Formed through Life Together

As Thompson reminds us, "Children learn what they live. They absorb knowledge of the world by what they experience and observe. . . . [They] learn more from what adults do than from what adults say; they are sensi-

14. Irene Cheung, a student at Trinity University, found this to be true in a study she conducted with Asian children in Toronto.

15. This observation comes from Cathy's work with children in worship over several years.

16. Robert Coles, *The Moral Life of Children* (Boston: Houghton Mifflin, 1986), pp. 105, 120.

17. Coles, *Moral Life,* pp. 33-34, 133.

tive to the hidden curriculum."[18] Children whose parents speak to them respectfully grow up speaking to others with respect. Those who are read to from an early age and watch Mommy and Daddy enjoying good books will likely develop a love for reading. They internalize values as they see and live them.

Children notice, in detail, what adults do. Early on they become aware of any difference between what we teach them and how we act. On her way to a church event, a pastor's wife needed to pick something up at a downtown office. "Pray that we'll find a parking place right in front of the office, honey," she said to her daughter. When they arrived, there was one parking space in front of the office — but another car had begun turning in to it. Undaunted, the pastor's wife nosed into the space and cheerfully turned off the car.

"But Mommy," her daughter exclaimed in disbelief, "he was turning in here."

"We prayed for a place, didn't we? It's ours," her mother responded. More than fifty years later, that daughter remembers her disappointment over her mother's lack of integrity.

Children are troubled by double standards and lose respect for parents who continue to demand of them what they are unwilling to do themselves. But if we listen to our children and take a look at ourselves through their eyes, they can help us grow and build greater consistency into our life. In some cases we need to conform to the standards we set for our children, but in other situations we will realize that our demands on the children are unreasonable and we need to relax them.

Children also observe and are affected by how the significant adults around them live out their relationship with God. In the early morning while the rest of the family sleeps, Ged spends time with God, his Bible, and a challenging book. One morning three-year-old Drew, still sleepy, padded across the living room and crawled up on his grandpa's lap. While Drew snuggled contentedly, Ged continued to read, pray, and enjoy God's presence. Drew may not remember this event, but he will grow up knowing that God and spending time with God at home each day are important to his grandpa, whom he loves dearly. Children need to discover through observation that religion is not just for Sunday at church: God is important to the adults they love all week long at home and at work.

18. Thompson, *Family: The Forming Center,* p. 22.

Children are blessed when families enjoy God together. Music celebrating God's goodness may draw the family into God's presence as it provides a backdrop for life or screens out distracting noises so that a little one can fall asleep. During times together outdoors parents and children can naturally enter into worship. One fall afternoon as Rita exclaimed over a little tree whose leaves flamed with brilliance, her young daughter Candace cried out, "I *love* God."[19] And in regular or special times of prayer, families can invite and enjoy God's presence.

Children are also deeply influenced by how the significant adults in their lives respond to unexpected events. When special blessings come our way, do we thank God and those who had a part in blessing us? In times of stress and grief, do our children see us turning to God and God's people for strength and guidance? Are we willing to process with the children the hard questions we have about where God is in our pain? In times of war and tragedy do they hear us pray for all those who suffer, including our enemies? Do they see a real faith being refined in the crucible of life?

One single mother told Cathy, "All my kids have a real understanding of God because we're a family that lives by faith. There have been times when we've just been hanging on by our teeth and I've said, 'OK, God, there's nothing I can do,' and God always comes through. The kids know that. I mean, I don't keep it a big secret."[20] Thompson believes such experiences "create indelible impressions on children whose spirits are being formed in the web of family interaction."[21] Encourage single parents to believe that this is true for their children. The visible reliance of any parent on God will point children toward the One who can be trusted, and it will strengthen their faith.

Formation through Intentional Activities

Our spirits are formed subtly and powerfully through the spontaneous interactions of everyday life and relationships. Realizing the full potential for spiritual formation in the family, however, calls for the intentional planning of ways to be together with God. Hectic busyness and constant

19. True account provided by Ruth Goring, 2004.
20. Catherine Stonehouse, unpublished interview with Shelly Baker, 2000.
21. Thompson, *Family: The Forming Center,* p. 112.

noise tend to engulf us as families, leaving us with limited time for one another or God and making it difficult for us to speak our questions or hear words of love. It takes thought, planning, and discipline to make the space and stillness needed for quality time together.

When is the family together? When could they be together? What adjustments could make those together times more meaningful? Many parents spend several hours a week *driving* children to and from school, music lessons, sports, or church events. This "wasted" time can be frustrating or a good time for conversation and presence. Leave the car radio off, focus your attention on the children, and give them a chance to talk about their day. Listen for their questions and make time to process them, coming back to a topic later if need be. Some children seem to find it easier to raise their questions in the car than in other settings. And the car may be a comfortable place for parents to address a concern with a child. One family purchased a large van so that they could take their sons and their friends to soccer games. They want the privilege of being with their boys, knowing their friends, celebrating victories with them, and helping them learn from their losses.

Eating together, without the distraction of television, helps a family bond and provides time for conversation. Could your family eat one meal a day together, or even three or four meals a week? Decide what is possible and build those family meals into the weekly pattern of life.

Children treasure *time alone with a parent.* As the oldest of four children, Cathy fondly remembers the times when she had her mother to herself. That usually happened on shopping trips. The activity wasn't that exciting, but it was special to be a young girl one on one with her mother.

Once a month Roger gave each of his four children an evening of his time. The child chose what he or she wanted to do with Daddy, and they did it, even if the child planned a picnic on a cold November evening.

What about *family fun times,* camping trips, a day at a national park, or a vacation? Given the busy schedules of most parents, it will be difficult to find time for these quality experiences if they are not scheduled before business commitments and other responsibilities fill the calendar. Intentionally making space for time together strengthens family bonds and sets the stage for processing questions, learning, and enjoying God.

Rituals are also important means of spiritual formation. God's instructions for passing on the faith to Jewish children involved rituals such as the Feast of the Passover and the Feast of Booths (Deut. 16:1-8; Lev.

23:39-43). Using concrete objects, questions and answers, drama, and physical movement for expressing praise, whole families reenacted the story of God's deliverance from slavery and made the story their own.

How do we celebrate Advent and Christmas, Lent and Easter — seasons intended for the retelling of the Christian story? Santa Claus, the Easter bunny, and materialism will squeeze out spiritual meaning unless Christians choose to establish their own family and faith community traditions for remembering God's actions on our behalf. Here are just a few traditions that friends have shared with me.[22]

One family purchased a hands-on nativity scene when their oldest son was just a toddler. Each year during Advent they build the scene piece by piece, telling another part of the story as each figure is added. The children may handle the figures, working through the story, whenever they wish. For Christmas morning a small manger with the baby Jesus in it is wrapped in a box, covered with brown paper, and tied with string. The box is hidden in the room where the Christmas tree stands. Before anyone opens presents, the young children search for the box. When it is found, the children open it and the family talks about how God's best present was hidden away in a small town, in a stable, and this focuses their attention on the wonderful gift of Jesus.

Many families use an Advent calendar as they move toward Christmas. Behind each door in one family's calendar is a name for Jesus. Together the family talks about each of the names, growing in their understanding of and love for Jesus. Many families have an Advent wreath, light the candles each Sunday in Advent, and share thoughts about the meaning of each one.

"We always have an Easter egg hunt," a mother told me. "I fill the eggs with some candy but also include symbols of Easter such as a small cross, a stone, a thorn, a flower, or a butterfly. These items set the stage for us to discuss the Easter story and its meaning."

In another family, Thanksgiving is celebrated for several days using a "countdown turkey." Each child is given a picture of a turkey with as many feathers as there are days until Thanksgiving. Each day the children color a feather, and on lines under the picture they write one blessing that is important to them. When Thanksgiving arrives, they have a colorful turkey and a page full of blessings for which to be thankful.

22. These ideas come from Cheryl Schell and Lenore Sweigard.

Daily and weekly rituals are also important means of spiritual formation. Taking the idea of a Sabbath candle from Jewish tradition, one family set up a lighted six-inch set of praying hands that their boys turn on each Sunday morning and turn off Sunday night. While it is on, it reminds them that the day is a special one, different from other days.

Interviews with children and their parents reveal that for many, bedtime is a special time for spiritual sharing.[23] Some parents read a passage from a children's Bible or Bible storybook each night and take time to discuss questions the children raise. Parents pray with each child and sometimes process concerns raised by their son or daughter based on the events of the day. Bedtime rituals give parents opportunities to assure children of the parents' love and God's love for them. In the quiet of their room, many children experience a sense of God's presence. This is more likely when rituals built into the nightly routine focus on God's love and constant presence.

Some families engage in *devotional activities* at other times in the day. This may involve reading a Bible story and singing, acting out, or discussing it. One family allowed the children to take turns deciding what the family would do in the devotional time. Having a special place set up for family worship and lighting a candle as a reminder of God's presence can turn the practice into a ritual, heightening the children's sense of its significance.

During Cathy's growing-up years, her dad traveled a lot with his work, but when he was home he would fix breakfast. When the children were ready to run out the door on their way to school, they paused and their dad briefly prayed for them. You could call it "devotions on the run," but this father wanted his children to begin each day knowing that God was an important part of their life.

Jesus blessed the children who came to him with special words and an accepting, affirming touch. How might we *bless our children?* One grandmother prepared a beautiful blessing for her grandchildren. With appropriate hand motions, she says:

> May the light of God shine over you.
> May the Holy Spirit fill you.
> May the blood of Jesus cover you.
> May you sleep in peace.

23. Research done by Catherine Stonehouse.

May you always know just how much the Lord Jesus loves you.
May you learn to see God, even when your eyes are closed.[24]

Parents may want to write their own evening blessing for their children or prepare a special birthday blessing for each child each year. Many parents make a practice of going into their children's rooms after they are asleep and praying for them. This can be a special time for the parents and an unknown blessing to the child.

The possibilities for nurturing the faith of our children are many, but we face a challenge, the demands on our time. In our busy lives we cannot "do it all"; we must set priorities and make choices. Will we choose to take time for our children and create the rituals and traditions through which their faith and ours will grow?

We have the great privilege of walking with our children on the spiritual journey, but we must remember, "Faith is a gift only God can draw from the human heart. We merely affirm, support, and encourage faith in one another at whatever stage of growth it is expressed. Children must find faith for themselves."[25]

Church and Home: A Team

Who is ultimately responsible for the spiritual care of children? Families are important, but as Herbert Anderson and Susan Johnson remind us, "raising children is a communal activity. Families do not and cannot do it alone."[26] We best serve the next generation when church and parents work together as a team, celebrating the crucial role of parents and the essential support role of the faith community.

Biblical evidence highlights the need for partnership between home and church. Moses' instructions in Deuteronomy were given to the whole faith community. Parents and children were to talk about and live out God's commands and keep the feasts in their home. But they would also

24. A blessing Scottie May prays over her grandchildren. It is her adaptation of a blessing Christina Kang developed from a prayer in Richard Foster's book *Prayers from the Heart* (New York: HarperCollins, 1994), p. xv.

25. Thompson, *Family: The Forming Center,* pp. 69-70.

26. Herbert Anderson and Susan B. W. Johnson, *Regarding Children: A New Respect for Childhood and Families* (Louisville: Westminster/John Knox, 1994), p. 4.

gather for corporate celebrations of the feasts and observe other families in the community living God's laws. The children's faith questions would arise out of family and faith community experiences. In the New Testament we find insights on family life and parenting in Paul's letters to the Ephesians and Colossians. Through these letters Paul equipped the church to give guidance to families (see Eph. 6:1-4; Col. 3:20-21).

Families need the church, but when young parents do not seem to be teaching their children about spiritual matters and values, the church often assumes the responsibility for teaching the faith to children rather than equipping and supporting parents for their indispensable role. Parents need the church, not to do their work for them but to affirm their crucial role in nurturing the faith of their children and partner with them in the task.

What should the church contribute to this partnership? We will look at how the congregation can provide support and equipping for parents, planned instruction and corporate worship opportunities, Christian peer groups, and a place in the extended family, the family of God.[27]

Support and Equipping for Parents

We have seen that some of the most potent spiritual formation takes place through the relationships between children and their parents. The most significant gift the church can give to children is *the spiritual nurture of their parents*. Young parents need a place where they can come to know Christ and grow in their love for God and others, a place of worship where they are renewed in the presence of God and given opportunities to learn more about the character of God and God's ways of integrity, love, and wholeness.

Young adults will be encouraged to take up their task of spiritual nurture in the home when the church affirms and celebrates them as chosen by God for that role and when the church makes covenant with parents to support and guide them as needed, to be there for them. In premarital counseling, when exploring views of the family, pastors can name for the couple the privilege they will have to guide their children on the spiritual journey. Infant baptism or dedication provides another opportunity to articulate and develop understandings regarding the spiritual nurture of

27. These categories are based on plans from the *Youth and Family Ministry Congregational Planning Manual* (Bloomington, Minn.: Youth and Family Institute, 2002).

children. As the pastor and parents prepare for the sacred ritual, they can examine the covenant to be made. They can discuss means to keep that covenant, the privileges, the challenges to be faced, and the resources available to the parents through the church.

Following an infant baptism or dedication, some pastors carry the baby down the sanctuary aisles so that the congregation can look in the face of the child they have promised to support and nurture. This act emphasizes the commitment the congregation is making to support the family. But what if the pastor went one step further and preached a sermon affirming the importance of parents as they walk with their children on the spiritual journey, and calling the congregation to faithfully support young families? The theme of the church-and-home partnership could be woven into other sermons throughout the year, building within the faith community an understanding of this partnership. Pastors also need to help the Christian education leaders of the church understand their role as one of supporting families.

Young parents often need equipping for their role in passing on the faith. Many of them have not experienced the nurture they want to give their children. They may not have known the kind of discipline that could have prepared them to understand God's love, law, mercy, and grace. They do not have memories of parents patiently exploring with them questions about life and God. Look at the practices identified in the section "Family: The Primary Context for Spiritual Formation," and think of the families in your church. What do they need to be able to provide a wholesome context for their children?

Wanting to support young parents, one suburban church in western Canada set up a reception area near the church nursery. Someone was on duty each Sunday morning to welcome parents when they arrived with their baby. That person did not provide care for the infants but focused on getting acquainted with the parents, helping them connect with other young couples and letting them know what resources and activities the church had to offer. Children's ministry leaders listened for the parents' comments and questions and, based on their felt needs, offered workshops on a wide range of topics including nutrition and formative discipline. They identified good books both for the parents and for the children. When a new baby arrived, the coordinator sent a card to the family and followed up with a contact to be sure the family knew of all the early childhood ministries the church offered.

Periodic workshops for parents could be offered to address topics such as age-level characteristics, bedtime rituals, enjoying times with God in the family, "what to do when children frustrate me to death," and other topics identified by the parents. Instruction can be built into a weekly "Mothers' Morning Out," a weekly or monthly men's breakfast, an intergenerational small group, a midweek family night, or a Sunday school class for young couples, to mention only a few possibilities.

Whenever parenting training is provided, it is crucial to stress the difficulty of being a parent. Good enough parenting is not simple; it is challenging, and everyone fails at some points. If our instruction comes across as "Ten Easy Steps to Perfect Parenting" and the young mothers or fathers have difficulty applying those steps, they may become discouraged, believe they can't be good parents, stop trying, and avoid further instruction that would create more guilt for them. But if they know that what they are called to do is hard, they don't feel so devastated when they fail and are more open to trying again.

It is also important to help parents realize that there are many ways to be a good Christian parent. Encourage them to discover the parenting that fits them and their children.

Teaching parents is most effective when they are part of a small group where they can process what they are learning, share their successes and failures, and encourage one another to get up and try again. Each time you offer a parenting workshop, encourage couples to join or continue in a small group. These groups should focus on the whole life of their members, their relationship with God, their spiritual growth, struggles they face at work, the challenges of marriage and parenting, and the resources of God's grace available for all their needs. Such groups, especially if they include a mix of ages and spiritual maturity levels, can become a significant extended family of care and support.

Another excellent means of instruction for parents is family events that model practices to be incorporated into the home. Gather families for an evening of fun. Design the devotions as a time for families to enjoy activities they could use at home. Just before Thanksgiving, Advent, or Lent, let the families experience a new tradition and make what they need to implement the tradition in their home. For example, provide materials for each family to make an Advent wreath, give them ideas for using it, and together enjoy a story and liturgy to launch the Advent season.

Planned Instruction and Corporate Worship

Learning and worship in the home are intimate, beautiful, and formative, but they are not the whole story. In our day, emphasis on the family can be taken to an extreme: for some, family has become an idol, valued above everyone and everything else. Some parents, in their desire not to shirk their spiritual responsibilities for their children, have fallen into the error of believing their children need no one but them. Spiritually healthy families, however, value the faith community and participate fully in it. When Elijah thought he was the only one left who served the Lord, he became very discouraged (1 Kings 19:4, 10). Families need to worship and learn regularly with others to know that they belong to a large family of people who love and serve God.

In the area of instruction, it is helpful for children to hear other adults affirming what their parents have taught them about God and Christian values. Much learning in the home comes through a spontaneous, unplanned "curriculum" that is relevant and powerful. However, there is a place for a planned curriculum designed to help children see the whole story of God and explore topics important to them at certain points in their lives. It is easier for the church to provide the planned curriculum than for most parents to try to develop it for the family.

In classes or small groups at church, children develop friendships with adults and other children that enrich their lives. And in times of crisis, when sickness, divorce, or death strikes the family, the church should be there for the children with love, support, and help with making sense out of what is happening. When crisis comes, children are blessed if they already have warm relationships with their pastor and Christian adults who will walk with them through their dark valley. A larger church may even bring together groups of children dealing with similar crises to support one another.

Christian Peer Groups

Peer friendships are important to children. In many cases if children do not develop friendships with age mates in the church, they drop out during their teen years, when they are old enough to choose whether to attend church.

Children need friends with whom to develop social skills and experiment with launching out beyond the family. As they grow and peer pressure increases, a Christian peer group with wise, caring adult leaders can be a great place to discuss the challenges they face and find courage to stand for what they believe.

The Extended Family of God

In our historical past and in many parts of the world today, the extended family has been an important means of support, nurture, and learning for children and their parents. But most North American families live at a distance from their extended family. The church has greater potential than any other institution for serving as an extended family for isolated nuclear families and singles. And yet very few churches have effectively stepped into that role.

Intentionality and initiative are essential if the church is to be all it can be for families. How do we help a congregation be the family of God for one another? Here are just a few examples.

Weddings and baby dedications or baptisms provide opportunities for making connections. Some churches offer young couples the option of having *godparents or sponsors,* an older couple who will get to know them, plan activities with them, and serve as friends and mentors in this new phase of life. As parents prepare for their baby's baptism or dedication, the pastor could talk with them about selecting godparents or sponsors who will take an active role in the spiritual mentoring of their child. The church could also provide godparents and sponsors with ideas on how to participate in the life of the young family, enjoying and contributing to the spiritual nurture of the child.

Some pastors recruit *mentors* for all the children in confirmation or church membership classes. The mentors attend classes with the children, share their spiritual journey stories, do fun activities with the kids, and continue to take a special interest in "their" child in later years. Sunday school teachers can also set up family-like relationships between children and adults in the church. One fourth-grade teacher enlisted adults as secret aunts and uncles for her students each year. Another class adopted a grandparent whom they visited and for whom they did special things.

Several years ago an international student came to Cathy and asked if she would be willing to do things from time to time with his six-year-old daughter. In his homeland aunts and uncles, grandparents and cousins would surround his children and help to raise them and form them. Now that blood relatives were not present for his child, he took the initiative to provide her with a surrogate auntie.

How could we help people in our churches connect as surrogate families? We might begin with some intergenerational events where people of all ages, married and single, can have fun being together and getting to know one another — in chapter 13 we will discuss ideas for such events. The next step would be to encourage families to adopt an older couple as grandparents, a couple or singles as aunts or uncles, inviting them to share holidays and special events with the family. Older couples could also take the initiative to gather an adopted family into their home. One pastor's wife made a practice, each time her family moved to a new church, of asking God, "Who are the grandparents for our son in this congregation?" As she felt drawn to a particular couple, she would invite them over and begin to get acquainted, and often that initiated a beautiful relationship.

We have been talking about providing rich relationships for families in the church, but it is also important not to overlook children who come to church without their parents. They need to be drawn into the church and be given a sense of belonging to the family of God. Find families, couples, or singles who will take a special interest in these children, inviting them to sit together in the worship service and at church events. Encourage these adult church friends and Sunday school teachers to visit the children in their homes and meet their parents. Seek ways to draw the parents into the family of God. But whether or not they ever come to church, care for the spiritual welfare of their children over the years.

God's Family in a Broken World

One of the harsh realities of our day is that many families are in crisis. In the crisis of divorce, an extended illness, or the death of a family member, it takes all the energy a parent has just to do what must be done. He or she has little emotional or physical energy with which to care for the children. At such times parents and children need the church to be there for them, to be their extended family. The church can provide a surrogate family to care for a ten-year-old boy while his mom and dad are with his sister as she battles cancer in a children's hospital several hundred miles away. When all efforts to save the marriage have failed and a husband leaves, are there close friends from church to sit with the grieving wife late into that first night? As the family of God, do we make sure that the life of the church provides fatherless children with opportunities to experience the friendship and care of godly men? How often do we find a way to lift the burden of the single mother who works full time and tries to be both father and mother to her children? Do we support the single father, regularly inviting him and his children to share a meal with other families? Is there a woman in the church who will help his daughter shop for school clothes?

Often at the time of divorce or death, the church is beautifully present. But very quickly we drift back into our busy routines, assuming the grieving family is "getting over it." Initially the family is in shock, and by the time they begin to feel the full stab of their pain and grief, we have left them to struggle alone.

In the past we too often assumed that children are resilient: "They'll be fine, especially if they have one stable parent." But children need more than one parent; they need an extended family. And they need that family not just at the initial point of crisis but across the months and years. As the family of God, will we take these parents and children into our hearts and love them as our own, with the love of Jesus?

Who is responsible for the spiritual nurture of children, the family or the church? Yes, healthy families, growing in their love for God, bless their children and assist in their spiritual formation. But those families need the support and participation of the church in the nurture of children and parents. The best environment for spiritual growth exists where home and church work together as a team.

Chapter 9

CHILDREN AND STORY

The one who tells the story shapes the society.

PLATO

One of Beth's strongest memories of childhood is curling up in a soft armchair and losing herself in a book. Eventually "from far away across the world" she would faintly hear a voice calling her name. She then had to give up being a princess and "sailed back over a year and in and out of weeks and through a day"[1] to where her mother was waiting for her to wash the dishes.

Stories can be delicious. Good stories nourish the imagination toward goodness. A good story tells the truth — truth about human experience, about enduring values, about what is right and good and worthy. The best stories "affirm honesty, fidelity, and generosity while exposing the deadliness of self-centered, greedy behavior."[2]

"The oldest written description of a storytelling event is found in the Egyptian Westcar Papyrus, dated 2000-1300 B.C.E. In it, the sons of Cheops, the great pyramid builder, entertain their father by telling him tales."[3] No doubt stories had been told in families and communities long

1. Maurice Sendak, *Where the Wild Things Are* (New York: Harper and Row, 1963).

2. William R. White, *Stories for Telling: A Treasury for Christian Storytellers* (Minneapolis: Augsburg, 1986), p. 12.

3. Susan Shaw, *Storytelling in Religious Education* (Birmingham, Ala.: Religious Education Press, 1999), p. 37.

before this time. Storytelling is a universal human activity. Oral and then written stories are found in every culture. They tell the history of a people. They embody the values and mores of the community. They teach, they entertain, they inspire, they encourage, they warn. Indeed, as Plato has said, they shape the society.

Although there are many places to find good stories, the Bible is a distinguished source. Narrative is a dominant form in the Bible. In the beginning there is the creation story. There are stories of kings, queens, prophets, priests, servant girls, midwives, fishermen, young people and old people, rich and poor, wise and foolish people. Then there are the parable gems that delight and inform. Generations of parents and educators have retold to their children the Bible stories they remember from their own childhood. Through the years a limited set of popular Bible stories has been established, with many important stories regrettably being ignored. Storytellers do well to return to the biblical source and rediscover its great wealth of stories.

Biblical stories tell us about God's will, works, and people. The biblical narrative tells us what happened and what happens. We find ourselves and our situations mirrored in the text. We relate to stories because they embody themes that resonate with us. Bible stories are rooted in reality and have the ring of truth.

Consider Daniel and his friends in Babylon (Dan. 1). The Babylonian King Nebuchadnezzar besieges Jerusalem, ransacking the "house of God" and taking some of the vessels dedicated for worship back to the land of Shinar. Along with the religious treasures, people are captured, among them the most promising young Judean men. The king commands that the best of them, the most handsome and those with the most natural ability, be selected to be educated in the Chaldean literature and language. Daniel, Hananiah, Mishael, and Azariah are chosen. It may appear to be a privilege for these four young men to be picked for special training, but they are captives, far from home, and likely have no idea what is going to happen to them.

The first thing that happens is that their names are changed. Their captors find their names strange and unpronounceable, so they start calling them Belteshazzar, Shadrach, Meshach, and Abednego. Their parents had given them names that were especially meaningful. The endings of their Hebrew names, *-el* and *-iah,* link them to the name of Israel's God. So when their names are changed, their identity as followers of God is also challenged.

Many of our students who were born in faraway places have had to learn to answer to a new name. Their name, which had been carefully chosen by their parents and meaningful in the community of their birth, is considered a tongue-twister for the English speaker, so it is changed to a name that is easier to pronounce. The new name often doesn't carry the meaning of the birth name. These students can readily identify with the experience of Daniel and his friends.

The program set up for Daniel, Hananiah, Mishael, Azariah, and the other young people in training includes gourmet meals. The king requires them to eat the same food as he does. Unfortunately, since this food has been offered to idols, for the Hebrews it is defiled — abhorrent. Daniel resolves that he will not eat this food or drink the wine; he approaches the palace master, asking to be given water and vegetables instead. The palace master is reluctant to put his job and life on the line by making an exception for these young men, but finally he agrees to a ten-day trial period. At the end of the trial, the Hebrew young men are healthier than the others.

It is noteworthy that Daniel and his friends do not object to the language, literature, and cultural content of the program. It seems that they receive top grades for their studies, for they end up with significant positions. They must have worked as hard as they could.

Young people can identify with the dilemmas of when to object to something they see as wrong, how to deal respectfully and effectively with authority, and when to dig in and comply with work expectations. Daniel, Hananiah, Mishael, and Azariah are inspiring for their courage and good judgment.

Of course, this is just the beginning of the story. A fiery furnace, raging lions, dreams and interpretation of dreams, prayers and visions follow. Daniel is a hero to emulate. Children need heroes, and Daniel and his friends are inspiring ones.

The connecting points in the story do not need to be pointed out overtly. The listener is wrapped up in the atmosphere and action and emotion of the story. Even if the principles are never talked about directly, the listener is touched by the challenges and courage and faith of Daniel, Hananiah, Mishael, and Azariah.

This chapter will explore reasons for telling stories of God's faithfulness and of the people who follow him. Then we will consider ways to tell great stories.

Why Tell Stories?

Storytelling is a primary tool of the Christian educator. Although stories are generally assumed to be for children, in fact they appeal to people of all ages. This was brought home to Beth one winter night when she joined friends to attend a concert of music and storytelling. Spellbinding stories told by a professional storyteller were interspersed with music from a string quartet. Beth's friends' enjoyment of the evening was a surprise: they had thought they had outgrown listening to fairytales. What became clear is that story is common ground for children, youth, and adults. Story has power to free people of all ages to participate and to draw out meaning. When we are asked to speak to a group that includes a range of ages, the best course of action is to "think story."

We tell stories for multiple reasons. In particular, we tell the stories of Scripture because through them children comprehend the deep truths about God and the world. Through stories they understand realities that they would not grasp through abstract explanations, propositional statements, or theological concepts. Stories touch the heart and mind and inspire us to believe in God and live as God's children. We express our faith through the stories we remember and tell about God. We tell Bible stories because the Scriptures instruct us to, because Jesus told stories, and because they are worth telling. As children come to know the stories of the Bible, they develop their identity as part of the Christian community.

Touching the Heart and Mind

Stories "tickle the imagination. They have a way of sneaking past the defenses of the heart."[4] When a story begins, the atmosphere in the room changes. Restless children quiet down to listen. They enter the story world with its sights and smells and sounds. They relive the struggles and triumphs of the characters. They discover that God is "not far from each one of us" (Acts 17:27).

A good story points to meaning beyond its particular characters and events, for the story tells not just *what happened* but *what happens.* Children

4. Reg Grant and John Reed, *Telling Stories to Touch the Heart: How to Use Stories to Communicate God's Truth* (Wheaton, Ill.: Victor Books, 1990), p. 7.

can find their own dilemmas, their own dreams, mirrored in the lives of the characters. "What is learned in story is not so much information or knowledge in the usual sense but is far closer to wisdom, understanding, or lived truth. Story, then, is a unique medium that both creates and explains experience. The meaning of the story is to be found in experiencing it."[5]

Further, as William Yount claims, "A good story, carried emotionally from speaker to listener by presence, voice, and body language, can connect with listeners in a way that literally alters thought patterns, reorders value systems, and changes behavior."[6]

Expressing Our Faith

For the Christian community, storytelling is a part of worshiping and learning. We listen year after year to the story of God's work in history. When we take Communion, we hear again how Jesus took a cup of wine and a loaf of bread, gave thanks, and shared with his disciples (Luke 22:17-19). At Christmas we retell the thrilling stories of the incarnation of Jesus. As we listen, we worship along with Mary and Joseph, the angels, the shepherds, the wise men.

Hearing and telling the stories of faith reinforces our memories of those stories. At times we have the delight of telling them for the first time to our children.

Belonging to the Community of Faith

Belonging to the Christian community involves knowing the biblical story. John Westerhoff III identifies *affiliative faith* as a critical style of faith that is particularly evident in school-age children. During this time, children in the church come to know the stories of the community — both people's stories and Bible stories. If the stories are compellingly told, children experience a "sense of the awe, wonder, mystery and acts of God in history." They come to recognize and love the biblical story as belonging to them.[7]

5. Shaw, *Storytelling in Religious Education,* p. 56.

6. William Yount, *Called to Teach* (Nashville: Broadman and Holman, 1999), p. 119.

7. John Westerhoff III, *Will Our Children Have Faith?* (New York: Seabury, 1976), p. 95.

Storytelling can be an effective tool for teaching children about what it means to be a follower of Jesus and part of the Christian family.

Reclaiming Lost Memory

Children who do not know the stories of the Bible are at sea when it comes to understanding the art, music, and literature of Western civilization. For example, understanding all of the following requires knowledge of the biblical story: "the patience of Job," "as wise as Solomon," Aslan and the stone table in Narnia,[8] Rembrandt van Rijn's magnificent painting *The Return of the Prodigal Son.*

Biblical literacy is on the decline. People in our society no longer have a common understanding of Bible stories as they once did. Other stories from the popular media are much more familiar. Children are more likely to know about Harry Potter, Luke Skywalker, or the Little Mermaid than Joseph, Queen Esther, or King David.[9]

One of the central roles of the church is to share the rich tapestry of Bible stories with each generation of children. The challenge is to tell the great stories of the Bible in interactively powerful ways that can capture the attention of children who are used to the stories popularized by the media. The stories children love will shape what they believe.

The Scriptural Call to Tell Stories

The social structures of biblical times were very different from those of the contemporary West. The Hebrew people not only lived with extended family but were organized by tribes as they traveled in the wilderness and then settled in the Promised Land. Intergenerational relationships were woven into the fabric of life. This is in sharp contrast to the generational isolation that is typical in much of North America today.

In the midst of the Israelites' communal living, they were given instruction on how to live together. Psalm 78 describes the older generation's responsibility to pass the biblical story on to the younger ones.

8. C. S. Lewis, *The Lion, the Witch and the Wardrobe* (London: Geoffrey Bles, 1950).

9. David A. Hogue, *Remembering the Future, Imagining the Past: Story, Ritual, and the Human Brain* (Cleveland: Pilgrim, 2003), p. 101.

> Give ear, O my people, to my teaching:
> incline your ears to the words of my mouth.
> I will open my mouth in a parable;
> I will utter dark sayings from of old,
> things that we have heard and known,
> that our ancestors have told us.
> We will not hide them from their children;
> we will tell to the coming generation
> the glorious deeds of the LORD, and his might,
> and the wonders that he has done.
>
> He established a decree in Jacob,
> and appointed a law in Israel,
> which he commanded our ancestors
> to teach to their children;
> that the next generation might know them,
> the children yet unborn,
> and rise up and tell them to their children,
> so that they should set their hope in God,
> and not forget the works of God,
> but keep his commandments;
> and that they should not be like their ancestors,
> a stubborn and rebellious generation,
> a generation whose heart was not steadfast,
> whose spirit was not faithful to God. (vv. 1-8)

The psalm instructs that the whole story be told: even the dark or unpleasant stories are to be told to the children, so that they might learn from the mistakes of their ancestors. But the children are also to learn of God's power and saving acts so that they remember his covenant to them.

The book of Deuteronomy is full of instructions in a similar vein. When children ask about God and religious observances, the response should be the story of what God has done:

> When your children ask you in time to come, "What is the meaning of the decrees and the statutes and the ordinances that the LORD our God has commanded you?" then you shall say to your children, "We were Pharaoh's slaves in Egypt, but the LORD brought us out of Egypt with a

> mighty hand. The LORD displayed before our eyes great and awesome signs and wonders against Egypt, against Pharaoh and all his household. He brought us out from there in order to bring us in, to give us the land that he promised on oath to our ancestors." (Deut. 6:20-22)

Although the context into which the Bible was written was different from ours, Christian parents and church communities today have inherited this responsibility of sharing the stories of faith with our children.

Jesus Told Stories

Jesus was a master storyteller. His parables reach beyond the original occasions for their telling and speak to people across the ages and to us today. For example, the stories of the prodigal son and the good Samaritan tell us who God is and what God expects of us more compellingly than a hundred sermons. They are not only poignant stories; they reveal layers of deep meaning.

The Gospel writers record many of Jesus' remarkable stories within their compelling tellings of the story of Jesus' birth, life, teaching, death, and resurrection. As we look to Jesus for direction in teaching people of all ages, we find that becoming skilled at the art of storytelling is fundamental.

Contemporary Sources of Story

Beyond the wonderful stories in the Bible, there are countless other great books to share with children.

Browsing the children's books at a library or bookstore will soon reveal that there are good books and not-so-good books. The important thing is to tell the difference. Some books have shoddy design; many have exquisite design. Some have pedestrian text; many have engaging text. Some have ordinary illustrations; some have extraordinary illustrations. Some have themes of great value; unfortunately, some have themes of lesser value. Those of us who delight in children's books look for the highest level of craftsmanship within all of these dimensions.

How then do we choose books for children, whether Bible storybooks or other storybooks? First, pick a book that looks interesting and start reading it to see if it captures the mind and imagination. Since it is adults who often will be reading the book aloud, perhaps reading it over and over again, it matters whether we like it. Medieval literature scholar C. S. Lewis, author of the Narnia stories, suggests that when adults enjoy a book intended for children, it is an initial indication that this is a good book: "I am almost inclined to set it up as a canon that a children's story which is enjoyed only by children is a bad children's story."[10]

Look for stories that are worth telling, that nurture the imagination toward goodness.[11] Good stories are found in many genres: fantasy, biography, fable, Bible story, and others.

Most children's Bibles use an abridged format. Before investing in a children's Bible or Bible story collection, consider what is included and what is left out or added. Ask what atmosphere is projected by the text and pictures. Do they evoke awe and mystery, epic heroism, whimsical charm, novelistic realism, or sentimental sweetness?[12]

Pay attention to how the story is told. Try reading it out loud and listen for language that speaks clearly to the mind and the heart. If this is a Bible story, consider how carefully the scriptural text is represented. If it is a picture book, note whether the text and illustrations work in harmony to tell the story. Think about both the artistry of the illustrations and how real life is depicted.

Watch for elder, gender, cultural, or ethnic stereotypes. One of the most frustrating things for non-Caucasian Christian families is finding that many Bible storybooks depict Middle Easterners essentially as Europeans. The clothes might be accurate but the skin color and features are not.

Children's enjoyment of books becomes increasingly individual as they get older. In choosing books, consider the children — how old they are, what their interests are. There are so many books available for children that it can be overwhelming trying to decide which to buy or to borrow from the library. Award-winning books are a place to start.

Biographies of people of faith across the centuries and from many places in the world will resonate with older children if they are written in an accessible style. Children should know about some of the remarkable

10. C. S. Lewis, *Of Other Worlds: Essays and Stories,* ed. Walter Hooper (New York: Harcourt Brace Jovanovich, 1966), p. 24.

11. Conversation with Laurel Gasque, Toronto, October 1996.

12. Gretchen Wolff Pritchard, *Offering the Gospel to Children* (Cambridge, Mass.: Cowley, 1992), p. 45.

people in the continuing story of God's work. The list is long but includes Catherine of Sienna, St. Francis of Assisi, George Müller, Susanna and John Wesley, Martin Luther, Amy Carmichael, Dwight L. Moody, Hudson Taylor, George Washington Carver, Harriet Tubman, Corrie ten Boom, Ruby Bridges, Mother Teresa, Billy Graham.

Many Bible storybooks offer compelling presentations of God's creation, covenant, and care. One such book is *Psalm Twenty-Three,* illustrated by Tim Ladwig.[13] The well-loved psalm is interpreted through Ladwig's rich illustrations of urban children living in a neighborhood of danger and temptation. The story begins at home in the morning and ends at home at the close of the day. The children go to school, play with friends, and then come home to a caring extended family. Throughout their day it is evident in the pictures that the Good Shepherd is watching over them. The psalm, thousands of years old, comes alive for city children and for adults meditating on the words and pictures with them.

There are also wonderful books for children that tell the truth more indirectly. A favorite is *The Runaway Bunny* by Margaret Wise Brown with pictures by Clement Hurd.[14] This book has delighted children for more than half a century. It begins thus:

> Once there was a little bunny who wanted to run away.
> So he said to his mother, "I am running away."
> "If you run away," said his mother, "I will run after you.
> For you are my little bunny."

The little bunny proceeds to run away to become a fisherman, a mountain climber, a sailboat, and to join the circus. But wherever he goes, his mother follows and finds him. The story communicates a mother's unfailing love, a reflection of the love that God has for us. This story reminds Beth of Psalm 139:

> Where can I go from your spirit?
> Or where can I flee from your presence?

13. Tim Ladwig, illus., *Psalm Twenty-Three* (Grand Rapids: Eerdmans Books for Young Readers, 1997).

14. Margaret Wise Brown, illus. Clement Hurd, *The Runaway Bunny* (New York: Harper and Brothers, 1942).

If I ascend to heaven, you are there;
  if I make my bed in Sheol, you are there.
If I take the wings of the morning
  and settle at the farthest limits of the sea,
even there your hand shall lead me,
  and your right hand shall hold me fast. (vv. 7-11)

Children's books can enrich our ministry with children, whether we read them to one child or to many. A good book can spark creative ideas for a devotional message for children or be the basis for the design of a whole program.

Good books nourish the moral imagination. They stimulate reflection on our own feelings, conflicts, relationships, character, and commitments. Stories can console us by letting us know that we are not alone in our problems. They can expand our view of the world. They can arouse longing to do what is good and right and inspire us to action. Bible stories, in particular, have the power to ground our children in what is "true, noble, reputable, authentic, compelling, gracious — the best, not the worst; the beautiful, not the ugly; things to praise, not things to curse" (Phil. 4:8 *The Message*).

How to Tell Good Stories

Of course, good stories can be poorly told. Pritchard contends that

> we can rob the (gospel) story of its power by telling it badly, by sentimentalizing or sensationalizing or distorting it, or by analyzing or reducing it to a theological formula, or a lesson to be learned to please the teacher. We cannot rob it of its power merely by telling it too often. It deserves to be told — our children deserve to experience it — over and over again.[15]

Since telling stories is a common everyday activity, we may assume that it is easy to do. The reality is that telling a story well takes hard work, discipline, and practice. Madeleine L'Engle, 1963 Newberry Medal winner

15. Pritchard, *Offering the Gospel,* p. 14.

for her *A Wrinkle in Time*, prods us to take storytelling seriously as a craft: "The storyteller is a storyteller because the storyteller cares about truth, searching for truth, expressing truth, sharing truth. But that cannot be done unless we know our craft, any more than a violinist can play Sibelius's Violin Concerto unless the techniques are there, learned, until they are deep in the fingertips as well as the mind."[16]

What then is involved in mastering the craft of storytelling?

Choosing the Story to Tell

Telling a story begins with deciding what story to tell. Obviously we will choose stories with the listeners in mind. Who are the children? How old are they? What stories do they already know? Are they dealing with a particular crisis in their lives? As we select Bible stories to tell to children, we will pay attention to what the story is about, who the characters are, and what the story tells us about God and what God expects of his people. The storyteller also matters. Stories that resonate with our experience and understanding can be told with special warmth and passion.

Telling a story is always a process of interpretation and selection. We bring our own experience, our own history, and our own spin on things when we tell stories.[17] When we consider which stories to tell, we tend to first think of some of our own favorites. The theme of the story stands out as meaningful to us, the characters are compelling and remind us of people we know, the storyline is exciting or inspiring or challenging. Then it is tempting to keep retelling the stories that are familiar to us to the neglect of others. When that is done, many important stories are left out and the continuity of the greater biblical story is lost.

Does it matter if we give children a patchwork quilt of Bible stories? It is difficult to form a clear picture of how the discrete stories we know fit together in the full narrative of God's work in history. The biblical record spans thousands of years. The challenge is to give our children a more complete narrative than we might have ourselves. We can do this only if we expand our own repertoire of stories. One way to do this is for parents,

16. Madeleine L'Engle, *Story as Truth: The Rock That Is Higher* (Wheaton, Ill.: Harold Shaw, 1993), p. 103.

17. Hogue, *Remembering the Future*, p. 92.

teachers, and children's ministry leaders to take a good biblical overview course. We need to come back again to the Scriptures and discover the stories that we have passed over or never noticed before. Of course the Bible is a big book. It takes a lifetime — at least — to master all the stories that we find there. But we can help our children make a start on the journey, set them on the way of discovering God's story for themselves. This journey will be enhanced if we set out to give children an overview of the full Bible story.

Are there some stories that are not appropriate for children? Although many parts of Scripture are completely comprehensible to children, some stories are beyond the understanding of younger children. In some cases we can reframe the story so that it is meaningful for the child. However, if we end up neutralizing the story by removing all violence, sexual content, or other elements we consider inappropriate, we should conclude that this story should be saved until the child is older.

Ask yourself, *With whom will the children identify in this story?* Using this question as a guide will affect the choice of story, the telling of the story, and the response to it. Consider the well-loved story of the infant Moses. As a baby, he is hidden by his mother in a basket among the bulrushes of the Nile River to protect him from becoming a victim of Pharaoh's edict to kill all Hebrew baby boys. Moses' sister, Miriam, is given the responsibility of watching out for him. Imagine her distress when the baby starts to cry just as Pharaoh's daughter and her attendants arrive at the river to bathe.

To Miriam's surprise, the princess is enchanted with the baby and decides to take him as a son. But the baby keeps crying — he is probably hungry. Miriam is watching and thinking fast. She has an idea. As if she were just passing by, she runs up to the princess and asks, "'Shall I go and get you a nurse from the Hebrew women to nurse the child for you?' . . . So the girl went and called the child's mother" (Exod. 1:8–2:10). This is a thrilling story of the way God protects the one who later would lead the Hebrews from slavery to a promised land.

When children hear this story, with whom will they feel the most affinity? Will it be the baby, his sister, or the princess? Older listeners might identify with the midwives, Shiphrah and Puah,[18] or with the parents of

18. It is noteworthy that the midwives, Shiphrah and Puah, are named but the pharaoh and his daughter are not.

the children. Perhaps some will connect with one character and some with others. Likely everyone will see Pharaoh as the villain. Since the youngest children will likely identify with the infant Moses, the storyteller should pay attention to the things that might concern them if they were left adrift in a basket. The narrator can assure the children that the baby was safe because God was caring for him but also that he might have gotten hungry and hot in the basket. School-age children will likely connect with Miriam, so the storyteller might highlight the weight of the responsibility she felt in caring for her baby brother. Identification with a story creates space for the listeners to learn from the characters' experience as if they had actually participated in the story — which they have, imaginatively.

Preparing to Tell a Great Story

"Those who present an unforgettable story have taken time to prepare an unforgettable story."[19] What preparations do you need to make to effectively tell a great story? The storyteller must make a number of initial decisions. After deciding what story to tell, you must determine how much of it to tell, from whose point of view, and how to present it.

Stories in the Bible are most often concise. Usually just the essential information is given. The language is rich in imagery and rhythm yet spare. Events that took hours or days may be recorded in a few sentences or paragraphs. The stories are in freeze-dried form but can be reconstituted in the telling.

How much freedom does the storyteller have? In telling biblical stories, keep the core of the story intact. Retain the fundamental elements of the plot, the characters, and the atmosphere. Pay careful attention to the details that are mentioned; they are there for a reason. Read between the lines to envision the event. Research in other sources will extend understanding of the particulars of the story's social, religious, and historical context.

With this in place, the storyteller can use his or her creative juices to push the story off the page and bring it to life. Listeners are invited to

19. John Walsh, *The Art of Storytelling: Easy Steps to Presenting an Unforgettable Story* (Chicago: Moody Press, 2003), p. 21.

imagine the sounds, smells, and sights around the event. To explore the feelings of the characters. To consider the problem or situation the characters are facing. To compare the story's dilemma to a dilemma that children might encounter today. Although stories can be told with puppets, costumes, or props, they are most powerful when the storyteller disappears and the listeners see the story unfold in their own mind's eye.

Preparing to tell Bible stories requires analyzing the text. Prayerfully read and reread the text, searching for the most important idea in the story. What is the theme that binds the story together? What do the children you teach need to hear about God in this story? These questions may help you decide where to begin and end the story. Although many Bible stories, like the parables of Jesus, are short, some, like the life and times of Moses, go on for chapters or books. The storyteller must figure out what the first and last scenes of this particular presentation will be.

As you become familiar with the atmosphere, scenes, and characters in the story, you decide the point of view from which the story will be told. Will the voice be that of a narrator or of a character in the story — perhaps a minor character who observes the whole event? The same story will take a different shape when told from the perspective of a different character. The essential story can be lengthened or shortened depending on the audience and the situation.

Rehearsal can make the difference between serviceable storytelling and terrific storytelling. Although storytelling is often freer and more natural when the text is not memorized, the first and last words are worth writing down and remembering. In rehearsal, prepare to tell the story as if you were a radio sportscaster doing the play-by-play of an international soccer game.

Telling the Story

Every telling of a story is a unique experience. It is almost impossible to reproduce exactly. Not only is the story told slightly differently each time, it is also heard in a personal way by each listener.

The way you begin is critical. Give yourself and the children time to get comfortable and focused. The first sentence should make listeners want to hear what happens next. Lengthy introductory comments spend the listener's attention allotment unnecessarily.

Certain practices will make the story live:

- letting the characters describe themselves through their words and actions
- using action verbs
- leaving out unnecessary details
- presenting characters who meet struggles and challenges with strength, courage, and compassion, so that children are given heroes worth emulating
- keeping the outcome hanging in the balance as long as possible to create suspense
- pacing your words, slowing them when the suspense builds, speeding up when the action quickens
- not rushing the story to get to the point; the story gets to the point better than any explanation can
- using pauses and silence
- creating an experience
- ending with an unforgettable statement

Like all good speeches or sermons, a good story has *focus* (a significant idea that binds it together) and *specificity* (unique characters who have particular experiences). The *shape and sequence* are carefully structured so that one scene builds on the next, creating tension up to the climax and resolution. The storyteller has *contextual awareness,* paying attention to how the story is being heard and making adjustments to rekindle any lost attention. A great story *engages the listener* because it offers a new idea, takes a fresh approach, makes us laugh or uses memorable turns of phrase, and is told with passion and conviction.

Responding to the Story

A good story doesn't permit casual observation. It wraps you up in truth and recognition and won't let go. You are there, in the story; your imagination is kindled; you are involved; you interact with truth on a deep and personal level because you are in the story and now the story is in you. Then it's over, and you sit in the embrace of truth. The story is still resonating in the deepest part of you. For the moment, you are still

> because it simply takes some time to "get back." And once you emerge from the story, you are never the same again. That's what stories can do.[20]

Stories can stand on their own without interpretation. Meaning is embedded in the story itself. One of the remarkable things about story is that listeners hear and interpret a story as it connects with their own understanding, experience, and need. For this reason, explaining what the story means may short-circuit its impact for the hearers. As Edith Schaeffer once said, "A sermon is always improved with a story, but a story is never improved with a sermon."

Story is a gift. Telling a story well is offering a gift to God and to others.[21] If we are observant, we will see that many of our children have storytelling talent. We can extend the power of story by offering them opportunities to develop their own storytelling abilities.

20. Grant and Reed, *Telling Stories,* p. 9.
21. Susan Shaw, *Storytelling in Religious Education,* p. 17.

Chapter 10

CHILDREN AND CURRICULUM

Terri loved children and believed in their potential to grasp deep spiritual realities. As a volunteer director of children's ministries for her church, she invested heavily in the children. Every Sunday she taught a class of older elementary children, and most Sundays she led children's worship. Each week she prepared her own lesson for the worship time, wanting to give the children some spiritual "meat."

But Terri was tired and discouraged. No one would help shoulder the leadership of children's worship. People would assist her for a Sunday, but they were sure they could not do what she did and were not willing to try on their own.

Then Terri learned of a curriculum resource designed to give children a time and a quiet place to be with God, to enter the stories of Scripture and meet God there.[1] Excited at the prospect of what the children she loved could experience through this approach, she introduced the curriculum to others in a demonstration session. When potential leaders saw their children engaged in the hands-on, reflective, creative activities of the new approach, they became excited along with her. Seeing that the curriculum plan was packaged in a book with clear instructions for guiding children into this time to be with God, they gained the needed confidence to volunteer for the children's worship team. Tiredness, discouragement, and reticence were transformed into joyful ministry and worship as these

1. The curriculum resource was Sonja M. Stewart and Jerome W. Berryman, *Young Children and Worship* (Louisville: Westminster/John Knox, 1989).

dedicated people of God began using this sound curriculum resource with their children.

Curriculum: What is it, and what role does it play in nurturing the faith of children? In this chapter we will examine understandings of curriculum, components of curriculum, and the curriculum planning process.

Understanding Curriculum

As a group of seminarians left a class, one of them asked his friend, "What was she talking about? What is curriculum?" The friend replied, "It's that book you buy for Sunday school teachers to use." That is a common understanding of curriculum, but not the one the professor had intended to communicate in that class session. Although materials used by teachers are part of any curriculum, they are not the whole.

The word *curriculum* comes from the Latin *currere,* which means a course to be run.[2] Curriculum, then, is a course or journey to be traversed together. Maria Harris sees curriculum as "the entire course of the church's life." Since every element in the life of a church educates in some way, she believes all activities should be considered part of the curriculum.[3] Similarly, John Lynn Carr claims that Christians are formed through the total life of the church, so a church's life is its curriculum.[4] Ted Ward defines curriculum as what happens to people through people in the learning environment.[5] These definitions give a much broader understanding of curriculum than the one held by the student quoted above.

The word *curriculum* carries a variety of meanings. Harris and Carr identify curriculum as *experiences in the faith community.* Curriculum may also refer to *activities intentionally designed to nurture the faith of children.* Ward's definition fits into this second vision of curriculum, but in addition to the experiences intentionally planned for the learning environment, it calls us

2. Maria Harris, *Fashion Me a People: Curriculum in the Church* (Louisville: Westminster/John Knox, 1989), p. 55.

3. Harris, *Fashion Me a People,* pp. 51, 59.

4. John Lynn Carr, "Needed: A Pastoral Curriculum for the Congregation," in *The Pastor as Religious Educator,* ed. Robert L. Browning (Birmingham, Ala.: Religious Education Press, 1989), p. 35.

5. Notes taken in a class taught by Ted Ward at Michigan State University, East Lansing, 1974.

to also consider unplanned interactions that take place. The seminarian's definition, meanwhile, was simply *resource materials*. In this book, *curriculum* is used under the first definition, the experiential big picture of what is involved in teaching and nurturing children. Much of the material in the book's curriculum-planning sections addresses intentionally designed plans for nurture. Teachers' guides and other materials will be referred to as "curriculum resources" or "materials."

Curriculum in History

How important are curriculum plans and resources for the effective Christian instruction of children? What role did curriculum play in past institutions that nurtured the faith of children? A brief review of curriculum's place in the Sunday school provides a glimpse of its importance and the motivations that led to curriculum development.

Within a few years of the Sunday school's founding in 1780, it became apparent that the teachers of these schools needed support.[6] In 1803 the Sunday School Union was formed in London, and by 1805 it had begun publishing curriculum resources: teachers' guides, a catechism in verse, a list of Bible verses, a reading primer, songbooks, and in 1813 the *Sunday School Teacher's Magazine*.

Sunday school began to take root in America by 1785, and it expanded rapidly thereafter. Between 1790 and 1815 the basic resource for religious instruction in Sunday schools was the catechism, a set of questions and answers designed to teach the basics of the Christian faith to children and new adult Christians. At this time the Bible was beyond the reach of most families. In 1816 the American Bible Society was founded, however, and soon the Bible became an affordable book for the common people and an important resource for the Sunday school. Still, no system existed for the study of the Bible in the Sunday school. Sunday school leaders realized that teachers needed a curriculum plan.

In 1872 a committee was appointed to prepare lesson plans that would

6. More information on the history of the Sunday school may be found in James E. Reed and Ronnie Prevost, *A History of Christian Education* (Nashville: Broadman and Holman, 1993), pp. 255-63, and Clarence H. Benson, *A Popular History of Christian Education* (Chicago: Moody Press, 1943), pp. 119-233.

lead students to study the whole Bible in seven years. This first curriculum provided uniform lessons, meaning that students of all ages studied the same Scripture passage each week. Within three years of their publication, 2 million users in nineteen countries were studying these lessons. The number of users increased to 17 million by 1895. Obviously the guidance offered by these curriculum resources was meeting a real need.

It soon became apparent to educators that young children were often not well served by a uniform curriculum. They needed lesson plans designed with their abilities and experiences in mind. Graded Sunday school curriculum resources for children were first published in the early 1900s. However, since the educators developing these first graded lessons accepted the liberal theology coming into prominence at that time, churches that rejected liberal theology also rejected the graded curriculum resources and the educational innovations they contained. These churches placed high priority on the theological content of curriculum.

New curriculum development has frequently come as a response to perceived need. In the late 1800s David C. Cook worked alongside D. L. Moody as he stood on the street corners of Chicago to evangelize. Realizing that the people needed something to help them remember the gospel message they had heard, Cook printed leaflets for them to take home. It was helpful that Cook's father was a printer and made a printing press available. This was the beginning of David C. Cook Publishing, now Cook Communications Ministry International.[7]

Henrietta Mears, a Christian educator in California, believed the needs of preschool children in her church were not being met by uniform lessons. In 1933 she and her staff began developing new Bible-based graded curriculum resources, first for five-year-olds and then for all the children of the church. When leaders in other churches learned about these new resources, they wanted to use them also, and out of this local church endeavor came Gospel Light Publications.[8]

After beginning to publish resources for youth workers in the 1970s, Tom and Joani Schultz recognized a need for children to be actively engaged in Bible learning. They believed curriculum resources that depended heavily on paper-and-pencil responses to biblical teaching were not effective in forming the faith of children. Setting out to provide

7. See www.cookministries.com.
8. See www.gospellight.com.

Sunday school teachers with a new vision of effective teaching and the resources to implement it, they began producing the Hands On Bible Curriculum in 1994 through Group Publishing.[9]

Several denominations currently place a high priority on providing their people with curriculum resources that are consistent with their theological tradition. They continually study the needs of the children in their churches and of the adults who work with them. They develop resources for the Christian formation of children in many different learning settings, regularly refining the materials to better serve the children.

At the turn of the twenty-first century, several large churches began developing their own curriculum resources, making their materials and training for using them available to other churches. Many smaller churches also choose to develop their own curriculum, in the belief that what they design will serve their children better than anything else that is available, or because they do not have funds to purchase curriculum materials.

Throughout history, curriculum resources have been valued for the plan they provide, bringing meaningful order to the study of Scripture. They have also enhanced the effectiveness of teachers, expanding their understanding of the Bible, the learners, and teaching methods that engage the learners. At no other time in history has there been the plethora of available curriculum resources that there is today. They come from many more sources than those mentioned above and in many forms: print, video, CD, and downloads from the Internet.

Surveying today's curriculum world can be overwhelming. Often teachers are allowed to choose any resource they want to use from this vast array. When this occurs, the curriculum experienced by children in the church has no overarching plan, there is no map for the journey, and the children may miss essential learning experiences that could have enhanced their spiritual growth. As Sunday school leaders throughout history have found, there is value in a coherent curriculum plan.

Components of Curriculum

Although the curriculum resources used in teaching have a significant influence on children, it is important to remember that they are just one

9. See www.handsonbible.com.

part of the curriculum and are very limited without the rest. What are some of the elements that make up a church's curriculum for children?

To discuss the forms of church curriculum, Maria Harris turns to the second chapter of Acts.

> "This Jesus God raised up, and of that all of us are witnesses." . . . They devoted themselves to the apostles' teaching and fellowship, to the breaking of bread and the prayers. . . . All who believed were together and had all things in common; they would sell their possessions and goods and distribute the proceeds to all, as any had need. Day by day, as they spent much time together in the temple, they broke bread at home and ate their food with glad and generous hearts, praising God and having the goodwill of all the people. And day by day the Lord added to their number those who were being saved. (vv. 32, 42-47)

In these verses Harris sees "the first Christian community" doing the essential activities of the church and identifies them as the classical elements of the church's curriculum: "*kerygma,* proclaiming the word of Jesus' resurrection; *didache,* the activity of teaching; *leiturgia,* coming together to pray and re-present Jesus in the breaking of bread; *koinonia,* community; and *diakonia,* caring for those in need."[10]

As it was in the early church, so it is today: children as well as adults are nurtured through a curriculum that gives them opportunities to experience the faith community and communion, worship and prayer, to hear the word of God and live out that word. They are formed as they engage in service to others and through teaching and learning. These are essential elements in a faith-nurturing curriculum.

Another way to look at curriculum is to see it as the dynamic interaction of six curricular elements: aim, learner, content, teacher/shepherd, environment, and evaluation.[11]

Curriculum planning begins when we seek answers to several key questions. Why are we providing a curriculum for children? What do we hope will result from what children experience in the church, in classes, clubs, choirs, or intergenerational gatherings? What can be learned best in a particular setting or at a certain age?

10. Harris, *Fashion Me a People,* p. 16.

11. Harold Burgess introduces these categories for analyzing religious education in *Models of Religious Education* (Nappanee, Ind.: Evangel, 2001).

Without clear *aims,* curriculum is directionless and its effect may be negligible or even negative. When those working with children know the aims of the church's ministry with the young, they can intentionally work toward those aims in all they do with the children. Churches often depend on curriculum resources to determine the aims and subject matter content for much of their curriculum. It is important, however, to *decide* which aims we believe God wants the children of our church to be moving toward. Those aims should then guide the planning and evaluation of the total curriculum, including curriculum resources.

Effective curriculum takes into account who the *learners* — the children — are, and it seeks to connect with them and the reality of their lives. The children themselves are part of the curriculum. They each bring their experiences to church, and these influence what they hear and learn. Their responses and relationships with the other children become part of the curriculum for all.

For example, some children seem to enjoy teasing others. When teachers allow that behavior, the tease or bully learns to be mean, and the child being picked on learns that church is not a safe place but a place of rejection and vulnerability. In contrast, children can learn to lovingly accept and encourage those who are often rejected by other peers. By their acceptance of one another they develop empathy and create a safe place for all to ask questions, learn, and grow.

When we select, develop, or evaluate curriculum resources, one of the first questions we tend to ask is, What should we teach? What should the *content* be? What Bible stories will we tell? Will we explore life experiences? If so, which ones? Our thoughts about content generally focus on subject matter and factual learning. However, content includes everything that the children experience in the faith community, including the lives of the adults they get to know, love, and observe. The processes and methods used in teaching also affect what is learned and are part of the content.

Content is very important in the teaching and nurture of children. They need to learn and come to love the stories of God and the people of God. The ways they are taught should lead them into biblical events, to meet God there and to reflect on life. They need a curriculum rich in experiences and interactions with others, giving meaning to the words of the faith and opportunities to ask their questions and share their insights.

Teachers, shepherds, or mentors play an important role in the curriculum. They choose what the children will learn about and experience, and they establish the learning environment. The heart and life of the teacher are also part of the curriculum. Teachers who have a joyous, intimate relationship with Jesus bring a sense of God's presence and love into the ministry setting. Their relationships with the children can demonstrate the meaning of the words they say.

When we think of curriculum as everything that goes on in the church, those appointed to specific Christian education roles are not the only teachers. Pastors and the whole congregation become teachers, contributing to the curriculum.

The *environment* is the context of the curriculum. The welcome, or lack of it, that children feel in the congregation may enhance or undermine the effect of what they experience in age-graded gatherings. Within a class, club, or worship setting, both the physical environment and the relational environment contribute to or detract from learning and nurture. Until strong, accepting, supportive relationships are built, the learning of many children reaches only a superficial level.

Public schools place heavy emphasis on *evaluation* to determine whether or not students are meeting the aims of the curriculum. Most churches, however, invest little time and effort in evaluation. Evaluation begins with establishing aims for the children and ministries of our church. We must know what we intend to accomplish before we can judge how effective the curriculum is.

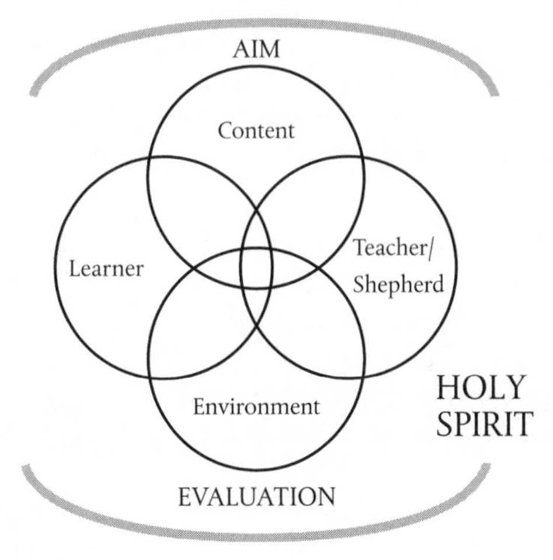

Figure 10.1 Curriculum

One major element of life-changing curriculum is missing from what we have discussed to this point. Only God can change lives, and our curriculum is ineffective unless *God's Spirit* is at work in and through us, our students, and all that we do. Without God at work with us and in us, we might as well be teaching social studies or ancient history. But Jesus promised to send the Holy Spirit to be with us, so we do not work alone.

Curriculum in Many Forms

Several other terms can help us think about the dynamics of curriculum. Maria Harris discusses *explicit, implicit,* and *null curricula.*

The explicit curriculum is what we intentionally present in our teaching. We teach children the Lord's Prayer so that they can participate, reciting it with adults and teens in worship; we enlist both men and women as shepherds to guide small groups of children to communicate that the Christian faith is important to both women and men.

Harris defines the implicit curriculum as "the patterns or organization or procedures that frame the explicit curriculum." Such things as the attitude and personality of leaders, the look of the meeting room — whether it is messy, orderly and sterile, or orderly and inviting — and who gets preferential treatment are part of the implicit curriculum.

The null curriculum is what we leave out, what we ignore. In some settings much of the Bible is null curriculum, since only a narrow selection of biblical events is explored. Cooperation and community are null when competition is the major motivation used in children's ministries. The value of all God's children is missing from curriculum when middle-class white North Americans are the focus of all illustrations and applications. Important teaching takes place through all three curricula.[12]

One last set of definitions is helpful: the *envisioned,* the *enacted,* and the *experienced curricula.* The envisioned curriculum is the plan we prepare, the enacted curriculum is what actually happens in the teaching/learning session, and the experienced curriculum is what the child walks away with.[13] To evaluate the curriculum offered to our children, we must be alert to what is happening through all of these expressions of the curriculum.

12. Harris, *Fashion Me a People,* pp. 68-69. Harris draws her insights from Elliot Eisner, *The Educational Imagination* (New York: Macmillan, 1979), chapter 5, pp. 74-92.

13. From a conversation with Linda Cameron, December 4, 2004.

Curriculum Planning

In the busyness of many churches, curriculum just happens. Children are involved in at least part of the life of the church, and we hope that is good. Program leaders select the curriculum resources they like to use and think the children will enjoy. Others may decide to design their own plans, but as time passes they may find it increasingly difficult to decide on relevant topics and come up with meaningful learning activities. Little attention is given to how all the programs for the young fit together or what may be missing from their curriculum.

God can do good things through curriculum that just happens, but offering children the best requires curriculum planning. One way to approach the planning process is to think through the six components of curriculum discussed earlier: aim, student/learner, content, teacher, environment, and evaluation.

Articulate Aims — Core Values

Before charting a curriculum course or path, we need to know where we are going and what is important for a meaningful journey. The first step in planning, therefore, is to articulate the aims or core values of the church's curriculum. You might begin the process by reflecting on the following questions — questions explored in this book — and jotting down your thoughts.

- What do I believe God wants to accomplish in the lives of the children in our church?
- What does Scripture teach about God's desires — core values — for children?
- What experiences are important to spiritual formation during childhood?
- What do we know about child development and how children learn that suggests aims or values for curriculum?
- What are the values and aims I hear the authors of *Children Matter* articulating?

The process of articulating aims or core values for the church is best done in community. Form a group of two to five persons to explore the above questions with you. You might choose the children's ministry leadership team or a group of teachers and parents who care about what happens with children in the church. A creative public school teacher experienced in curriculum planning could be a helpful resource in such a group. After beginning with your own brainstorming, look at what others have identified as their core values, aims, or key curricular elements.

One day Linda and Scottie were discussing the need for core values to drive the education within faith communities. From that conversation flowed a learning paradigm of core values:

- experiencing encounters with God
- gaining a sense of awe and wonder
- knowing God's character and actions
- knowing and being formed in the character of God's people
- owning an identity as part of the people of God
- engaging in service and mission

Figure 10.2 A Learning Paradigm's Core Values

In figure 10.2 encounters with God are at the hub, with arrows moving toward all the outer circles. These arrows picture the work of the Holy Spirit. Every encounter with God is initiated by God's Spirit, reaching out to draw children — and persons of all ages — into the experience of God's loving, transforming presence. We may design activities intended to accomplish the goals identified in the outer circles, but without God's initiating activity those experiences are spiritually sterile. On the other hand, teachers, leaders, and shepherds can prayerfully set up means for reaching these goals and experience the joy of partnering with God as they facilitate the child's transforming encounters with God.

Any of the outer circle elements may lead to encounters with God. Over time, in fact, the maturing child's encounter with God will grow through experiences and learning in the outer circles. Notice the reference to the child's encounters with God as "transformational." These encounters involve some type of conversion — a new or renewed turning toward the Lord Jesus, a deeper way of allowing Christ to be formed within. This paradigm identifies core values for a curriculum focused on seeing children meet God and be increasingly transformed and conformed to the image of Christ (Rom. 12:2; Eph. 2:8-10).

Earlier in this chapter we saw what Maria Harris values: opportunities for God's people, including children, to participate in

Koinonia (community and communion), engaging in the forms of community and communion;
Leiturgia (worship and prayer), engaging in the forms of prayer, worship, and spirituality;
Kerygma (proclaiming the word of God), attention to preaching and practicing and incarnating the kerygma, "Jesus is risen," in the speech of their own lives;
Diakonia (service and outreach), attention to service and reaching out to other persons, personally and communally, locally and globally;
Didache (teaching and learning), attention to the most appropriate forms of teaching and learning (including schooling) in our own communities.[14]

14. Harris, *Fashion Me a People,* pp. 43-44.

She would claim that curriculum is incomplete without significant experience in each of these five activities.

A well-known megachurch articulates six core values for its ministry with children:

> a) safe physically, emotionally, and spiritually; b) fun place for kids to go; c) child-targeted in our approach to make sure this is the BEST hour in every kid's week; d) relevant teaching that kids can apply to their everyday lives; e) intentional shepherding through group interaction facilitated by volunteers in small groups; and f) teaching the Bible creatively through curriculum programs designed to reach today's kids.[15]

Another list of possible aims is worth considering. Here children will have a number of key experiences:

- experience God and gain language for that experience of God
- know and love the stories of Scripture
- be confident of God's unconditional love
- know Jesus as Savior and friend
- experience being loved and nurtured in the faith community
- grow in understanding God's call to live in just and righteous ways
- join God in serving others

It is critical for every church to wrestle with and articulate its aims or core values for children. The ideas listed here may be helpful in that process but probably do not include some values important in your context. Drawing on these ideas, other sources, and your own thinking, select and articulate a set of core values or aims to guide the development and evaluation of your church's curriculum for children. Then put the values to work. Lead the volunteer teams for all areas of children's ministry in discussing the values or aims, helping volunteers more fully understand the purpose of their investment in children's lives. You may want to print the values on attractive bookmarks to keep them before the staff.

Find ways to make the pastoral staff and the congregation aware of the core values of the church's curriculum for children. This may begin to

15. "Core Values," Willow Creek Church Promiseland brochure, Willow Creek, Ill., 2004.

open their eyes to the fact that they are part of the curriculum that children experience. The ministry values should become the church's compass to keep curriculum planning on course and to guide the assessment of all elements of the curriculum.

Knowing the Learner

Planning meaningful curriculum requires that we know the learners/students. Assumptions about our young students color our thinking on all aspects of teaching or leading them. Unexamined assumptions are not good enough. Curriculum planning needs to begin with an intentional focus on the young learners. Children bring with them a mix of characteristics common to most youngsters their age and an array of unique gifts, interests, and challenges. Understanding the general characteristics of children along the developmental journey assists curriculum planners in selecting subject matter, learning activities, and experiences that are likely to connect with most children.

In addition to a general understanding of children, however, to develop or adapt existing curriculum plans we need to know the specific children in our community, church, and class or group. With this knowledge, caring adults can assist them in connecting with transformational learning.

To focus on the children they serve, a ministry team could spend profitable time discussing questions such as the following.[16]

- Who are the children (students) we serve?
- What gifts do they bring to the spiritual journey?
- What do they most need to receive from God?
- What are their interests and learning styles?
- What challenges do they face?
- What are the socioeconomic and cultural realities of our children?
- What gifts do their families offer to their spiritual nurture?
- What challenges do their families face?

16. These questions tie in with question B in the Frankena Model discussed in chapter 13 ("Specialized Ministries").

- Who are the children we should be serving who are not present in our church?
- What resources are available to help the ministry staff understand better how to serve the children of our church and community (books, videos, local professionals)?

Yet it is not enough to simply know about our children. Based on that knowledge, elements must be built into the curriculum to allow children to use their gifts and to address the challenges of their lives as caring adults point them to God's resources and support them in their struggles.

Selecting Content

Certain essentials of life-forming and transforming curriculum make the content Christian and relevant. We will briefly discuss just four: experiencing God, coming to know and love the whole of God's story, connecting with real life, and experiencing the joy of service.

1. Christian formation requires that children *experience God.* Curriculum planners cannot program this first essential, but we can set the environment and make quiet time and space for children to encounter God. And we can pray that our children will sense God's presence as we meet together.

2. Children meet God as they *come to know and love the whole of God's story.* We are not suggesting that children be taught every verse of Leviticus, the Minor Prophets, and Revelation, but that we make it possible for them to learn the flow of the story from creation through the birth, life, death, resurrection, and ascension of Jesus to the promise of Christ's return. They need to enter the stories and see God interacting with the characters of Scripture to discover God's power, love, justice, mercy, and grace and to understand the character God desires to form in the people of God. Children profit greatly from time to wonder, reflect, discuss, and, as they mature, dig into the meaning of Bible stories.

There is a place for fun presentations of biblical events through puppets and video. These, however, should not be the child's only exposure to Scripture. They should build on the child's firsthand experience with the essence of the biblical stories, simply told, with opportunity to wonder about them and explore the child's questions.

3. Meaningful curriculum *connects with the realities of children's lives.* Although Sunday school teachers endeavor to help children relate biblical material to their lives, often the curriculum for midweek club programs focuses even more fully on guiding children to discover God's plan for living. Through varied activities children learn how to relate constructively with others, love and care for God's creation, and face the challenges and pressures of a non-Christian society.

Many children in our congregations deal with deep traumas — the divorce of their parents, the extended illness or death of a loved one, or abuse, to mention only a few. Where in the curriculum of our churches can children find help and healing for their pain?

4. Followers of Jesus are called to be servants like their Master (Mark 10:43-45). In a self-centered society the curriculum of the church must provide children with opportunities *to experience the joy of service.* Through such a curriculum, children can early learn the joy of service, making it a habit of life.

A one-hour-a-week program will have difficulty providing children with all these essentials. Many churches offer several ministries for children — Sunday morning or evening learning hour, worship, clubs, and choirs — all of which can contribute elements to the curriculum.[17] When the whole life of the church is planned as curriculum, children find many more opportunities to explore these essentials. So far in this chapter we have not explored the curriculum of the home; however, the home offers great potential for experiencing the essentials of faith formation.

Deciding on Curriculum Resources

This chapter begins with an account of a worship team that was equipped to offer meaningful worship for their children through the use of a published resource. In chapter 13 you will read accounts of learning experiences that unfolded through curriculum plans designed by members of local churches. How does one decide which approach to take? Considering some of the strengths and weaknesses of each type of curriculum may help in the decision process.

17. Ideas for a wide range of ministries are found in chapter 13, "Specialized Ministries."

Strengths of prepared curriculum plans:

- They provide a plan of action, a map to follow.
- Much of the intensive curriculum planning work is done for the church.
- They offer a carefully designed sequence of biblical material and important concepts to be explored.
- Materials are designed to lead children into the basics of the faith, taking into account what is best explored in the preschool, younger, and older elementary years.
- Activities appropriate for each age level are presented.
- They give teachers a variety of learning activities crafted to facilitate leaning and formation, in many cases endeavoring to connect with all learning style preferences.
- Resources often contain insights from a team of persons with children's ministry experience, understanding of how children learn, and knowledge of the Bible and theology. The materials Terri's team used, for example, had been field-tested in thirteen churches prior to publication and refined based on their feedback.
- Many publishing houses offer options — resources for different settings and learning formats.
- Some resources are designed to support a certain theological perspective.
- They provide busy teachers with a place to start, a plan to adapt to the specific needs of the children in their classes.
- They offer new and inexperienced teachers plans and methods to help them implement theories they have never heard of.

Weaknesses of prepared curriculum plans:

- Not all printed resources are strong in the ways listed above. Some are based on inadequate understandings of teaching and formation. They may contain uncreative ideas or a theology you would not want to teach.
- Teachers may depend too heavily on the printed resources, simply teaching materials rather than knowing and facilitating the learning of their students.
- Teachers may use only the paper-and-pencil resources, not taking the time to develop the more active, creative ideas suggested.
- Churches — and teachers themselves — tend to think the "Leader's

Guide" and "Resource Packet" are all teachers need, and teachers are left on their own to sink or swim, to bore the children or lead them in exciting learning.

Strengths of curriculum plans designed within a local church:

- Creative planners have the satisfaction of designing curriculum that they believe is meaningful for their children and contains the elements they see as essential for the children's spiritual formation.
- They creatively use the space available and the special gifts of leaders, teachers, and children.
- Designers tend to major on experiential learning.
- Without paper-and-pencil resources to depend on, the staff is more willing to engage the children in a wide range of experiential activities.
- A team guides the learning, allowing persons to work in areas of giftedness and invest the amount of time and energy that is possible for them.
- Often these approaches are broadly graded, allowing the volunteers for all school-age children to pool their resources and work together.
- The special needs of a church's children and topics no one else seems to care about can be addressed through locally designed curriculum plans.
- Churches may choose what portion of their curriculum to design themselves.

Weaknesses of curriculum plans designed within a local church:

- Designing curriculum requires leaders with creativity and planning skills that are not present in all churches.
- Designing learning units for a three- to six-year journey calls for persons with a good grounding in and understanding of children, the Bible, and theology. It is also time-consuming and creatively demanding.
- In some cases, those who have great ideas for fun experiences do not understand the essentials of the child's spiritual formation.
- Innovative approaches often falter when the key designer moves or can no longer give leadership.

A third alternative is possible. A church may adopt a variety of approaches to the design and use of curriculum resources. Leaders may find materials that perfectly fit the needs in one area of their curriculum, while another ministry may choose to use prepared curriculum materials as its map and idea source but adapt them significantly. In another area of children's ministry the team may decide to develop its own curriculum plans and resources. This varied approach will work well if those overseeing each area of the curriculum keep in mind the core values and the curricular essentials they are committed to providing for the children of their church.

Empowering Teachers, Shepherds, and Leaders

The vast majority of adults who work with children in the church genuinely love children and enjoy seeing them learn and grow in their relationship with Jesus. But how many of them see *themselves* as a significant part of the curriculum that forms the children of their church? Curriculum is more effective when teachers grasp the significance of their role. Children's pastors can help the volunteer staff realize that curriculum is "what happens to people, through people, in the learning environment" and that they are key influencers in the formation of children.

Because of the significant role teachers play, curriculum planning must include attention to their support, encouragement, and equipping. Their contributions are greatest when they are being nurtured spiritually and know that their ministry is valued by the church. Many adults enjoy being part of a team whose members have fun and encourage one another as they serve. The effectiveness of such teams will be enhanced as they take time to pray for their ministry and one another.

During a graduate course, Ted Ward burned into the thinking of his students the principle that "curriculum change is people change." One afternoon Cathy was touring a church in California. As her guide led her into one department room, she commented, "These teachers went to a workshop last fall and decided they needed new curriculum resources, but nothing has changed." If the *people* have not changed, they continue to teach and relate to students in old ways, even if the curriculum resources and the format have been changed.

In *Diffusion of Innovations* Everett Rogers identifies three kinds of knowledge necessary to bring about long-term change: awareness knowledge, "how to" knowledge, and principles knowledge.[18] Preparing our

18. Everett M. Rogers, *Diffusion of Innovations,* 3rd ed. (New York: Free Press, 1983), pp. 164-68.

staff for curriculum change calls for leading them to become aware of the need for change, equipping them with the how-to skills required to minister effectively with the new approach, and helping them to understand the principles, core values, and aims behind new curriculum.

For broad, long-term change to occur in the curriculum for children, changes must be understood and owned by the whole children's ministry team and the leaders of the church. New approaches may be pilot tested by one teacher who has a vision for the desired innovation, or by the ministry team for one program or event. Trying out a new paradigm on a small scale gives opportunity to learn from the experience and refine the approach for one's church. It also provides a setting in which others can see the innovation in action and observe its effectiveness. This permits the team members to understand the new way of doing ministry and opens up their willingness to change.

If church leaders are to own and support major changes, they must be informed about the innovation being tested. Help them understand the need for change and, using illustrations from the pilot test in your own setting, the effectiveness of the new paradigm. Significant change requires the support of not just children's ministry leaders but also the church's leaders.[19]

Attention to the Environment

The physical and relational environment influences learning dynamics and thus is part of the curriculum. Messy rooms, and even rooms that are orderly but contain irrelevant toys and visuals, distract from learning.

The ordering of space can communicate certain expectations to children. For several years Cathy led children's worship in the room where some of the children also met for choir and Sunday school. Before church began, the worship leaders moved the Sunday school furniture to a corner, set out a circle of carpet squares on the floor, and moved in the children's worship materials. As the children reentered the room, they knew they were in a different space with different expectations and anticipated

19. Your effectiveness as a children's ministry leader will be greatly increased as you grow in understanding of how to lead change and how the systems within a church interact when one of them undergoes change. A helpful resource is Rogers's *Diffusion of Innovations.*

different experiences and responses. That change in the physical environment was a necessary part of the worship curriculum.

The space available for children's ministries influences the format of the curriculum. Often one of the challenges in curriculum innovation is finding creative ways to use available space to accommodate new forms of teaching and learning.

Another crucial aspect of curriculum planning is providing for the building of significant relationships between children and adults and among peers. The ratio of children to adult volunteers, whether or not time is provided for sharing and interaction, and the adults' ability to relate warmly with children all affect the relational environment and whether or not the curriculum communicates a sense of belonging to the children. Children also sense and respond to the environment of the church as a whole.

Planning for Accountability

Evaluation of spiritual development involves more than finding out what facts children know; it is not simple. However, we do not want to waste precious time inflicting ineffective programs on children. We do not want to discover, when teenagers drop out of church, that as children they never had a sense of belonging to the church. Effective ministry calls for regular evaluation of our curriculum and willingness to make changes that enhance children's learning and spiritual growth.

Regular review of the curriculum is part of good curriculum planning. Every few years, have the leadership team for each area of children's ministry evaluate their envisioned curriculum — what they intend to do and teach — in light of the children's ministry aims or core values. Does the envisioned curriculum capture aspects of the core values, or are adjustments needed to bring it more in line with them? Ask the ministry teams to annually consider the question, How does the actualized curriculum compare with the one envisioned?

Leaders who are present to support volunteers during their ministry time can observe what is actually taking place and judge whether the intent of the curriculum is being lived out. Encourage ministry leaders, teachers, and shepherds of small groups to be continually looking for evidence of the real curriculum. How are the children responding? What concepts and commitments are they making their own? Is there evidence that they are growing in their love for Jesus and their commitment to live in God's ways?

Life in the Congregation: Curriculum for Children

At the beginning of this chapter we defined curriculum as "the entire course of the church's life," or "the total life of the church." So far we have focused mainly on curriculum in the context of children's ministries. How might we begin to influence the congregation more broadly, for the sake of the children?

As we saw, John Carr believes that "the whole life of the church is the school for faith," and if this is so, "then the pastor becomes pivotal for what kind of school it is."[20] Many pastors care deeply about children and even hire staff members to work with them; however, few seem to be aware of how the curriculum of the whole church influences the young. Most pastors need intentional, ongoing teaching and guidance from the children's pastor or other concerned children's workers if the curriculum of the whole church is to become what is best for children.

Regular communication between the pastor and the children's pastor — or volunteer children's ministry leader — sets the stage for influencing the pastor's perspective and the view of the congregation regarding children. In some cases the pastor will establish a regular pattern of meetings; in other situations the children's pastor or leader will need to request these regular times of communication.

Curriculum can be the topic for some of these meetings. Explain and discuss with the pastor the understandings of curriculum presented in this chapter. Lead the pastor, and possibly the pastoral team, to reflect on what children may be learning through the explicit, implicit, and null curricula of the church. As the core values or aims of the children's ministries are developed, these should be discussed with the pastor and other church leaders, considering in what ways the life of the church encourages or hinders the progress of children toward those aims.

With the pastor, explore ways of leading the congregation to understand the importance of the total life of the church in the spiritual formation of children. The pastor might be willing to preach a sermon, or even a

20. Carr, "Needed: A Pastoral Curriculum," p. 36.

sermon series, on nurturing the faith of children, reminding the congregation of God's plan for the church to be a faith-forming curriculum for all ages. Through this sermon, and possibly by placing notes in the church bulletin, newsletter, or website from time to time, encourage adults and teens to reach out to children and give suggestions for how to do that.

In most congregations the mission of being the faith-forming curriculum for children will not be taken up and understood instantly. But with God's help and with thoughtful planning and teamwork, we can see congregations move in that direction.

PART III

HOW WE DO IT MATTERS

Chapter 11

IN WORSHIP

Ascribe to the LORD the glory of his name;
worship the LORD in holy splendor.

PSALM 29:2

New Year's night, 2003, some of Scottie's family, including five grandchildren ages five to twelve, went together to a monthly Taizé service in a nearby suburb. Scottie and her husband had been attending these ecumenical prayer services for about three years, but this was the first time family had come along. During the service these normally active, restless, busy children became calm and still without parental intervention, melting into comfortable positions, gazing at the beauty of the church, enjoying the gentle pacing of the service and the repetition of the simple prayer songs. Knowing that children would be invited to pass the light of Christ throughout the congregation, using thin taper candles, made them eager for this point in the service. The ten minutes of silence that followed was no problem for them in this environment. When the hour-long service ended, the grandchildren were in no hurry to leave but moved forward to sit near the altar, gazing at the symbols and the flood of light from amassed candles.

It is not likely that the children would have used the word *worship* to describe what they were experiencing, but their expressions and actions gave evidence of a sense of peace and wonder. They appeared to be worshiping the God whose presence they seemed to sense. Watching them made Scottie wonder what worship is really like for children. She wondered in what way this New Year's evening experience with hundreds of other people enabled them to experience the numenous.[1]

This chapter looks at worship and children's ability to engage in this activity in ways that bring great pleasure to our God. We will consider children's worship experiences in various church contexts and evidence of children's spiritual experiences. The chapter concludes with examples of various worship experiences with children as well as suggestions to include children in responsible ways in corporate worship.

Worship Is a Verb — and a Noun

Worship is a multifaceted, complex concept. Many aspects of worship involve action, requiring verbs to describe what is taking place. Other perspectives of worship identify encounters or experiences with God. These are nouns.

The dictionary definition of *worship* includes action terms like "bow low," "prostrate oneself," "pay honor or homage," "show reverence," "kneel down." Some of these actions are not commonly experienced in much contemporary worship in our culture; it takes some thought to realize how these actions might look. It seems that Scottie's grandchildren were showing reverence to God during the Taizé prayer service; they were honoring him. They also may have been telling him what was in their heart.

The Old Testament's first use of the word *worship* occurs in Genesis 22:5, when Abraham and Isaac are going up Mount Moriah because God has asked Abraham to sacrifice his son there. Abraham tells the two servants with them to wait while Abraham and Isaac go ahead *to worship*. After that lone occurrence in Genesis, the word *worship* and its derivatives occur scores and scores of times throughout the biblical text. It is very evident that worship is important to God and to God's people.

The book of Exodus is replete with detailed descriptions of God's expectations for worship — especially regarding the tabernacle, the special space where the people of Israel gathered to celebrate God's goodness.

1. *Numenous* is a term used by Rudolf Otto in *The Idea of the Holy: An Inquiry into the Non-rational Factor in the Idea of the Divine and Its Relation to the Rational* (New York: Oxford University Press, 1958) to describe a spiritual experience.

Even though the Bible does not provide a concise definition, Scripture is full of examples of worship and the actions involved in it. Consider the portion of 1 Chronicles 16 where David speaks praise to God for enabling the Ark of the Covenant to be returned to Jerusalem:

> O *give thanks* to the LORD, *call on* his name;
> *make known* his deeds among the peoples.
> *Sing* to him, sing praises to him,
> *tell of* all his wonderful works.
> *Glory* in his holy name;
> let the hearts of those who seek the LORD *rejoice*.
> *Seek* the LORD and his strength;
> *seek* his presence continually.
> *Remember* the wonderful works he has done,
> his miracles and the judgments he uttered. . . .
>
> *Ascribe* to the LORD, O families of the peoples,
> *ascribe* to the LORD glory and strength.
> *Ascribe* to the LORD the glory due his name;
> *bring* an offering, and *come* before him.
> *Worship* the LORD in holy splendor;
> *tremble* before him, all the earth. . . .
> O *give* thanks to the LORD, for he is good;
> for his steadfast love endures forever.
>
> *Say* also:
> "Save us, O God of our salvation,
> and gather us and rescue us from among the nations,
> that we may give thanks to your holy name,
> and glory in your praise."
> Blessed be the LORD, the God of Israel,
> from everlasting to everlasting."
> Then all the people *said* "Amen!" and *praised* the LORD.
> (vv. 8-12, 28-30, 34-36)

Many of these same verbs appear in the Psalter, in chapters 95, 96, 100, 105, and 106 as well as in other psalms. Psalm 148 is entirely about praising the Lord. All creation is to praise him. All God's people are to participate in this praise, according to verse 12 — young men and maidens, old men *and children.*

A beautiful picture of worship is painted in the apostle John's vision in the book of Revelation:

> Then I looked, and I heard the voice of many angels surrounding the throne and the living creatures and the elders; they numbered myriads of myriads and thousands of thousands, singing with full voice:
>
> "Worthy is the Lamb that was slaughtered
> to receive power and wealth and wisdom and might
> and honor and glory and praise!"
>
> Then I heard every creature in heaven and on earth and under the earth and in the sea, and all that is in them, singing,
>
> "To the one seated on the throne and to the Lamb
> be blessing and honor and glory and might
> forever and ever!"
>
> And the four living creatures said, "Amen!" And the elders fell down and worshiped. (5:11-14)

Frederick Buechner describes worship this way:

> To worship God means to serve him. Basically there are two ways to do it. One way is to do things for him that he needs to have done — run errands for him, carry messages for him, fight on his side, feed his lambs, and so on. The other way is to do things for him that you need to do — sing songs for him, create beautiful things for him, give things up for him, tell him what's on your mind and in your heart, in general rejoice in him and make a fool of yourself for him the way lovers have always made fools of themselves for the one they love.[2]

According to Buechner, service to God is an essential component of worship. One way that is done is by serving others, something even young children can do. Another way to worship or serve God is to do things that

2. Frederick Buechner, *Listening to Your Life* (San Francisco: HarperCollins, 1992), p. 182.

show our love for him or that display his glory. These are also things children can do through appropriate music, art, liturgical dance, and drama.

The Significance of the Verbs of Worship

When we focus on the verbs of worship, it helps us discern the abilities of children to participate in acts of worship: give thanks, call on him, make him known, sing to him, glory in him, rejoice, remember, bring offerings, praise. How many of these are children capable of doing and at what age? Even little ones — two- and three-year-olds — can sing, praise, and give thanks. They also can show reverence on their own.

Recently four-year-old Trevor chose to spend time in solitude in the prayer corner, a curtained-off area of the church's classroom for fours and fives. After he sat quietly in the lone chair for several minutes, his little body showed under the curtain. He was on his knees with his face to the floor and maintained that posture for some time. All told, for about eight to ten minutes he was prostrate in what appeared to be an act of worship of God, even though he was unable to articulate what he was doing. If given the opportunity and appropriate environment, older children who are nurtured in the faith are able to act in all the ways identified earlier as well.[3]

In scriptural accounts, children are often involved in the verbs of worship. Here are some passages describing their actions of hearing, standing, rejoicing, and shouting:

- Joshua 8:34-35: Joshua reads all the words of the law, the blessings and the curses, to the whole assembly of Israel, including women and children.
- 2 Chronicles 20:13: All the men of Judah, with their wives and children and little ones, stand before the Lord.
- Nehemiah 12:43: Women and children rejoice because God has given them great joy.

3. Current usage of the term *worship* often connotes music or singing. In settings for people of all ages these phrases are common: "worship leader," "worship team," "now it's time for worship" (meaning singing). We must ask what implicit lessons might be learned from this language. Might the breadth of meaning of worship be diminished by this narrow usage?

- Matthew 21:15-16: Children shout in the temple area, "Hosanna to the Son of David." Jesus hears them and quotes Scripture: "From the lips of children and infants you have ordained praise."

We need to ask: How do the verbs of worship involve our children? What place are we giving to children when our faith communities gather to worship our God? Do we see children actively involved in corporate worship as the Israelites in Scripture did? Do our congregations welcome children and enable their full participation in worship? Later parts of this chapter will focus on ways to equip congregations as well as parents to provide opportunities for children to participate fully in the verbs of worship.

Children's Encounters with God — the Noun of Worship

During fall 2003, Scottie and three graduate students conducted a study of young children's responses in an environment that had been intentionally prepared to help them worship or to encounter God. Every week fifteen to twenty four- and five-year-olds focused on a different attribute of the Good Shepherd as he relates to the sheep in his flock, based on John 10. Symbols were used: a special candle designated as the Christ candle and figures and art of the Good Shepherd.

For the most part these young children could not verbalize what was happening within them, but their actions and attitudes spoke volumes. Scottie and the students watched the children respond with an increasing ability to be calm and reflective, often choosing to interact on their own with the story of the Good Shepherd. The children appeared eager to enter this specially prepared space for two hours each Wednesday morning while their mothers attended a women's Bible study. Here the noun of worship intermingled with worship's verbs.

Like Trevor, five-year-old Conrad chose to spend time in the prayer corner one day. Conrad sat quietly for five or six minutes. When he emerged, he said, "God touched me." A leader asked him what he meant. He replied, "I don't know what happened. I just know that God touched me."

Teresa, also five years old, firmly declared that this special time was not like her Sunday morning class: "This is God's class."

Week after week the children spent up to forty minutes of the morning responding to the story through various art forms, solitude, and retelling the story. Their work often expressed deep reflective connections.

According to C. Ellis Nelson, a primary image of "god" is established in very young children by the end of their third year.[4] The toddler "carries on a conversation" with this "god," who is initially formed by the child through interaction with the parents. She may be fond of this "god," or she may fear or dislike "god." If a parent dies or abandons the family, the child may blame "god." By five or six the child may be able to speak of this "god." This image is significant for children of this age, more than faith statements they may be taught.

Others see the child's connection to God as less defined by the parents. Walter Wangerin in the prologue to *The Orphean Passages* uses poetic language to describe a young child's experience with the God of Christian faith:

> Who can say when, in a child, the dance with God begins? No one. Not even the child can later look back and remember the beginning of it, because it is as natural an experience . . . as the child's relationship with the sun or with his bedroom. And the beginning, specifically, cannot be remembered because in the beginning there are no words for it. The language to name, contain, and to explain the experience comes afterward. The dance, then, the relationship with God, faithing, begins in a mist.[5]

Sofia Cavalletti relates a three-year-old's experience. This child was growing up in an atheistic home in which no one ever spoke of God.

> One day she questioned her father about the origin of the world: "Where does the world come from?" Her father replied, in a manner consistent with his ideas, with a discourse that was materialistic in nature; then he added: "However, there are those who say that all this comes from a very powerful being, and they call him God." At this point the little girl began to run like a whirlwind around the room in a burst of joy, and exclaimed: "I knew what you told me wasn't true; it is Him, it is Him!"[6]

4. C. Ellis Nelson, "Formation of a God Representation," *Religious Education Journal* 91, no. 1 (1996): 22-39.

5. Walter Wangerin, *The Orphean Passages* (Grand Rapids: Zondervan, 1986), p. 20.

6. Sofia Cavalletti, *The Religious Potential of the Child* (New York: Paulist, 1983), p. 31.

Psychologist/theologian James Loder, supporting the latter view, articulates the difference between a view of God shaped by parents and one that is not. He stresses how important it is "to make the crucial distinction between a person whose god is created out of the self and parental images and one whose image of God is derived from *an actual encounter* with the living God to whom humans do not give birth."[7] When a child comprehends God only from human images, that comprehension "deprives the spirit of the person of the transcendence and the 'beyond-one's-self' toward which it is drives. Worship of one who is truly other is cut off," and the spirit of the person "is turned back into its own imagination where 'god' becomes at best an aid to social adjustment."[8] If Loder is correct, absence of transcendent, divine images of God may ultimately lead to deforming the spirit or soul of the child, although Cavalletti's story indicates that is not always the case. It may also be true that *both* human and divine encounters influence the formation of the child's perception of God.

Loder further discusses the implications of the spirit of the child relating to the Spirit of God. "It adds up to the developmental origins of an act of worship. Rather than being driven by primordial lust and violence, development is driven by the human spirit toward the worship of God, an expression of the highest form of human behavior."[9] Cavalletti writes that the "language" of the child engaging in spiritual realities "is often composed of actions and interior attitudes more than words."[10] She has noted that these actions and attitudes recur in children in widely different contexts and cultures, often engaging children intensely even when something presumed to be more appealing is also available.

The study of four- and five-year-olds referred to earlier in this section seems to affirm Loder's view. Creating a special environment to enable children to experience God, the researchers were able to develop appropriate liturgies, rituals, and symbols that might bring the divine alongside the child even though this study was taking place in a church that does not use symbols or follow an established liturgy. Symbols, like a Christ candle to remind children that Jesus is present and is the light of the world, are more easily and richly grasped by children than are metaphors. Rituals, such as

7. James Loder, *The Logic of the Spirit* (San Francisco: Jossey-Bass, 1998), p. 169, emphasis added.

8. Loder, *Logic of the Spirit,* p. 169.

9. Loder, *Logic of the Spirit,* p. 169.

10. Cavalletti, *Religious Potential of the Child,* p. 37.

the way each child is welcomed and the way the group prays and eats together, help children sense continuity and familiarity. Liturgy, literally the work of the people, prepares children for Spirit-to-spirit encounters.

Scottie's team developed liturgies for the morning, including music in which the adults and children made graceful motions to God; preparation for the story presentation (the "sermon"); and blessings to prepare the children to depart for home. The components were repeated each week. The children grew to anticipate and welcome the repetition. G. K. Chesterton has delightful insights regarding this love of repetition:

> Because children have abounding vitality, because they are in spirit fierce and free, therefore they want things repeated and unchanged. They always say, "Do it again"; and the grown-up person does it again until he is nearly dead. But perhaps God is strong enough to exult in monotony. It is possible that God says every morning, "Do it again" to the sun; and every evening, "Do it again" to the moon. It may not be automatic necessity that makes all daisies alike; it may be that God makes every daisy separately, but has never got tired of making them. It may be that He has the eternal appetite of infancy; for we have sinned and grown old, and our Father is younger than we.[11]

Referring to theologian Wolfhart Pannenberg, Loder identifies the significance of the context of worship for the child: Christian liturgy is sacred play. He describes worship as a "creative response" — a response by the remarkable human spirit that the whole created world is a daily gift from God. "This drive is a longing that anticipates but does not yet know the Face of God until it is revealed in the image of God in Jesus Christ."[12] This is how children have encounters with God: Spirit to spirit.

Worship and Insights from Neuroscience

It may seem strange to find a section on neuroscience in a chapter on children's worship, but remarkable technological developments in recent

11. G. K. Chesterton, *Orthodoxy: The Romance of Faith* (New York: Doubleday, 1959), p. 60.

12. Loder, *Logic of the Spirit*, p. 170.

years have brought physiological findings that have led scientists to make some fascinating relevant hypotheses. For decades the functions of the hemispheres of the brain have been common knowledge. The left hemisphere functions rather analytically and contains the speech center; the right brain operates more analogically, allowing creative expression. In recent years scientists have realized, however, that all parts of the brain function far more interdependently with greater interconnectedness than once thought. For some fifty years a unique role of a third area of the brain, the limbic system, has been recognized — regulating emotions, feelings about memories, value judgments, and attachments to people. The function of this "third" brain or limbic system is less familiar to people in ministry with children. If the understanding of the limbic system is valid, the implications for ministry are significant.

Of particular interest for Christians is an observation made by neurologist Antonio Damasio, chair of the neurology department at the University of Iowa, that moral behaviors such as compassion have emotional grounding in the limbic system as well as other parts of the brain.[13] The interworkings of the brain have relevance for those in ministry, since one of ministry's goals is obedience to biblical mandates.

Some neuroscientists see a connection between the limbic system and religious experiences. According to Loder, the limbic system is in charge of regulating and distributing emotions. In complex ways it unifies messages that come through the right and left hemispheres when passion is present, as is often the case in religious experiences. Neurologically speaking, the limbic system enables mystical visions to be transforming.[14] Neuropsychologist Rhawn Joseph says boldly, "The limbic system may well be the seat of the soul or may serve as the neural transmitter to God."[15] This view is supported by Andrew Newberg, Eugene d'Aquili, and Vince Rause in their work *Why God Won't Go Away.* They studied the spiritual experiences of deeply religious people and found that these experiences were associated with observable neurological activity. The researchers hypothesize that there is "a link between mystical experience and

13. Antonio Damasio, interview, www.harcourtbooks.com/authorinterviews/bookinterviews_damasio.asp#top, accessed May 20, 2004.

14. Loder, *Logic of the Spirit,* p. 58. A mystical experience may be defined as a conscious relation with the Absolute.

15. Rhawn Joseph, "The Limbic System and the Soul: Evolution and the Neuroanatomy of Religious Experience," *Zygon* 36, no. 1 (2001): 105-35.

observable brain function. In simplest terms, the brain seems to have the built-in ability to transcend the perception of an individual self."[16] They place their subjects' spiritual experiences on a continuum from deep mystical encounters to more common uplifting moments while praying or singing a hymn.

Jerome Berryman's extensive work with young children and their spiritual development has made him aware of the need to recognize nonverbal limbic responses as well as verbal neocortex responses. In Berryman's words, "falling in love [with the Lord Jesus] through grace" happens through the limbic system, whereas the experience is articulated through the left hemisphere of the neocortex.[17]

Since the onset of rationalism a couple of centuries ago, there has been an emphasis on *speculative* knowing — a process of thinking about what is to be known. In the church this would mean learning *about* God. In recent years some scholars in religious education are seeing the need to recognize *connatural* knowing — an innate or inborn form of knowing. This form of knowing comes through emotions and relational responses through the limbic system rather than neocortex-oriented speculative knowing. These scholars advocate letting young children *know God* initially rather than focusing on helping children know *about* him.[18] They call for opportunities for children to experience God.

One researcher, Karen-Marie Yust, writes that children must be permitted to encounter the living God directly. Adults must *wonder* with children about personal spiritual experiences and their faith tradition's understanding of who God is rather than merely instructing them in faith. "Children's faith formation is fundamentally about nurturing their relationships with God, and in all aspects of children's ministries, we would do well to let children meet God face to face."[19]

16. Andrew Newberg, Eugene d'Aquili, and Vince Rause, *Why God Won't Go Away* (New York: Ballantine, 2002), p. 174.

17. Jerome Berryman, "Children and Mature Spirituality," in *Children's Spirituality: Christian Perspective, Research, and Application,* ed. Donald Ratcliff (Eugene, Ore.: Cascade, 2004).

18. Christopher Renz, "Christian Education and the Confirmation Debate: Towards a Theology of Catechesis," *Journal of Christian Education* 41, no. 1 (1998): 53-65.

19. Karen-Marie Yust, "Theology, Educational Theory, and Children's Faith Formation: Findings from the Faith Formation in Children's Ministry Project," *Association of Professors and Researchers in Religious Education Proceedings,* Philadelphia, 2002, p. 163.

Damasio, in an interview conducted by Steven Johnson, recounts recent findings that provide physiological support for some of the above observations as well as ministry approaches based on them. He notes that parts of the brain operate at different speeds: the cognitive system can be trained to function faster and faster because the neurons are myelinated.[20] The unmyelinated emotional system works more slowly, and "there is no evidence that the emotional system is going to speed up."[21] Damasio fears that as cognition continues to speed up, emotional neutrality may result. This underscores the need Cavalletti, Berryman, and others see for children to have time and space where they can be present thoughtfully and without haste, in order to provide emotional grounding and encourage desire for an ongoing relationship with the Good Shepherd, the "Other."

Findings such as these help us realize that the interaction of all parts of the brain — especially the two cerebral hemispheres and the limbic system — enabled by the Holy Spirit of God, helps children worship. Thus we who create worship opportunities for children need to recognize the role of emotions and experience with God (connatural knowing) as much as the cognitive and creative aspects of children's learning (speculative knowing).

Forms of Worship Experiences for Children

Children's capacity for worship often surprises adults. Children have significant potential for experiencing deep joy in worship, through both the verbs or acts of worship and its noun, an encounter with God. They desire the assurance of their relationship with God that comes through worship, through connatural more than speculative knowing.

Seeking a different type of worship experience, seven-year-old Anna's family began attending a church that was unlike their former church. After being part of the new church for about three weeks, Anna said to her mother that she missed her friends at the old church but was able to "feel" God better in her new church.

20. Myelin is a whitish protein material that encases some neurons in a sheath, serving as insulation and enabling transmission of nerve impulses.

21. Steven Johnson, "Antonio Damasio's Theory of Thinking Faster and Faster: Are the Brain's Emotional Circuits Hardwired for Speed?" *Discover* 25, no. 5 (2004): 49.

What was Anna "feeling"? What was different about the setting and the worship experiences that prompted her comment? Considerable research attention is currently being given to questions such as these. Building on evidence in Scripture that even infants and the preborn may have awareness of God (see Ps. 22:9-10 and Luke 1:41) and the work of Robert Coles in *The Spiritual Life of Children,* some Christian scholars believe that even the youngest children have a sense of God's presence.[22]

It is primarily through the acts of worship that a congregation communicates faith to children. "Children themselves are worshipers, who like other worshipers praise God, seek God's forgiveness and restoration of relationship, and receive God's Word through the sacraments and preaching. . . . Children practice and proclaim faith and share love and joy during worship. They express trust and can encourage others to be trusting."[23] The presence of children in worship helps the whole congregation keep its promises to each other.[24] Yet children are still children. They can know the God they worship even though not every worship experience will have the same effect on all children, just as it doesn't on adults.

Now let's examine ways different churches approach children's worship: when children are welcome in the worship service, when they are present for part of the service, when they have their own separate worship experience, and when the church offers family-oriented services. The chapter concludes with suggestions for helping children worship more effectively, regardless of the church's approach, as well as strategies for implementing change.[25]

22. See works such as Robert Coles, *The Spiritual Life of Children* (Boston: Houghton Mifflin, 1990); David Hay and Rebecca Nye, *The Spirit of the Child* (London: Fount, 1998); Sofia Cavalletti, *Religious Potential of the Child,* and also Cavalletti, *The Religious Potential of the Child Six to Twelve Years Old* (Oak Park, Ill.: Catechesis of the Good Shepherd, 2002); Jerome Berryman, *Godly Play: A Way of Religious Education* (San Francisco: Harper, 1991); as well as many journal articles on faith formation in children and children's spiritual development.

23. Barbara Kines Myers and William Myers, *Engaging in Transcendence: The Church's Ministry and Covenant with Young Children* (Cleveland: Pilgrim, 1992), p. xxi.

24. See chapter 7 for a description of promise-keeping congregations.

25. From Scottie's investigation of church practice it appears that theology or faith tradition influences children's worship experiences more than church size does.

Children Are Present throughout Congregational Worship

Most churches that encourage children to be present throughout the worship service are in liturgical traditions, but they can also be found in other traditions. They believe that children must intentionally be included as responsible participants and contributors in worship. This is especially true for traditions in which the whole congregation holds itself responsible before God for the faith nurture of the child. Through their participation children come to understand the significance of the acts of worship, but only if the adults actively participate in meaningful ways. These corporate worship times tend to have an order of service or liturgy that enables every person to participate at various points by acting out some of the verbs of worship seen earlier in Old Testament passages — responding through hymns, prayers, readings, reciting creeds, coming to the altar to present tithes and offerings or to receive the Eucharist or Lord's Supper. The established liturgy of a faith tradition may become as familiar and comfortable as a child's own bedtime ritual, especially when the worship is meaningful to the parents. (In these churches a separate experience may be provided for children under the age of five.)

Pastors of these churches recognize the presence of children, and often include engaging illustrations referring to children during the sermon or homily. Some also have the children gather around the altar for a special message just for them; this may be constructed with thoughtful intent, or it may simply occur because "it's always been done this way." Or the pastor might suggest something for children to draw during the message. Symbols and rituals such as infant baptism or dedication in these churches allow all to see and understand their significance. Altar cloths and banners may be used, corresponding to the church calendar or Christian holidays, providing visual stimuli that often evoke questions from children.

When all the faith community is gathered together and the verbs of worship (singing, praising, praying, offering gifts, and so forth) involve everyone, there is great vitality. A child may respond by saying, "Wow! I met God there." Children may be enfolded corporately in the presence of God. These encounters may come through visual symbols, through gestures such as kneeling, through music, or through the power of story.

Increasingly, many pastors are realizing the significance of narrative preaching — the use of biblical narratives from which the sermon develops. Well-crafted narrative preaching helps a congregation grasp the significance of a particular biblical story as it relates to the biblical metanarrative — the overarching story of the redemption of God's people beginning in Genesis and concluding in Revelation. Thomas Groome speaks of the power of seeing "my story" (that of the individual) and "our story" (that of the faith community) within "The Story" (the biblical narrative), past, present, and future.[26] Such preaching enables all generations of hearers to find their own story within God's story.

Helpful Resources

Many churches that keep children within the worship services are part of denominations in the liturgical tradition. These denominations publish a range of resources that leaders may use to enhance worship experiences with children. You can use an Internet search engine to find such a denomination's web page, or call its headquarters to ask what resources are available.

Some churches provide resources to help parents explain the liturgy to younger children and to allow older children to follow along and gain their own understanding. Early childhood specialist Shirley Morgenthaler with her staff has developed a variety of materials for parents and children to use. She identifies numerous ways congregations can encourage children in worship: provide booster seats so young children can see better; point out when a Bible story corresponds to stained-glass and other images in the church; shake hands with a child during Sharing of the Peace. There is also a hymnal marker that parents may refer to for reminders of how to help their children worship.[27]

Let's face it: worship services can be boring for children without any way for them to be involved. In their helpful book *Children in the Worshiping Community,* David Ng and Virginia Thomas identify ways adults can help children participate in worship more fully.[28] The following adaptation of

26. Thomas Groome, *Christian Religious Education: Sharing Our Story and Vision* (San Francisco: Harper and Row, 1980).

27. These materials are available from KidFaith, www.kidfaith@curf.edu. Other helpful resources for parents are Robbie Castleman's *Parenting in the Pew* (Downers Grove, Ill.: InterVarsity Press, 1994) and *A Children's Guide to Worship,* by Ruth Boling et al. (Louisville: Geneva Press, 1997).

28. David Ng and Virginia Thomas, *Children in the Worshiping Community* (Atlanta: Westminster/John Knox, 1981), pp. 82-102.

their suggestions is applicable to a congregation of any size where children are welcome in the worship service, but especially when children are present for the entire service. These ideas might become topics for a special class on worship for children and parents:

- talking about the vocabulary of worship — words such as *hymn, alleluia, doxology, praise, confess, dedicate, holy,* and others that are specific to your tradition
- discussing the significance of prayer — when one speaks to and listens to God — and how to pray
- participating in corporate worship: using a hymnal and following the lyrics, finding Bible passages, listening to a sermon, following the liturgy, and reading responsively
- learning common worship responses such as the Apostles' Creed, the Doxology, and the Lord's Prayer
- preparing children for the worship service: "walking them through" the service so that they will know what to expect
- discussing the meaning of special events such as Communion and baptism

Consider including older children as participants in the service by leading the call to worship, reading Scripture, taking part in liturgical dance or drama, playing an instrument, ushering, greeting, walking in a procession, lighting candles, offering a prayer, and giving testimony, among other things.[29]

Multicultural Worship

In recent decades North America has become increasingly multicultural. Metropolitan areas are dotted with churches representing ethnic groups from many parts of the world. As these people gather for corporate worship, many from communal societies, the children are almost always present throughout the service.

The centuries-old presence of African American churches in the

29. See also Elizabeth Francis Caldwell, *Come unto Me: Rethinking the Sacraments for Children* (Cleveland: United Church Press, 1996), for more specific ideas about involving children in worship.

United States is a historical exception to the more recent influx of people from many different nations. Longstanding African American churches, regardless of their denomination, tend to conduct worship services with all ages gathered together. This is the time everyone rehearses and celebrates God's goodness and is reminded of God's abundant resources that bring them through the trials of life. Even the youngest of children are held in parents' arms as the congregation rejoices in singing that is often rhythmic and jubilant. Gifts and offerings may be brought forward processionally. Congregants may gather around the altar for intercession or prayers of repentance. Children observe and even participate in the "call and response" style of sermons. When infants are welcomed into the faith community, they may be "put on display," held overhead for all to see and "claim." Many elements allow everyone to be fully engaged in acts of worship. The church is a haven where children are valued and nurtured as the generations interact. These faith communities seem truly to live out being the family of God as they worship together.

Children Are Present for Part of the Worship Service

Churches where children attend part of the service have the widest variation in ways children participate. Most common is for children to leave the sanctuary during the sermon or homily. This means that children are present for the other parts of the service, so that the resources and suggestions noted in the above section are also applicable here.

Models exist for large churches, even "megachurches." A liturgical church in the Chicago area that qualifies as a megachurch has five weekend services, most of which have close to a thousand people in attendance. Children of all ages are present except during the twenty-minute homily or sermon.

Every generation, from infants to octogenarians, is represented equally. The liturgy of the service is designed in such a way that every person participates frequently and actively. Teens and adults lead the music, which includes contemporary songs with percussion but also traditional reflective music. Children participate in the liturgical worship procession; they help prepare the altar. People (all ages) stand and also kneel together at different points. Before the children leave the sanctuary for their own liturgy of the Word (sermon), they come forward around the altar for a children's story from the pastor. This certainly is not innovative or unusual, but what happens next is much less common. The children turn and face the congregation, extend their arms and proclaim a blessing over the adults that they might hear the word from God that he has for them that day. Then in turn the congregation stands and extends a similar blessing over the children.

About two hundred children then leave the sanctuary to go to the church's chapel for the message designed just for them. After the homily, the children return to partake in the Eucharist. The service ends with the entire congregation joining hands, boldly stating together, "Christ was born; Christ has died; Christ is risen; Christ will come again." Everyone lifts joined hands on the last phrase. This very large church has found ways to involve the entire faith family actively in corporate worship.

In some liturgical or sacramental churches, especially smaller ones, children may be part of the main worship service only during the weekly Communion, which is the culmination of worship and usually occurs toward the end of the service. Very young children spend most of the service in specially prepared spaces.

Although nonliturgical churches tend not to have children present for the entire worship service, many want children to experience worship with the congregation until it is time for the sermon. At that point the children are dismissed to their own space for the remainder of the time.

Some churches replicate the "adult" worship time and space, including miniature pews, in order to "train" children for "big church." Fortunately, this approach is not as common as it once was. Most children's ministry leaders realize that a future focus is not as helpful as aiming for children to worship God in the present and to grow in understanding of and joy in worship. Other churches engage in promising practices that replicate a portion of the worship service in an age-appropriate manner. After the children have been dismissed to their own space, they have their own call to worship, a welcome, a time for prayer, silence and reflection, and a message from the Word that might be presented through any number of media.

A greater tendency among larger nonliturgical churches is to use puppets, skits, videos, and other entertainment forms to engage the children in a theme that may or may not correlate with what they have just experienced in the worship setting. Setups for this time may be very elaborate. This approach is not bad or wrong, but it may diminish children's sense of

God's transcendence and their reverent response. It seems some leaders feel that children are incapable of, or not willing to engage in, the acts of worship described at the outset of this chapter. These children may be deprived of time and space to reflect on and experience God with awe and wonder.

Helpful Resources

Increasing numbers of liturgical churches offer Catechesis of the Good Shepherd, developed by Sofia Cavalletti, or *Young Children and Worship* by Sonja Stewart and Jerome Berryman, or Godly Play materials developed by Jerome Berryman. In Catechesis of the Good Shepherd worship is the main focus, accompanied by learning appropriate to the age of the child. Cavalletti advocates creating a holistic environment called an atrium in which the child can be in relationship with God and have a sense of belonging. Like Maria Montessori, Cavalletti believes that children need space between the setting of the classroom and of the sanctuary in which they can experience God and his story and wonder about those things. The atrium is "a place for celebrating the Word of God, for listening, praying, and reflecting together, for meditation and work. It is a place where the child is able to do everything at his own rhythm, which is slower than the adult's; this is how the child can prepare himself to participate more consciously in the community life of the adults."[30]

The atrium experience includes silence — a full silence rather than an empty one.[31] This is a critical part of every atrium, and to the surprise of many adults, children love it. Cavalletti describes the experiences in an atrium as providing "a deep joy that makes the child peaceful and serene." Catechesis of the Good Shepherd has three levels of atria, each with a three-year curriculum with themes paralleling the church calendar; materials for older children help them gain an understanding of all of redemption history. Thus it is possible for a child to participate in Catechesis of the Good Shepherd from age three through age twelve.[32]

30. Cavalletti, *Religious Potential of the Child*, p. 23.

31. In a full silence children are quiet because they have engaged or entered into a story with wonder; an empty silence is when children are told to be quiet or to stop talking.

32. For more information about Catechesis of the Good Shepherd, see Cavalletti's *Religious Potential of the Child* and *Religious Potential of the Child Six to Twelve Years Old*. You

Jerome Berryman developed Godly Play out of Catechesis of the Good Shepherd and the work of Montessori. Though similar to Catechesis in many principles, Godly Play is more easily modified for nonliturgical churches. Godly Play is becoming increasingly widespread in North America.[33] In a session of Godly Play, after being greeted, children sit in a circle on the floor for a brief time of talking to God through prayer and singing. Then they are invited into a Bible story, told simply using the essential words of the text. The storyteller uses only voice, simple objects, and hand movements, telling the story while keeping eyes focused on the materials. The lack of eye contact with the children keeps the story, not the storyteller, central, and the children enter the story to live in it for a time — to meet God and to hear what God has to say to them. At the end of the story, children and adult leaders wonder together about its meaning. The storyteller does not "teach" the meaning. By inviting the children to wonder about the story, we imply that God can speak to them, that God's Spirit will guide them to grasp meaning in the story, a meaning that the storyteller may not realize is important to the child. After this time of wondering, the children decide how they wish to respond to the story. They may choose to work with the materials the storyteller used, telling the story to themselves and living in it again, or they may express their feelings and thoughts through art. Whatever their choice, they have time and a place to process their response to God's story and presence without distractions.

Both Catechesis of the Good Shepherd and Godly Play integrate worship and learning, but the emphasis is on worship. The pace is slow and gentle, allowing children of all ages time to reflect. About twenty children is maximum for an atrium or for Godly Play. Both approaches are thus more suitable for smaller churches, although a few very large churches are beginning to introduce such a model during one or more of their services.

Sources of print materials for nonliturgical churches that have children present for part of the service can be found in the next section.

---

may also wish to contact the national training headquarters: Catechesis of the Good Shepherd, PO Box 1084, Oak Park, IL 60304; www.cgsusa.org.

For reasons not fully understood, there appear to be many more level I atria than level III.

33. For more information about Godly Play, see Berryman's *Godly Play* plus other of his books. Also see Sonja Stewart and Jerome Berryman, *Young Children and Worship* (Louisville: Westminster/John Knox Press, 1989), as well as Sonja Stewart, *Following Jesus* (Louisville: Geneva, 2000).

Children's Separate Worship Experience

Another pattern for churches of various traditions is to have Sunday school and worship at the same time with children attending only Sunday school and adults only worship.

Churches that keep children separate throughout the worship service may make this time much like an extended Sunday school, with an opening assembly including singing, followed by a Bible lesson and an activity or craft. Or it may be an hour-long version of the entertainment-style approach just described, or in some cases it is a miniature adult service.[34]

Many large, "contemporary" churches that attract heretofore unchurched people offer parallel experiences for children. These churches often do not provide a teaching hour for adults on Sunday morning, so children and parents are at church only one hour. The children's experience may begin with an activity time, followed by a large group time in which a worship band leads singing and a contemporary drama sets the stage for the Bible story. The final part of this hour is usually spent in small groups with a leader assigned to meet with them each week. This is a time for application of the story and prayer.

Some churches intentionally create an experience where children can be involved and lead in acts of worship. In the 1990s one large church in the St. Louis area developed what might be called the "Learn by Doing" model.[35] Elementary-age children are divided into five groups of mixed ages. A shepherd, who stays with that group for the whole year, guides each group. The groups are assigned to different stations — Prayer, Leading Worship, Service, Missions, and Drama — each led by a teacher with a heart for that area. The children spend half of the hour at their stations, preparing their portion of the worship service. During the second half, the children conduct their own worship time, with each group contributing, and an adult gives a ten-minute sermon.

34. Occasionally we've heard an adult volunteer in such a setting say, "You're here so you won't be bored in the service." That should never be the explanation children hear for why they meet separately; that attitude simply sets them up to anticipate boredom when they're older. Most churches, though, put forth considerable effort to engage children effectively in their own age-designed worship experiences.

35. Karen Woolsey is the director of children's ministry at First Evangelical Free Church, Manchester, Missouri. She began the Kids Worship with fifty children attending; it has grown to several hundred each week. See www.efree.org.

The Prayer group compiles prayer needs from the children and the church at large to include in the "pastoral" prayer time. They also study a prayer from Scripture and create prayer journals, among other things. The Leading Worship group prepares the order of service, selects the music to be used, and practices leading it. The Service group makes sure that the worship area is tidy and ready for the service. They set up any needed equipment, prepare the "bulletin," and serve as ushers. This group also meets the needs of others within the church and the community through acts of age-appropriate service, from fixing sandwiches for a local shelter to cleaning church coffeepots during part of this time. The Missions group focuses on the needs of the world. This group may learn about a missionary the church supports and the country where he or she serves. Or they may visit a church that conducts its service in a different language, to get a sense of what it means to enter another culture. They present a missions report during their service. The Drama Group prepares a creative presentation of the Bible message or story of the day. This may or may not correlate with the teaching in the adult service.

Each group spends six weeks at one station, and then rotates to the next. Through the school year, every child experiences each station for six weeks, making contributions to each aspect of the worship services.

As the church has grown and more children participate in this worship time, more stations have been added. Now there are stations called Children's Choir, Our Church's Doctrine, Scripture (where memorization takes place), and Faith Stories (where faith-filled adults and teens tell stories of God's work in their life). This model takes children's abilities seriously and allows them to develop and lead their own worship time aligned with their church's tradition.

Helpful Resources

Most major denominational and independent Sunday school curriculum publishers offer materials for children's church, a separate worship experience for children. Information about these materials may be obtained from the publishers' websites or from their area representatives. Other sources for materials may be uncovered by the creative use of an Internet search engine. Resources of this kind are also available from many Christian/religious bookstores.

It is important to determine the purpose and goal for the children's worship experience before looking for materials. Let your purpose determine what you select rather than what may appear to be the most clever or fun theme.

Intentionally Family-Oriented Worship

Some churches are increasingly realizing the need for families to experience worship together. Worship is more meaningful, they believe, if families can participate actively together. The forms of all family services will not necessarily have the same look, and rightly so. Some churches that have multiple services choose to gear one of them to children and families. For example, a church that has three worship services may shape the early service to be "traditional," the middle service "contemporary," and the third a family service that focuses on multigenerational involvement. This model provides choices for members of the congregation, but it can be challenging for church staff to develop and oversee three completely different services each week.

Churches may choose to have a family service once a month at a set time rather than every Sunday. A church in Toronto has been doing this for ten years. Although persons of all ages are invited to attend, the intent is to draw families. From humble beginnings of fifteen in attendance, more than 150 people now regularly attend this special Sunday service.

A member of the congregation describes it like this:

> The premise of the All Age Liturgy is simple — a family-centered worship service, where breakfast and the Gospel story are shared and enjoyed by all. The setting is like a family gathered — with tables and chairs in a big circle around the outside of the room — a simple altar in the center. Paper placemats double as the order of service — in the center of each table are copies of the morning hymns and pictures from today's Gospel story for coloring (by artists of all ages).[36]

The Gospel story sets this service apart. Often drama is used. Once, to focus on the apostle Peter's life, a good-sized boat was created out of a refrigerator box for retelling the story of the miraculous catch of fish. A brief

36. Donna Quantz, unpublished document, c. 1990.

flashback vignette shows Peter's betrayal of Jesus, including the sound of a cock crowing. Then the fishing incident is portrayed. Next, the story moves to the beach around a "campfire." There the power of forgiveness is portrayed as Jesus three times asks Peter to care for his sheep, thus making the connection to Peter's three denials of Jesus.

> The service moves beautifully into the Eucharist, which is celebrated with the entire church family coming forward into one large circle around the altar. . . . The bread and wine are shared around the room. This [special] moment is carried through into a favorite hymn, "Go Now in Peace," sung in closing as a three-part round. As the final strains of the round fade away, one truly feels that the love of God will surround you "everywhere, everywhere you may go."[37]

Children too young to be given the elements of the Eucharist receive individual blessings. After the final hymn, everyone helps clean up and put things away, just like a big family.

A third model for family-oriented worship works for churches that do things differently in the summer. Some churches suspend children's ministry for a couple of months to give a respite to volunteer staff, but family worship services are held during those months. These corporate worship times are carefully planned to engage and value every generation present. Many points in the worship service allow for this: generational[38] passages of Scripture (such as Genesis 17:1-9; Exodus 3:14, 15; Luke 1:46-55); different generations taking turns singing verses of a hymn such as "May the Mind of Christ My Savior"; greeting or "passing the peace" between generations; generational storytelling, as well as the suggestions made earlier in this chapter (page 230).

Developing Intergenerational Worship: An Example

Sometimes fresh strategies must be used to open spaces for corporate family worship. Sunday worship services at one Illinois church are pri-

37. Quantz, unpublished document.

38. For our purposes here, "generational" refers to settings that have at least two and preferably three generations of people referred to. In biblical terms it would refer to "your children and your children's children" (Prov. 17:6; Joel 1:3).

marily intended for adults. Unable to find a workable time on Sunday evening, the director of children's and family ministry thought creatively and chose Thursday early evening for families to gather for a simple meal followed by intergenerational worship. Though this church does not follow a traditional liturgy, a simple one was established for this gathering because children respond especially well to rhythm and repetition, as previously noted, and because it provides structure for the experience.

After the planning team established a vision for this weekly experience — to provide opportunities for families to worship at church with other families and also to worship more meaningfully at home — the purpose and goals were delineated. Next, the team determined a structure for these family worship times, one that would provide a model that families might use for their times of worship at home. Here is what was decided:

- *Celebrate* by sharing a simple meal; end the meal by singing the Doxology.
- *Prepare* individually for the worship experience to follow through brief reflection or journaling.
- *Gather* for corporate worship. Have each household light a candle from the lit Christ candle.[39] Process into the worship space following the Christ candle and Bible held aloft, reciting Psalm 100 antiphonally. Place those objects on the altar, each household placing its candle there as well.
- *Center* on the theme for the service through thoughtfully selected music, Scripture, or liturgy.[40]
- *Encounter* God through the story from Scripture.
- *Respond* to the story in clusters through interaction or a creative activity.
- *Close* the time with a recessional, reversing how the worship time began; proclaim a blessing over all participating households.

39. The term *household* was used rather than *family* so that single parents and people without children in their home would also feel welcome.

40. This family worship experience followed a curricular scope and sequence that was appropriate for all ages. A nine-week series focused on different ways the Good Shepherd provides for his sheep. Another series focused on the many "I am" statements of Jesus — for example, "I am the light of the world," "I am the living water."

Multigenerational experiences provide intentional opportunities for the whole family of God to worship together, but they also become prime teaching opportunities. Parents experience worship with their children in ways that may be replicated at home. As Marjorie Thompson, a specialist in family spiritual formation, writes, "Adults need assistance with ways to pray and worship at home, as well as concrete helps with ritual and faith celebration. The best way to teach such practices is through events provided for the whole family instead of age-segregated groups."[41]

Ideas for Using This Model

Consider having family units serve as greeters, ushers, readers, and musical ensemble or drama participants. Members of a family unit also could lead the congregation in corporate prayer.

Creative elements in worship services can underline the importance of the generations within the faith community. Here are a variety of suggestions:

1. Showcase well-loved family treasures or life-stage markers. One example: on the Sunday before school starts in the fall, have school-age children bring their backpacks and come forward with their families to stand together for prayer for the new school year.[42]
2. Invite families to create banners or murals for display that represent God's work among them.
3. Give an interactive sermon, inviting children to come forward and participate in the message discussion style. The pastor might ask questions such as: Why do you think Jesus said that adults need to become like children? Why do you think it was so hard for some grown-ups to realize who Jesus was while he lived here on earth?
4. During a prayer time, have congregants stand around a certain age group to pray for them. For example, gather around parents who have

41. Marjorie J. Thompson, *Family: The Forming Center* (Nashville: Upper Room, 1996), p. 141.

42. Dick Hardel of the Youth and Family Institute calls this the "Blessing of the Backpacks." For more information about his work and the Child in Our Hands conferences that he conducts, see www.youthandfamilyinstitute.org.

children still at home; gather around teens, or children, or couples whose children are now grown.

5. Have children distribute to worshipers symbols or gifts that relate to the theme or message of the day — bookmarks, balloons, flowers, or bread, for example.
6. Use bolts of wide florist ribbon to "connect" all worshipers during a song or prayer, for a visual sense of community.
7. Make space at the rear of the worship space for rocking chairs for parents to cradle or nurse infants. Set up a "quiet play" area for crawlers.

Challenges for Ministry Leaders

Several challenges presently face leaders in ministry with children, not the least of which is the need to counter assumptions many North American church leaders hold regarding children and worship:

- Worship is an adult activity that should meet the needs and interests of that population (such as quality or excellence to the point where the worship service may appear to be performance).
- Reverent worship is beyond children's abilities and will bore them. (Granted, some services also bore adults, but more important, this may indicate an inability or unwillingness to make worship engaging for children.)
- Worship for children must be fun, active, and entertaining. (Highly influenced by contemporary culture's assumptions about children, many leaders feel it is necessary to ape popular media forms.)
- If the church is growing, space must be made for adults in worship services. (Often driven by the assumption that reaching the adult is the prime task of the church, this implicitly devalues the soul and spirituality of the child.)

These assumptions will not be easily unseated, because they are widespread even if held subconsciously. The children's ministry leader will need to pray for wisdom and sensitivity to cast a vision that will enable church leaders to see children with new eyes — the eyes of Jesus. Thoughtful, patient work will be required to prepare statements that will help leaders to consider why a change of view may be necessary.

The media saturation of our culture poses another challenge. Because media are highly engaging, there is a tendency to seek engagement of the children without critically evaluating and seeking to retrieve what may be lost because of the power of media.[43]

Another challenge is unfolding at the time of this writing: the view that the current missional or emerging church may have regarding children. This newer trend in church philosophy rejects many of the programs and approaches of recent generations, desiring to return to certain forms of worship and mission of the early church.[44] Since this movement is led by a younger generation, if the leaders have children, they are still quite young. The leaders of this movement must thoughtfully consider the role their children will play in the worship experiences of their faith communities.

Diana Garland, a scholar who focuses on family ministry, describes the situation regarding worship in too many North American churches:

> Sometimes services of worship become so oriented toward the quality of performance — beautiful music, flawless liturgy, eloquent sermon — that the active participation of the congregation seems secondary. Yet everything leaders do in worship should guide participants in experiencing and giving glory to God. Worship therefore needs to engage everyone present, including the youngest of children, in active ways. . . .
>
> Children's presence in the church service represents the inclusion of all who want to worship, regardless of their ability to sit still or fully understand everything that we do together. More than that, however, their presence challenges us to change our style of worship so that everyone is a part. Worship should actively include the whole congregation.[45]

43. Many resources on the topic of media are available. Here are a couple of them: Marva Dawn's *Is It a Lost Cause? Having the Heart of God for the Church's Children* (Grand Rapids: Eerdmans, 1997), and Neil Postman's *Technopoly: The Surrender of Culture to Technology* (New York: Vintage, 1993).

44. The emerging or missional church is described in books such as Darrell Guder, ed., *Missional Church: A Vision for the Sending of the Church in North America* (Grand Rapids: Eerdmans, 1998), and Robert E. Webber, *The Younger Evangelicals* (Grand Rapids: Baker, 2002), among others.

45. Diana Garland, *Family Ministry* (Downers Grove, Ill.: InterVarsity Press, 1999), p. 467.

All Christian churches share common desires for their children — that they love and commit themselves to the Lord Jesus Christ, obey the commands of the Word of God, and have a heart for worshiping God. Churches realize that because children are children, worship experience needs to be conducted so as to be relevant and meaningful. Churches interpret "relevant and meaningful" in very different ways. Herein lies our challenge.

Essentials for Children at Worship

Scripture calls for children's presence and involvement in worship. Therefore it is crucial for church leaders and parents to receive training on children's ability to worship and to encounter God. The same education is needed by the entire congregation, for to consider involving children in authentic worship runs counter to much of current North American church culture. That is why the educational aspect of this task is vital. If only adults are valued in worship services, those adults will likely never achieve full spiritual maturity.

For those who resonate with the concepts presented in this chapter, there is now a responsibility — a mission — to raise awareness within the congregation. The strategy for this task will depend on experience and level of responsibility at the church. Those who are experienced in children's ministry with a high level of responsibility may want to begin by writing a position paper for the church leaders that articulates significant biblical concepts and relevant principles from this chapter. Then gather a small task force to pray and seek God's direction regarding the role of children at worship in that setting. The task force might present to the leadership steps to implement change, if that is deemed appropriate, with a possible timetable. Create opportunities for the task force to worship together through various means, including silence and reflection. Implement varied worship practices in small groups or Bible studies. Then consider creating a six-week worship experience for a specific group, even the church leaders.

Those who are inexperienced, or who have less responsibility but feel the significance of this issue, will want to pray for guidance. They should look for someone who shares this concern. They can pray together, encourage each other, and then decide on steps to implement change. In any ministry that involves children, provide authentic worship opportunities for them, even if it is simply in a Sunday school class of six or seven children.

Whatever form of worship a church practices, taking seriously the following principles can help children worship well. First and foremost, children must feel that they belong and that their ability to participate in worship is respected. Elements of a family-friendly church may be adapted to help children in worship:

- Welcome and show respect to children of all ages.
- Model love and care for children as part of the worshiping community, so that the congregation will see it and respond in like ways.
- See church life as similar to life in a large family.
- Emphasize children's ability to worship God more than programs that will engage them.
- Empower people to create their own ways of including children in worship.
- Allow children to be present for every aspect of church life at least some of the time, so that they may be formed by all the ways the faith community members relate to each other.

For those who serve in a ministry setting where children are separated for their own worship time, here are some components that are important to include each week:

- a focal point such as a Christ candle to remind children of God's presence
- songs that address God's character and actions and our praise and love for him
- presentation of the Word — God's story
- offering praise to God and praying to him, including listening prayer
- reflection on the significance of what was heard about God
- consideration of ways to serve others and the world
- response to the Word that will help form God's people individually and corporately

Establish an order of worship to follow that is appropriate for the faith tradition. Children take delight and comfort in the familiar, the rhythm of the expected.

Christians everywhere long for children to find their identity as part of the people of God. Even the youngest children contain an openness that allows them to receive the mystery of our living God. Here are questions to consider:

- What happens when the faith community worships together in your setting?
- How do people there encounter God?

Children and adults bring their particular gifts to create a rich mutual experience. Adults learn from children's fresh insights and the immediacy of their responses. Children learn from adults' experience and understanding. Together their time with God is enriched and their faith is strengthened as they carry out the verbs or actions of worship and experience the noun or encounter of worship.

It is our deep desire that all people in our faith communities, including children, know the joy of worshiping God together. Can the church truly be in worship to our God if children are not present?

Chapter 12

IN LEARNING AND TEACHING

The church must teach or die.

L. Rinmawia, *Looking Ahead in Christian Education,* Delhi, India

The role of teaching in the church is crucial. If the stories and truths of redemption history are not taught, the church will die. Redemption history is the Story that must be at the center of all our teaching in the church.

In this chapter we attempt to demonstrate educationally how the Story might be taught with and learned by children. We begin with Scottie May's and Linda Cannell's stories of how they developed as Christian educators — how the ability to teach the Story unfolded in their own lives. Their stories lead into principles and methods that may facilitate teaching in ways that attract children to the Story. The sections that follow discuss the nature of teaching, the nature of learning, church-based models of learning, and the characteristics of effective teaching and its challenges.

Scottie's Story

My mother was my kindergarten teacher. I have clear memories of that first year of school. We made things that were "real," though child-sized. Using small hammers, nails, and saws, we built a house, a greenhouse, and even a church (this was in a public school decades ago). We built furniture for the house, planted seeds and grew plants in the greenhouse, and pretended to be in church with the pews and altar we made. Later, in second grade my class took a field trip to a farm, where I got to steer the tractor and try to milk a cow.

These early experiences are still vivid. They involved *experiences using real materials, doing authentic tasks.* Reflecting as an adult, I became aware that in spite of the lived faith of my parents and our Christian home, my childhood church education rarely offered authentic tasks or experiential learning — but I had gotten lots of points and recognition for doing Bible worksheets correctly.

When I was in my twenties, I was asked to teach a week of vacation Bible school for upper-elementary-aged children. The materials focused on Jesus' life from Palm Sunday to Easter, but the lessons were extremely boring even to me. I wanted to make this important section of Scripture come to life for the children, though I had no training in how to do that. My early experiences of experiential learning were residing only in my subconscious. But they were enough to prod me to think outside the box for this week of VBS.

On the first day I gathered the more than twenty-five fourth- through sixth-graders to explain the plan for the week. "We are going to create a newspaper, the *Jerusalem Gazette,* about the events of Holy Week and life at that time," I told them. We took the sections of a regular newspaper and assigned them according to interest, including front-page news, editorials, comics, want ads, sports, fashions, even a "Dear Abby" column. From experience with my own children, I realized that not everyone would enjoy this task, so there was a choice. Those who didn't want to work on the newspaper could build a replica of the tomb where Jesus' body was placed.

Soon I was peppered with questions: "How should we do this?" "What should we write?" "What did it look like?" Intuitively my response was "We have to figure it out." Little did I realize that by not answering them directly I was *empowering these kids to research and investigate* — to become curious about the subject, Holy Week in the life of the Lord Jesus.

The children took the tasks seriously. Before I arrived at church the next morning, a pickup truck had pulled up loaded with scrap lumber and appliance boxes. Some of the boys had scavenged for materials and persuaded a dad to haul their treasures to the church. Construction began, and so did publishing. Learning happened as the kids read about the events in the Bible and used reference books to fill in details as they wrote pieces for the various sections of the newspaper. The biblical story was the focal point for all of us, including me. Yet I did virtually no "teaching." I wanted to *create the setting for them to want to learn and teach themselves.* By the end of the week, the *Jerusalem Gazette* was ready for distribution to the congregation, and the tomb was ready for inspection.

Wanting a capstone experience for the week, I used part of the last day to re-create Jesus' walk from Pilate's hall to Golgotha (see John 19). It took eight children at a time to carry the full-sized cross that our church used during Easter up a half-mile dirt road near the church to a cemetery atop the hill. The kids complained about the heat and the weight of the cross. All the while, I recounted for them the experiences Jesus had endured out of love for them. Then we had a time of worship and prayer in the cemetery.

Many years later I returned to that church for a visit. A tall man carrying a child in each arm came up to me and said, "Do your remember that summer when . . . ?" He had been one of the tomb builders. *Authentic, experiential learning is memorable.*

A Hands-On Bible-Time Museum

Years passed. I continued serving in the church, mainly with youth and adults. Then in the mid-1980s I went back to school. As I worked toward a master's degree in educational ministries, I began to understand educational process and how learning best happens. I found support for some of the ideas I had intuitively implemented earlier. I also became increasingly frustrated with the dominant mode of church education — the schooling model. It is not bad or wrong, but it does not encourage the kinds of experiences or learning that had become significant to me.

One day I visited a children's museum in a Chicago suburb. Part of it looked like any other children's museum. But a significant section made me feel as if I had stepped back into biblical times. There was an Old Testament–style village equipped with tools and household items; there was a large sailing vessel like the one on which Paul traveled. As I looked at these wonderful settings, touching things, using the oars, hoisting the sail, in my imagination I entered several biblical stories. Then light bulbs started going off in my head. *Why can't a church do things like this? Sometimes they are done during vacation Bible school, but why not every Sunday?*[1]

Now I had a mission: to think through how to create a church-based, Sunday, hands-on, living Bible-time museum. Providentially, I was soon asked by my church to teach the upper elementary children during summer Sunday school. Our church was small at the time; the fifteen to twenty fourth- through sixth-graders would be a manageable group. A couple of days later, I received an apologetic phone call stating that there was no one to teach the first- through third-graders, so could I teach them too? That would make about forty children. I said that I couldn't teach that many by myself, but if I could have three or four helpers, I would like to try some ideas I'd been thinking about. I was given free rein in the Sunday school hour if only I would help. (Summer, by the way, is a great time to try new ideas.)

The June curriculum was on the book of Nehemiah — a wonderful context for a children's Bible-time museum. I started planning from the published materials but adapted and expanded them to better serve my experimental model as I developed lesson aims and stories. I brainstormed projects that would make this an authentic hands-on Bible-time museum. We planned to make a large clay/play dough model of the walls of the city of Jerusalem, create a mural depicting the capture of Jerusalem by the Babylonians, fashion period costumes for us all to wear, write reenactments to be performed by the children, and prepare foods that the Israelites of Nehemiah's time may have eaten. We were determined that the activities not be simply "crafts" but ways to engage children in the life and setting of that biblical period. As I met with the three helpers who agreed to work with me, excitement began to build even though we were not sure how it would all work.[2]

Desiring to create a lifelike setting, we kept children of all ages together for most of the hour. We sought to re-create life in that day as much as possible. Of course there were many obstacles that challenged that goal, such as time and space constraints — we had sixty-five minutes and one medium-sized room, and parents were not involved.

1. Some years earlier I had reviewed an experiential vacation Bible school curriculum, Betty Goetz's *Marketplace 29 AD*, self-published at the time. Currently it is available from Group Publishing, Loveland, Colorado, 2004.

2. Note that no one would agree to "teach," but finding "helpers" was not a problem.

We wanted the children to recognize as they first arrived that something different was about to happen.[3] We draped the room's entrance to make it look like a market booth; the leaders wore simple Bible-time headpieces. All the projects were set up early so that each child could pick a project and begin working right away — no waiting for things to begin. We realized that *the ministry begins when the first child arrives.*

We divided the hour into three twenty-minute segments. First the children worked on projects. Then we gathered everyone together for the "teaching" time, done through first-person narrative.

The first week a helper was the storyteller, providing an exile experience for everyone. This "Babylonian captor," wearing a makeshift costume, carrying a long rope and full-sized bow and arrow, barged into the room declaring that he was taking all these "children of Israel" captive — they were being exiled. Then he ordered us all to grab hold of the rope. He led us outside the church, barking orders at us — no talking, stay in line, don't touch anyone — and marched us around for ten minutes. Then he led us back inside to an unfinished area of the basement, where we huddled under a bare light bulb. We talked about how it felt to be taken captive. How long would it take to walk from Jerusalem to Babylon? (About the same as walking from New York City to Chicago.) How many possessions would they be able to take with them? We wanted the children to "feel" the Israelites' experience.

After this came small group time. Within each cluster, an adult helper guided the children to discuss the experience and identify similar things that might happen to them today. This was also when children prayed for and encouraged each other.

In subsequent weeks the storyteller was Nehemiah himself giving his perspective on events; another week it was Ezra the priest/teacher; another week it was a mother of some of the people helping to rebuild the walls of Jerusalem. A modern-day family from Liberia who were actually living in exile came to talk to the children about how their experiences were like the Israelites'. Instead of the memory verses suggested in the materials, we chose Deuteronomy 6:4-9, a passage that all Hebrew children of Nehemiah's day would have known. We put rhythm and motions to it. Nearly everyone knew it by the end of the six weeks.

3. The major adjustments: we eliminated the rows of chairs for the opening time, as well as the low tables around which the children normally sat during class time.

The weeks went by quickly. We had fun; we learned together. Children kept arriving earlier and earlier to work on projects. Behavior problems virtually disappeared.

But as a leader, I learned a very important lesson. After the "museum" experience was over, I peered into the space where we had experienced Nehemiah and saw chairs in straight rows and low tables with stacks of workbooks. I had failed to *cast a vision* that learning the Bible experientially could be a valid model for Sunday learning. I knew it because I had been part of it and watched it work, but I had not communicated why and how it worked.

In 1990, however, we implemented a significant paradigm shift from a traditional age-graded, workbook-oriented Sunday school to an experiential approach. This time I was careful to develop a strategy that would inform and instruct all volunteer teachers about the change and the philosophy behind it. I also said that we would evaluate how things were going after six weeks; if the fruits were not satisfactory, we would return to the old model. Today the experiential model is still in place.

A Crucial Lesson

After I began teaching at Wheaton College, the Japanese mother of one of my students visited our church. She watched everything we did and visited all the places where children were working and learning. At the end of the morning, in very broken English, she said to me, "Scottie, your children have a wonderful time here. They learn lots of things. They have fun here, but Scottie, *when do your children meet God?*"

It was a profound wakeup call for me. I suddenly realized that we had developed and refined a significant, effective model for engaging children in the biblical story, but we had not left space for them to experience God. Not that we hadn't prayed for the work, the teaching, the curriculum, and the children, but we had not made *time* and *space* for God. When the children of God are gathered together, awareness of God's presence evokes the natural response of worship. Therefore though the main emphasis of the Sunday-morning hour is to help children understand the biblical story, learning should not be separated from worship, just as worship cannot be completely separated from learning.

The leadership team began discussing how this might look in our nonliturgical church context. These were challenging discussions: most of us assumed you met God at church and when you prayed, but no intentional time or space in which to encounter God was actually provided. Gradually we found ways to help the children become aware of God's presence. We introduced silence, symbols such as an altar and Christ candle, and music that focused on God's presence.

We began to see a change in the children and in ourselves. Ever since that day when a woman from halfway around the world taught me a profound lesson, my highest priority as a teacher of children has been to help them encounter God. I'm still learning how to do that.

I now realize that *the preparation of the space or environment profoundly affects the learning that takes place.* If the goal is to help children meet God and experience God's story, the space will look different from the way it looks if the goal is to teach the Bible to children. Neither goal is wrong, but they are very different and must be accomplished through different ways of teaching. As a teacher, I must be aware of that difference.

It was during the development of this model that Linda and I met. As we conversed about children and teaching and learning, we realized that we had similar views. She had been experimenting with ministry models in Canada as I experimented in the United States.

Linda's Story

Through an "accident" of real estate I became a member of a certain church. If my parents had chosen the house at the south end of Garfield Street, they might have sent me to a different church, and my religious upbringing undoubtedly would have been very different. Because a pastor's family lived across the lane from us, I met their daughter through a neighborhood Sunday school canvass. Thus my church life began.

At the time I didn't know that this particular church group was rather narrow theologically and tended to define Christian faith in relation to taboos such as movies and dancing. The important thing was that Sunday school opened a door to youth group and camp and gave me something to do on Sundays. Scottie and I have been in the front lines for many years critiquing the traditional Sunday school and its curriculum, yet we are not surprised that a great many women and men of our generation have fond memories of Sunday school experiences. We share stories of the adults who did their best to teach and to love us, or we tell stories about the trouble we got into. Even though for many of us Sunday school seemed like a visit to another era, something stuck.

As I grew older, my church experiences broadened. I finished advanced degree work at a seminary, left my childhood church, and joined a church where I encountered a more thoughtful view of the church's educational ministry. Influenced by my childhood church experiences, I still felt that knowing the Bible, or more accurately knowing biblical information, was important. I equated mastery of Bible information with growth in Christian maturity. Gradually through my graduate education I came to realize that there was more to the Christian life than that.

I questioned the approach of a popular weekday Bible club program for children because its organizers insisted that only the King James Version (KJV) could be used for memorization of Bible verses. The KJV's language is basically foreign to most English-speaking children, so by insisting on its use, this program was essentially keeping the Word of God from being accessible to children. I became concerned that children were learning Bible verses with little attention to their meaning, in or out of context. In time the organization conceded that the New International Version of the Bible could be used, but simple memorization and competitive games continued to be its main approach to learning.

As I developed increasing awareness through my continuing studies of what it means to be a Christian educator, I turned my attention to Canadian Sunday schools and began a campaign to help churches understand the limitations of the traditional format and the available published curricula. I traveled from coast to coast, advising church leaders and parents that attending Sunday school is no guarantee of biblical literacy.

I discovered that most editorial guidelines for curricula required writers to prepare lessons for teachers who were assumed to be inexperienced, would spend no more than fifteen to thirty minutes in preparation, lived in a small town in rural North America, and understood vocabulary and concepts at essentially an eighth-grade level. No wonder the resulting lessons were introductory at best. The publishers, however, cannot be blamed for the material they produced. Church leaders were also at fault for not seeking to understand the nature of education and learning, and for largely ignoring the need for teacher development. The publishers were simply writing for the market that the churches had produced.

To challenge the Sunday school and its curriculum in the early 1970s in Canada was almost like challenging the faith itself! One denominational executive even sent a letter to his churches warning them to have nothing to do with me. By the mid-1970s, however, some were realizing that there were flaws in the traditional system. The audience of children from unchurched families who needed to be introduced to the Bible and to Jesus as Savior had changed to an audience of children from churched families. By school age, these children had heard the familiar Bible stories over and over, and as soon as they could drop out of Sunday school they did. The mass defections typically took place during junior high years, when parents became less willing to force their children to attend what the children often perceived as a boring program. The notion that the Sunday school, as we knew it then, would produce expert Bible knowledge and mature faith could not be sustained. A grassroots movement was born as concerned laity began to prepare resource materials and programming initiatives for their own churches. That is when I made the transition from critic to consultant who helped churches plan alternatives.

Since I wasn't a trained childhood specialist, I visited public schools and sat in the classrooms of teachers who were acknowledged by their colleagues to be the most capable. I introduced myself to school principals as a church professional who wanted to learn by watching their best teachers. I was welcomed into schools and spent several months in some of the finest Canadian public schools, learning skills, teaching approaches, classroom management techniques, effective use of resources, and ways to create a classroom environment conducive to learning. I investigated learning centers; I saw walls covered with materials that helped children learn; I experienced whole environments created to enhance learning in a particular unit. Most of what I learned is now commonplace, certainly in the better schools and in well-led children's ministries, but an important principle I internalized at this point in my career was that *children have to be engaged in their own learning.*

At this point I became a staff member of my church. I learned new things by trial and error. I made the same mistakes nearly everyone makes when they are new to church ministry. I misjudged people; I planned vacation Bible school programs that were marred by snags and problems. In time, though, through my work I discovered that I was able to design, lead, and administer programs competently. I could work with a group of volunteers and create with them a variety of experiences in teaching children.

It was satisfying to see children interested and involved in Bible learning. And since the children's ministry in most churches is the largest consumer of volunteer time, and since happy children tend to lead to satisfied parents, a well-run children's program means that there are fewer disgruntled adults in ministry roles in the church.

In this pragmatic spirit, I was determined to help foster children's biblical literacy, so I worked with simple teaching and learning approaches such as large group projects, learning centers, and family or intergenerational experiences that I felt church volunteers could manage. A large group project might include creating the village of Bethany out of appliance boxes as a setting for stories that took place there, or developing a giant floor map of Paul's journeys on which children could move objects that they made to retell those exciting adventures. Popular learning centers included art and puppet centers and a game center at which children helped develop board games based on a Bible story series. (A rule of thumb is that a center is needed for every five to seven children.) Intergenerational experiences included gathering clusters of families or people of all ages in which value-laden stories were read aloud, developing learning activities for all participants of all ages, and having multi-age groups or families enact a story or lead a group in music. None of these approaches seems new today, but at the time, in the small communities where I worked, they were seen as revolutionary in children's education in the church.[4]

Ongoing Development

Churches were responding to the different approaches, but I was still in a program-management mode. Having mastered this, I needed to be taken to another leadership level altogether to learn some additional principles related to the development of children. In 1990, at the invitation of Ted Ward, an innovative, thoughtful Christian educator/scholar, I moved to Chicago to take a faculty position at Trinity Evangelical Divinity School. I wasn't interested in leaving Canada, nor was I excited about returning to a theological school, since I felt that theological education had largely failed

4. For further reading on these approaches, see Linda Cannell and Scottie May, "Kids' Community: Children's Ministry for the New Millennium," *Christian Education Journal* 4, no. 1 (2000): 41-55.

the church. However, I couldn't imagine passing up a chance to work with Ted, and it was time for a change. After almost twenty years of church work and consulting, I was tired and needed a new stimulus for my professional development.

Reflecting on children's ministry, I came to realize that children are not just the church of tomorrow; they are part of the church of today. In Chicago I worked with a superb team of volunteers in a local church, where I learned that the whole church is children's faith community. Children are learning from the totality of their experiences in the congregation. We began to seek ways for children to be involved in the life of the congregation as ushers and as participants in the worship services — reading Scripture, leading in music, praying, and so on. Children do need to be involved in learning geared to their development stage, but I became convinced that children learn *as part of a community* that is committed to their development. This community doesn't replace the family or the child's primary caregiver(s) but serves as a context within which families and caregivers can learn together what it means to nurture children.

Adults (including those who lead many of today's churches) greatly underestimate the capacity of children for learning, for meaningful worship, and for responsible service. My orientation in children's ministry shifted from program management to a more holistic emphasis on ways children can be participants in the life of the congregation. I realized that children are too often simply attached to the church through programming — or that programming is used to keep children occupied so that they won't bother adults. I am still learning.

Some Key Principles

Scottie and Linda have sought to highlight significant insights as they told their stories. Certain key principles and values that they have gleaned through the years have become normative in their work with children.

- Experiences and authentic tasks using real materials (rather than coloring pages or "refrigerator art" made of craft sticks) enhance the value and relevance of the learning.
- Authentic experiential learning is memorable.
- Empowering children to research and investigate subjects for them-

selves increases their desire to learn and helps them to own their learning.
- In order to implement change effectively, leaders must cast a vision that is then owned by others.
- The way space is used affects the quality of the learning.
- For learning to be effective, children must be engaged in their own learning about the subject. This helps them feel valued.
- The content being taught should be meaningful at the time to the child.
- Cooperation and community create a safe learning environment that facilitates Christian formation.
- Allowing children choices shows them that they are valued and can be trusted.
- Methods must flow from purpose; therefore, know your purpose before choosing methods or materials.
- People enjoy serving when their gifts and their interests are utilized.
- Creativity enhances learning, making the familiar fresh and engaging both for children and the volunteers who work with them.

The Nature of Learning

How can you tell when someone has learned something? How do you know when *you* have learned something? What does it mean to "know"? Parents and teachers of little ones can virtually see learning happening daily as new skills and vocabulary are acquired. But in many cases, as time goes on parents and teachers need more discernment to notice evidence of learning.

The Bible says a great deal about learning and knowing. If we are truly to learn, actions must follow that are in accordance with what has been learned: for example, to revere God (Deut. 4:10), to follow God's commands (Deut. 5:1), to fear the Lord (Deut. 31:12), to do right (Isa. 1:17), and to continue doing these things (2 Tim. 3:14). Some people are "always learning but never able to acknowledge the truth" (2 Tim. 3:7); in other words, if learning does not result in change toward godliness, it is not true learning.[5]

5. Consider the definition by O. Sanders, "Learning," in *Baker Encyclopedia of Psychology,* ed. David Benner (Grand Rapids: Baker, 1985): "Learning is . . . the process responsible for relatively permanent changes in behavior, . . . distinguished from behavioral changes that are transient" (p. 634).

This perspective on learning is reflected in the biblical meaning of the word *know.* In English, to know something may or may not mean that true learning has happened. It may simply mean that I know *about* something: for example, I know about Abraham Lincoln, but I don't truly know him. Usually when Scripture uses the word *know,* it implies a relationship or experience with the object or concept that is known, not merely information about it.

A wonderful example of how God wants people to learn can be found in Isaiah 41. Beginning at verse 17, God identifies a serious need of the people: they need water. To assure them that they have not been forsaken, God explains how their need will be supplied. Then in verse 20 a series of verbs — *see, know, consider, understand* — is used to reveal that the hand of the Lord has provided the water that met their need. Hebrew scholars say that that sequence is not mere coincidence. Think about how that sequence leads to learning. To *see* means to have a concrete, sensory, real-life experience. To *know* involves an encounter or relationship with what God has provided. To *consider* indicates the ability to reflect on, meditate, or think about that provision. Then finally, to *understand* means "Aha! I get it."

What a precise sequence God has given us to help us know how to help children learn. For example, in order for children to learn about the Feast of the Passover, let them *see* the various ingredients of a Seder; then they can *know* them as they hear the Passover story and taste the food. Next, they can *consider* or reflect on the significance of these foods and, with the help of a teacher, connect the Old Testament story to the sacrifice of the Lord Jesus. Hopefully they will then *understand* more fully God's redemptive story through Jesus Christ.

Many contemporary educators reflect the verbs of Isaiah in their practice. Learners discover, build, and reorganize images, creating a grasp of truth. These actions are filtered by their worldview, cognitive development, and affective state. Drawing on past experience, the learner makes meaning of new interactions and experiences. The teacher helps learners process these meanings by guiding the connections. In the Christian setting, *God's story must be kept at the center of these connections.* This view of learning is complex, hard to describe, interrelated, and holistic. It seems to leave space for the work of the Holy Spirit in learners' lives.

Insights about Learning

Edgar Dale has designed a helpful tool that provides general observations about the retention of information.[6] For learning to happen, concepts, ideas, or facts must be retained; the more that is retained, the more helpful the learning. Dale's research reveals that after a reasonable period of time (about two weeks), retention of information occurs at the following rates:

- 10 percent of a text that is read.
- 20 percent of what is heard.
- 30 percent of what is seen.
- 50 percent of what is seen and heard.
- 70 percent of what is said and written.
- 90 percent of what is performed as a task.

According to Dale's research, the least effective method involves learning from written and verbal symbols. The most effective methods involve direct, active, purposeful learning experiences, such as hands-on or field experience that represents reality as closely as possible. Dale's findings are usually represented as a cone — the further you progress down the cone, the greater the learning that is likely to take place. "Action-learning" techniques result in up to 90 percent retention. The majority of people seem to learn best when there is sensory involvement — sight, sound, smell, touch, and taste. According to Dale, learning should be designed around real-life experiences as much as possible. His analysis of retention helps us see why that is the case.

Learning is complex. True learning, learning that results in life change, is holistic. Ward uses a helpful metaphor to describe holistic learning, which also means the development of a person. He likens a person to a hand.[7] You may want to look at your hand, palm toward you, to help you envision this metaphor. The thumb represents physical development, with very observable, distinctive qualities. "Pointer" (the index finger) stands for cognitive development, significant and capable. "Tall man"

6. Edgar Dale, *Audio-Visual Methods in Teaching*, 3rd ed. (New York: Holt, Rinehart and Winston, 1969), p. 108.

7. From class notes taken during "Spiritual Ecology," a course taught by Ted Ward at Trinity Evangelical Divinity School, Deerfield, Ill., spring 1989.

(middle finger) is emotional development, while "ring finger" is social development. "Pinky" is moral development, often neglected but remarkably strong though sensitive. If you wish, picture the joints of the fingers as stages of development for each area.

Note that spiritual development is not assigned to a finger. That is because Ward represents it with the palm of the hand. Spiritual development, he says, cannot be directly addressed or taught. This development occurs when the whole person is involved in learning in ways that evoke awe and wonder and encounters with the living God and his story. Deformation of any of the "fingers" adds extra challenge to spiritual development.[8] Ward adds, however, "Useless is not the same as worthless. Though we often teach children in ways that make information useless to them (such as rote learning), that does not mean that the information we give them is worthless. It's just that they can't do anything with it in the form they received it."

Each Learner Is Unique

Sometimes in teaching settings adults have the same expectation for children of like ages, and thus they tend to provide the same experiences for them. Fortunately, significant strides have been made toward awareness of the uniqueness of each child's ability and style of learning. In the past decades extensive research has sought to identify patterns and categories that influence learning. Since 1967, Rita and Kenneth Dunn have explored how various factors affect different learners.[9] The general categories of factors are (1) the environment (such things as lighting, noise, and temperature), (2) emotional (e.g., motivation and responsibility), (3) social (alone, in pairs, or in a group), (4) physical (time of day, mobility, food intake), and (5) psychological (global or analytic, action or reflection). There are also different modalities of learning: people may be auditory, visual, tactual, or kinesthetic learners or a combination. Insights from the Dunns' work are

8. Given the waves of rationalism in recent centuries, it is not uncommon to have hugely inflated "index fingers" in our North American churches. Cognitive knowledge of the content of the Bible has been emphasized to the neglect of other aspects of character development.

9. For more information about the work of Rita Dunn and Kenneth Dunn, see www.geocities.com/~educationplace/element.html.

helpful, but many learning preferences cannot easily be accommodated in church-based ministry — factors such as lighting, time of day, noise, and social factors.

The experiential learning theory of David Kolb is a practical tool for thinking about ways to help children learn. Kolb's theory relates to cognitive style, how the brain perceives or takes in and processes information.[10] Kolb sees this as a learning cycle in which one may begin at any point; see figure 12.1.[11]

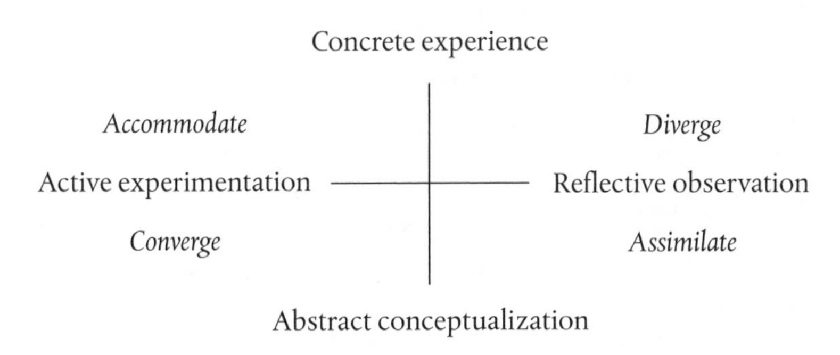

Figure 12.1 Kolb's Learning Cycle

For Kolb, the primary components included in learning are (a) to experience, (b) to reflect, (c) to think, and (d) to do.[12] These four actions indicate ways people tend to *perceive* data — to take in information and the world around them. In his scheme Kolb places *concrete experience* and *abstract thinking* or *conceiving* on opposite ends of a vertical axis; *reflect* and *do* are on opposing ends of a horizontal axis. This instrument allows people to visualize graphically their learning style. If points are plotted on each axis demonstrating the degree to which a person prefers each of those four actions, a learning "kite" will result. According to the theory, a balanced kite would indicate the "ideal" style, but that balance is not com-

10. For an in-depth look at David Kolb's theory, see his *Experiential Learning: Experience as the Source of Learning and Development* (Englewood Cliffs, N.J.: Prentice Hall, 1984). Though parts of the book are less relevant for children's ministry, the sections on the four basic learning styles are helpful.

11. Kolb, *Experiential Learning*, p. 42.

12. Although not directly parallel, these four verbs have a measure of correlation with Isaiah 41:20.

mon. Most people, including children, have learning preferences — ways they are most comfortable learning — even though we all use the various ways to perceive information at different times. Every learning style is accompanied by its own strengths and weaknesses.

According to Kolb, "Learning is the process whereby knowledge is created through the transformation of experience."[13] He uses four terms to identify the ways the brain *processes* data it has just perceived: *diverging, assimilating, converging,* and *accommodating.* The learning kite for people who prefer to *diverge* as they process information would be weighted toward the upper right quadrant of the learning cycle — toward experiencing and reflecting on experiences by coming up with creative, diverging ideas. These people enjoy artistic expression and enjoy learning through their creativity; they thrive on interaction, tending to be highly relational. Those who prefer to *assimilate* emphasize the bottom right quadrant — reflecting and thinking. This group enjoys ideas — thinking about them, analyzing them — especially if an expert presents the ideas in an ordered fashion. If there were a learner who is the proverbial sponge, it would be one who prefers this way of learning. Because the traditional schooling system often affirms this style, these people are comfortable in that system and often become teachers, particularly in higher education. Learners who *converge* enjoy thinking and doing. They want to work with materials and concepts, create plans and strategies, not simply read or hear about them. They need to do something with what they are learning. Note: assimilators and convergers are likely to be less people-oriented than divergers. The last group prefers to *accommodate* while learning by doing and experiencing. These people enjoy active learning and experimenting, but most of all, they thrive in flexible settings devoid of rigid routines.

If Kolb's theory is valid, it is significant to reflect on factors that facilitate learning for most people — settings in which there is dialogue and interaction, activity and strategizing to make application. This contrasts with the modus operandi in many settings: in order to learn, sit still with your hands in your lap and your mouth shut.

Two things about Kolb's theory are especially helpful for working with children. First, acknowledge the strengths and weaknesses of one's own preferred way to learn. In so doing, realize that some things that help you learn may actually hinder someone else's learning. Therefore, in

13. Kolb, *Experiential Learning,* p. 38.

teaching be intentional about including learning activities that are uncomfortable for you so that you don't exclude someone whose style might be opposite. Second, don't worry about identifying the learning styles of the children in your ministry. Whether or not you should match or mix children according to their learning styles doesn't need to be an issue in ministry settings. Involvement in a variety of types of learning can be a growing experience for most children. As the teacher, be sure to include or design an activity that will be enjoyed by learners of each style at some point in each session. This is not as difficult as it may seem.[14]

A well-designed lesson plan includes a sequence of activities, a sequence that can intentionally vary. Here is a way to use learning styles to set up experiences for a lesson or class. After determining the aim of the session, at some point help children realize a felt need or problem they have that relates to the aim. Such an affective activity often appeals to those who prefer to diverge. Then let the children investigate what Scripture says about that problem. Assimilators enjoy this research-like task. Then it's time for a converging activity, in which the children figure out how to apply the truth of Scripture to the problem. Finally, accommodators get into the act and help each other be accountable for acting on the insight gleaned from the lesson.

Kolb's theory of learning styles integrates nicely with a structure for developing lesson plans that Scottie devised for a curriculum she teaches. She calls it "the 5-ATES to EducATE." The steps are LocATE, ElaborATE, IlluminATE, IntegrATE, and ActivATE. The word *educate* means to lead or draw out. In ministry we want to lead children out into a deeper relationship with Jesus Christ. The LocATE step is to identify what God wants the children to know about him from the passage being studied. The ElaborATE step helps children see an issue or problem in their lives that relates to the text. This experiential, feelings-oriented step speaks to the diverging learning style. The IlluminATE step shines the "light" of God's Word onto the problem — an assimilating task. Then IntegrATE connects the text back to the life of the children through application, which is attractive for convergers. Last, to ActivATE or motivate each other toward changed behavior is a step that appeals to the accommodating learner.

14. For additional help in how learning styles relate to ministry, see Marlene LeFever, *Learning Styles: Reaching Everyone God Gave You to Teach* (Elgin, Ill.: Cook Communications, 1995).

As helpful as awareness of various learning theories can be, there is still much that we do not know. For sure we cannot say, "Here is how children learn." While we must recognize and honor the fact that cultures and traditions make differing choices about how learning happens, we can encourage every group to explore various ways of learning and then choose what they feel will be most effective for their context. We want to demonstrate the positive effect on children of people who model godly living. We can take to heart the words of Jesus when he said, "Learn from me" (Matt. 11:29). He can be our example (John 13:15) of how to help people learn. We also do well to be vigilant about elements in our educational settings that might hinder children's learning from and coming to Jesus (Matt. 19:14).

The Nature of Teaching

Jesus is a master teacher. The pages of the Gospels provide glimpses of him teaching large groups of people, small groups, and individuals (Matt. 7:28; 10:1-14; John 3:1-21 are just a few examples). A passage that clearly shows Jesus' style of teaching is Luke 10:25-37: he listens, asks questions, and uses story.[15] In this passage an expert lawyer tests Jesus with a question; Jesus listens to the question and, without answering it, replies with another question. The lawyer answers; Jesus comments; the man asks another question. Then Jesus tells a story, the parable of the Good Samaritan, in order to drive home the point he wanted to make — all the while never explaining the underlying meaning of the questions. Jesus follows the story with another question, which the man answers. Jesus ends the interaction by simply stating, "Go and do likewise." What a remarkable example of teaching by *listening, questioning,* and *telling a story.*

Robert Pazmino, a professor of Christian education, says, "Teaching at its best can foster a sense of wonder and awe about God and the amazing variety of God's creation."[16] Parker Palmer describes teaching this way: "To teach is to create a space in which obedience to truth is prac-

15. Ted Ward in a workshop presented this simple, clear analysis of Jesus' teaching for curriculum developers for the Free Methodist denomination at Winona, Indiana, in the early 1980s.

16. Robert Pazmino, *The Basics of Teaching for Christians: Preparation, Instruction, Evaluation* (Grand Rapids: Baker, 1998), p. 50.

ticed."[17] How would these definitions be applied in children's ministry? Our purpose in teaching is to facilitate spiritual growth and transformation, to familiarize learners with scriptural texts and truths in such a way that they can make a personal connection with the material and its core subject, Jesus Christ. Because the Holy Spirit is the only One to cause true transformation, the human teacher is best defined as one who provides space for the learner to encounter the Holy Spirit. The educator plays an important role in providing the framework for this encounter.

Critical Strategies for Teaching

Using Jesus as our model, consider the three skills he uses in Luke 10 — listening, questioning, and storytelling — skills that also are effective in teaching children. (See chapter 9 for more about storytelling.)

Listening

Many of us have much to learn about listening. Far too often people assume that to teach means to talk and to learn means to listen. This certainly is not always the case. Someone has said that listening is a love gift to another. Therefore be quick to listen, slow to speak. This applies even in teaching.

Listening can be hard work. To listen well means to be actively involved, staying focused without preparing what you want to say in response. It also requires listening carefully to what the child is saying rather than for the answer you had expected or desired. Listening means becoming comfortable with silence so that learners have time to formulate their thoughts and to say all that they have to say. This skill will enable you to understand what a child is thinking, what is being understood, and what may need clarification.

Teachers need to practice increasing "wait time" after asking a question. Studies show that after asking a question, most teachers wait an average of only three seconds before answering it themselves. It takes discipline to learn to "listen" to silence.

17. Parker Palmer, *To Know as We Are Known: Education as a Spiritual Journey* (San Francisco: HarperSanFrancisco, 1993), p. 69.

Questioning

Experienced educators know that being able to ask meaningful questions — questions that promote thinking and reflection — is one of the most important skills a teacher can have. (Note the scores and scores of questions that Jesus asks throughout the Gospels.) Too many teachers feel that thinking just happens and that if it doesn't, something is wrong with the learners. In reality it may be that the questions being asked do not engage learners' thinking.

Here is an example of a poor question: What is the name of the Pharisee in John 3:1? The question requires the learners to look in their Bibles, but it requires no thinking on their part because the answer is clearly stated in the verse. Children quickly become disinterested in that type of question if there are not follow-up questions that go deeper.

In the 1950s Benjamin Bloom, a professor of education at the University of Chicago, along with some colleagues, developed a tool for organizing and structuring learning objectives. Bloom's Taxonomy is useful for developing sets of questions that help learners move through different levels of cognitive tasks to think more deeply.[18] It's a way of helping learners process content:

Level 1, *information acquisition,* involves memorizing and recalling. To help children think at this level, ask questions such as these: Who? What? When? Where? How? What happened? What did you see?

Level 2, *comprehension,* is reached when the child understands the meaning of the text. It involves translating and interpreting the meaning as well as inferring — much more sophisticated tasks than those of level 1. To help children achieve this level, ask them to restate the content or retell the story in their own words. Follow up with questions that allow for new expression and understanding. Ask: What is the point of this story?

Level 3, *application,* identifies how this new information and understanding may be useful. You might create an experience in which learners actually do what has been learned. Ask How and Why questions:

How is __________ an example of __________?
How is __________ related to __________?

18. Benjamin Bloom, ed., *Taxonomy of Educational Objectives: The Classification of Educational Goals* (New York: D. McKay, 1956).

Why is __________ significant?
How would you use __________?
What if __________?

Level 4, *analysis,* takes apart a story or concept in order to identify its components or relationships and the functions or principles behind them (a challenging task for many adults). It may include identifying assumptions behind arguments or positions. Ask:

What are the parts of __________?
How would you arrange __________ according to __________?
What evidence do you have for __________?

Ask learners to compare and contrast elements or concepts.

Level 5, *evaluation,* involves making value judgments. Help learners evaluate the analysis they just did to determine worth and priorities and to identify values.

What criteria would you use to assess __________?
How would you decide about __________?
Explain why you agree or disagree.
What do you feel is most important?

Level 6, *synthesis,* requires combining old and new understandings to build new, larger, more complex concepts. It produces relevant new ideas, procedures, or methods. Because creativity is involved, creative writing or artistic expressions may result. Ask:

What solutions would you suggest for __________?
What would you suggest about __________?
What can you add to __________?
Create a new __________.[19]

19. David Krathwohl, who worked with Bloom in developing the taxonomy, met with a team of educators and revised the original taxonomy to the form presented here. They reversed the order of levels 5 and 6. The revision is explained in Lorin W. Anderson, David R. Krathwohl, Peter W. Airasian, et al., *Taxonomy for Learning, Teaching, and Assessing: A Revision of Bloom's Taxonomy of Educational Objectives* (New York: Longman, 2000).

These important levels are sequential; a weakness at one level will produce a weakness at the following levels. More advanced uses of the cognitive mind cannot be developed effectively apart from the foundations of lower levels of thinking processes. The first three levels are regarded as lower-order thinking, while levels 4-6 are of a higher order, requiring critical thinking. Surprising to many, even elementary-age children are capable of higher-order thinking, though it is different from adult thinking. When you are guiding children through these levels of thinking, use familiar content rather than material that is new to them.

Based on Bloom's Taxonomy, here are some questions that might help children think deeply about Jesus' healing the paralytic in Mark 2.

- Level 1: What happened in this story? Who are the people who were involved? Has any detail been forgotten?
- Level 2: What would Jesus want us to learn from this story? Or, What do we learn about Jesus from this story?
- Level 3: What other stories in the Bible teach us something similar? In what way is this story important for you?
- Level 4: What did you hear in this story that makes it different from other stories or different from what has happened to you? How is it similar?
- Level 5: How would you decide who was honoring God in this story and who was not? What is an important thing about God that you learn here?
- Level 6: Imagine that this event happened today. How would it look different? Who might be the paralytic? Who might be teachers of the law?

Although no one child would likely be able or want to answer all of these questions, when an atmosphere of open discussion is created children are capable of deep, insightful responses.

Here are some simple, practical tips for teachers that may encourage learners' thinking:

- Use follow-up questions and statements, even repeating them: "What else?" "Give an example." "Tell me more." "Please explain."
- Allow learners time to think on their own and write down their thoughts, then time with a partner to discuss their thoughts. Finally, bring the whole group together for a discussion.

- Withhold judgment on a learner's response; delay evaluation. Or ask the group to respond: What do you think about that? Do you see it differently?
- Ask one learner to summarize what another has just said.
- Survey the group for agreement or disagreement.
- Play "devil's advocate," taking an opposing position to deepen discussion.
- Ask learners to think out loud — to unpack how they are thinking.
- Set aside time for learners to formulate their own questions.
- Encourage alternative responses when appropriate.

Teaching Very Young Children

Little ones bring some people great joy and delight while they nearly paralyze others, especially when it comes to teaching. If the teacher expects them to behave differently from the way God designed them, those expectations will lead to frustration and most likely ineffectiveness as well. Young children have a remarkable ability to meet the expectations of authority figures, whether those expectations are high or low. We affect the child's attitudes, actions, and spiritual responses first by our own attitudes, then by our actions, and only then by what we say.

Young children are highly affected by factors of which adults may be oblivious — for example, space, pace, and volume. The way the space for learning experiences is laid out demonstrates the powerful effect that space has on little ones. If bookcases and furniture are used to divide the learning environment into small spaces, nooks and crannies containing interesting things, little ones will explore and investigate those spaces. If the area is large and open, they may run wildly through the room or hover in a corner.

The pace of activity also has the power to affect young children. If lots of energy is expended in leading the children, if the experiences are fast paced, and if leaders move quickly because they are behind schedule or feeling stressed, the children will respond by increasing their own activity level.

The same is true for the noise level: the volume of sound has power over children. Soft voices, gentle tones, and well-modulated music will help little ones maintain a calm sense of self-control. Loud voices, intense rhythmic music, and heavy percussive sounds, on the other hand, will elevate the noisiness and activity level of young children.

Those who teach young children will want to put thought and careful planning into the experiences they desire for the children. If children begin to get out of control, it can be difficult to help them regain focus and more appropriate behavior. It is much easier to prevent these problems by intentionally planning the desired use of space, pace, and volume than it is to correct them.

Young children do not have the life experience to "walk in our shoes," so it is our responsibility to try to see the world from their perspective. Their understanding of time and space is quite different from that of adults. For four-year-olds, one year is a quarter of their lifetime. When children have not yet learned to tell time, the passing of time is more about feel than about seconds and minutes. So children need to be given real-life clues about time: "When we finish our snack, it will be time to . . ." In the same way, a young child's measure for distance might be how far it is to the store or to church or to Grandpa's place. What this means is that starting a story with "A long time ago in a place far away" or "When Jesus walked the road to the big city called Jerusalem" is specific enough.

Young children's language is expanding daily but is grounded in the here and now. Figurative language and even object lessons are confusing for preschool children. For example, they will often picture "fishers of men" as men on hooks or in nets rather than as a call to share the gospel of Christ. When adults speak about faith issues we often use terms that are abstract. Even the word *faith* is difficult to understand. The challenge then is to speak to young children about God's story without lapsing into religious terminology but using simple language structures.

Play is the way young children learn. Sometimes adults consider play a waste of time, but the Christian educator who understands that children learn by doing and not simply by listening will find ways to integrate their natural way of learning into the classroom. Plan to act out Bible stories using simple props and encouraging children to participate with the adults in the story. Design activities that use all the senses. The process of drawing, cutting, painting, pasting, manipulating clay, building towers, blowing bubbles, or studying pictures in a book is more important than the finished product.

Young children who have experienced loving care trust easily. They have a simple trust in God. They basically want to please their parents and their teachers. This makes them vulnerable to manipulation. When preschool children are asked if they would like to accept Jesus into their heart, many will respond, "Yes," because they think that is the answer the teacher wants. However, some may then object to drinking their milk because it might "splash on Jesus in my heart." That is, they have given the desired response but really don't understand what it means. What then should we do? Affirm a child's belief in God. Worship and pray with children. Plan learning experiences that translate the love of God into everyday living.

In spite of the example of Jesus to guide us, to teach may seem almost frightening when we read what James writes: "We who teach will be judged with greater strictness" (James 3:1). But the task is less onerous if we pray *and* keep our eyes on the Lord Jesus. Teaching is a privilege, a calling (Eph. 4:11), and a responsibility.

New and Not-So-New Ways of Teaching and Learning

In recent years, many children's ministers and volunteers have worked to create alternate ways of teaching children in the church, approaches that engage children in actively learning through meaningful experiences designed by thoughtful adults. Here are brief descriptions of some of those models.

Focused Learning Rooms

This well-received model is known by several names: Multidimensional Learning, the Rotation Model, and Workshop Rotation Model. We use "Focused Learning Rooms" because it describes the key concept behind the model: each room is designed to have children focus on a different way of learning. When first conceived in a northern Illinois Presbyterian church in 1990, this model was built on the theory of learning styles described earlier in this chapter. The same Bible story was taught in each room in a different way. Each week children would rotate to a different room, where they would experience the story through a different learning modality. As Howard Gardner's theory of multiple intelligences became popular, focused learning expanded to address those eight "intelligences," embracing music, movement, and other art forms. Gardner's eight categories of intelligence include word/language, mathematical, intrapersonal, interpersonal, musical, bodily/kinesthetic, naturalist, and spatial.[20]

This model works well for the church whose building contains classrooms with a central hallway rather than large multipurpose rooms. Many churches using this model decorate each room accordingly and often very elaborately. The story room might look like a synagogue, the craft room might look like a Bible-time home, the drama room like a stage; Bible-learning game, video, and computer rooms may have a contemporary look. As with the Bible-time museum model, adults enjoy using their gifts in the various foci of the rooms.

The same Bible story is taught for a series of weeks, usually six, so children become familiar with that story thoroughly and in diverse ways. Most churches age-grade the rotation groups. During a story series a teacher will eventually teach every grade level. However, since the same Bible story is taught throughout the rotation, only small, week-to-week adjustments in the lesson plan are needed to accommodate the varying ages of the students. Thus weekly lesson preparation for the series is relatively easy once the initial work is completed.[21]

Promiseland

The components of this model — large group and small group — have stood the test of time. It is especially helpful for managing very large numbers of children. Though the format is not new, the spin that Willow Creek Community Church in suburban Chicago gives to it is fresh and invigorating. The church's children's ministry is called Promiseland, and its model is being replicated all over North America and even internationally. (The original Promiseland has about one thousand children for each of three weekend services.)[22]

20. See Howard Gardner's *Frames of Mind* (New York: Basic Books, 1993).

21. For more information about this model and dates of an annual conference, see www.cmamerica.com. Information is also available at www.rotation.org (accessed August, 2004). *Workshop Rotation Model,* a book by the originators Melissa Hansche and Neil MacQueen, may be ordered at www.sundaysoftware.com/rotationbook/bookorder.htm.

22. For information about Promiseland conferences, see www.promiselandonline.com.

As children from toddlers to fifth-graders arrive, they select an activity, game, or craft to do for a period of time. Children are carefully divided by age, with activities chosen for their specific appropriateness. These fun activities do not usually reinforce the learning theme of the session. Then the children gather with their assigned small group leader for music and teaching in a large group. This format is used for all age levels. The large group experience, with excellent production even for the little ones, includes electronic music, lights, staging, and some choreography. The teaching usually includes a well-rehearsed drama and a Bible lesson. The seventy-five-minute session ends with small group time, in which an adult or teen leads a discussion of the relevance of the story they just heard for their own lives.

Kids' Community — A Hands-On Bible-Time Museum Model

The way this model developed is described earlier in this chapter; Linda and Scottie have made refinements, but the basic structure is unchanged. There are three twenty-minute components.[23] (1) In project time, the children engage in the context of the biblical story. (2) In large group or story time, children hear the biblical story, usually through a dramatic, first-person retelling, and begin to learn the theme verse. (3) In small group time, the shepherds (they are not called teachers)[24] help the children apply the story and the key verse to their own lives, and pray for each other. The sequence of the components is flexible, though ending with small group time is preferable.[25]

Each year Scottie's church incorporates a series that emphasizes mis-

23. Thirty minutes for each component would be ideal, but the original setting is limited to a total of sixty-five minutes.

24. The difference between a "teacher" and a "shepherd" is more than semantic. A shepherd is a guide, facilitator, relationship builder who helps a small group of children apply the story and then pray and care for each other. "Teacher" conjures images of a deliverer or instructor of the content. Therefore for this model the name change is very significant.

25. When missionaries and internationals have viewed the Bible museum model, they see immediate cross-cultural application. This is due primarily to the fact that the focus is on the culture and stories of the Bible with as little influence from Western culture as possible.

sions. The space is arranged and decorated to look as much as possible like a specific country in which the church is involved. Instead of Bible-time projects, the children work at various stations relating to life in that country: language, food, education, recreation and play, art and culture, marketing and the economy, the effect the gospel has had, and the church. Missionaries to that country are often the storytellers during the series.

One of the strengths of this learning setting is that it allows volunteers to minister according to their giftedness. Because of the unique ways volunteers are used in this model, we sometimes have waiting lists, especially for small group leaders. Volunteers are responsible for each of the three components. It is helpful to have three coordinators, one each for a team of storytellers, a team of project leaders, and a team of small group leaders (shepherds). Storytellers are teens and adults who enjoy drama — those who can create a story from the text that comes alive for children. Project leaders are people with special skills — woodworkers, sewers, artists, cooks, biologists, historians, computer experts, builders, researchers, map experts — that often are not utilized in traditional ministries. Qualifications for shepherds are that they love the Lord Jesus and love kids.

This model is flexible enough to accommodate the busy lifestyles of suburbanites. Expectations of the volunteers look like this:

Responsibility	**Level of commitment**	**Amount of preparation**
Storytellers	low	high
Project leaders	moderate	moderate
Shepherds	high	low

A storyteller is expected to spend at least two hours developing the story, gathering a costume and props, and rehearsing. But that person may tell a story only two or three times in a year. The project leader is committed to helping through an entire six- to eight-week series but perhaps only one series a year. These people, with the help of the coordinator, develop the project, finding the best way for the children to accomplish the task. They need to arrive early enough each week to have everything set up and ready for the children.

Shepherds are the key to the effectiveness of Kids' Community. They greet the children in their group, watch to see which project each child chooses so they can talk about it, and sit with their group during large group time. Though a yearlong commitment is desired for consistent presence to build relationships within each small group, there is only minimal weekly preparation once a shepherd becomes comfortable leading discussions with children.

Kids' Community is published under the product name Jubilation Station. More than twenty story series from both Testaments are available, but as with all published materials, adaptations must be made for each church's setting.[26]

"Contained Classroom" Model

Sunday school has served the church of Jesus Christ well for more than two centuries.[27] It is the epitome of the "contained classroom" model. Although this chapter has pointed out weaknesses of traditional Sunday school because our culture has changed and insights about teaching and learning have unfolded, that does not negate the value that the "contained classroom" model can have. It provides space without interruptions or distractions for learning to happen.

Anytime a Sunday school teacher using published material in a classroom modifies it using his or her own creativity, an effective learning experience can result. The classroom model is least effective when volunteers follow the lesson plan as if it were a recipe and "the cake will flop" if not followed exactly. Also, it is important to avoid school-like tasks such as quizzes, a task that is usually counterproductive. Engaging learning can come from such simple activities as using Bible-time figures from the resource kit as puppets or characters for a mock TV program, with the children creating the scripts.

Current church security policies can actually make this model more effective. Since in many churches one adult is not allowed to be alone with children, teaching teams are often employed in classrooms. This leads easily to using the gifts of the team in creative ways to enhance learning. Even the Bible-time museum model can be modified to work in a contained classroom. Set up two projects germane to the Bible story, allowing chil-

26. Jubilation Station is available electronically at www.cookministries.com/nexgen/Jubilation.

27. For a rich description of the history of Sunday school, see Robert Lynn and Elliott Wright, *Big Little School* (Birmingham, Ala.: Religious Education Press, 1980).

dren to choose which task they prefer. Then one of the adults can be the first-person storyteller. Next, the whole class can be the small group that discusses and applies the story.

Special Days Model

Many churches prefer to maintain a more traditional Sunday-morning church education. This does not mean that their children don't enjoy rich, authentic learning experiences; they just may not have them on Sunday mornings. The seasons of the calendar and of the church year provide a structure to enable children's ministry to provide wonderful times of engagement and education that go beyond the norm. And the calendar structure begs these experiences to be repeated each year.

The rhythm of the festivals, feasts, and fasts that Scripture relates allows salvation history to be rehearsed with children (and grownups as well). These special day celebrations are a way for children to enter into and experience God's story. Rather than simply learning about the Passover, they can experience it by celebrating a Seder. This is true holistic education. Special day celebrations based on the church calendar are easier for a liturgical church to implement, because these congregations are usually more familiar with these holy days (holidays) and their sequence. There may be more challenges for a nonliturgical church to celebrate events in the church calendar, but the common calendar can also be used.

Gretchen Wolff Pritchard, in her creative, helpful book *Offering the Gospel to Children,* describes how she implements special Saturday celebrations at her church.[28] Because she ministers in a context that follows the church calendar, she carefully describes how these festivals and commemorations unfold. She includes an intergenerational Christmas pageant, a Palm Saturday event, and a prayer walk during Holy Week, among others. Her examples may inspire new ways of thinking about Christian celebrations for the education of all God's people. Pritchard's church is located in the inner city, and she says the ministry approach she describes has provided continuity and nurture for neighborhood children who have many

28. Gretchen Wolff Pritchard, *Offering the Gospel to Children* (Cambridge, Mass.: Cowley, 1992).

unmet needs. The result: a sense of security and trust among children who are considered to be "at risk."

Training Teachers for Alternative Models

Traditional terms such as *Sunday school* and *classes* are not as common as they once were. Many programs have replaced the word *teacher* with *shepherd*. The intent is to help prepare parents and volunteers for an experience that is different. Yet most models use a similar format — large group time, small group time, and "activity" time — though the sequence varies.

For newer models to be effective, there must be a focus on team building. None of these formats is effective without that. Ministry leaders must work hard to build and support teams that allow for a wonderful variety of ways to serve. Successful recruitment and retention of teams requires a coordinator who has zeal for communication and team building.[29]

It should come as no surprise that traditional ways of training teachers will not be as helpful with these newer models of learning and teaching.[30] Teacher training meetings have traditionally been used to explain administrative policies and help volunteers know how to use curriculum materials and how to manage children's behavior. The team approach at the core of many newer models uses "teachers" very differently, as already explained. The change in roles is partly behind the name change from *teacher* to *shepherd*. These changes require a different approach to equipping volunteers.

It is helpful to gather new volunteers with those who are more experienced, to help them get acquainted with each other but also to explain the vision and approach behind the new model. (This step is especially important for those who have experienced traditional Sunday school.) This event should include time for new staff to ask questions of those who are more seasoned. The experienced staff might also relate anecdotes and testimonials of their experiences with the model. Next, new volunteers

29. See chapter 15, pp. 344-50, for help with these tasks. Develop a list of resource people in the congregation who could give help and insight to specific teams. For example, instead of using your professional teachers as church teachers, find out what they do best and invite them to come alongside a teaching team for a period. Identify people in other types of work who have particular skills you can use in equipping others.

30. For additional guidelines, see chapter 15, pp. 345-49.

should be assigned at least a couple of sessions to watch "master" teachers or shepherds in action, to see how they lead and relate to the children. Then for a couple of weeks the new volunteers and the experienced ones should collaborate, preparing together and then leading the session together. In the last step, the "master" teachers should watch the new staff do it all, providing input, affirmation, and suggestions as appropriate.

Such a procedure works well if the ministry model is well established and has generated an experienced staff of volunteers. But if the intent is to initiate a new model, a different strategy is needed. The leadership team needs to carefully develop the vision for the new model, including the biblical and philosophical thinking behind it, and then present it in thoughtful stages to the volunteers. If possible, each stage should include a demonstration or experience for the volunteers so that they can envision how the model will work. The more the volunteers can enter into and own the new learning setting, the more they will feel comfortable in their new roles.

Effective Teaching — Whatever the Model

Many factors help ensure that positive learning is happening. Here are some of them.

The Content

We who call ourselves Christian, followers of the Lord Jesus Christ, have access to and responsibility for the world's most remarkable story — the story of the actions and character of God as proclaimed in both Testaments. We want children to see that the Bible is about God's actions with real people at a real place in time. This content, when adequately understood and interpreted in light of relevant insights into teaching and learning, will engage children in formational, even transformational encounters.

We dare not devalue this story by "dumbing it down," assuming it cannot be grasped by children. Nor dare we reduce the stories about God and his Son to moralisms: for example, "This story teaches us that we are to be kind." God is the center of his story! Yes, we are to be kind, but the point is that it is God who wants us to be kind; God wants us to learn how to do this through the Holy Spirit.

Cooperation and Community

Children relax and engage in learning activities with greater focus and depth when the environment is cooperative rather than competitive — when it has a community-like feel. This may seem counterintuitive, since the chance to be "winners" can elicit considerable enthusiasm and determination among children.[31] Competition is effective for short-term retention of facts but rarely results in long-term internalization of content or in character formation. It is very, very difficult to teach children to be compassionate while they are participating in competitive activities. Children of all ages enjoy working together toward a common goal, however, when they are with adults who value cooperation. *Community* means "with unity," a New Testament goal for the church, to be sure.

Choice

Allowing each child to be able to choose work at times enables children to make decisions in a safe, welcoming environment. Many children rarely have that opportunity; adults make most decisions for them. They are told what to do, when to do it, and how to do it.

Choice honors the different ways children like to learn and the unique ways they are gifted, but it should not be a rigid value. Because cooperation and community are also important, sometimes children should be assigned to work on tasks together.

View of Children

Because establishing and nurturing relationships with children is a value, their behavior is managed differently. The goal is to help children develop self-control rather than to impose external control on them. That job is made easier by the fact that fewer behavior problems develop when chil-

31. See Scottie May, "A Look at the Effects of Extrinsic Motivation on the Internalization of Biblical Truth," *Christian Education Journal* 7, no. 1 (2003): 47-65; also Alfie Kohn, *Punished by Rewards* (Boston: Houghton Mifflin, 1993), and *No Contest: The Case Against Competition* (Boston: Houghton Mifflin, 1986).

dren are actively engaged in their learning. Long lists of behavior rules discourage some children and challenge others to become defiant. Still, guidelines are necessary. Stated positively, they may be as simple as "Respect people, respect property, stay where you belong, and walk in this place."[32]

Children's own interests and abilities can be utilized as resources. With adult guidance and encouragement, children can become leaders of learning teams, peer encouragers, mentors of younger children, worship leaders, ministry leaders, and so on.

Effectiveness in Multiple Settings

Effective teaching often has cross-cultural relevance. Because some of the models described here rely on the biblical context for the story and for projects (especially the Bible-time museum), they may be used in any culture. Though the project-oriented models require materials, they are economical. Little print curriculum is needed, and with a bit of ingenuity most materials can be gathered from volunteers' households and yards. Nonchurched children too feel comfortable in these settings, because learning is not necessarily based on prior knowledge.

Challenges to Effective Teaching

The shift in teaching and learning models in the church has driven us away from the comfortable, familiar model of Sunday school. Many churches have left the familiar but are floundering, looking for what should replace it. It's as if we left Egypt but many of us have not yet reached the Promised Land.

We must remember the past and the efforts and values embodied there. These values seem to have been forgotten in many cases, nor have they been effectively replaced. Unfortunately, in recent years some church leaders have assumed that a core value for children's ministry is that it must be fun. There is no problem with church being fun for children, but

32. This approach comes from Barbara Colorosa's *Kids Are Worth It: Giving Your Child the Gift of Inner Discipline* (New York: Avon, 1994).

when it becomes a *core* value for the ministry many other biblical and spiritual values easily become secondary. It is difficult to help children experience God's presence with awe and wonder when the environment is intentionally designed for fun.

As with most things, weaknesses can be found in the new models. The unfamiliarity of these models may deter some churches from trying them even if they might lead to increased effectiveness. Generally more effort is required to create teams and to prepare for learning experiences. However, most ministry leaders find that busy volunteers will make time to do that which is interesting and purposeful. (Note that in many of these models, once a series or unit is set up the sessions run smoothly and easily. Creating new units or experiences takes time, coordination of teams, and administrative attention to detail. But our kids are worth it!)

It is essential to keep the purpose for these alternative experiences in mind: effective teaching and learning. Unless planned carefully according to a clearly defined and understood purpose with an eye to children's capacity for learning, the projects and activities can become busywork and the experiences trivial.

* * *

As this chapter has unfolded, you have encountered models, concepts, and theories of learning and teaching that, we hope and believe, are worth consideration. At the same time, you have probably seen some familiar, tried-and-true principles and methods. Attention has been given to several learning models that differ conceptually from traditional forms of church-based learning such as Sunday school. Through personal stories we have tried to explain the rationales, structures, and processes of these models. We hope these concepts can be catalysts for your own thinking, because *how you do it matters!*

A significant challenge for the children's pastor is to discern which model is most appropriate for the vision and purposes of his or her church's ministry. Just because First Community Church has six hundred children in its Sunday ministry does not mean that it is using the right model for your congregation.[33]

33. In chapter 13, pp. 285-88, William Frankena's tool for helping discern such a decision is presented.

Chapter 13

IN SPECIALIZED MINISTRIES

Ministry opportunities abound. Ministry is a mindset of continually being the hands and feet of Jesus Christ and seeing others through his eyes. When we are aware of what is happening in the lives of children, we realize that children's ministry calls for more than offering them Sunday morning worship and learning. These are very important experiences, but usually they are not enough for the child's Christian formation, particularly if children struggle with complex issues, lack nurturing caregivers, or know very little about the gospel. This chapter explores forms and ideas for responses and ministries, other than regular Sunday learning and worship, that may enrich the spiritual life of children and support them as they deal with difficult realities. We also attempt to articulate strategies for developing and sustaining such ministries.

Compassion-Based Ministry

As we examine the ministry of Jesus on earth, we see that he reached out to both the wealthy and the poor, to those who were physically or spiritually broken as well as to those who lived as faithful believers. There is no reference to Jesus turning someone away. He ministered holistically as he responded to the needs of the people he encountered. While the Gospels do not outline a specific plan that Jesus followed in his ministry, the compassion of his responses is key.

Compassion means "with passion," or empathy that results in action.

Someone has defined it as "your pain in my heart." Compassion also means to care. To minister means to care. Henri Nouwen, noted scholar and writer on spiritual formation, says that to care we must empty ourselves and allow others to come close, removing any barriers that would prevent them from communing with us. The ministry of the Lord Jesus was marked by compassion just as our ministries with today's children should be — full of empathy and caring with action.

The Gospels make explicit references to Jesus' compassion as he moved among people during his three brief years of ministry on earth. Compassion was often his response when he saw a crowd of people. Sometimes his compassionate action resulted in healing; other times he met physical needs such as hunger; still others he met spiritual needs. He allowed situations around him to become natural ministry opportunities. His ministry — to preach, teach, and heal — flowed creatively from his context. As we consider shaping children's ministries for special contexts, it is important to keep Jesus' example in mind and allow it to shape the framework of our thinking.

Seeing Children's Need for Compassion

Josh is a handsome fourth-grader who is profoundly deaf. He also has ADHD and a bipolar disorder. Only recently have physicians been able to balance his medications to allow him to interact with his peers. Josh and his family came to a church in the Midwest looking for a place where they could be a part of the body of Christ. At first the staff was ill prepared to minister to Josh's needs, but as the church family came around them in a response of Christlike compassion, everyone settled in. A fourth-grader who had an inner-ear implant is fluent in sign language. She makes sure that Josh understands classroom projects and teachers' instructions. Josh's mom, Janeen, is working now with the children's choir, teaching signs for their songs. When the children sing in worship, they often sign the words. These choir members are learning kinesthetically and developing valuable skills in signing. They are also gaining a greater awareness of the life that Josh, their brother in Christ, lives every day. So while there was no formal ministry in place for Josh and his mom, the church family responded with compassion and created a space for them.

Seven-year-old Anthony's family dog died. Anthony's parents, unable to console him, called upon the church for help. Although no seminary or education classes prepare a minister for ministering to a child bereaved of a pet, the church was asked to respond to a hurting Anthony with the love and compassion of Jesus. They assured Anthony that if God knows how many hairs are on his head, surely God understands the importance of the family pet; God understands his sadness and continues to have a good plan for all things.

Katy, who is twelve, broke down in tears during a church gathering because of her pain over her parents' divorce. Katy was assured that the church is a safe place to express her feelings. She was encouraged by the constant support of her church family and reassured that she could trust in the faithfulness of the Lord, particularly during this difficult time.

Local news broke the story that on a park outing a tragedy had taken the life of a ten-year-old girl. Though the family was unknown to the staff of a large nearby church, upon hearing the news the children's pastor immediately went to the family's home to offer comfort and support. The church family provided meals and transportation for this family. The pastor made the church building available for the child's funeral. He also made sure the other children in the family received compassionate, listening support. The congregation embraced this family in ongoing ways — a family that would have been strangers to them but for the tragedy.

These four real-life situations provided children's ministry staff with opportunities and a context for ministry. All of them were unplanned, informal ministry situations, but each could become the catalyst for intentional specialized ministries. Working with Josh might lead to an outreach to other families with deaf children and the enlisting of a sign-language interpreter to teach hearing children basic signs to communicate with their deaf friends. Anthony's need might encourage ministers to take regular time to talk through the high and low points in children's lives and to help children understand God's daily presence. Katy's example might lay the groundwork for a support group with a trained facilitator to help children make sense of their family struggles and realize the presence of Jesus Christ in the midst of them. The ten-year-old's death brought an opportunity for the faith community to reach out to a family that was not part of a church, so that the family could be comforted, welcomed, and nurtured in the faith.

Rather than understanding the experiences of these children as isolated events, leaders need to consider that many other children may be experiencing similar struggles. Those who minister to children need to be prayerful about their responses and consider how Christ himself would work in these situations. Godly leaders who provide compassionate care will enable children to see that the need of their souls can be truly filled only by Jesus Christ.

As we consider all the needs of today's children (and we've barely scratched the surface with these examples), one thing becomes obvious quickly: children's ministry demands flexibility! No one in children's ministry begins work anticipating such situations and the ministry opportunities they provide. No prepackaged curriculum can respond to the uniqueness of these needs. Thus it is the heart of the leader and the readiness to respond that are most significant.

A Tool for Discerning Ministry Purposes: The Frankena Model

An effective Christian children's ministry needs a Christian philosophy — a Christian worldview that develops from incorporating the principles and values of Scripture into every aspect of the ministry. *God* must be the center. Not teaching the Bible, not knowing *about* God, not attracting large numbers of kids, not having fun, but *knowing God.* This must be the driving purpose in all that we do in the name of ministry with children. The other things are important and should be included in the ministry, but they must not be its heart. The philosophical model described here is known as the Frankena Model.[1]

Five interrelated sets of questions can help us form a philosophy of children's ministry for any setting.

A. What is the ultimate purpose of the ministry — the big-picture goal? Why do we have a children's ministry?
B. What is the nature of the ministry context? What do we believe about God? About children? About salvation? What are the children like, including their spiritual condition? What is the community like, including economic, demographic, social, and cultural aspects?
C. What values or qualities need to be developed within the children? If

1. Adapted from William K. Frankena, *Philosophy of Education* (New York: Macmillan, 1965), pp. 4-10.

seeing Christlikeness develop within children is part of our purpose, what needs to be cultivated within them? What else needs to happen in the children? Do they have a special need for self-discipline? If they are in an at-risk setting, do they need to learn to read?

D. In what ways do learning and character development best happen for children? What educational theories and methodologies are most helpful here? In other words, what are the best practices for accomplishing questions A and C?

E. What ministry experiences should be created to achieve these purposes? When and how should they happen?

We ministry leaders must constantly ask ourselves, "What are we doing? Why are we doing it? How should we do it?" The above five sets of questions help in that process. Questions A and C are "what" questions: What are we trying to accomplish here? Questions B and D are "why" questions: Why is a specific children's ministry needed here? Why are these methods the most effective ones to use? Question E asks the "how" question: How are we going to accomplish our purposes? Also, questions A and C address "ought" issues: What *ought* to be accomplished here? What ought to be developed within the learners? Questions B and D identify "is" concerns: What is the reality of our ministry? What is the most effective theory or method, given our current state of knowledge, for accomplishing our purposes?

People in the United States tend to be pragmatic. They often prefer to start with the "how" question in many areas of life: How can I lose more weight? How can I gain more from my investments? How can I overcome depression? This same tendency can be found in the church. Children's leaders may ask: How can I attract more kids to our ministry? How can I get kids to memorize more Scripture? How can I help children learn about God? When you start with the "how" question, it is easy to overlook the important issues that the "what" and "why" questions raise. In other words, "how" should be the last question to be asked in the series "what," "why," and "how." When the sequence is out of order, discontinuity may develop between how the ministry is unfolding and what its actual purposes are.

When Scottie worked with churches as a Christian education consultant, she would sometimes find a discontinuity between the mission statement or purpose of the children's ministry (question A) and what was actually happening within the ministries (question E). "Whatever works" would sometimes be assumed to suffice. Time and thought are required to address questions B and C, to assure that the needs of the children are thoroughly understood. Question D demands that ministry leaders keep abreast of findings about learning, teaching, and spiritual formation that may make the ministry more effective. This is especially true when specialized ministries are being developed. What we do and how we do it *must* flow from our purposes and values.

If these questions were visualized as shapes that "talk" to each other, they might look like figure 13.1.

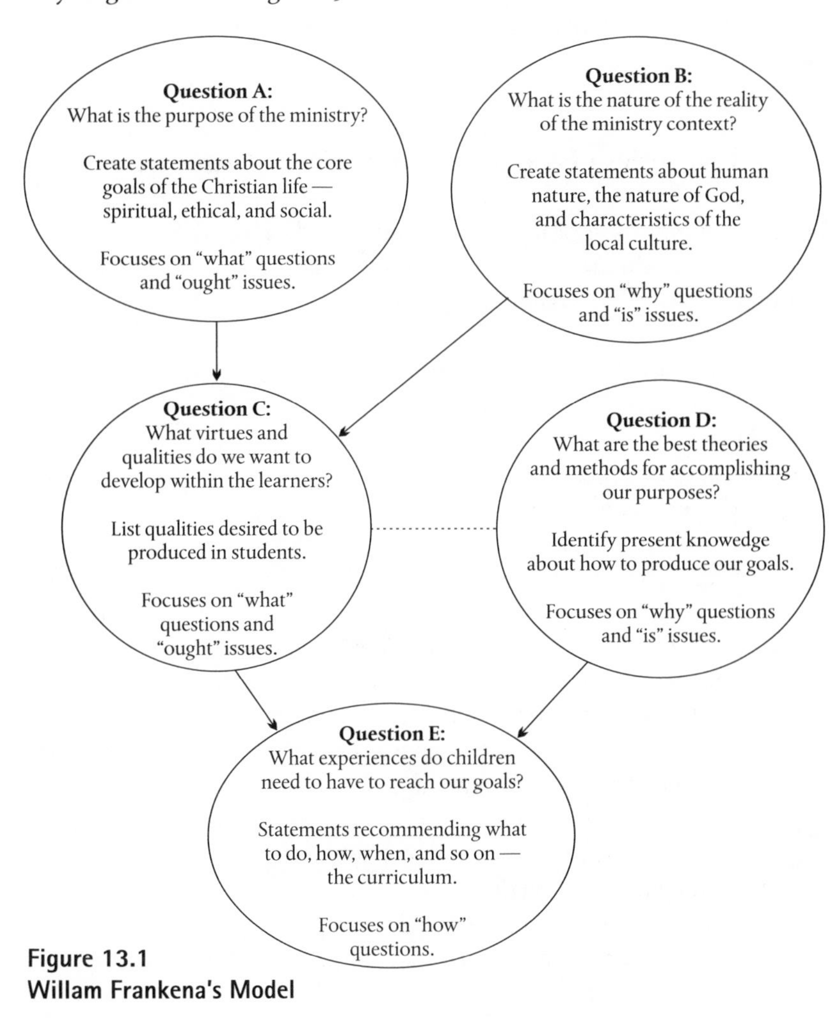

Figure 13.1
Willam Frankena's Model

This series of questions can be used to help formulate a philosophy of children's ministry and to determine the special ministries needed to reach and nurture the children within our sphere of influence. These questions can also aid in the evaluation of existing ministries and programs to see if they really are serving the church's vision. A strength of this model is that it can be used on many different levels: Frankena's questions may be used to create or assess the ministry purposes of the whole church, of the entire children's ministry, of one facet of children's ministry, or even of one session. This model provides a valuable tool to ensure that what we do in ministry is consistent with our ultimate purposes and values.

Categories of and Ideas for Specialized Ministries

Since the compassion of Jesus knows no boundaries, neither should our ministries with children. Some categories of ministries can help us think through the range of possibilities:

- nurture/growth
- social
- outreach
- need based/caring
- intergenerational
- crisis driven
- service

Some ideas falling under each category are general, while others are specific to a particular church or ministry. In no way are the ideas listed here intended to be exhaustive or even representative. There are countless possibilities within each category. These ideas may be ministry resources or a means of sparking your own creativity.

Christian Nurture and Growth

In addition to Sunday ministries of learning and worship, there are other ways of promoting spiritual nurture and growth in children. Several of these involve preparation for rites of passage such as baptism or partaking in the Lord's Supper for the first time.

Confirmation or Doctrine Classes

This time-honored experience for older children and young adolescents can be profound or it can be perfunctory. Such classes can be sustained with vigor when approached with fresh ideas and energy. The length and content of such courses vary among church traditions, but in any case it can be the source of much nurture and growth. If conducted at an age when children are asking deep questions, and in a manner that engages children in their own learning rather than merely sets them to memorizing a set of prescribed questions and answers, confirmation can have rich meaning.

Let the children help develop the questions, filling in where important gaps may exist; with guidance, allow them to investigate the answers. Then celebrate their learning during the course by having each create an expression of his or her own faith to be shared with the entire congregation. These expressions might include artwork, original music composition, creative writing such as poetry or story, or an exposition on why the child chooses to be Christian.

Each child could be connected with an adult mentor who might even attend the classes with him or her. Hold a confirmation retreat. Present the children to the congregation or to a small group for prayer.

The Child in Our Hands

This model partners the home and the congregation in nurturing the faith of children and youth. It places children and youth in the center of faith formation and surrounds them with family as the primary place for formation, while the role of the congregation is to come alongside and assist the adults in the home to teach and nurture faith in the young ones. If this model is envisioned as a series of concentric circles, children and youth are the center circle of faith formation, surrounded by family; the family is surrounded by congregation, the congregation is surrounded by community, and the community by culture. This is a discipling or nurturing process, with the Holy Spirit working from the inside out to transform culture.

One church has teams of adults trained to visit each child two weeks before the anniversary of his or her baptism. The team helps the family prepare to celebrate this special event, interacts with children old enough to be conversant about the anniversary's significance, and leaves a symbolic gift as a memento.[2]

Club or Midweek Programs

In addition to Sunday learning and worship ministries, many churches offer weekly sessions on Wednesday or Sunday evenings. These tend to be children's club-type programs, often affiliated with national organizations and using their published materials.

Some club programs are patterned after scouting. Many of them are very popular and time-tested. In addition to encouraging Christian nurture and growth in the children, club programs often have an outreach and evangelism thrust. They also may be highly developed, volunteer intensive, and sometimes quite costly because of uniforms and paraphernalia for each leader and child. Ministry leaders should take care to ensure that the program fits the purpose and values of the church's overall ministry with children. No matter what program is selected, the children's minister needs to equip the volunteers to be able to adjust and modify the curriculum to fit these children and this context.

Some churches schedule a weekly family supper, following which children go to the club program and adults attend their own activities. Examples of these programs include Adventure Club, AWANA, Christian Service Brigade, Logos, Missionettes, Pioneer Clubs, Royal Rangers, and denominational clubs. An Internet search will yield web addresses of these organizations.[3]

Other churches choose not to follow a prescribed program. They may combine a weekly children's choir rehearsal with a light meal and a game time. A customized weekly ministry offers much room for creativity.

A word of caution is needed here: the ministry leader needs to monitor the time and energy necessary to sustain a church's own midweek event. Weekly club meetings may also happen after school at church and in homes and back yards of church family members.

2. For more information on "The Child in Our Hands," contact Dick Hardel, Youth and Family Institute, 1401 E. 100th St., Bloomington, MN 55425, or e-mail rhardel@theinstitutefrw.org.

3. A range of club materials may be accessed at www.childrensministry.net.

Summer Ministries

Vacation Bible School and church-based day camps tend to be the mainstay of summer ministries, often including an intent of reaching out to nonchurched children. VBS has had a resurgence of popularity since about 1990. Publishers go to great lengths to produce VBS materials with exciting, innovative themes. Churches tend to select what appears to be the newest and best. Rarely does a church reuse a VBS kit; therefore VBS is big business.

Once again, the ministry leader needs discernment to ascertain if the flashy materials really "deliver the goods" that will accomplish the ministry goals. In many places preschoolers make up the majority of children attending VBS, a fact that must not be lost on the curriculum decision-maker.

As in other areas of children's ministry, there is much room for creativity in weeklong summer ministries. Many churches create alternatives to traditional VBS, drawing on the gifts and expertise of congregants. One church has a Celebration Arts Festival, where artists from the community who are skilled in art forms including watercolor, sculpting, woodworking, ballet, percussion, and even martial arts guide children to develop their abilities in the form of their choice. All the children gather for a teaching time that focuses on the biblical qualities important to developing the discipline to create. Another church has a science camp led by science teachers and professional scientists from the church. Another church VBS studies insects, making parallels with biblical texts. Still another created its own Narnia, developing a curriculum that led children through C. S. Lewis's series and its biblical allegory. Churches have cooking camps, music camps, or the increasingly popular sports camps — soccer, volleyball, football, and basketball. These alternative approaches are dual-purposed: most of them teach a skill or a knowledge base that then is integrated into biblical truths for the edification of the churched child and the evangelism of the nonchurched child.

Daystar School, a Creative Model

Daystar School is an unusual example of a Christian elementary school. Its unique character offers an example of how a specialized ministry might look. This culturally engaged school located in downtown Chicago uses the entire city as its classroom. Socially, economically, and racially diverse, it combines age groups in learning and has a strong emphasis on visual and performing arts. Cooperative learning and small group work are valued. The children take field trips to countless sites to learn within the authentic contexts of the city.

Children's ministries might nurture and grow children by providing similar experiences for several weeks during the summer or on Saturdays. Though such ministry requires extensive advance planning and administration, the benefits reaped for the children would be well worth the efforts extended.[4]

Relational Ministries

The only limit to what can be included in this category is one's imagination. Gather the children of the faith community for any reason at all. The more the children of the church are able to play together outside of other church activities, the more it will feel like a family. Deep friendships within the faith community may provide a shelter to help children through the adolescent years.

The church might become an after-school drop-off site for children whose parents work. Imagine what it might be like if the church rather than the mall were the gathering place for kids. What might it take to accomplish that? Susan Lennartson, formerly a children's pastor at a church in Minnesota, encapsulated the goal with a catchy slogan: "When school is off, church is on." That sentence epitomizes the possibilities that relational ministries present.

Parties

Any kind of a party works: a preschool pool party (wading pools set up on the church yard), trike/bike parking-lot rallies, an annual birthday party to celebrate the birthdays of all the children, holiday parties, table-game parties, scavenger hunts, play night parties in coordination with a parents' night out. The local library is a helpful source for additional party ideas.

4. Contact information is available at www.daystarschool.com.

Skill Mentoring

Mentoring can take many forms. In the area of relational ministry, mentors can impart skills to children. People within the congregation who have skills can meet with a small group of children for a series of sessions in woodworking, gardening, baking, fitness conditioning, martial arts, ballet, sewing, art, knitting/crocheting, design, or graphic arts and animation. These intentionally planned though informal times may lead to interaction that nurtures the children and also the mentor.

Outreach Ministries

Because many churches struggle with outreach, extra attention is given here to special ministries intended to reach children who are not yet followers of Jesus and do not know about the gospel. Taking the gospel story to those who don't know it is a significant emphasis in the New Testament. A special challenge accompanies this work, especially when ministering with at-risk children: these children need people who are willing to make long-term commitments to being there. Because many have been abandoned, rejected, or relocated over and over, they desperately need consistency and compassion from the people who minister among them.

Sometimes a church views successful outreach as having children pray to "ask Jesus into their heart." Other churches see outreach as simply providing food and clothing for those without. This is an area in which leaders in children's ministry need clear biblical and theological vision.

Francis Bridger, visiting professor of pastoral care and counseling at Fuller Theological Seminary, illumines ways to reach out to children outside the faith community. In a review of his work he is quoted as saying, "Individual *belief* cannot be separated from social *belonging.*" Traditional evangelism, he notes, acknowledges a child as part of the group only after the child comes to personal faith in Christ. In the view of many, belonging follows belief: you can belong after you believe. Bridger proposes that this be turned around. "It may be that in today's world, the majority of unchurched children will be reached by an approach which aims first and foremost at developing a sense of group belonging before it invites individual commitment to Christ."[5] Bridger's position deserves careful consideration when we are developing outreach strategies and events.

Carefully conceived outreach can have breadth, depth, and creativity, qualities evident in the variety of ministries described below.

Great Family Fun Fair

Since 1990 this community outreach event has been held at Wheaton Bible Church, Wheaton, Illinois, at the end of October. The director of children's ministry, Joan Whitlock, oversees the development of a theme that changes each year, elaborately transforming the entire church into the world of Noah's Ark, Treasure Island, or a medieval kingdom. Church members of all ages get involved in creating the spectacular environments. One purpose of this event is as the title suggests: fun for the church family, but especially fun for those in the community who don't attend church. The main purpose of GFFF is for families and individuals to reach out to those outside the church by inviting them to this event. Some 4,300 people flocked to the fair in 2003. Those who attend leave with a bag of goodies, including the gospel story and a description of the church's ministries.[6]

Inner-City Outreach Ministry

Children in the heart of our cities are sometimes out of the shadows of our church building, but they are not beyond our reach. Inner-city children are sometimes perceived as challenging and potentially disruptive to established children's ministries, but they are made in God's image and deeply loved by him. The compassion of our model, the Lord Jesus, compels us to reach out to areas underserved by churches with significant financial and human resources.

Gary Newton, a professor of Christian ministry at Huntington College in Indiana, directs a ministry to primarily nonchurched, at-risk urban children. Because of his longstanding interest in the inner city, he conducted a research project targeting fifteen such ministries in North Amer-

5. Ron Buckland, "Round Table" (review of Francis Bridger, *Children Finding Faith: Exploring a Child's Response to God,* rev. ed. [Bletchley, U.K.: Scripture Union, 2000]), *Journal of Christian Education* 44, no. 1 (2001): 59-60.

6. For more information: info@wheatonbible.org.

ica.[7] As he surveyed the directors, he discerned that such outreach ministries were most effective at developing quality relationships with children but weakest at recruiting enough people to develop those relationships. With enough volunteers to build relationships that extended to adults within an inner-city community, work with the families could be carried out more effectively — making home visits, helping with practical needs, and involving the families in the ministry. If invited, churches could partner with an existing inner-city ministry, encouraging members to come alongside the ministry with their resources of people and supplies.

Sidewalk Sunday School

This outreach idea is not new, but it can still be effective in urban areas. According to Newton, helping children get established in a church is crucial for their nurture and spiritual growth, but existing ministries are often not very effective in doing so. When members of a church go into an area and hold Bible classes on the sidewalks, it can be the beginning of connecting the children who attend with a church. But these sidewalk ministries must be a long-term commitment.

Newton adds: "One of the most aggressive strategies to assimilate kids into the church is to plant indigenous churches in the communities where the children and their families live. While this option will take the most time and resources, it seems to promise the greatest results."[8] An outdoor class just might become the beginning of an urban church.

Teaching like Jesus

A contextual model for urban children's ministry has been developed by La Verne Tolbert. The core of the model is found in a handbook titled *Teaching like Jesus,* available from Christian bookstores or from Zondervan. Suitable for Christian education in local churches, it applies Jesus' methods to making the Bible culturally relevant for today. The focus is on the teaching methods of Jesus as the model to help learners know God inti-

7. Gary Newton, "Ministering to Unchurched Urban, At-Risk Children," in *Children's Spirituality: Christian Perspectives, Research, and Applications,* ed. Donald Ratcliff (Eugene, Ore.: Cascade, 2004).

8. Newton, "Ministering to Unchurched Urban, At-Risk Children," p. 385.

mately and apply biblical principles to their daily life. A Spanish version, *Enseñemos como Jesús,* is also available. This ministry also has trainers for Latino and Asian churches.[9]

Tutoring as Outreach

Frazer Memorial United Methodist Church in Montgomery, Alabama, is a 7,200-member congregation where "every member [is] a minister." With a purpose statement like this, it is no surprise that the congregation reaches out to support many community services. The leaders of this church empower the laity to do the work of the ministry. If a member identifies a need within the congregation or the community, the church considers that person as able to provide the vision and compassion for meeting the need, enlisting a team and developing a specialized ministry. The church staff supports the birth of the new ministry.

One of Frazer Memorial's more extensive forms of outreach is a tutoring program for inner-city school-age children, an ongoing ministry for over thirty years. After Frazer relocated, the church began busing inner-city children to its larger new site on Wednesday nights for supper and then tutoring by church members. The church shares its resources of tutors, space, and materials. Frazer Memorial also partners with Bell Street Church within the inner city. For several years Charlie Kendall, a member of Frazer's staff, has worked primarily at Bell Street. Kendall oversees an extensive outreach-tutoring program among first- through third-grade children from the neighborhoods surrounding Bell Street Church. Remarkably, the tutors for these early elementary children are the middle school kids and young teens who attend Frazer's tutoring classes on Wednesday evenings. Kendall hires the older kids, providing them their first paid jobs, to work with six-, seven-, and eight-year-olds. Kendall reports significant changes in the children's reading ability, grades, and attitudes. The young tutors learn important job skills such as reliability and punctuality. Since they are paid for their work, age-appropriate job performance is expected. Although at this writing not enough time had passed to assess long-term success of children who have gone through this tutoring program, at the six-year mark there had been no dropouts or failures to succeed in school.

9. For information or to order materials: www.teachinglikejesus.org.

During the summer Frazer sends teams of members to Bell Street to conduct vacation Bible school. The inner-city children are more comfortable staying within their own community for this type of experience.

More recently a Latino pastor has joined the Frazer staff to minister to that population. Extensive opportunities to learn English as a second language are made available at the church. These classes also become an outreach ministry.[10]

Beulah Land

Gretchen Wolff Pritchard has developed an inner-city outreach model to introduce and enhance storytelling. Working in downtown New Haven, Connecticut, she developed fabric storytelling materials that she uses with children from a wide range of cultural backgrounds. Her approach is appropriate for ages three through ten and engages children through sight, sound, touch, and participation. Although this approach initially seems similar to familiar flannel graph, the shapes are scriptural images and symbols rather than literal representations of a Bible story. Children see and hear the significance of the shapes and are invited to wonder and discover as they connect storytelling to the liturgy through symbols. Beulah Land invites children to enter the biblical narrative with imagination, by asking questions, and by interacting with fabric art on a storyboard. The continuity of God's plan is evident as the children see images and symbols move from one narrative to another. They discover for themselves God's presence in the story and in their lives.[11]

KIDS HOPE USA

"One child, one hour" is the motto at the heart of this church-based ministry that reaches out to needy children. It matches one church with one school. The goal is to have one caring adult mentor one at-risk child one hour at school every week. The directors of this program realize that when kids feel loved and valued they are better able to learn, grow, and succeed.

10. Contact www.frazerumc.org. At the time of writing, Marsha McGehee was the director of children's ministry at Frazer Memorial UMC.

11. Contact information: 57 Olive Street, New Haven, CT 06511, www.BeulahEnterprises.org. See also Gretchen Wolff Pritchard's book *Offering the Gospel to Children* (Cambridge, Mass.: Cowley, 1992).

Churches are better positioned than other organizations to recruit volunteer mentors who will be faithful over the long haul. Volunteers are loyal to the program since their own church operates and funds their segment. KIDS HOPE USA is provided for schools free of cost; thus it meets an urgent need for intervention that fits limited budgets. KIDS HOPE USA sees the opportunity as vast and the need great. "How many other children do you see at my school?" is a question most KHUSA kids ask their mentors. It demonstrates the desperate longing of at-risk children to be "the one and only" in the life of a caring adult. This need for love can be met only one child at a time. The idea is simple: One Child, One Hour, One Church, One School.[12]

Ministry with the World's Children

We who are Christian must be aware of children beyond our reach. This requires a global perspective, seeing the world's children as part of the church's responsibility. We who have much can provide resources — people, finances, and supplies. For children not in Christian contexts, we can build bridges by focusing on beliefs and values that we do hold in common. But most of all we can pray. Here are some organizations that can help churches become more global in their ministry with children.

Viva Network

This organization facilitates worldwide connections for strategic work with children. Through its website a church is able to make contacts, find information, and join initiatives. Viva is a global movement of Christians concerned for children who are at risk, and it is committed to every child's having the opportunity to become all that God intends. Rather than starting more children's projects, Viva creates and sustains networks among people who are already working with children at risk, so that more children get better assistance.

Viva Network provides a prayer diary containing specific prayer requests from children's projects around the world, to help churches pray regularly and effectively for needy children and for the Christians caring

12. Information is available at www.kidshopeusa.org.

for them. It also administers a "World Wide Day of Prayer for Children at Risk" that takes place on the first Saturday of June each year. Viva produces an information pack that enables and invites all Christians to participate.

Ideas and resources for encouraging the church's children to pray for children at risk are also available. An international initiative is being developed that will raise awareness of the significance of children's prayer.[13]

Rainbows of Hope

Through training, involvement in community- and church-based projects, and demonstrating Jesus' love to the children in every way possible, Rainbows of Hope seeks to restore children's losses and extend to them the gift of hope.

The organization can inform a church of the needs of suffering children around the world, and it can encourage the church to become involved in meeting those needs and helping other children know of the hope and new life they can have through Jesus Christ. Its website explains the organization and how to become involved. It also identifies resources that describe the conditions that millions of children face around the world. Rainbows of Hope's publications will help a congregation stay informed. Finally, this organization can help equip a church team to minister directly to needy children by means of rapid-response, short-term, or long-term mission trips.[14]

Needs-Based Caring Ministries

There is a great need for ministries to provide loving, caring environments to help children deal with hard issues and the unfairness of life. Ministry leaders will serve children well if they carefully watch and listen for the children's longings and yearnings rather than creating ministries around their surface wants and presumed "needs."

Unfortunately, a common need for specialized ministry occurs when children suffer the loss of a significant person through death, divorce, or

13. More information about Viva Network may be obtained at www.viva.org.
14. For additional information see www.wec-int.org/rainbows.

sometimes simply relocation. Because of the frequency of this need in recent decades, materials are available now to help local churches establish support groups for children such as Katy, whose situation was described earlier. Listed below are three organizations that help churches establish support groups for children. Each has created materials a church can use to assist children and parents who are experiencing significant loss.

Center for Single-Parent Family Ministry

When his parents divorced in the 1960s, Gary Sprague felt he was the only person who had suffered such a loss. Now it is much more common. Because of his early experience, Gary created a ministry center that specializes in single-parent situations. Through resources designed to help children realize that they are not the only children of divorce and that the divorce was not their fault, the center helps churches support these kids. In group settings where they can hear other kids express feelings about their divorce, children begin to heal and recover from their loss. Some resources, like "Help for the Modern-Day Orphan," can be downloaded from the center's website.[15]

Rainbows for All God's Children

This ecumenical organization fosters emotional healing among children grieving a loss from a life-altering crisis. Rainbows is nonprofit and international in scope. It offers training and curricula for establishing peer-support groups in churches, synagogues, schools, and social agencies. These curricula are available for children and adults of all ages and religious denominations who are grieving a death, divorce, or any other painful transition in their family.[16]

Confident Kids

The materials available through this ministry cover a somewhat broader perspective. During the years that Linda Kondracki-Sibley served as direc-

15. See www.spfm.org.

16. Rainbows for All God's Children: toll-free 800.266.3206; www.rainbows.org; e-mail info@rainbows.org.

tor of children's ministry at a large California church, she encountered scores of children living challenging, stress-filled lives. In many cases simply surviving has become a complicated task. Growing up with divorce, stepparents and stepsiblings, drugs and alcohol, gangs, community violence, absent parents, and more is taking its toll. Kondracki-Sibley feels that few groups within our society, and even fewer within our churches, are reaching out to help elementary-age children deal with the complexities of living in their world. So she designed materials for hurting children and struggling parents.

Confident Kids is a biblically based support program offering life skills for children ages four to twelve to deal with the stresses of living in today's world. Through games, skits, and small group discussions, children learn while experiencing a safe place to talk about their life experiences. In a concurrent group, parents learn to apply these same skills in their home while they also experience a safe place to tell their stories. In their separate groups, children and parents grow as they discover they are not alone in their struggles.[17]

Disability Ministry

For many years College Church in Wheaton, Illinois, has offered a "Disability Ministry" for children and young adolescents. The ministry is open to those with a wide range of disabilities. Under some circumstances a child like Josh (described earlier in this chapter) may be more comfortable in such an environment. The church offers two special Sunday school classes, one for those with developmental disabilities, another for autistic children. Inclusion is encouraged as much as possible.

Twice a month on Friday evenings there is a dinner for them at the church followed by a time of fun and games. There is also a monthly support ministry for parents or caregivers of these children. The church offers autoharp and chime classes and provides scholarships for summer camps for special-needs children. Respite care is available for the families through arrangements made with nearby Wheaton College students.[18]

17. See www.confidentkids.com.
18. For contact information see www.college-church.org/disability.asp.

Service Ministries

This is another branch of specialized ministry that is limited only by a leader's imagination. The more often children have the privilege of serving and the younger they are when they begin having those experiences, the more likely it is that serving others will continue through life, especially if the joy of serving is evident in adults whom the children admire. In serving others we are emulating the Lord Jesus (see Matt. 20:28; Luke 22:27; Phil. 2:7).

Princeton professor of Christian education James Loder writes that for the school-age child, theologically speaking, "persons work not for reward, intrinsic pleasure, or sublimated sexual gratification. Work . . . is motivated by persons' being given a vision of what God is doing in the world."[19] Loder feels that a child's awareness of the presence of the Spirit of Christ helps resolve loneliness and increases desire for relationship. Acts of service done in the name of Jesus Christ can facilitate such relational growth. If Loder is correct, ministries of service may be an invaluable corrective to what North American culture tends to do to children of this age: make them passive consumers. Our ministries with children, then, must help them sense the Spirit of Christ. We must help them serve as we give them a vision of God at work globally.

Here are some ideas for service that groups of children in a local church might learn to offer. Think about how you might expand this rudimentary list.

Service to the Church Family

- wash nursery toys
- empty trash containers
- weed flowerbeds
- hold doors open as people enter
- pick up trash in the church yard
- make simple gifts for sick church members
- adopt an elderly person to provide assistance for and play games with
- serve during worship services in ways listed in chapter 11

19. James Loder, *The Logic of the Spirit* (San Francisco: Jossey-Bass, 1998), p. 177.

Two of the most common ways of involving children through worship — music and art — are worthy of special mention here. When training children to perform music, pay careful attention to the integrity of the text and the construction of the music so that children can access its meaning. The music must enhance the text and not detract from it; both should be memorable. Selections should not be below their abilities and intellect and should cover the whole range of human experience. Avoid using music to "get the wiggles out"; this tends to devalue the music for them. Consider multi-ethnic music and instruments. Be passionate about directing the children in this way of serving.[20]

With proper guidance, children's artistic expressions can assist the whole congregation in worship. Tissue-paper window art can make ordinary windows look like stained glass. Designing and creating these pieces become acts of worship for the creators. In the process children can realize the source of their own creativity — their creative God. Provide a beginning piece of art for their inspiration, one that connects with the worship theme or story. Various media can be used to add richness in worship. Art can transcend what even young artists intended, allowing others to see additional meaning.[21]

Community Service

- pick up trash in the neighborhood
- ask area merchants if pairs of children may help with simple tasks
- taller children can wash car windows (for free, of course)
- ask to help clean up construction sites
- with permission, help moms at a park with their toddlers
- spend time regularly visiting residents of a nursing home (not just during the holidays)
- at Christmas sing carols through the neighborhood
- participate in Earth Day (April 22) activities such as planting trees or a

20. Source of these guidelines: Brad Jones, a music educator, former high school choir director, and minister of worship and music, as well as director of the children's choir of a church.

21. These suggestions were gleaned from an interview with James Breckenridge, an artist for major children's animation studios for more than twelve years and a volunteer artist at his church.

garden at your church or in your neighborhood, or clean up a nearby park[22]

Regional Service

Accompanied by adults, a group of older children who show appropriate maturity might travel a couple of hundred miles to work on a project with Habitat for Humanity or a similar group. A puppet team could develop a program to present to inner-city children or other underserved populations.

Family Missions Trips

Clusters of two to four families can plan and execute a cross-cultural service ministry. A missionary supported by the church can help with logistics, language, and cultural orientation. All members of the families should be prepared to be part of a work crew or a ministry team, whatever is needed. Work crews can build or repair facilities. Ministry teams could hold special events for children or families and build relationships. (In spite of the language barriers, friendships spring up quite easily when children are involved.)

A word of caution is in order: Be sure children realize that regularly serving others in the neighborhood is just as important to God as going on a yearly mission trip to a different country.

Intergenerational Ministries

Finally, special ministry to children may be approached in a way appropriate for a multigenerational group. It is curious that our church culture spends so much time dividing children into age-level groups for programming, given that faith formation for everyone could be deepened when the generations are enabled to interact with each other.

Multigenerational ministry can take different shapes. The easiest and most frequent probably occurs when a meal to which everyone is welcome is held at the church. Weekly potlucks or catered casual suppers re-

22. For further information about Earth Day visit www.earthday.net.

quire minimal effort; rotating designated cooks might also provide the meal. Throughout the year events can be offered that would appeal to a wide range of age groupings: a picnic, sock hop, game night, roller-skating party, hayrack ride, or sledding. In these settings the presence of people of all ages allows for interaction of the entire church body. Each member has the opportunity of seeing faith lived out in a different generation of life, and each is given the chance to see themselves as a member of a larger whole. Rather than being simply one of the third-graders, a child will come to see him- or herself as one member of a very large family. Gathering for Sunday worship may then feel less like a formal obligation and take on the warmth of a family gathering.

A more specialized form of intergenerational ministry occurs when parents are included as learners. Sometimes one of the best things a church can do for children is to help equip their parents with skills for parenting. Here are a couple of programs developed to do just that.

Equipping the Saints: A Model for Christian Parenting

Chris Boyatzis, a Christian child development psychologist at Bucknell University, developed a model that attempts to revise parents' vision of parenting — to help them see their task through new eyes — as well as offer concrete strategies for Christian family life. His model emphasizes three crucial components: integrity, intentionality, and accountability. First, parents must live as integrated rather than disintegrated, fragmented beings. We must articulate our values *and* live them. Second, to achieve integrity, we must live intentionally and mindfully examine our priorities: What kind of Christian do I want my child to be? Am I helping my child grow into this person? Am *I* the Christian I want my child to be? Third, we are accountable to God and our faith community, since parents are the most influential Christian witnesses in children's lives, "on display 24/7." To inform and inspire parents, this model integrates knowledge from faith development theory, Christian Scripture and faith traditions, and developmental psychology and family relations.[23]

23. For more information, e-mail boyatzis@bucknell.edu.

Family Faith Formation

A suburban Chicago church has developed a family-led, intergenerational alternative to classroom religious education. The intent is to offer families an opportunity to share their faith "family style" in a flexible, familiar environment.

First comes a Family Covenant, signed by each family, signifying that the parish community and the family are committed to working together. Family Packets of eight lessons are provided quarterly to guide the parent and leader. Families fill in "How Are We Doing?" review sheets or keep a journal of their learning experiences. Family Service Projects are another component. Each family does two projects during the year and then turns in a reflective feedback form. The last key component is a monthly Family Gathering, at which families interact with each other, connect through activities, and dialogue about faith questions.[24]

Structures for Specialized Ministries

When planning for ministry events and preparing the calendar, we must remember that the possibilities and opportunities are limitless. Too often ministries are structured parallel to the school schedule and calendar. Churches need to consider the potential of working opposite hours, since many children end up in front of television after school and when they are on summer break. Children's time away from school creates special ministry prospects. Programs may be offered on a weekly basis on Sunday mornings, on Sunday evenings, or during the week. Some ministries are conducted during a particular season, such as a traditional vacation Bible school or a summer soccer club. Other ministries may be a onetime or an annual event.

Special ministry events may be seasonal or may correlate with the church year. Take advantage of events by including children — events such as anniversaries of the church and of those in ministry leadership or weddings of people well known to the church's children. The children could even be allowed to host a shower for the bridal couple. The same

24. Contact information: St. Isidore Roman Catholic Church, 427 W. Army Trail Road, Bloomingdale, IL 60108; www.stisidoreparish.org/religious_education.htm.

could be done for a special couple upon the birth of a baby. When appropriate, prepare children to attend the funeral of a person significant to them, or plan a special gathering for the children to celebrate and memorialize the life of that person.

In times of crisis, provide special time to help children work through the crisis. For example, during a time of war or political unrest, offer children a special series on Christ the Prince of Peace. After a tragic event like September 11, 2001, a series on God's faithfulness or a support group for children to discuss fears could be set up on short notice and conducted only as long as the children need. Other short-term crisis needs would be a parent's going to war, a tragedy within the church family, the death of a school friend, or a regional flood or fire. Any event that shakes the security of children can be dealt with through a specialized crisis ministry. In some situations this might take the place of a regular ministry like Sunday school for a time.

Administration Issues

Specialized ministries to children are truly endless; any life situation can be adapted into an opportunity for ministry, providing it supports the ultimate purpose of the ministry. (For the significance of an ultimate purpose see the Frankena Model, pp. 285-88 in this chapter.) Administration of the details of these ministries is a significant responsibility of the leader. Foremost, those who minister need to prayerfully discern what is the best type of ministry to offer in a particular setting. It takes time and a commitment to know the congregation before a church leader is truly able to sense its pulse and to imagine how Jesus would respond if he were to walk the halls of the church building. Creating specialized ministries takes time, but a consistent commitment to discerning the best direction for a congregation will lay the groundwork for ministries that are relevant to the needs of the people.

Staffing specialized children's ministries in some ways is one of a leader's biggest challenges. "How will I ever find and train enough people to run this special program?" is a common concern, even if it's not said aloud. A prime way for leaders to staff ministries is to get to know people within the congregation — to know their interests, passions, skills, and giftings. Keep a computer log of these people and their abilities that can be accessed easily when a need arises for a particular skill set.

Some practical tips for inviting people to serve can be helpful.

- Affirm what you see as their strengths and abilities.
- Don't take the first no as the final answer. Come back to that person a couple more times and ask again.
- When asking someone to serve in a ministry, offer choices of opportunities. You might say, "I have a need for __________, __________, or __________. Do you see yourself helping in one of those areas?"
- Consider asking the obvious: "How would you like to be involved in this special ministry coming up?"

Leaders need to work with the expectations of the congregation to appropriately screen volunteers and then prayerfully consider what training is most fitting to equip them for service. Leaders need to be clear about the commitment a person (paid or volunteer) is making when he or she accepts a position. As the ministry grows and matures, it is important to continually be in conversation with the church staff about any changing roles.

Regarding other administrative needs, those who minister must begin with an understanding of the facilities and the budget available to support their efforts. While the four walls of a church building certainly ought not limit the space of a ministry, it is important to have a realistic understanding of the resources available before moving ahead.

Conclusion

The door is wide open for the message of God's love to be communicated through special ministries. Therefore the church needs to approach each opportunity with a plan in mind. Consider the format of the ministry. How would the most critical elements of faith best be incorporated?

For example, when a soccer camp is being held, how will the message of Christ be included? Sessions might begin with the sports activity and conclude with a devotional message under the agreement that if "you come to play, you come to stay." Or coaches might look for opportunities to weave in intentional moments of faith learning. In the middle of a game when a dispute arises, it may well be appropriate to stop the game and discuss the issue from a Christian perspective. This allows faith to meet a real-life conflict and gives learners the opportunity to see the difference faith in Christ makes in the everyday.

Even in a traditional context like a Sunday school or vacation Bible school, those ministering still need to be intentional about the message they are communicating. Leaders need to determine what will be their primary focus, what spiritual truths will be highlighted, and what children will hopefully glean from their participation in the ministry.

With the compassion of Jesus as our model and the boundless needs of today's children as our motivation, special ministries with children just might become the heartbeat of the faith community. For that to happen we must keep in mind several non-negotiables:

- Whatever form these ministries take, they must be done in Jesus' name.
- They must place a high value on relationships.
- They must include a prayer or word of blessing for each child.
- They must help each child connect with the larger faith community.

From the examples included, so many that it may seem overwhelming, it is evident that special ministries may occur anywhere — in a church building, a public school, a park, a crisis center. But it is important to remember that it is just as important to decide what *not* to do as it is to decide what to do. No church can or should do everything. As leaders, we should be less concerned about having our ministries full of children and more concerned about helping the children be full of God.

The words that God spoke to Isaiah have particular relevance to the needs of children and the creative ways that God's people, his ministers, are endeavoring to meet them:

> The LORD has anointed me . . . to bring good news to the oppressed,
> to bind up the brokenhearted,
> to proclaim liberty to the captives,
> and release to the prisoners; . . .
> to comfort all who mourn;
> to provide for those who grieve in Zion —
> to give them a garland instead of ashes,
> the oil of gladness instead of mourning,
> the mantle of praise instead of a faint spirit.

They will be called oaks of righteousness,
  a planting of the LORD, to display his glory. . . .
But you shall be called priests of the LORD,
  you shall be named ministers of our God. (Isa. 61:1-3, 6)

Chapter 14

ALL CHILDREN MATTER

In the Gospels we see that Jesus pays special attention to people on the margins. He notices people whom others would rather avoid.[1] He has time for people who are sick, outcast, hungry, old, or young. As followers of Jesus ministering with children, we have the challenge of responding to all the children the Lord brings to our attention, whatever their circumstances. Children with special needs or who are in crisis are among the people to whom we need to open our ears and eyes, mind and heart. This chapter will focus on some concerns related to ministry to hurting children and will explore ways to make sure that the church is a sanctuary and a place of welcome for all children.

Children with Special Needs

What is special about ministry to children with special needs? What do we mean by special needs? How can we respond to the spiritual needs of children with special needs?

Ministry with children with special needs is in some ways no different from ministry with other children. Each child is at a different place on his or her spiritual journey and will know more or less of the Scriptures. Although we often think of children's ministry as working with groups of

1. Stewart D. Govig, *Strong at the Broken Places* (Louisville: Westminster/John Knox Press, 1989), p. 15.

children, individual children may need unique attention. Children's ministry is about welcoming, listening to, responding to, and teaching every child in the name of Jesus. But the welcome, listening, response, and teaching may be more complicated for the exceptional child.

The special education literature defines exceptional children as those who have difficulty reaching their full potential without special help. A person may be considered to have special needs because of intellectual differences, sensory handicaps, communication or behavior disorders, physical handicaps, or special healthcare needs. The disability may be mild or severe or somewhere in between and may be a disadvantage in some situations but not in others. For example, a person may not be able to walk but be a mathematical whiz. Some disabilities are invisible, like many learning disabilities; others are visible to all.

The impact of the disability varies depending on its severity, the personality of the child, whether the disability is visible or invisible, the social, physical, and spiritual support available, and the acceptance of the person by family and friends. If people around the child are able to see the person first, the disability is put in its proper place.

In reality none of us are perfect. All walk with a "limp" of some kind — interpersonal, emotional, physical, spiritual. The limitations of most of us are not immediately obvious, so there is little handicapping impact for the world to see. But for some the need for special support is obvious.

Terminology used in special education has changed over the years. Children with special needs have been called "exceptional," "impaired," "handicapped," "atypical," "physically challenged," "developmentally disabled" or "differently abled." The problem with all of these labels is that they tend to focus on the limitation rather than on the person him- or herself. Everyone has some gifts to offer to his or her family and the community; this includes the child with special needs. Who we are clearly goes beyond what we look like or what our specific ability or inability is. A high school student who was paralyzed as a result of a gymnastics accident says it well: "I don't come with the wheelchair. The wheelchair comes with me."

It is respectful to ask the person involved what terms he or she prefers and what language is offensive to him or her.

Ministry Barriers

In spite of the many accounts in the Gospels of Jesus connecting with "exceptional" people, people with disabilities are underrepresented in the church. Why might this be? Are we sending subtle "not welcome" messages to families who have children with special needs? There *are* many churches that offer an intentional welcome to children with all kinds of disabilities. We celebrate these churches.

Again, we who minister to children must consider the master Story. When Jesus' disciples attempted to protect Jesus from the interruption of children, Jesus rebuked them: "Let the little children come to me, and do not stop them: for it is to such as these that the kingdom of heaven belongs" (Matthew 19:13-14). In even stronger terms, he said, "Whoever welcomes one such child in my name welcomes me. If any of you put a stumbling block before one of these little ones who believe in me, it would be better for you if a great millstone were fastened around your neck and you drowned in the depth of the sea" (Matthew 18:5-6).

One might ask if Jesus meant all children — including children with special needs. We are convinced that he did. If so, it is right for us to ask whether we are hindering these children from coming to Jesus by setting up barriers that keep them away.

Barriers we set up, or at least allow, may include insensitive or ill-formed religious views, prejudicial attitudes, inaccessible buildings, or inhospitable programs. Usually we don't intentionally block access to our ministry, but whether we mean to or not, the impact is the same.

Religious Barriers

The most crushing obstacles keeping families with children who have disabilities away from the church are insensitive and ill-formed religious views that belittle their children. These views are sometimes expressed as questions. Families ask or are asked, *Why did God do this to me? Is my child a blessing from God or not? What did I do to have a child with disabilities? Is my child, like other children, created in the image of God? Is there a place in the kingdom of God for my child?*

Henri Nouwen gives some light to these difficult questions in his account of his experience living in the L'Arche community in Toronto, called Daybreak. In 1985 Nouwen moved from the academic world — he had been a theology professor at Harvard Divinity School — to live at Daybreak in a household of ten, some who were disabled and some not. He writes movingly about living with Adam.

> Adam is the weakest member of our family. He is a 25-year-old man who cannot dress himself, walk or eat without help. He cannot speak. His back is curved, and his arm and leg movements are spastic. . . .
>
> Whoever sees in Adam merely a burden to society misses the sacred mystery that Adam is fully capable of receiving and giving love. He is fully human, not half human, not nearly human, but fully, completely human because he is all heart. And it is our heart that is made in the image of God. . . .
>
> After months of being with Adam, I am discovering in myself an inner quiet that I did not know before. Adam is one of the most broken persons among us, but without any doubt our strongest bond. Because of Adam there is always someone home; because of Adam there are always words of affection, gentleness and tenderness; because of Adam there are smiles and tears visible to all; because of Adam there is always time and space for forgiveness and healing. Yes, because of Adam there is peace among us.[2]

Sometimes parents wonder whether they have done something to cause the disability of their child. They wonder why God let this happen. Sometimes religious friends or strangers even suggest that if they just had enough faith the disability would be healed. Jesus confronted this idea in the context of restoring the sight of a blind man: "As he walked along, he saw a man blind from birth. His disciples asked him, 'Rabbi, who sinned, this man or his parents, that he was born blind?' Jesus answered, 'Neither this man nor his parents sinned; he was born blind so that God's works might be revealed in him'" (John 9:1-3).

Jesus is clear that the disability of this man was not due to either his sin or the sin of his parents. His blindness happened, Jesus said, "so that God's works might be revealed." In this situation, Jesus healed the man, and the man became his follower, drawing attention to who Jesus was. In Adam's situation, the Daybreak community was spiritually enriched by Adam's presence.

2. Henri J. M. Nouwen, "Because of Adam," *Reader's Digest,* October 1988, pp. 51-52.

Causes of disabilities are often hard to identify. Some are simply inexplicable. We may never know why they occur, but there is every reason to support the family and to help display God's mercy, kindness, love, and hope in their lives and the life of the child.[3]

Architectural Barriers

Our church buildings may be excluding children simply because they are physically inaccessible. Modern building codes in most cities require that new buildings be accessible to persons in a wheelchair. However, older buildings, including many churches, are often difficult for a person in a wheelchair to enter. Stairs, narrow doors to washrooms, and curbs are all hard or impossible to maneuver. Classrooms may be too crowded to accommodate a wheelchair. The sanctuary may not be designed for a person in a wheelchair to worship inconspicuously. Sitting in the aisle is isolating.

An architectural movement featuring universal design that is also aesthetically pleasing is gaining prominence. Those of us who are charged with making decisions about new construction or remodeling of older buildings would do well to consider the design ideas coming out of this work.

Attitudinal Barriers

It seems obvious that we should design buildings that are accessible for everyone. Why does this not always happen? The cost of elevators, ramps, and other structures is part of the answer but not the whole. Advocates of accessibility contend that noninclusive *attitudes* at every level of society keep physically and intellectually challenged people on the outside. They argue that these attitudes are pervasive in our culture, rooted in what they call an "aesthetic anxiety," a fear of others whose traits are perceived to be disturbing or unpleasant. "Our society has little use for weakness, humility or silence."[4] This way of thinking affects persons with disabilities even more than the physical environment.

3. Jim Pierson, *Exceptional Teaching: A Comprehensive Guide for Including Students with Disabilities* (Cincinnati: Standard Publishing, 2002), p. 215.

4. "Imago Dei and People with Disabilities," *Context: Research to Make Religion Relevant* 6, no. 2 (Fall 1996).

An important responsibility of parents, teachers, and ministry leaders is to enable children to understand and experience the lives of children who are different from them, whether the difference lies in ethnicity, denomination, home country, ability, or disability. "As children's cognitive capacities grow, they not only have an increasing ability to categorize, but also an increasing ability to place themselves in the place of the other person. It is adults who guide and encourage each of these capacities in either prosocial or antisocial ways."[5]

Program Barriers

Another ministry barrier for a child with special needs may be the programs offered by the church. He or she may not have the skills or abilities to participate fully. The attendance of some children will be irregular because of health or treatment needs. Unless adjustments are made for these children, not only will they be left behind but they will feel alienated. Sometimes new programs will need to be developed to accommodate a number of exceptional children.

Clearly, to minister to children with special needs and their families, we will need to look carefully at our attitudes — including those supported by or reflected in our religious arguments, our buildings, and our programs. We will need to address barriers that may be hindering some children from participating fully in the life of the church. Do we see each child as a blessing? Do we value each child? Is our facility totally accessible? If not, what can we do to make it so? Do we see the child or the disability? Do we consider each child when we are designing programs, so that all may worship and learn to love the Lord and glorify God with their lives? May we never be accused of hindering any child from coming to Jesus.

Including Children with Special Needs

Although each child has individual needs and will need to be responded to in unique ways, the following ideas may be helpful in integrating a child with special needs into ongoing ministry.

5. Viva Network Working Group: Child Perspectives for the 2004 Forum for World Evangelization, June 2003.

If you know in advance that a child with a disability is moving into the program, prepare the teachers and children. Introduce the child. Explain what is special about this person. Talk about what is helpful and what is not helpful for the child to be a participant in the program.

The leaders especially will need to know how to respond to medical concerns. Some children have dietary restrictions that must be strictly adhered to. Everyone who cares for the child must be vigilant in protecting the child from harm. The family is usually the best source for this information about what care the child requires and what to do in an emergency.

Recognize the expertise in the congregation and ask for help when appropriate. Professional people may need a break from their work when they come to church, but most would be more than willing to participate as consultants. Sometimes they are eager to contribute their professional expertise to the church's ministry to children and only need to be asked.

Develop a file or binder of community resources that you can call upon and use for family referrals. A library of books (for children and adults), videos, and tapes can be helpful to families and adults working with all children. The local library is a place to start to find the needed information.

A helping friend or teacher assistant who participates alongside the child will release the leader to care for the whole group. This person can help the child to take part as fully as possible and can design learning experiences that are specific to the child when necessary. Parents should be able to trust that the teaching assistant will enjoy and protect their child, so that they are free to join in worship or other activities.

Children, whatever their abilities, enjoy music and drama and the other arts. Even children who have severe disabilities can participate in their own ways.

As we get to know and enjoy more of the children in the church and community who are challenged by special needs, we will find ways to join them in the spiritual journey.[6]

6. Catherine Stonehouse, *Joining Children on the Spiritual Journey* (Grand Rapids: Baker, 1998).

Children at Risk

Who are the children at risk in our community? How do we helpfully minister to them in the name of Jesus?

A child at risk is one who has undergone or is facing a life-changing experience that could have an effect (positive or negative) on his or her development. Every family experiences crises, but some are especially devastating for children. "Children are particularly vulnerable, simply because they are children."[7]

The child may be dealing with death, abuse, illness, parents who are divorcing, poverty, war, homelessness, or any number of other crises or tragedies. The impact of the crisis is directly related to the losses the child experiences. Such losses may include family members, home, country, friends, safety, identity, status, security, self-worth, school, necessities of life, even childhood itself. Not surprisingly, children dealing with an accumulation of losses and resulting change or adaptation to new situations often show their distress in their behavior.

Different children cope differently with crises. The magnitude of the loss plays a part in how the child copes, but there are other factors as well. Norman Garmezy determined that certain protective factors help children deal with life stresses. Some children just have better coping skills; their temperament, ability to think reflectively, and interpersonal skills make them more able to respond positively to others and deal with new situations. Children who are fortunate enough to have a warm, cohesive family are much more able to handle crises.[8] This means that *crises within the family* are especially difficult for children.

Of special interest to those of us in ministry with children is that research indicates that the presence of a caring adult and connections to a supportive community such as a church can be a major factor in a child's staying afloat in the troubled waters of a life crisis. "One consistent characteristic of resilient children is the faith that things will work out. This belief can be sustained if children encounter people who give meaning to their lives and a reason for commitment and caring."[9]

7. Linda Moorcroft, Lecture at Tyndale University College, April 2003.

8. N. Garmezy, "Resiliency and Vulnerability to Adverse Development Outcomes Associated with Poverty, *American Behavioral Scientist* 34, no. 4 (1991): 416-30.

9. Grace Craig, Marguerite Kermis, and Nancy Digdon, *Children Today,* Canadian

As caring adults, we can make a difference in the lives of children who are in unfair circumstances. Programs that offer peer support for grieving children and those whose parents are divorcing, homework and other after-school programs, arts and sports programs, and intergenerational celebrations can provide stability and nurture for children in difficult times. Of course we need to know our limits and recognize when a child needs professional help beyond our expertise. Knowing what resources are available in the community will enable us to connect families with the support they need.

When we lift our eyes beyond our own circles of ministry to the world's children, new issues emerge. Linda Moorcroft, director of the World Vision Refugee Reception Centre in Toronto, Canada, gives some perspective on ministry with children who have been uprooted from their home because of imminent danger to their family.[10] The Refugee Reception Centre receives people from around the world who are seeking asylum for their family. People come from countries engulfed in war, political instability, and the resulting disruption of access to food and other life necessities. Some of the children are dealing with severe trauma. Apart from the trauma is the sadness of their many losses. They have lost connections with their families, lost their country, lost what is familiar to them.

When asked what helps children who are adjusting to their new life, Linda replied, "How the children manage really depends on how the parents are handling the transition." Also whether the family is intact makes a big difference. Sometimes a family arrives without a father, for he was killed in a conflict or was captured and tortured. Or the family may have lost other members in war. Children in such situations have a great deal of trauma, grieving, and loss to work through.

Family is of primary importance for all children, including refugee children. Children tend to do well when their family does well. Even if children from a country in conflict have had to deal with great trauma, their family can sometimes protect them from the trauma's worst aspects.

Families often immigrate to provide a more hopeful future for their children. When children move to a new town or a new country, whatever

---

edition (Scarborough, Ont.: Prentice Hall/Allyn and Bacon Canada, 1998), p. 308. Referring to E. E. Werner, "Resilient Children," *Young Children*, November 1984, pp. 68-72.

10. Interview with Linda Moorcroft, director of World Vision's Refugee Reception Centre. Toronto, March 27, 2002.

the reasons, they leave a lot behind. There is sadness and grief. They miss their friends, their family, their school, and their community. If they don't understand the local language, their life is more complicated. However, especially if they are still at an age of sensitivity to language learning — under eight years old — they learn the language quickly. Often children acquire the new language long before their parents do. This puts them in the awkward position of being translators for their parents, which turns the responsibility relationship upside down.

Some refugee children may have had little experience with toys, games, and stories that are very familiar to North American children. For example, they may never have done a puzzle. On the other hand, they may have a number of other valuable skills. For example, most American children in grade two or three would be lost if they were asked to prepare a meal for the family or care for their younger siblings. In children's ministry, we should recognize and value the abilities of young newcomers, even if they are different from what we expect.

In some countries — especially in the developing world where resources are restricted — Christian or other minority religious groups are persecuted. Children are often the means through which parents are persecuted: a child is removed from school or is denied equal access to other services. In these situations children are disproportionately affected.

It must be said that the vast majority of children in countries of conflict or other trauma do not have the chance to move to a more peaceful place. Increasing numbers of children around the world have the responsibility of being the main caregivers for younger siblings, even if their parents are alive, and there is a growing number of child-headed households where both parents have died from the HIV/AIDS crisis. Further, many have inadequate food, water, or housing, and thousands of children die of preventable diseases. The church has a critical responsibility to advocate for the well-being of children everywhere. Even the smallest church can find ways to respond to the needs of children in other parts of the world.

Many families that move to North America have strong Christian beliefs, although some have other religious backgrounds. All are looking for a place to belong, a place to contribute, a place for their children to be valued and to learn. Refugees are very isolated people, and many of them have lost extended-family members who had been intimately involved in helping them raise their children. The church has a special opportunity to welcome, befriend, and pray for these children and their families.

Welcome and Sanctuary for All Children

Churches have a spiritual, moral, and legal obligation to be a sanctuary for all children who come to learn, to worship, to serve, to make friends. The abuse of any child is a criminal act as well as a violation of God's moral law. It is especially shameful when it happens within the trusted relational context of the church, and it can have a devastating effect on the credibility of the church and the gospel of Christ.[11]

Children are naturally trusting and thus vulnerable to manipulation and abuse. Although churches are generally considered to be places where children are safe, they also unfortunately have features that make them attractive to people bent on molesting children. Child molesters are attracted to places where they have immediate access to potential victims in an atmosphere of complete trust. The risk to children increases dramatically during overnight activities. Also, most churches struggle to get adequate help for children and youth programs; turnover among volunteers is high. Thus a willing volunteer worker provides welcome relief.

What can we do to protect the children to whom we minister? Every church should have a clear policy and plan to safeguard children and to protect church staff and volunteer workers from potential allegations of sexual abuse. Many sample policies are available that can provide a framework for a policy and procedure plan for an individual church. However, a policy is useful only if it is taken off the shelf and applied in the situation.

A plan to protect children needs to be built on basic principles such as the following:

- Screen all employees who work with preschoolers, children, or youth, including ministerial staff and volunteers. Check references and do criminal record checks.
- Train staff about child abuse, how to carry out policies, appropriate and inappropriate touch, reporting procedures.
- Set up the two-adult rule: two adults should be present during any children's activity.
- Establish the six-month rule: adults will be considered as potential

11. Based on materials produced by the Pentecostal Assemblies of Canada, Mississauga, Ontario.

volunteers to work with preschoolers, children, or youth only after they have attended the church regularly for six months.

- Keep doors open or install unobstructed windows in doors to rooms where child and youth activities take place.

One issue that sometimes surfaces is what to do about the person who has been guilty of child molestation in the past but has had a religious conversion. The person may insist that he or she has changed and now poses no risk to children. But putting this person in a position involving access to children is taking an enormous risk, no matter how long ago the incident occurred. There are other places in the church where the person could volunteer — places where he or she will not be in contact with children and youth.

Vigilance about protection of children sometimes leads to a "hands off" policy. But touch is an essential responsibility in nurturing lives. Respect and care for young children can be expressed in the following appropriate ways:[12]

- bending down to the child's eye level and speaking kindly, listening to him or her carefully
- taking a child's hand and leading him or her to an activity
- putting an arm around the shoulder of a child who needs quieting or comforting
- holding a child by the shoulders or hand to keep his or her attention while you redirect the child's behavior
- holding a preschool child who is crying

Inappropriate touch to be avoided:

- kissing a child, coaxing a child to kiss you, extended hugging and tickling
- touching a child in any area that would be covered by a bathing suit (except when assisting a very young child with toileting)
- carrying older children or having them sit on your lap
- being alone with a child

12. Policies and Procedures Manual: *A Plan to Protect the Children, Youth and Leaders of Royal View Church,* London, Ontario, 2002.

In some cases, a strong policy for the protection of children has led to men feeling unwelcome as leaders. This reinforces the status quo: women are most often responsible for the care, nurture, teaching of children in churches and parachurch organizations. There are implications for both boys and girls. A committed faith can come to be seen as something that women experience and talk about but not men. Children are strongly influenced by people with whom they have an ongoing relationship. If their friendships with adults in the church are mostly with women, they miss the modeling that needs to be provided by Christian men.

Classroom Management

Feeling compassion for the children with whom we serve, we are sometimes caught off guard by difficult behaviors in the classroom. How do we support children in developing the self-control needed for effective learning and for building durable friendships?

Haim Ginott puts into perspective the power and responsibility that teachers have over children in the classroom:

> I have come to a frightening conclusion. I am the decisive element in the classroom. It is my personal approach that creates the climate. It is my daily mood that makes the weather. As a teacher I possess tremendous power to make a child's life miserable or joyous. I can be a tool of torture or an instrument of inspiration. I can humiliate or humor, hurt or heal. In all situations, it is my response that decides whether a crisis will be escalated or de-escalated, and a child humanized or dehumanized.[13]

Discipline is often an issue for teachers, but we need to be careful that it doesn't overtake our agenda. Ministry with children is like school in some ways but unlike it in others. Everyone can meet Jesus here — not just the bright and able but those who struggle in school and those with disabilities; those who are facing crises at home and in the community and those who are in happy, healthy homes. In the church we are not about passing to the next grade but about coming to know Jesus. Still, the

13. Haim Ginott, *Teacher and Child* (New York: Avon Books, 1975).

teacher or children's leader is the person who can give the children the gift of knowing there is someone in control, of knowing that behavior will not become destructive or hurtful, because the teacher will not allow it.

We can make it easier or harder for children to be courteous and respectful of others and of things around them by how we set up the environment, by our choice of curriculum and how we teach it, by managing our own behavior, and by understanding the individual child's situation.

The way a classroom or meeting space is set up can help children feel safe and able to focus, or it can be distracting. A messy space encourages adding to the mess. The principle of using beautiful materials rather than "leftover stuff" lets children know that their work is valuable. A relational climate of respect, welcome, and fun helps children want to participate.

Selecting a curriculum — whether purchased or developed by the local church — that is appropriate for these particular children will result (one hopes) in productive learning and meaningful worship. How the curriculum is implemented is, of course, important. The teacher can err by focusing intently on getting through the lesson and losing track of the students' concerns. The opposite error is also possible: losing focus on the purpose of the time together and letting time be used up with disorganized chatter and activity.

As Ginott says, the teacher sets the standard for behavior. People tend to respond in the way they are treated. Sarcasm and rudeness gets a similar response. A friendly welcome is usually received with a smile. There are particular times when behavior can be especially disruptive — when people are arriving and leaving and during transitions. The disruption will be minimized if the teacher plans for creative ways for children to move from one place or activity to the next. A principle to remember is *The ministry begins when the first child arrives.* One person might be given the responsibility of welcoming children and introducing them to an interesting activity to do before the formal program begins.

Children's poor behavior often has a physical or emotional starting place. The child may be sick or tired or in crisis or under pressure. Or the child may be feeling "stupid" because he or she doesn't have the background of the other children or lacks the skills to do what is asked and thus the behavior masks embarrassment. Some children enjoy the limelight and "clown around" in the classroom to elicit laughter. Some children are a trial and their behavior is difficult to handle. All these children are precious to God and we must not give up on any one of them. Our care for them may make a lasting difference in their lives.

What then do we do?

- Be firm. Have as few rules as necessary, but stick to them. Don't be picky; everyone has a tough day now and then. But consistency is important. Students need to be able to depend on the teacher for protection and direction.
- Be fair. Avoid punishing the whole group for the misbehavior of one or two. School-age children are especially sensitive to fairness, and they perceive this as gross unfairness. Use sensible consequences that fit the action. Deal with a problem situation promptly — although sometimes we need to cool off before we take action — and then carry on with the program.
- Be friendly. Enthusiasm is contagious. A sense of humor is appealing. Students respond as much to who we are as to what we say. Use the mildest response possible to disruptive behavior. Authority is like soap: the more you use, the less you have.

People who work with children in the church need to know what strategies are recommended and what is prohibited in dealing with behavior problems. The church should develop a policy about behavior management, and it needs to be made clear to everyone who works with children. Of course hitting a child is both unethical and illegal. Time out is often seen as an appropriate discipline strategy, but it can be poorly used. In one instance a child was given a time out and put outside the classroom door. Across from the classroom, however, was an elevator. In this instance the child was safe and was brought back into the classroom, but the result could have been much different. *Time out should preferably happen in the meeting room, where the child can be seen by the adult leaders and continue to listen to what is going on. If it is necessary to remove children from the room, an adult should accompany them, talk with them, and help them regain their control.*

It's a fact of life that children sometimes misbehave; so do adults. Establishing a framework of routines and expectations will give support to all the children and encourage them to take responsibility for their own actions.

Potential Danger Ahead

A safe and welcoming place in the faith community for all children is important, but those who love children must also think about the years beyond childhood. For many, the adolescent journey is fraught with risk and danger.

At the turn of the twenty-first century "a group of 33 children's doctors, research scientists, and mental health and youth service professionals," disturbed by the increasing mental and emotional distress they were seeing in U.S. children and adolescents, banded together to study the causes of the distress and look for answers.[14] These researchers believe that human beings are "hardwired for close attachments to other people" — mothers, fathers, extended family, and then the broader community — and for "meaning." They believe that to meet these needs for connectedness and meaning, children and adolescents must live in "authoritative communities — groups of people who are committed to one another over time and who model and pass on at least part of what it means to be a good person and live a good life."[15] Children who lack such a community are at risk.

Recent studies on violence in schools have focused attention on bullying and the devastating impact it can have on children and adolescents. Ronald Cram reports that in the United States "almost two-thirds of the thirty-seven school shootings over the past twenty-five years were the result of persons seeking revenge" because they "felt persecuted, bullied, threatened, attacked, or injured." The school and the youth culture did not provide them a safe and welcoming place.[16]

In the 1990s researchers began to notice worrisome symptoms in girls, with many preteen girls manifesting a sudden change. At nine or ten years of age they enjoyed many activities, freely expressed their thoughts, were confident and comfortable with who they were. But around eleven years of age they suddenly became uncertain about what they thought

14. *Hardwired to Connect: The New Scientific Case for Authoritative Communities.* A Report to the Nation from the Commission on Children at Risk. YMCA of the USA, Dartmouth Medical School, and the Institute for American Values (New York: Institute for American Values, 2003), p. 5.

15. *Hardwired to Connect,* p. 14.

16. Ronald Hecker Cram, *Bullying: A Spiritual Crisis* (St. Louis: Chalice Press, 2003), p. 50

and what they wanted to do. Instead of standing up for what they knew was right, they gave in to peer pressure, they lost touch with their real self, and relationships became complicated and often painful.[17]

North American children grow up in a media-saturated world, and hour after hour the images they see tell them girls must be thin, beautiful, sexy, and sophisticated, while boys must be muscular, tall, tough, and cool. Eating disorders are rampant as adolescent girls try to be thin and beautiful enough to be accepted.[18] Adolescent boys may do damage to their bodies with obsessive exercise and weightlifting and through unhealthy eating.

Those who feel that there is no use trying to meet appearance standards, or whose families do not have money for the "right" kind of clothes, often find themselves rejected, ridiculed, or bullied.[19] Preteens may be teased for being too smart and eager to learn or for being dumb, enjoying the wrong activities, or choosing the wrong friends. Often adolescents are faced with the choice of being rejected or denying their true self in order to be accepted.[20]

A Safe Place to Prepare for the Journey

What can the family of God do to prepare the next generation of children for this risky adolescent journey? Within the church we can provide preteens with a safe and supportive place to prepare for adolescence. They need a congregation that is an authoritative community, one that is warm and nurturing, communicates clear expectations and values, models what it means to be a good person, and in which children and youth feel truly included.[21]

17. Carol Gilligan, Nona P. Lyons, and Trudy J. Hanmer, eds., *Making Connections: The Relational Worlds of Adolescent Girls at Emma Willard School* (Cambridge, Mass.: Harvard University Press, 1990).

18. Mary Pipher, *Reviving Ophelia: Saving the Selves of Adolescent Girls* (New York: Ballantine, 1994), p. 12.

19. Wendy Murray Zoba, *Day of Reckoning: Columbine and the Search for America's Soul* (Grand Rapids: Brazos, 2000), pp. 69-70.

20. Pipher, *Reviving Ophelia*, pp. 22, 37.

21. *Hardwired to Connect*, p. 34. Consult this resource for additional characteristics of an "authoritative community."

Such a community must have zero tolerance for bullying. Teachers and leaders may need help in understanding bullying, its various forms and devastating results, how to lead children to embrace the value of respect for all, and how to consistently call children to respond with empathy for one another and interact respectfully.[22]

The church can help preteens affirm or discover their worth in God's eyes and in the eyes of others. We might provide fifth- or sixth-graders with a curriculum designed to help them prepare for adolescence. Here are some goals that could be included.

- know themselves as God's highly valued sons and daughters
- see themselves as made in the image of God, not in the image of the culture
- know that God is with them, providing strength to stand for what is right and true
- discover and celebrate their gifts
- understand peer pressure and how to deal with it
- see human sexuality as a precious gift from God to be expressed as God planned
- model and teach "manhood that is caring and bold, courageous and gentle, and strengthen the taboos against violence"[23]
- model capable, thoughtful, adventurous, creative, caring womanhood
- model how women and men can minister together in mutual respect
- strengthen family ties through fun activities for the families of preteens, possibly including a family retreat or camp

A confirmation-like segment could aim to guide preteens in exploring their faith questions, provide them with language to articulate their faith, and offer opportunity for new or renewed commitments. A sense of belonging to the faith community could be enhanced through mentors and participation in the larger community.[24]

The church also has the privilege and responsibility of supporting

22. Cram provides helpful suggestions for developing and living out a "No Bullying" policy, pp. 79-82.

23. Pipher, *Reviving Ophelia*, p. 290.

24. For additional ideas, see Robert L. Browning, *The Pastor as Religious Educator* (Birmingham, Ala.: Religious Education Press, 1989), pp. 65-70.

adults who are about to become parents of teenagers. Preteens need parents who are warm, understanding, and involved in their lives and who clearly communicate guidelines, limits, and expectations.[25] Get to know parents of the preteens and what they want from the church. They may want to learn more about adolescent development and challenges, how to strengthen their family through effective communication, how to set boundaries with love, or how to have fun with their children. Some may be open to forming a small group of parents who meet regularly to enhance their own spiritual growth, support one another as they seek to live as Christians at home, and pray for their children.[26]

We can do more than hope for the best as our children move toward adolescence. We can offer them a safe, authoritative community of adults and peers to support them on the journey.

* * *

As we minister with children, we need to be intentional about offering sanctuary to them, about providing a place that not only is safe but also *feels* safe to all children — a place where each child can grow to be the person God created him or her to be. We celebrate the value of all children and our privilege of walking with them in the faith journey.

25. *Hardwired to Connect*, p. 34.

26. Walter Wangerin, Jr., *Little Lamb Who Made Thee?* (Grand Rapids: Zondervan, 1993), pp. 143-47. In this chapter Wangerin provides some excellent insights for parents.

Chapter 15

IN LEADERSHIP

Many persons who love children and sense a strong call to minister with them are dismayed to discover that extensive administration is required of the children's pastor. Those who learn to creatively guide ministry planning and empower a team of volunteers, however, experience great joy as they watch increasingly effective ministry with children unfold. In this chapter we will look in on the experiences of a seasoned children's pastor, examine the principles guiding leadership decisions, and identify additional strategies for implementing some of the principles.

The Case Example: Building a Children's Ministry Team

Several years ago, conflict among members of the pastoral staff threatened the vitality of Community Church. After several interim pastors, the loss of several members, and the formation of a new board, however, the church was beginning to find its way. Through the turmoil, a core of volunteers sustained a reasonably vital children's ministry. However, as new families joined the church and the children's ministry grew, volunteers' time and energy were strained, and they were beginning to question their continued involvement. Community Church decided it was time to hire a children's pastor. After a long search and several interviews, the church board invited Chris, a veteran children's pastor with significant experience in other churches, to take the position.[1]

During the interviews, the lingering effects of the leadership trauma were discussed. Chris knew that building trust would be a major issue within both the congregation and the pastoral staff. The new senior pastor seemed to be a man of integrity and committed to the development of people. Also, Chris had learned that the children's ministry volunteers cared for children and that many parents would be willing to help. Chris decided to accept the church's offer to join its staff. Though familiar with the conflict and its effects, Chris had much to learn about the history and dynamics of this congregation. As the new children's pastor, Chris confronted a complex network of choices and had to make decisions about how and when to act.

Knowing that some immediate, visible action was expected to assure the congregation that they had made a wise choice in hiring a children's pastor, Chris assessed what could be done without committing the children's ministry to a new direction before necessary groundwork was laid. Since a children's ministry has the potential to affect the climate of an entire congregation, Chris wanted to avoid moving into full-scale program change right away — if ever.

Chris could have taken one or more of several actions: evaluating existing programs, conducting workshops, analyzing the demographics of the community around the church and attendance patterns over the previous five years, visiting other churches in the area, changing the curriculum, reconfiguring the space, ordering new equipment, and so on.

Developing a Base of Support

Chris decided to spend the first three months establishing effective communication channels and building rapport. The first step was simply walking around to visit all the programs that involved children. Chris carried 3 × 5 index cards to make note of concerns or easy-to-resolve dif-

1. The church and Chris are fictional. Though a particular style and abilities are reflected in Chris's decisions and actions, a volunteer children's ministry leader will confront many of the issues and challenges presented in this case example. Further, some of the principles that guide Chris's leadership may be transferable to other cultural contexts, even though leadership strategies and specific ministry formats may differ.

ficulties expressed by the volunteers on site. Chris made sure that the volunteer observed the note-taking and the content of the notes, to prevent the assumption that the notes were critical or judgmental in nature. From experience Chris had learned that in the absence of genuine feedback, many volunteers typically assume that they are doing an inadequate job.

Where appropriate, Chris asked questions such as "What is working well for you? If you could change something, what would it be?" Questions asked on site should elicit information quickly, not be perceived as critical, and not commit a leader to major changes or premature judgment about people or programs.

While walking around, Chris observed how the children and adults moved around the areas before, during, and after the various programs; the state of the equipment and how it was used; the resources that had been purchased and how they were used; and how the volunteers related to each other and to the children. To avoid threatening any insecure volunteers, Chris did not stay too long in any one area.

In the first few weeks, Chris encountered a difficulty that is common in working with volunteers, especially for new staff members. One of the long-term volunteer leaders was angered (or threatened) that Chris was being paid to do what the volunteer had been doing for years without pay. He felt that Chris would displace him and that his work was no longer valued. This volunteer attempted to undermine the children's ministry by using his relationships in the church to turn other volunteers against Chris. Should Chris confront this person in public or in private, or simply move ahead without provoking a confrontation? Private confrontation is seldom effective before a relationship is established, because words and meanings can be twisted. Public confrontation can be perceived as mean-spirited, especially when one is the newcomer. Chris chose to simply move ahead and continue building a base of support and rapport. If the situation worsened, Chris would ask the senior pastor, and the board if necessary, to deal with the individual.

Chris asked the office staff how resources and supplies were ordered for the children's ministry and what the policies were for making expenditures (the size and patterns of increase or decrease of the budget had been discussed during the initial interviews). Chris also called the volunteer leaders for the various program areas and invited their input on several matters:

The place of children's ministry in the church

Children's ministry is typically the largest consumer of volunteer labor, space, and resources among a church's ministries. Yet it is often the least visible ministry in the church. Frequently children are dismissed from worship or excluded altogether; they are seldom involved in the ministry and significant fellowship activities of the congregation. In some churches, the children's ministry leader is considered less than a bona fide leader or staff member. If the children's minister is a woman, she is often not paid at the same level as a male staff member, even though her workload is equal to or greater than those of other staff members.

One of the characteristics of a growing church is a large number of families with children. However, the first person to be hired by a growing church, after the senior pastor, is either a worship leader or a youth minister. When the church board consists primarily of men and women with adolescent children, they want to hire a youth pastor. (This pressure can be problematic if the pastor, for his or her part, wants to hire a worship/music leader.)

Children's ministry is one of the most complex and time-consuming ministries in the congregation. The children's minister works with children but usually is also the leader of a large group of *adult* volunteers. Complicating the role is the need to communicate often and clearly with parents, some of whom can be demanding. Add to these responsibilities the need to be an advocate for the children's ministry, a director of ministry development and evaluation, a cheerleader for volunteers, a supervisor of custodial care in the children's area, a security watchdog, a facility designer, an equipment procurer, an evaluator of resources, and a representative of the church to the community. One wonders why anyone would aspire to the role but for the love of children. Children matter! ❑

- *Communication:* Can you get answers to your questions easily? Are your concerns or ideas heard?
- *Suitability of resources, space, and equipment:* Are the resources helpful? Is the space and equipment adequate? What one thing would you suggest that might increase the satisfaction level of volunteers during the program time?

- *Movement patterns:* Describe how children move in and out of the program areas. What consistent behaviors do you observe at the beginning of the program, during the program, and at the end?
- *Ordering procedures:* How do you get the supplies you need, and how easy is it to get them? Who has control over your area of the budget?
- *Budgeting procedures:* What involvement have you had in establishing the children's ministry budget? Are the line items in the budget realistic for the way your program functions? What additional line items are needed?

Chris knew that a personal base of support was needed outside the church as well. Fortunately, there was an active network of children's pastors in the city, and Chris became an enthusiastic member.

Chris learned that the church's Christian Education (CE) Committee was responsible for oversight of the children's ministry. The youth ministry had its own committee, and there was little to no communication be-

---

Where does one begin?

In the early stages of ministry development, leaders often feel that one of their primary tasks is to determine and meet needs. However, needs-based assessment is problematic for several reasons. Ted Ward warns that a leader concerned only about meeting needs will be focused on short-term projects rather than long-term development. Further, inappropriate approaches to change and development can occur if strategy is based on an outsider's or newcomer's view of the situation. An outsider often begins with one of two premises: "I will tell you what your needs are and how to meet them," or "You tell me your needs, and I will fix them." The key to change and development is genuine relationship and/or partnership. Insiders and outsiders must collaborate in the assessment of the situation *and* in the development of strategy. Even when it is appropriate for the outsider to assume a prophetic role or a teaching role, the insider must be involved in identifying the application of the word from the outsider to the society.

(Ted Ward, "The Christian View of Development as Participation," lectures presented at the Daystar Conference on the Church's Role in Development, Nairobi, Kenya, 1980)

---

tween the leaders in the children's ministry and the youth ministry. One member of the CE Committee organized the adult Sunday school program; all other members represented various programs in the children's ministry. Inevitably, most of the work of the committee was related to planning programs for children. At this point Chris simply noted these realities without offering an opinion or suggesting alternatives; to do that would have been to initiate structural change before organizational and relational dynamics were understood.

During the next three to four weeks, Chris spent several hours on the phone, contacting the volunteer leaders and as many of the volunteer staff as possible and engaging them in brief conversations about their work. Chris sought to learn what they enjoyed about children's ministry, how it had gone that week, and any suggestions they might have for improvement. Chris made personal visits to each member of the CE Committee, learning its history, how it functioned, how new members were added, how the committee communicated with the congregation, how volunteers were recruited, and so on.

Initial Structural Changes

From the visits and conversations, Chris learned enough about the committee structure to realize that before any further development in the children's ministry was possible, one of the following actions was necessary: (1) disband the existing CE Committee and rename it the Children's Ministry Team, or (2) leave the CE Committee as a committee, strip it of its children's ministry members, and form a new group, the Children's Ministry Team. To decide how to proceed, Chris had to work through some important questions:

- What is at stake in this decision?
- Why identify the group as a team rather than as a committee?
- Who should be involved in this change and why?
- What action(s) would have to be taken concerning the adult ministry person on the committee?

Chris recommended that the CE Committee be disbanded, a Children's Ministry Team be formed, and a small group of laity be gathered to work

Learning from Experienced Others

A great deal can be learned by interacting purposefully with men and women who have been in the ministry for some time. Seek out more seasoned colleagues and ask such questions as these:

- What significant tensions exist between the ideal image you had of yourself as a children's minister and the reality, as you've experienced it, over the years of your ministry?
- What have been your most significant shifts in perspective about children's ministry, and how do you feel about those shifts?
- What principles guide your conduct as a children's minister?
- What fundamental values or principles shape your ministry?
- What are the hardest lessons you've had to learn in this work?
- If you moved to another church next month, what would be some of the first things you would do in that new situation?

At some point the new children's pastor should engage in professional reflection. This is often best done with a group of colleagues in the church or the children's pastors' network in the area. Questions that are helpful for reflection include these:

- What good things are happening in the children's ministry and why?
- What needs improvement, and what could hinder or aid this improvement?
- What criteria would indicate that constructive change is happening in the areas identified?
- What needs to be accomplished in personal ministry development over the next year?
- What decisions need to be made today to begin movement in the areas identified? ❑

with the person planning the adult Sunday school program. Chris understood the potential and complexity of the adult ministry, but felt it would be unwise to take on responsibility in this area. In time, perhaps some constructive conversations might be held with the pastor and board concerning the educational development of the whole congregation.

For now, Chris concentrated on helping the children's ministry leaders become a functioning team. As the Children's Ministry Team, they would learn to foster change and suggest new ventures without offending leaders and staff of existing programs or creating the impression that the new venture was now the unchangeable direction for the ministry. They would evaluate existing ministries, study new resources, share ideas, and interact with other children's ministry leaders. Chris added a line item to the budget: "Children's Ministry Team Development." One of the team's first experiences would be to attend a leadership conference together.

After a few weeks leading team meetings, Chris recommended that a member of the team chair the meetings and that the agenda be created in consultation with each member of the team. Chris believed that the best way to learn responsibility and develop one's abilities is to be personally involved. As a participant, Chris could encourage the chairperson, helping her to reflect on her leadership. Chris could also share ideas, communicate values, suggest new ventures, and so on. However, Chris avoided the trap of submitting *every* action or decision to team discussion and decision. Since the team met only monthly, and not at all during the summer and holiday periods, the work of the children's pastor could not be held hostage by unnecessary commitments to team process. In areas of fundamental program or policy change, team input was necessary. Strategy and decisions concerning personnel were most often discussed in the team meetings. Chris felt freedom to approach volunteers for ministry, to consult with volunteer leaders about their responsibilities, to streamline communication and other administrative processes, and to delegate certain tasks (such as previewing resources). As the team members learned to trust in one another, they were less likely to perceive activity undertaken outside team meetings as threatening.

In these early stages of leadership, Chris, without much effort, was able to streamline communication and ordering procedures. What had been minor irritants in program areas were addressed as well — for example, advising the custodian of desired room setup arrangements and cleanup procedures; purchasing supply cabinets and storage equipment; enlisting persons to sharpen pencils and tidy and restock supplies; organizing a process to have linens and toys in the nursery taken home and washed by members of a weekday Bible study. These and other simple changes had an immediate and positive effect on volunteers. Most volunteers have lives beyond the church. They are easily frustrated by small matters that waste time or take time away from their ministry. Chris gained considerable goodwill by removing some of these necessary but more menial tasks.

Foundations for Effective Leadership

Chris made time to reflect on important foundations for children's ministry leadership. However, it was also important to nurture spiritual vitality in the team. Chris had several suggestions. Each member of the team was encouraged to select and read a book or article that focused on prayer, Scripture, or contemporary culture. Some of the team meeting time would be spent discussing ideas from these books and praying for one another.

Leadership Responsibilities in Children's Ministry

The major areas of leadership responsibility in children's ministry include creating climate, anticipating direction, promoting the ministry, and discerning and equipping leaders.

Creating climate has to do with embodying the values and spirit of the ministry. The personal presence of the children's leader is important, as are the attitudes and concrete behaviors of support, encouragement, and a "can do" spirit. The *most difficult tasks* of the leader include helping the church understand that children are part of the church and not just attached to it through programs; developing ministries that do not simply take care of children but foster growth, participation, and responsibility; developing leaders and not getting bogged down in program details; and educating the staff about the importance of the ministry.

Anticipating direction entails noting trends and patterns in the ministry — in other words, being alert to indicators that signal it is time for something new or time to assess an existing ministry. The children's leader is a skilled observer and listener, able to name issues and the realities of a situation.

Promoting the ministry is largely about modeling what you want to see others doing with children. If a "slogan" for the ministry exists, the leader embodies it. The children's leader also takes responsibility for helping volunteers with oral and written expressions that are presented to the con-

---

Chris also encouraged the team to pray for the volunteers who served the children in various ministries. A simple sheet with names and areas of responsibility served as a reminder. Part of the spiritual development of the team involved authentic sharing of their spiritual journeys and commitment to encourage others.

Moving beyond Programs

Several of the first conversations with the newly formed Children's Ministry Team concerned values and purpose. Chris wanted the team to begin thinking about something larger than program maintenance and planning but

gregation. If the leader is not skilled at speaking or writing, then he or she should seek out someone in the congregation or community who is.

Discerning and equipping leaders is one of the more vital responsibilities of the children's leader. To avoid the danger of becoming a micromanager, the children's leader must soon recognize (discern) those capable of leadership. The children's pastor, because he or she is committed to the development of people, provides experiences for growth and empowers the person to undertake leadership tasks. The skill of passing on responsibility to another while staying in touch for support and ideas is difficult to learn but necessary. The children's leader facilitates the formation of children's teams, so that no volunteer leader is alone in the ministry. Finally, when leaders are involved in ministry and dealing with matters that were once the responsibility of the children's pastor, he or she is free to move on to new ministry — to blaze new trails.

Managing details is one of the more difficult of the children's minister's roles. The leader will either take over all the details for the volunteers (assuming he or she is being paid and that the volunteers are busy people) or leave too many details, or the wrong sorts of details, to volunteers. Certain details or tasks further the growth and development of volunteers' ministry skills (for example, searching through resource books for fresh ideas for teaching and learning). Other details are more or less routine and can be taken care of by support people (such as getting craft supplies ready and distributed to classrooms by Sunday morning). ❑

What then might the work of a children's ministry leader look like?

In consultation with others, the children's minister . . .

- articulates a philosophy of children's ministry and the values undergirding the ministry
- develops long-range Bible learning and Christian life development goals for children's curriculum
- represents the children's ministry for children, volunteers, parents, staff, church board, and congregation
- profiles the children's ministry in the congregation
- helps the congregation see the relationship of children's ministry to the total ministry of the church
- gives direction to curricular development and learning opportunities for children
- calls out and/or develops persons for leadership in major ministry positions
- discerns and enlists those interested in and able to serve in the children's ministry
- works with ministry leaders to fill the staffing gaps that occur through the year
- gives direction to the children's ministry team
- encourages volunteers in their ministry with children
- plans/coordinates equipping opportunities for volunteer staff
- consults with volunteer leaders in coordinating the various ministries
- works with ministry leaders to evaluate the various aspects of children's ministry
- recognizes and resolves problems
- manages the children's ministry budget
- coordinates special events
- manages the children's ministry facilities
- oversees the acquisition of supplies and equipment
- develops new initiatives in children's ministry as lay leaders take on existing administrative functions
- networks with other children's ministry professionals
- keeps abreast of resources and development in children's ministry ❑

had to facilitate these conversations without disempowering the lay leaders or taking over the group. It was important to move the children's ministry from preoccupation with programs to a concern for the personal and spiritual development of people — the children, those who worked with the children, parents, and people in the community who were touched by the ministry. In time Chris would lead the team to expand its vision about what could be done in the present to shape a desired future for the ministry.

As the Children's Ministry Team became more active and visible, Chris found ways to encourage the whole congregation to own the children's ministry. Many church members had assumed that the programs of the church existed simply to support the family and that each family was responsible for the spiritual nurture of its children. Chris appreciated this ideal but understood that the reality was quite different: with changing family patterns and pressures, parents or caregivers were often unwilling or unable to provide spiritual nurture for their children. Chris asserted that it was important for the congregation to be a welcoming place for children, but that it was *more* important for it to become a context for the development of families and intergenerational groups. As families and mixed generations learned, worshiped, and ministered together in the congregation and community, they would learn from one another the attitudes, skills, and resources essential for the nurture of children. However, before this could happen the congregation had to learn to embrace children as *part of* the community of faith and not just attached to it through programs. Chris began to refer to programs as "ministries" and discouraged jokes or language that depicted children's ministry as a battle to be fought or that typed children as miniature monsters.

Chris encouraged the team to think through and create a statement of values. Since values tend to reflect the governing metaphor of a children's ministry,[2] Chris asked the team to reflect on the metaphors that might describe *this* church's children's ministry. They considered the value statements of other churches but soon realized that they needed a statement that would reflect their specific context. Chris invited each member of the team to identify what he or she considered important values.

Many volunteer groups resist experiences that seem too "academic" and just want to get on with practical matters. This team, however, under Chris's urging, attempted to identify what is important for the personal and

2. See chapter 1 for a more complete discussion of metaphors.

Core Values for a Learning Community

The church is a holistic and dynamic learning community that integrates worship (liturgy), service, relationship, as well as learning, in a context that includes the family and the entire congregation. The core values of this learning community encompass the world's children and can be expressed in these ways:

- Every child should have (a) Christian faith, (b) a nurturing community, (c) an advocate where necessary, (d) positive, appropriate experiences in worship, learning, service, and relationship, and (e) a family that is supported by the faith community. *Therefore, we will involve the entire faith community in the development and nurture of children and the support of their parents or caregivers.*
- Children should be respected for (a) their unique gifts and their individual and cultural differences, (b) their individual capacities to respond to God in worship, (c) their various abilities to engage in responsible service, and (d) their multifaceted capacities for learning. *Therefore, we will create a variety of experiences to honor and fulfill this intention.*
- Children should be accepted as part of their congregation and not

spiritual development of children. They found it a difficult but rewarding task. In some cases a volunteer would state a value that was really an action (e.g., "Children need to learn Bible verses"). Chris would then ask, "Why do you want children to learn Bible verses?" By asking "Why?" or "What is driving that statement?" or "What is at the heart of that suggestion?" Chris was able to help the team clarify the non-negotiables in the children's ministry.

When talking with parents or interested members of the church, Chris would often ask them to name one or more values. In time, the team had a list of statements that they could refine and word as concisely and simply as possible.

The values were used to guide the development of more or less specific goals or purposes for the ministry. Chris discouraged the team from getting too specific at this point, since goals and purposes take more real-just attached to it through programs. *Therefore, we will commit ourselves to the development and nurture of children in the context of congregational communities.*

- Every child should be embraced within a responsive and responsible community. *Therefore, we will encourage the people of God in every part of the world to become advocates where necessary, and supporters of and participants in local community efforts on behalf of children where possible.*

In the Christian learning community, children and adults encounter God through the Scriptures, meet God in worship, take time for reflection, and obey God in life and service. Through experiences of worship, learning, and service, the members of the learning community connect the biblical story to today's world and to their personal worlds. Learning is interactive. Children are active participants in their own learning and not simply passive observers. To teach involves orchestrating, creating, and supporting a learning environment that nurtures the learning of all children. Curriculum developers support adult leaders and guides with the resources and training to understand how to effectively implement and execute the experiences of the learning community. (Developed by Richard Best, Linda Cannell, and Scottie May) ❑

istic shape as the ministry continues to unfold. See the "Core Values for a Learning Community" on pages 342 and 343 for an example.

Inviting Parental Involvement

As values were being clarified, Chris decided it was time to bring parents into the process. A series of meetings was organized in which Chris introduced the Children's Ministry Team and its responsibilities, presented the values and purpose statements, and invited parental feedback — impressions, concerns, and ideas. The meetings incorporated some time for the participants to celebrate the past while they anticipated future development.

The parents had strong feelings concerning the quality of programming for their children, but Chris was reluctant at this stage to propose the formation of a Parents' Council as some other churches had done. Time was needed to help parents gain a vision for the spiritual development of their children, development that would be nurtured in a variety of ways and not tied exclusively to age-specific programs. However, Chris made sure that the parents were affirmed as a vital part of the children's ministry and encouraged their input.

Educating the Congregation and Staff

The final activity that Chris identified for the first three months was to begin the process of educating the congregation and the other staff members about the children's ministry. Chris knew that though the children's ministry was the church's most volunteer-intensive ministry and had potential to affect the overall climate of the congregation, in too many churches it is not taken seriously. This church seemed to treat the staff members with some equity, but Chris knew of churches where the children's pastor was treated as little more than a paid babysitter rather than a legitimate member of the pastoral team, especially if the children's pastor was a woman.

The Children's Ministry Team determined that every communication, written or oral, would contain some value-laden slogan such as "Children are not just the church of tomorrow, they are part of the church of today." Or, "We respect our children highly." Chris prepared inserts for the bulletin and a letter to the congregation informing them of the new team and the values that would energize their efforts. Volunteers were affirmed publicly, and members of the congregation were invited to walk through the children's ministry area and talk to the volunteers and the children (appropriate security safeguards were already in place). On Sundays Chris was visible in the foyer, modeling attitudes toward children and introducing children to adult members of the church. All these activities were ongoing, to ensure that the children's ministry was kept before the congregation.

A "Visiting Member of the Congregation" process was instituted: individuals from the congregation were invited to take ten to fifteen minutes in one of the children's programs on a Sunday of their choice, to describe their work, a hobby, a special talent, and so on. The Children's Ministry

Team and the pastoral staff led the way, and no adult in the congregation refused the invitation. The stage was set for further development.

Chris would spend the next two years affirming the work that had been done with the children, helping the team emerge as an effective body in the church, beginning the process of evaluating and enhancing existing ministries, allowing new ventures to emerge, finding and developing leaders, involving children in the ministry, and launching a series of family development experiences.

Building the Ministry Team

Volunteers, even committed and able volunteers, have limited time and energy to give to leadership. Chris challenged and affirmed volunteer leaders but acknowledged that the members of the team had multiple demands on their time. Chris never took for granted the commitment of these leaders to the children's ministry. A genuine thank-you, a short note, a nod, a thumbs up, providing childcare as needed so that team members could have lunch together just for fun, sharing books with the team, inviting prayer from them and assuring them of prayer — these and other tokens of friendship and support were genuinely offered and gratefully received.

The attitudes and behaviors established in the team soon carried over to other volunteers in the children's ministry. The children's ministry came to be known as a place where children and adults had fun together, accomplished meaningful work, and made a difference. Who wouldn't want to be involved? Chris was not surprised when people offered to help.

Team meetings dealt with routine administrative matters, but time was set aside for creative thinking as well. Chris told stories of various formats for Bible learning, worship, and ministry with children. Other members of the team reported on what had been done in the past in the children's ministry. They discussed alternative possibilities for existing ministries and prayed that the Lord would bring new leaders into the ministry or would help them recognize those volunteers who were ready for leadership responsibility.

Chris encouraged the team to try one experiment in teaching and learning with children. Sunday was chosen, because most children are present on Sunday and the ministry is typically most visible to the rest of the congregation then. The team assumed responsibility for planning, but

Recruitment and Equipping of Volunteers

Several factors are important in the recruitment and equipping of volunteer leaders.

Climate. What is the nature of the church's climate? How does it "feel" to the volunteer? Ways you can affect climate include developing congregational awareness of the nature of the church and its ministry as revealed in Scripture. Be visible in your affirmation of people. Assume that people want to serve the Lord. Treat people as partners in ministry. (Many volunteers feel used by church leaders. But it is those who work in the ministry who are the most logical persons to evaluate it and offer suggestions for change.) Work on communication skills. Give spiritual support and direction. Show that you understand the real-life situation of persons. Say thank you often. Make recruiting a year-round, ongoing spiritual activity, replacing the "nominating committee" with a structure that allows people with discernment to seek out and encourage the gifts of others.

Recruitment Style. Paper-and-pencil "talent surveys" are seldom effective. Personal contact is always best. Experienced recruiters have learned that the primary reason people volunteer is that they are asked and that a no often changes to yes over time. People will enlarge their view if you talk with them. If they say no, ask them what else they would like to do. The problem with leaders who seek to recruit volunteers is that they simply want help, not input. Many volunteers leave because they are underutilized or because they perceive little meaning in their tasks. An experienced recruiter observed that volunteers are often not allowed to define what they are good at, what they are tired of doing, what they don't like to do, what they want to learn, where they are growing, and when they need a break. As you are speaking with volunteers, invite them to tell you of their own ministry dreams.

Job Descriptions. Many church leaders believe they should design job descriptions for the various ministry areas in the church. However, once designed, the descriptions are seldom used. Volunteers bring their own styles and experiences to the ministry. Job descriptions that use terms like *will* or *must* can produce conscious or unconscious resistance within the volunteer. Work out a way of doing ministry *with* the volunteer. Many times in such interchanges, aspects of ministry will emerge that expand and enrich the program beyond what the leader could have envisioned.

Equipping. We spend a great deal of time at the front end getting people into the system; we spend far less time in nurture and development. Plan for *basic* input suitable for a general audience. Ask, "What are the basic things that have to be learned if ministry is to be effective?"

For example:

- the nature of spirituality and personal discipleship
- input on spiritual gifts
- the basic purpose and nature of the "faith community"
- basic principles of communication
- the nature of group dynamics
- basic principles of Christian leadership
- biblical models of teaching

The *basic* (or foundational) input can be provided in short-term workshops, retreat settings, one-to-one relationships, and large group or small group exercises.

Plan for the *specific* input that will be required if persons are to be developed for their practical ministry, for example:

- teaching methods appropriate to a particular age group
- significant age-group characteristics that affect teaching
- specific aspects of preparing a teaching and learning experience
- leading an adult group
- specific skills in caregiving
- skill development in storytelling, leading a discussion, presenting a lecture
- the strengths and limitations of particular resource materials

Specific input is most effectively presented in long-term, "hands-on" experiences.

Here are some practical suggestions for equipping:

- Provide input at times when volunteers are already at church (for example, during the Sunday school hour or midweek program time, Sunday noon "tabletalks").
- Work with small groups of volunteers at times and in places that best suit their schedules.

(continued)

- Use prepared videotapes. Encourage volunteers to view the tapes on their own time at home. Provide a viewing guide or arrange a debriefing session at a later time.
- Design "make-it, take-it" workshops. For example, make it possible for teachers to actually prepare Bible learning games.
- Form ministry teams. Busy volunteers often find it difficult to function as "lone rangers" in ministry. When persons can work and plan together, ministry is often more effective.
- Talk with each volunteer about areas of growth he or she would like to explore over the next few months.
- Recommend books or articles for people to read. Ask them to report on what they have read or to share a ministry idea with the large group.
- Subscribe to magazines focused on ministry areas. Enlist someone who can clip relevant articles and circulate them.
- Purchase resource books. Select an idea from an idea book and try it out at a ministry meeting.
- Encourage people to participate in some community service training options. For example, some seniors' organizations provide workshops in how to involve seniors or communicate with seniors; some community colleges offer continuing education opportunities in a variety of areas relevant to the church's ministry. Provide scholarships to conferences or workshops that are related to the volunteers' ministry.
- Use the facilities of a camp (winter or summer). Invite ministry groups to the camp for a couple of days or a week for fellowship, fun, worship, and training.
- Develop an "Idea Sheet" pertinent to a particular ministry area and circulate it (use this sheet to affirm the people involved as well!).
- Provide workshops or skill-development options for some volunteers while other volunteers are in service; then rotate the groups.
- Enlist experienced volunteers to act as resource persons or spiritual mentors for less experienced volunteers.
- People tend to change over time. If you have been in a church for a long time, realize that your assumptions about people probably need to be updated. Provide opportunity for people to talk about what they would like to do differently.

- Celebrate contributions made and allow people to leave a position without feeling guilty.
- Training or equipping may be best done on the spot.
- Don't overload the volunteer with information too soon. Allow time for new ideas to become familiar. People are willing to listen to something they think might work, but when it comes to the implementation they will often hesitate. Allow time for debriefing. It could take as long as a year before there is a discernible difference in a volunteer's willingness to try something new.
- Recognize personal needs and problems and provide opportunities for conversation and prayer.
- Feature different ministries throughout the year and highlight the volunteers involved in the ministries. Plan annual ceremonial occasions that celebrate specific aspects of the ministry.
- Say thank you frequently. Take time to talk with people.

Volunteers are paid in a different coin from the pay of professionals. Their payment comes in the form of satisfaction with doing something important and appreciation extended by the people with whom they serve. Those who supervise volunteers do well to make certain they receive their "salaries."

Evaluation. The key to effective volunteer leadership is communication. Discuss the potential ministry with a prospective volunteer in detail. After a few months, schedule a conversation to determine the volunteer's perception of his or her fit. Establish ministry expectations up front (e.g., how children are to be treated, the ministry's educational philosophy). Propose a time limit for involvement in a given ministry. If a volunteer is proving difficult, you may be able to suggest another area of ministry. In an extreme case, a volunteer may be hurting the ministry. The difficult but necessary action is to describe the behavior and indicate why it is inappropriate. Ask the volunteer for a response. If the problem continues, involve one or more others in the action to remove the volunteer from the position (in other words, use the approach typically used in church discipline). At all times, work toward a relational environment characterized by trust and confidence. ❑

Chris took charge of the details for the first experiment, knowing that failure in the details could lead to future reluctance to try anything new. Ultimately, many of the details would be managed by the volunteers. Chris knew that children could be involved in their own learning and would respond positively, despite the worries of some adults that the children would become unruly and that something new would automatically create more work. The volunteers would have to see the positive results through actual experience, not a lecture. For this reason Chris encouraged at least one experiment in some aspect of the ministry each year.

Experimental projects became special memories for the congregation and signs that something was happening in the children's ministry. The team saw firsthand how children and volunteers responded to something different, and they felt empowered to try new things or to revamp existing ministries.

Chris made an effort to meet with volunteers who seemed to have particular interests or aptitudes. "Mary, you seem to have an interest in creating learning experiences for young children. Would you be interested in becoming part of a team that builds more meaningful activity into the curriculum?" "Myoung, I have noticed that you enjoy the summer ministries with children. Would you consider heading up the team that plans the . . . ?" Chris invited members of the Children's Ministry Team to participate in these focused recruitment visits and, in time, encouraged them to approach people in whom they discerned particular interest or ability.

Recruitment of volunteers is considered one of the most onerous tasks in a children's ministry. However, Chris knew that once three things were in place, recruitment would become almost a nonissue. First, the Children's Ministry Team had to model positive attitudes toward ministry and toward the children. Second, the congregation had to see that volunteers were supported and that children were enjoying the ministry. Third, parents and other members of the congregation had to see that children were learning important values, involved in meaningful service, engaged in worship, and learning that Bible stories are true, interesting, and helpful for their daily lives. As the ministry gained a reputation for encouraging personal and spiritual development and not just babysitting, people began to offer their services to the ministry. The growing interest and support of the congregation further encouraged the team and emboldened them as leaders of the ministry.

By the end of the first year, Chris was able to interest members of the team in assuming responsibilities that in the early stages had been part of the children's pastor's responsibility. Members of the team considered ways to provide training for volunteers. For example, two team members organized a Saturday brunch for fellowship and for developing the skill of storytelling. They invited the best storytellers in the congregation to share their techniques. Chris also encouraged on-the-job training. If a discipline problem emerged, Chris or another member of the team would go to the area and help with the problem. Afterward they would discuss with the volunteer what happened and what would be possible ways to deal with the difficulty should it recur. One member of the team invited a specialist to model questioning techniques during an actual teaching/learning session with children. These in-context training sessions were often particularly valuable and did not involve an extra day or evening out for the volunteer.

Team members became active in regular conversations with volunteers and parents as part of a process of evaluation.

Building for the Future

As the responsibility for various aspects of leaders was shared by members of the team, Chris was able to move into other areas of development. The next task was to consider ways to involve families and intergenerational groupings in learning, worship, and service.

After two years of building and learning, Chris used budgeted funds to take the whole team on a weekend retreat with any spouses and children who wanted to come. Part of the time was spent in simple fun and family or intergenerational activities. Chris indicated that these experiences were designed to "prime the pump" for the development of similar experiences in the congregation. Chris also used part of the time to think with the team about the future.

Conclusion

Teaching and nurturing the faith formation of children is one of the church's more challenging ministries. Chris's experience offers some insight into leadership practices and attitudes. However, there is more to learn than can be presented in a short chapter. Each person who takes up the mantle of children's ministry leader will have his or her own story to tell. Every situation presents its own opportunities and challenges. Each children's pastor will form a distinct understanding of the values, goals, or purposes for children's ministry and how to work these out in the presence of particular children.

Children who are part of a vital church community where people of all ages are engaged in meaningful worship, learning, and serving will be nurtured in their faith. Significant learning about the Scriptures and what it means to be a follower of Jesus is shaped in the context of a caring church community. The children will be guided in making faith and life commitments that are informed by God's precepts and principles. As they participate in the life of the congregation, they will be challenged and inspired and equipped for authentic service. Their relationships will be expanded to encompass people of all ages, social strata, ethnicity, and cultures.

The task of Christian education is not just about what a teacher does or delivers *to* children. The evidence of teaching is learning: how the children respond, the questions they ask, the attitudes they demonstrate in actual behavior, and the way they use Scripture to inform their lives and decisions. In the teaching/learning process, child and adult contribute something of value to each other's spiritual journey.

Many congregations assume that they hire a children's minister to lead programs. This assumption, however, will in time doom the children's ministry to failure. The role of leaders among the people of God is to equip other leaders who are in turn able to equip others. The apostle Paul gives this encouragement to Timothy: "You then, my child, be strong in the grace that is in Christ Jesus; and what you have heard from me through many witnesses entrust to faithful people who will be able to teach others as well" (2 Tim. 2:1-2).

In this way, the work of the Lord continues. Indeed leadership — the right kind of leadership — matters in the significant enterprise of teaching and nurturing the spiritual life of children.

A POSTLUDE — OUR PRAYER

Now to our loving and holy God, to the Lord Jesus,
our Good Shepherd, and to
the indwelling Holy Spirit, we pray for each person who
ministers with children. May they have —
Eyes to see your glory,
Ears to hear your voice,
A mouth to speak your truth,
Hands to do your work,
A heart to share your love,
Knees to bow before you,
And feet to follow you all the days of their lives.
In Jesus' name,
Amen and amen.

BIBLIOGRAPHY

Anderson, Herbert, and Susan B. W. Johnson. *Regarding Children: A New Respect for Childhood and Families.* Louisville: Westminster/John Knox, 1994.

Anthony, Michael, and Warren Benson. *Exploring the History and Philosophy of Christian Education.* Grand Rapids: Kregel, 2003.

Archer, Gleason, Jr. "Covenant," in *Evangelical Dictionary of Theology,* edited by Walter Elwell. Grand Rapids: Baker, 1984.

Barna, George. *The Second Coming of the Church.* Nashville: Word, 1998.

Benson, Clarence H. *A Popular History of Christian Education.* Chicago: Moody Press, 1943.

Berryman, Jerome W. *Godly Play: A Way of Religious Education.* San Francisco: Harper Collins, 1991.

Best, G. F. A. *Shaftesbury.* New York: ARCO Publishing, 1959.

Blocher, Henri. *Original Sin: Illuminating the Riddle.* Grand Rapids: Eerdmans, 1997.

Bloom, Benjamin, ed. *Taxonomy of Educational Objectives: The Classification of Educational Goals.* New York: D. McKay, 1956.

Boyd, Gregory, and Paul Eddy. *Across the Spectrum: Understanding Issues in Evangelical Theology.* Grand Rapids: Baker, 2002.

Bronfenbrenner, Uri. *The Ecology of Human Development.* Cambridge, Mass.: Harvard University Press, 1979.

Brown, Margaret Wise, illus. Clement Hurd. *The Runaway Bunny.* New York: Harper and Brothers, 1942.

Buckland, Ron. "Round Table" (review of Francis Bridger, *Children Finding Faith: Exploring a Child's Response to God,* rev. ed. Bletchley, U.K.: Scripture Union, 2000), *Journal of Christian Education* 44, no. 1, 2001.

Buechner, Frederick. *Listening to Your Life.* San Francisco: HarperCollins, 1992.

Bunge, Marcia, ed. *The Child in Christian Thought.* Grand Rapids: Eerdmans, 2001.

Burgess, Harold W. *Models of Religious Education*. Nappanee, Ind.: Evangel, 2001.

———. *The Role of Teaching in Sustaining the Church*. Anderson, Ind.: Bristol House, 2004.

Bushnell, Horace. *Christian Nurture*. (reprint) New Haven, Conn.: Yale University Press, 1967.

Caldwell, Elizabeth F. *Come unto Me: Rethinking the Sacraments for Children*. Cleveland: United Church Press, 1996.

Cannell, Linda, and Scottie May. "Kids' Community: Children's Ministry for the New Millennium," *Christian Education Journal* 4, no. 1, 2000.

Carr, John Lynn. "Needed: A Pastoral Curriculum for the Congregation," in *The Pastor as Religious Educator*, edited by Robert L. Browning. Birmingham, Ala.: Religious Education Press, 1989.

Cavalletti, Sofia. *The Religious Potential of the Child*. Chicago: Catechesis of the Good Shepherd Publications, 1992.

Chesterton, G. K. *Orthodoxy: The Romance of Faith*. New York: Doubleday, 1959.

Coles, Robert. *The Moral Life of Children*. Boston: Houghton Mifflin, 1986.

Colorosa, Barbara. *Kids Are Worth It: Giving Your Child the Gift of Inner Discipline*. New York: Avon, 1994.

Comstock, G. A. "The Medium and Society: The Role of Television in American Life," in *Children and Television*, edited by G. L. Berry and J. K. Asamen. Newbury Park, Calif.: Sage, 1993.

Craig, Grace, Marguerite Kermis, and Nancy Digdon. *Children Today*, Canadian edition. Scarborough, Ont.: Prentice Hall/Allyn and Bacon Canada, 1998.

Cram, Ronald Hecker. *Bullying: A Spiritual Crisis*. St. Louis: Chalice Press, 2003.

Dale, Edgar. *Audio-Visual Methods in Teaching*, 3rd ed. New York: Holt, Rinehart and Winston, 1969.

Dawn, Marva. *Is It a Lost Cause? Having the Heart of God for the Church's Children*. Grand Rapids: Eerdmans, 1997.

Dykstra, Craig. *Growing in the Faith: Education and the Christian Practices*. Louisville: Geneva, 1999.

Eavey, Charles B. *History of Christian Education*. Chicago: Moody Press, 1964.

Elias, John. *A History of Christian Education*. Malabar, Fla.: Krieger, 2002.

Erickson, Millard J. *Christian Theology*. Grand Rapids: Baker, 1985.

Foster, Richard. *Prayers from the Heart*. New York: HarperCollins, 1994.

Frankena, William K. *Philosophy of Education*. New York: Macmillan, 1965.

Gardner, Howard. *Frames of Mind*. New York: Basic Books, 1993.

Garland, Diana. *Family Ministry*. Downers Grove, Ill.: InterVarsity Press, 1999.

Garmezy, N. "Resiliency and Vulnerability to Adverse Development Outcomes Associated with Poverty," *American Behavioral Scientist* 34, no. 4 (1991).

Gilligan, Carol, Nona P. Lyons, and Trudy J. Hanmer, eds. *Making Connections: The*

Relational Worlds of Adolescent Girls at Emma Willard School. Cambridge, Mass.: Harvard University Press, 1990.

Ginott, Haim. *Teacher and Child.* New York: Avon Books, 1975.

Goleman, Daniel. *Emotional Intelligence.* New York: Bantam, 1995.

Govig, Stewart D. *Strong at the Broken Places.* Louisville: Westminster/John Knox, 1989.

Grant, Reg, and John Reed. *Telling Stories to Touch the Heart: How to Use Stories to Communicate God's Truth.* Wheaton, Ill.: Victor Books, 1990.

Green, Joel B. *The Gospel of Luke,* New International Commentary on the New Testament. Grand Rapids: Eerdmans, 1997.

Groome, Thomas. *Christian Religious Education: Sharing Our Story and Vision.* San Francisco: Harper and Row, 1980.

Hardwired to Connect: The New Scientific Case for Authoritative Communities. A Report to the Nation from the Commission on Children at Risk. YMCA of the USA, Dartmouth Medical School, and the Institute for American Values. New York: Institute for American Values, 2003.

Harris, Henry J. *Robert Raikes: The Man Who Founded Sunday School.* London: National Sunday School Union, 1959.

Harris, Maria. *Fashion Me a People: Curriculum in the Church.* Louisville: Westminster/John Knox, 1989.

Hay, David, and Rebecca Nye. *The Spirit of the Child.* London: Fount, 1998.

Hay, David, Rebecca Nye, and Roger Murphy. "Thinking About Childhood Spirituality: Review of Research and Current Directions," in *Research in Religious Education,* edited by Leslie J. Francis, William K. Kay, and William S. Campbell. Macon, Ga.: Smyth and Helwys, 1996.

Heitzenrater, Richard. "John Wesley and Children," in *The Child in Christian Thought,* edited by Marcia Bunge. Grand Rapids: Eerdmans, 2001.

Hogue, David A. *Remembering the Future, Imagining the Past: Story, Ritual, and the Human Brain.* Cleveland: Pilgrim, 2003.

Horton, Michael. "Reformation Piety," *Modern Reformation* 1, no. 4, 2002.

Hughes, P. E. "Grace," in *Evangelical Dictionary of Theology,* edited by Walter Elwell. Grand Rapids: Baker, 1984.

"Imago Dei and People with Disabilities," *Context: Research to Make Religion Relevant* 6, no. 2, Fall 1996.

Johnson, Steven. "Antonio Damasio's Theory of Thinking Faster and Faster: Are the Brain's Emotional Circuits Hardwired for Speed?" *Discover* 25, no. 5, 2004.

Johnson-Miller, Beverly. "Medieval Education," in *Dictionary of Christian Education,* edited by Michael Anthony. Grand Rapids: Baker, 2001.

Joseph, Rhawn. "The Limbic System and the Soul: Evolution and the Neuroanatomy of Religious Experience," *Zygon* 36, no. 1, 2001.

Knight, George R. *Philosophy and Education: An Introduction in Christian Perspective.* Berrien Springs, Mich.: Andrews University Press, 1988.

Kohn, Alfie. *No Contest: The Case Against Competition.* Boston: Houghton Mifflin, 1986.

———. *Punished by Rewards.* Boston: Houghton Mifflin, 1993.

Kolb, David. *Experiential Learning: Experience as the Source of Learning and Development.* Englewood Cliffs, N.J.: Prentice Hall, 1984.

Ladwig, Tim, illustrator. *Psalm Twenty-Three.* Grand Rapids: Eerdmans Books for Young Readers, 1997.

Lakoff, George, and Mark Johnson. *Metaphors We Live By.* Chicago: University of Chicago Press, 1980.

Lay, Robert F. *Foundational Documents for Christian Teachers and Ministers.* Upland, Ind.: Robert Lay and Taylor University, 2004.

LeFever, Marlene. *Learning Styles: Reaching Everyone God Gave You to Teach.* Elgin, Ill.: Cook Communications, 1995.

L'Engle, Madeleine. *Story as Truth: The Rock That Is Higher.* Wheaton, Ill.: Harold Shaw, 1993.

Lewis, C. S. *The Lion, the Witch and the Wardrobe.* London: Geoffrey Bles, 1950.

———. *Of Other Worlds: Essays and Stories.* Edited by Walter Hooper. New York: Harcourt Brace Jovanovich, 1966.

Loder, James. *The Logic of the Spirit.* San Francisco: Jossey-Bass, 1998.

Lynn, Robert W., and Elliott Wright. *The Big Little School.* Birmingham: Religious Education, 1980.

May, Scottie. "A Look at the Effects of Extrinsic Motivation on the Internalization of Biblical Truth," *Christian Education Journal* 7, no. 1 (2003): 47-65.

May, Scottie, and Donald Ratcliff. "Children's Spiritual Experience and the Brain," in *Children's Spirituality: Christian Perspectives, Research, and Applications,* edited by Donald Ratcliff. Eugene, Ore.: Cascade, 2004.

Mouw, Richard. *He Shines in All That's Fair: Culture and Common Grace.* Grand Rapids: Eerdmans, 2001.

Mulholland, M. Robert. *Shaped by the Word,* rev. ed. Nashville: Upper Room, 2000.

———. *Invitation to a Journey: A Road Map for Spiritual Formation.* Downers Grove, Ill.: InterVarsity Press, 1993.

Myers, Barbara Kines, and William Myers. *Engaging in Transcendence: The Church's Ministry and Covenant with Young Children.* Cleveland: Pilgrim, 1992.

Myers, Barbara Kines. *Young Children and Spirituality.* New York: Routledge, 1997.

Nelson, C. Ellis. "Formation of a God Representation," *Religious Education Journal* 91, no. 1, 1996.

Newberg, Andrew, Eugene d'Aquili, and Vince Rause. *Why God Won't Go Away.* New York: Ballantine, 2002.

Newton, Gary. "Ministering to Unchurched Urban, At-Risk Children," in *Children's*

Spirituality: Christian Perspectives, Research, and Applications, edited by Donald Ratcliff. Eugene, Ore.: Cascade, 2004.

Ng, David, and Virginia Thomas. *Children in the Worshiping Community.* Atlanta: Westminster/John Knox, 1981.

Nouwen, Henri J. M. "Because of Adam," *Reader's Digest,* October 1988.

Orme, Nicholas. *Medieval Children.* London: Yale University Press, 2001.

Ozment, Steven. *When Fathers Ruled: Family Life in Reformation Europe.* Cambridge, Mass.: Harvard University Press, 1983.

Palmer, Parker. *To Know as We Are Known: Education as a Spiritual Journey.* San Francisco: HarperSanFrancisco, 1993.

Pazmino, Robert. *The Basics of Teaching for Christians: Preparation, Instruction, Evaluation.* Grand Rapids: Baker, 1998.

Phillips, Timothy, and Dennis Okholm. *A Family of Faith: An Introduction to Evangelical Christianity.* Grand Rapids: Baker, 2001.

Pierson, Jim. *Exceptional Teaching: A Comprehensive Guide for Including Students with Disabilities.* Cincinnati: Standard Publishing, 2002.

Pipher, Mary. *Reviving Ophelia: Saving the Selves of Adolescent Girls.* New York: Ballantine Books, 1994.

Pohl, Christine. *Making Room: Recovering Hospitality as a Christian Tradition.* Grand Rapids: Eerdmans, 1999.

Postman, Neil. *The Disappearance of Childhood.* New York: Vintage, 1994.

———. *Technopoly: The Surrender of Culture to Technology.* New York: Vintage, 1993.

Pritchard, Gretchen Wolff. *Offering the Gospel to Children.* Cambridge, Mass.: Cowley, 1992.

Reed, James E., and Ronnie Prevost. *A History of Christian Education.* Nashville: Broadman and Holman, 1993.

Renz, Christopher. "Christian Education and the Confirmation Debate: Towards a Theology of Catechesis," *Journal of Christian Education* 41, no. 1, 1998.

Richards, Lawrence O. *Children's Ministry: Nuturing Faith within the Family of God.* Grand Rapids: Zondervan, 1983.

Rizzuto, Ana-Maria. *The Birth of the Living God: A Psychoanalytic Study.* Chicago: University of Chicago Press, 1979.

Rogers, Everett M. *Diffusion of Innovations,* 3rd ed. New York: Free Press, 1983.

Seamands, David. *Healing Grace: Let God Free You from the Performance Trap.* Wheaton, Ill.: Victor, 1988.

Sendak, Maurice. *Where the Wild Things Are.* New York: Harper and Row, 1963.

Shaw, Susan. *Storytelling in Religious Education.* Birmingham, Ala.: Religious Education Press, 1999.

Sherwood, Illadel. *200 Years of Sunday School in America.* Nashville: Dynamic Manuscripts, n.d.

Stewart, Sonja M., and Jerome W. Berryman. *Young Children and Worship.* Louisville: Westminster/John Knox, 1989.

Stewart, Sonja M. *Following Jesus: More About Young Children and Worship.* Louisville: Geneva Press, 2000.

Stonehouse, Catherine. *Joining Children on the Spiritual Journey.* Grand Rapids: Baker, 1998.

———. "Children in Wesleyan Thought," in *Children's Spirituality: Christian Perspectives, Research, and Applications,* edited by Donald Ratcliff. Eugene, Ore.: Cascade, 2004.

Stortz, Martha Ellen. "'Where or When Was Your Servant Innocent?': Augustine on Childhood," in *The Child in Christian Thought,* edited by Marcia J. Bunge. Grand Rapids: Eerdmans, 2001.

Strange, W. A. *Children in the Early Church.* Carlisle, Cumbria, U.K.: Paternoster, 1996.

Strohl, Jan. "The Child in Luther's Theology," in *The Child in Christian Thought,* edited by Marcia Bunge. Grand Rapids: Eerdmans, 2001.

Tamminen, Kalevi. "Religious Experiences in Childhood and Adolescence: A Viewpoint of Religious Development between the Ages of 7 and 20," *International Journal for the Psychology of Religion* 4, no. 2, 1994.

Thompson, Marjorie J. *Family: The Forming Center.* Nashville: Upper Room, 1996.

The United Methodist Book of Worship. Nashville: United Methodist Publishing House, 1992.

Vinovskis, Maris A. "Schooling and Poor Children in 19th-Century America," *American Behavioral Scientist* 35, no. 3, January/February 1992.

Walsh, John. *The Art of Storytelling: Easy Steps to Presenting an Unforgettable Story.* Chicago: Moody Press, 2003.

Wangerin, Walter, Jr. *The Orphean Passages.* Grand Rapids: Zondervan, 1986.

———. *Little Lamb Who Made Thee?* Grand Rapids: Zondervan, 1993.

Ward, Ted. "Metaphors of Spiritual Reality, Part 3," *Bibliotheca Sacra* 139, no. 556, 1982.

Weber, Hans-Ruedi. *Jesus and the Children.* Loveland, Ohio: Treehaus, 1994.

Wells, Gordon. *The Meaning Makers: Children Learning Language and Using Language to Learn.* Portsmouth, N.H.: Heinemann, 1986.

Wesley, John. *The Works of John Wesley: Complete and Unabridged,* 3rd ed., vol. 6. Peabody, Mass.: Hendrickson, 1984.

The Wesley Bible. Nashville: Thomas Nelson, 1990.

Westerhoff III, John H. *Will Our Children Have Faith?* rev. ed. Toronto: Morehouse, 2000.

White, William R., *Stories for Telling: A Treasury for Christian Storytellers.* Minneapolis: Augsburg, 1986.

Willhauck, Susan Etheridge. "John Wesley's View of Children: Foundations for

Contemporary Christian Education." Ph.D. diss., Catholic University of America, 1992.

Winnicott, Donald W. *The Maturational Processes and the Facilitating Environment: Studies in the Theory of Emotional Development.* London: Hogarth/Institute for Psychoanalysis, 1965.

Yount, William. *Called to Teach.* Nashville: Broadman and Holman, 1999.

Youth and Family Ministry Congregational Planning Manual. Bloomington, Minn.: Youth and Family Institute, 2002.

Yust, Karen-Marie. "Theology, Educational Theory, and Children's Faith Formation: Findings from the Faith Formation in Children's Ministry Project." *Association of Professors and Researchers in Religious Education Proceedings,* Philadelphia, 2002.

Zoba, Wendy Murray. *Day of Reckoning: Columbine and the Search for America's Soul.* Grand Rapids: Brazos, 2000.

INDEX OF NAMES AND SUBJECTS

INDEX OF SCRIPTURE REFERENCES

OLD TESTAMENT